TRAVELLERS THROUGH TIME

TRAVELLERS THROUGH TIME

A Gypsy History

Jeremy Harte

REAKTION BOOKS

In zi Ann Wilson (1959–2019)
miro Romani pen

Published by
Reaktion Books Ltd
Unit 32, Waterside
44–48 Wharf Road
London N1 7UX, UK
www.reaktionbooks.co.uk

First published 2023
Copyright © Jeremy Harte 2023

Printed and bound in Great Britain by TJ Books Ltd, Padstow, Cornwall

A catalogue record for this book is available from the British Library

ISBN 978 1 78914 716 2

CONTENTS

Prologue:
Writing a Gypsy History

A SECOND HELPING of Hilda's cinnamon tart put an end to conversation, but once plates had been cleared, the young man opposite me returned to the topic. He had the usual good manners of a Gypsy speaking to his elders, and our dinner had been hosted by someone with a formidable reputation in the community; but still, he wasn't going to be put off.

'So you're going to write a book about us, then.'

'Yes,' I said, and started to talk about sources and archives and what seemed to be new discoveries. But that wasn't what he wanted to hear.

'Impressive, I'm sure, but it doesn't change the facts. No offence, but you're not a Gypsy. We're the Romany. Shouldn't we be in charge of our own story?'

'Jeremy has been around for years,' said Ann in a conciliatory way. 'He knows a lot about us.'

'Your cousin's got a point, though,' I said. 'Yes, I might have picked up a bit about the community, but that's not the same as knowing from experience, is it? I'm not a Gypsy and I haven't had a Gypsy life. I've never been moved on. I've never been turned down in a pub. Nobody ever spat on *my* kids. But isn't that just the reason why there ought to be a book? I might not know the half of it, but I know enough – I've *seen* enough – of what people have to put up with. Anything I can do, that might tell the real story . . .'

'Like the Romany Days,' said Michael. 'He started them, and a lot of people came.'

'Yes,' I said. 'You know what it's like at an open day – music, a couple of old waggons, people sitting round the fire, endless supplies of bacon roll pudding. And the public love it. Fair enough, this is just a day out for them, but it's one that says something positive about Gypsies, and where else do you see that outside of *Travellers' Times*? If one day of people talking about the old times does that, then how much better it would be with a real history, a story right from the beginning, five hundred years . . . I don't deny it could be written by a Gypsy, perhaps it should be written by a Gypsy, but who? I don't see anyone with a degree in history. Suppose we wait till the little one grows up . . .'

'You leave my grandchildren out of this,' said Hilda. 'He tries to talk to them, you know,' she told the table, 'in that old Romanes, only talking posh. Poor things, they haven't all started on English yet.'

'Well, I hear what you're saying,' said the young man, who was smiling a bit but obviously not going to give in. 'But you're not the first to think, ooh, Gypsies, that's a bit exotic, isn't it – I could write a book about that. And then it's all about how the white man came along and explains *our* culture, *our* traditions . . .'

'No,' I said. 'If it's going to be a Gypsy history, then it's got to be a history *for* Gypsies. And that means writing it pretty much from the perspective of a Gypsy. Even though I'm not.'

'Worse and worse,' said my opposite number.

'You've got to choose which side you're on, haven't you? All the books, all the documents are written by strangers – hostile ones, as often as not. If you go along with the flow, if you don't deliberately take the other viewpoint, you end up thinking like . . . like people you wouldn't want to be. And I thought, well, damn me if I don't write a book in which it's the Gypsies who are the normal people, and my own breed the outsiders.'

'But it's still you that's telling the story.'

'To be sure. But isn't it more honest to tell that story through the voices of the people it happened to? Even if that means setting aside who I am for the moment.'

'Isn't there something you haven't thought of?' he said. 'Who's going to buy your book? You might know how we talk, maybe even have an idea how we'd think about things, but isn't that just going to put off the others?'

'I don't think so. They came to Romany Day to talk to Gypsies in Surrey here and now; why shouldn't they take the chance to meet the Gypsies that lived here before? If I can pull off one, then why not the other?'

'I don't know,' he said. 'If you can do it, I'm not sure that you should. And even if you should, I'm not sure you can.'

'I can give it my best. Let's try.'

Introduction:
Meetings on Epsom Downs

June days are long and the nights are mild. Even the dirty country roads of the 1930s were dry that month and there was sweet long grass to feed a weary horse, so the Gypsies were ready to travel to Epsom. For weeks they had come, from the Devil's Dyke overlooking the Sussex coast, from the cherry orchards of Kent, from the meadows of the Thames – there were dark faces from the South Shore at Blackpool and the Black Patch at Birmingham – everyone answering the call of the Derby, which is, they say, the greatest horse-race in the world. Under the gentle sunshine of an English summer, strong horses pulled living-waggons up Ashley Road and Wilmerhatch Lane, their owners walking alongside with a steady grip on the reins. Young mothers stared out through the waggon doors, the latest baby wrapped close in a shawl. Children jostled each other in excitement as the long journey came to an end. They drew slowly down Grand Stand Road past the Bushes, shouting greetings to old friends, looking for a level spot between the thorn trees and the furze. And there they stopped, for a while: they were Gypsies, and never stayed anywhere long.

Between the two world wars, the Derby attracted crowds of up to half a million people. The race was run on the first Wednesday in June, and for the week before it, Epsom Downs was home to a canvas city of touts, tarts, boxers and bookies; there were fried fish stalls, penny shows, coconut shies and missionary tents; everyone with something to sell or something to show came to get a profit out of the great crowd of foot-loose Londoners who headed up to the Hill, and wanted to make the most of their day out. Flitting in and out of this throng were the Gypsies, loud-voiced, vivacious, bright in their new clothes – the aristocrats of the road, and well aware of it. They were not many, in proportion to the vast crowd. Perhaps eighty waggons stood scattered around the Bushes and the roadside waste, bringing four or five hundred travellers to the Downs. But they were instantly recognizable and quite distinct from those around them. Every scruff-headed child from the waggons grew up knowing that. As elemental as the basic divisions of the world – night and day, summer and winter, man and woman – was the difference between those who were of the Romany and those who were not, between Gypsy and gorjer. That cleavage was part of the culture of the people of the road: in fact, it was a precondition for their having a culture at all.

And because Gypsies were different from gorjers, and knew very well how different they were, they made good copy for journalists. Before sunset, at the end of the idle hour between first arrival on the Downs and the preparations for race day, families could expect to be joined around the fire by a stranger clutching a notebook – well-dressed, a little hot in his suit after half an hour's walk uphill from suburban civilization, but still delighted to have found authentic nomads only 15 miles from Waterloo Station. It was a moment of cultural exchange, most of it stage-managed by the Gypsies.

Flattery, racing tips, much talk of luck and a persistent demand for shillings (or sixpence would do, or failing that, how about a twist of tobacco?) were mixed with casual generosity. 'Better stay and have a cup of tea now you've come this far,' said the Pidgeleys to their man from the *Daily Sketch*. Once the fire was going well, they put four chops in the frying pan with onions and wild thyme and let him eat his fill. Simple food but presented with care. Tea was served in bone china, laid out on a white crumbcloth; water was poured from a bright copper jug. It was an aesthetic of rich colours, with a kind of gleaming cleanliness. If the reporter had stepped into Mother Pidgeley's waggon – red, with black wheels picked out in yellow – he would have seen polished brass fenders and a tile-hung fire-back to the stove, and on either side lustrous mahogany panelling, done up with gilded scrolls, maybe, or cut-glass mirrored panels; at the back, on the raised platform for the bed, white sheets and coverlets with lace trim; everything delicate and decorative. If he had come expecting Gypsy squalor, this was not the place for it. Of course, there was a great deal of squalor around, though in Derby week it tended to disappear into the general chaos of the Downs. There were cans and bottles, rags and broken metal, and other waste as well, as might be expected when hundreds of people gather in an area with no toilets. But that was all kept well out of the way of the beautiful, coloured waggons. Cleanliness at the heart of things, dirt on the outskirts, that was the principle. The outskirts might be where the gorjers lived, but that was their problem.[1]

And what of the people who travelled in the bright waggons? Reporters who arrived with their heads full of *Carmen* and *The Hunchback of Notre Dame* were in for a disappointment. The people on the Downs were not stage-Gypsies and there were no jangling bracelets or silver-hilted daggers to be seen. In the mornings, young women dressed up with a colourful headscarf and draped a shawl over their shoulders, but that was all in the way of business, to identify them easily in the crowd as fortune-tellers. At day's end, around the fire, people wore the ordinary clothing of the English working class: the men in hardwearing suits with waistcoats and flat caps, the women in blouses and long skirts. Only the weather-beaten faces of old grandmothers, and the tenacity with which they tugged at the stems of their short clay pipes, suggested the hardships of the road. There were some dark faces to be seen, but individual Romanies did not look particularly exotic. It was only as the evening progressed, and other members of the community dropped by, that an observant newspaperman would become alert to the Gypsy physique. Brown eyes and glossy black hair were the rule; people were a little shorter and stockier than their gorjer counterparts.

Wealth on Epsom Downs, 1920s.

The traces of a common descent might not be obvious, but they were still visible.

And just as there was a common look among members of the community, there was also a Gypsy temperament. Whether this was something passed down by descent, or a manner acquired over a travelling life, it was enough to impress even the casual reporter. Self-confidence was part of it, along with versatility and the kind of dignity most obvious in someone like 65-year-old Perrin Lee, who was 'swarthy, composed and smiling. He holds himself erect, and his face, in youth, must have been very handsome.' Now he had grandchildren, more than he could count, and though he travelled with his son and son-in-law, he remained independent. As the man from the *Daily Herald* listened and took notes, Perrin carried on with his basket-making, running the reeds through his fingers and trimming them with a knife. 'There's not a foot of this land I don't know, or of Ireland.' He could take a rabbit in any field and hook a trout in any river. Could he ride? Why, certainly; as teenagers, he and his sister had been out on their ponies in the Carmarthenshire hills when they saw the hunt run by. For sheer devilment they joined in, bareback though they were, keeping up right until the kill, when he remembered that the gorjers had made a collection and gave them 25s for their bravery. But now he had other things to do. Good luck be with *you*, sir.[2]

'All the gipsies on the Downs seem to be called Lee,' said a plaintive journalist. 'I spoke to ten Lees before I discovered a Smith.'[3] That was a fair introduction to the intersecting paths of Romany genealogy. Another colleague fell in with Rosie, Mary and Eileen Lee, all down for the day in their bright shawls and dresses to try a little fortune-telling with their mother, Lucy, who sent him off to see her husband's aunt on the official pitch which she had hired for her waggon. Nancy Lee was born on the Downs in 1858, more or less. Eight decades later, and smarting from having just paid £3 12s to stop on her native turf, she reminisced: 'Yes, mister, Epsom Downs and a lot of other things was much freer when I was a young beauty. I've got seventy grandchildren, and most of 'em are here today, as well as about five great-grandchildren.'[4] Born into large families, and marrying among a small network of trusted allies, Gypsies had come to bear only a few surnames. In any case, as the overly inquisitive reporter would soon find, names were more negotiable among the Romany than they were for outsiders. A woman would use her surname interchangeably with that of her husband; children would take that of their mother or father, depending on who they were dealing with; and it was not unknown for a whole family line to throw over their old name and adopt a new one, if the circumstances seemed appropriate.

So it must have simplified things for the lady from the *Daily Mail* when she learnt that Bella Martha Boswell was indeed 'a Boswell, born and bred, both on me old man's side and me long-dead father's'.[5] Bella would never see eighty again, and her leathery complexion and hoarse voice bore witness to a life weathered by sun and wind and woodsmoke. Brushing half a dozen great-grandchildren away from her skirts, she headed unerringly for the gossip columnist, laying an arm heavy with rings on her shoulder and saying huskily 'You want to *know*, don't you, my lady. There's many'll tell you this, and tell you the other, but only Bella Martha knows the true Name.' She paused for effect and held the gorjer's palm tightly. Her brown eyes never wavered in their stare. 'Now if you have another piece of silver, my lady . . .' No? Then alas the name of the Derby winner must remain half-imparted. Every year, on the night before the Derby, Jem Boswell came to his daughter in a dream – and old Jem, he understood more about horseflesh than those toffs in the Grandstand would ever know – and he told her the Name, which could be imparted at very reasonable rates. Ah well, Bella had made something out of the exchange, and the journalist had her copy.

With her flowing black hair and golden earrings, Bella was a bit of a cliché, but stereotypes were good for business, and at least they were of her own making. As for the newspaper writers, they were happy enough to take part in their own exploitation. 'I bought some herbs to cure my rheumatism, a lucky charm, an ashplant walking stick and had both my hands read,' reported the man from the *Daily Express*.[6] He'd paid for a tip about the winner as well, leaving some very happy families behind him. In Derby week, the Downs were swollen with people pretending to be something that they were not: infallible tipsters, patent medicine doctors, blackface minstrels. But uniquely, the Gypsies were making a living out of pretending to be themselves.

Not one in ten of the journalists penetrated beyond the Gypsies' romantic mask to get a real insight into their world, although clues to it lay scattered everywhere for those who cared to look. Fortune-telling might be a rigmarole, but the mysteries of good and bad luck were genuinely recognized as guiding principles in life. Old Jem Boswell's posthumous knowledge of horseflesh was a convenient fiction, but it had been woven out of everyday fact, because Gypsies did know about horses, and cared for them. That was obvious from the sturdy condition of the animals grazing by the waggons, from the fathers proudly picking up toddlers to pose them on horseback, from the laughing children playing around the latest colt. As for Bella's patter about messages from a long-gone father, she could deliver it all the more plausibly because of her real respect for the dead. The Downs at Epsom lie just above the cemetery and in the early days of the race meeting, before trade picked up, families would trickle down in twos and threes to bring new flowers and leave a silent tear at the graves of the old people.

The memory of those long-gone grandparents and great-grandparents held the community together. To count as a Gypsy, you had to follow some at least of the traditional lifestyle – you had to associate and identify with fellow Romany – but most of all, you had to show Gypsy descent. That lineage might run through one parent only, for the community was not ethnically homogenous, and the occasional blonde head could be seen among the black; but everyone could trace their kinship from some respected ancestor, and so everybody was related. Where gorjers might speak of friends or mates at work, Gypsies spoke of brothers and cousins. Family ties were some support in a hard world, but they imposed their own requirements too. Things that were carefully kept out of the sight of the journalists with notebooks – the feuds, the debts of honour, the stand-up fights shielded by a ring of watchers behind the wood – usually came down, in the end, to some kind of family obligation.

Now and then, the authorities at Epsom would decide to ban the Gypsies from the Downs. And as one section of the respectable world tried to push the community off the roads and fields, another would leap to its defence with a string of Letters to the Editor: the Gypsies were colourful, they were traditional, they were the last truly free spirits in an increasingly drab and regimented world. Like fortune-tellers' patter, these protests had some truth behind them, but they said more about the writers than about the people they were trying to defend. Gypsies were not free. Rosie and Mary Lee, for all their fetching manners and flashing eyes, were more strictly chaperoned than any debutante in the Grandstand. They would not have dreamed of talking to a boy without a parent, uncle or aunt joining the conversation; for them, or for their mother, to be alone with a strange man in the family waggon would have merited a thrashing, or worse. There were fewer constraints on men's behaviour, but for all that they had very little free time in which to go whistling down the lane. Caring for the horse and feeding him, protecting the waggon against sunshine and damp, searching for water and firewood

The less well-off on Epsom Downs, 1920s.

– these took up the best part of the day, and at the end of it there was still a living to be made. The insistent begging which so annoyed the authorities, the offers of useless, expensive oddments, all helped to bring in a little precious money.

And as if the practical difficulties of a travelling existence were not enough, Gypsy life was hedged around with unspoken rules about propriety and decency. It was not enough for a girl to be modest and chaste, she had to make sure that her skirts never brushed against a man or came into contact with food. The water fetched with such labour from the standpipe must be carefully husbanded for two separate washing bowls, one for cleaning the person, the other for cups and plates and anything to do with cooking. The white crumbcloth which so impressed the Pidgeleys' guest was not just there to look good, but to keep food and china from contaminating contact with the ground. There were rules for how you should eat, rules for where you could sit, rules for what you should say: in short, a whole culture, separate from and different to that of the gorjers, and unsuspected by them though it took place only the width of a hedge from their own settled world.

And for those who lived within its rules, the culture of the Romany was not a constraint but a source of strength. It was something to celebrate if you had survived to the age of those revered Gypsy ancestors, and never given in to the uncleanliness and immorality of the gorjers, never failed to keep your family and maintain tradition. 'You see that little wood over there?' said a grandmother, pointing her withered finger beyond the Bushes. 'That's where I was born, in that wood, sixty years ago. I've been here every year since then – except when the war came. And every year till I die I shall come.'[7] She folded her arms and shook her head, as the golden sovereigns swung from her ears and glinted in the sun.

The Gypsies were different, and they were fiercely proud of that difference. That was obvious even to the newspaper people, as they sat and listened to the gossip among their hosts. If there was a brotherhood of the road, there was also a spirit of emulation, a desire for all the things that marked status in the Romany world: ornate waggons, sleek horses, the quick movements of an assured dancer or fighter, inexhaustible funds of songs, tunes and stories. And people were proud of their own language, too. If journalists let the rapid Gypsy talk ebb and flow uninterrupted around them, they would soon hear it peppered with unfamiliar expressions. Fortune-telling was *dukkering*, a horse was a *grai*, the waggon a *vardo*, the men and women *mushes* and *juvvels*. A word of interruption from a stranger, and the whole company would innocently revert to everyday English; but among themselves, when they felt confident in their Romany identity, they spoke in their own tongue. Language was the most distinct of their many distinctive traditions, and it is the thread of language, traced slowly back through the centuries, that tells who the Gypsies were, and what long paths had brought them to the English countryside.

1

Entertaining Strangers:
Tudor England

B efore any waggons hauled slowly up Wilmerhatch Lane, before
even the first Derby, when the green curve of Epsom Downs
hosted nothing but sheep, the Gypsy world had another centre
in southern England, a little further towards Kent on the Norwood hills.
Nowadays that seems absurd. Train announcements for stops on the line
may still ring out Balham, Streatham, West Norwood, Gipsy Hill – but
that is just one name among many, and it means nothing to those who live
there. Even the Gipsy Tavern, a pleasant little local down the road from
the station, has gone the way of so many other small pubs. The building
is converted and the naive signboard, with its waggon and cob standing
behind a Romany as he snoozes under the trees, has been taken away to
rust in some corner.[1]

But before the great suburban growth of London in the nineteenth
century, when you could still look down through clear Surrey air and
see the smoke of the capital many miles off, Norwood was a wild and
lonely place. London's highways, already beginning to transform the
old villages into a ribbon of suburbia, stopped at the hills of Penge and
the rising ground which had in medieval times been the Great North
Wood. Streatham lay to the west of it and Dulwich to the north; eastwards, on the Kentish side, were Sydenham and Beckenham. Scattered
along the slopes there were open glades in which to stop, woods for fuel
and unenclosed springs of water. The region belonged to the parishes of
Lambeth, Camberwell and Croydon, none of which had much interest
in their remote dependency, while the nearby county border made it easy
for an anonymous people to slip away from authority.

Like Hampstead Heath, Epping Forest and other wild places beyond
the urban limits, Norwood was as popular with excursionists as it was

with Gypsies. Visitors might not want to walk there on dark nights, unless armed with a stout stick and some knowledge of the winding pathways, but things were different on a summer Sunday afternoon. Then the Londoners would form little parties, hire some sort of carriage, pack lunch for the day and enjoy time in the open air far from the noise and dirt of the city. An encounter with the Gypsies was part of the entertainment, sauced with just a slight undercurrent of the risk that a true urbanite feels when venturing away from paved roads and streetlights. And the Gypsies were happy to oblige. As one of the Coopers said, remembering the good old days before the tide of building displaced them all:

> A number of gentry would come into the woods for a picnic or else a wedding party would make its appearance. The gypsies would be all out of sight, but keenly watchful. A cloth would be laid on the grass in some open field, and a hearty meal would be partaken of. That done the question would arise, 'What shall we do next?' This was the gypsies' chance. They would gather round them from all sides, begging, telling fortunes and selling trinkets. It was Mrs. Cooper's business on these occasions to bring up some donkeys for the ladies to ride on, and the fun once commenced would usually continue until nightfall. A good business was made out of this sort of thing, and they rarely did anything else for a living.[2]

In this kind of encounter, it was as difficult as it would be at Epsom one hundred years later for a gorjer to get beyond the standard patter and make real contact. 'No sooner does a stranger approach their fire on the heath, than a certain reserve spreads itself,' wrote Richard Bright in 1810. 'The women talk to him in mystic language – they endeavour to amuse him with secrets of futurity – they suspect him to be a spy on their actions – and he generally departs as little acquainted with their true character as he came.'[3] But Richard was not to be fooled like that. He was persistent, he had no prejudice against the community – quite the reverse, in fact – and it soon became clear that he was neither a parish officer nor a police nark. He had travelled widely and must have had a fund of interesting stories to tell. But there was one thing which marked him out from the other gentlemen who came to Norwood for the day. He could *rokker* Romanes – he could talk in the Gypsy way – and that was a direct path to people's confidence. They were amazed that he could speak the language of the road. And he was amazed to find the language being spoken at all.

For Richard had learnt his Romani, not in a glade of English oak trees, but on the shores of Lake Balaton in Hungary. These rolling hills held villages where the Roma could be numbered by their hundreds, where their language was the ordinary speech of home and work, and where a stranger could get the basics of it, as Richard had. And then returning home, to leafy Surrey, he was astonished 'to find, crouched beneath a hedge at Norwood, a family who expressed their ideas in the same words as those with whom I had conversed but a few weeks before, in the most distant corner of Europe'.[4]

It was not just that the two sets of people had words in common. Words travel easily between one language and another; they can be picked up as a code or slang, and with a little ingenuity (underworld groups are not short of ingenuity) you can put together a patter of code-words that an outsider is quite unable to grasp. But Romani was not like that. It was a language with its own grammar, phrasing and sentence order.

This is the kind of thing that people at Norwood said when they talked Romanes:

Chirikloi givella ako dives. 'The birds are singing today.'
Dikan e greski boshto? 'Have you seen the horse's saddle?'
Jova menga keti varingera. 'I will go to the fair.'
Tu hawsa kushko hawben ake rati. 'You will eat a good meal
    tonight.'[5]

You don't have to be a linguist to see that this is a fully formed language, with tenses and persons and case-endings. It was hard work for the Norwood Gypsies to help Richard with his enquiries; when you come from an oral culture, you speak as you think, and going back over your thoughts and trying to say them all over again, and in another language, does not come easily. But they kept at it, and as they talked first about food and then about horses (a natural topic of conversation for the Romany) slowly the outlines of a grammar began to emerge. Verbs, it seemed, varied much as they do in English, though with completely different endings – *hawsa*, 'you eat'; *hawla*, 'he eats'; *dikela*, 'he sees'; *dikan*, 'you saw' – though it took a while for Richard to realize that Romani had no future case, and relied on an anticipatory use of the present instead. Nouns were more complicated, for as well as the genitive *greski*, 'of the horse', there was a dative *gresti*, 'to the horse' (just as in Latin, Richard must have thought), together with other cases not familiar even to a classicist, such as the instrumental, used with the name of *Devel*, 'God', in the dignified farewell *Atch Develesa*, 'Remain with God.'

When he compared it with the language of the Hungarian Gypsies, though, Richard could see that in Norwood the old language – *puri jib* – was under siege from the English spoken all around it. People frequently talked of something happening to *o grai*, 'the horse', without giving the words their necessary ending, and several of the grammatical inflections were found only in certain fossilized, old-fashioned phrases. He had been just in time to catch a fully formed language at the point when it was being reduced to its vocabulary alone. Within a generation it would become impossible for anyone to make a similar collection under the trees at Norwood. The woods were felled, the Gypsies were dispersed and the old speech was lost.

But not quite, for the language spoken by the earliest generations of Gypsies in this country – what we may call Old Romani – survived in the remotest part of the country, among the woods of North Wales.[6] And it was there that, by one of the luckiest chances in the history of scholarship, Edward Wood met and befriended John Sampson of the University of Liverpool, and invited him to spend time with the extended clan until he had fully mastered the language.[7] Though John's masterwork, produced after thirty years of preparation, is called *The Dialect of the Gypsies of Wales*, it is really a study into the language as it existed throughout Britain up to the eighteenth century, when the Woods first made their way west of the Severn.[8]

Throughout the densely packed pages of *The Dialect*, the whole family can be heard gossiping and quarrelling and storytelling in a language that no living person now knows, for they were the last generation of native speakers. It was a subtle and dignified idiom which they had kept pure, and in it they were preserving, quite unawares, the secret history of the Gypsies. The Romany had no literature or chronicles, nothing but fallible tradition to pass down the communal story; but they did have a language, and this alone can unlock the story of who these people were, and where they came from.

The bedrock of the language was Indian. To come and go, *av* and *jell*; to live and die, *jiv* and *mer*; day and night and sun and fire, *divvus*, *rati*, *kam*, *yog*: these all came from the vernacular of north India, somewhere around Rajasthan, though it is difficult to be more precise since several different dialects seem to have gone into the making of the aboriginal language.[9] The grammar of Romani is Indo-Aryan as well, and the developments which it shares with other Indic languages date from before the tenth century, so the split from the parent tongue must have happened after then.[10] As the Gypsies travelled westward, new worlds opened up and the language adapted to keep pace with them. By the time that Romani reached England, *mol*, which once meant mead, had become 'wine'; the *rai* and the *rashai*, prince and sage in the old country, had dwindled into 'gentleman' and 'vicar'; and the word for mango, *ambrol*, was being used for 'pear'.[11] Well, they had to call it something.

Many other languages contributed to the Romani vocabulary – Armenian and Persian and Byzantine Greek, Romanian and the Slavic languages – but the last loanwords adopted before people crossed over the seas to Britain show that the ancestral group must have passed through France and Germany. Several Romani words taken from German dialects suggest that the Romani were mixing with a wandering underworld – people who judged strangers as *wafodi* (bad) or *fino* (shrewd), and who made their way over many a *stigga* (stile) in hope of winning a *horro* (penny). *Trin-gush*, the word for a shilling, is literally 'three groats', imitated from German *Dreigröschen*. The word *swegla* (pipe) came from

A woman with children in the Rhineland, *c.* 1480s.

these companions. It derives from the German *schwegel* or the Dutch *swegel*, which both mean pipe – but not the sort you smoke; they are words for a musician's pipe, played by entertainers with a tabor or little drum. This is exactly the sort of word Gypsies would have picked up as they mingled with fairground entertainers. Cheap tobacco didn't become available until later, and when it did, people referred to tobacco pipes by using the word for 'pipe' which was already in their vocabulary. This pun works in English but not in any Continental language.[12]

Some borrowings were distorted in the process, as if the Romany were not quite fluent in the languages spoken around them: *avonka* (before) began as the French *avant que*, and *nogo* (our) is a very clipped version of the German *mein eigen*.[13] The loans from French concentrate on the things most likely to be useful to a travelling people – the *granza* (barn) in which they slept, the *fuzyanri* (fern) with which they made their bedding and the *budika* (shop) where they bought provisions. These would have included *kas* (cheese), but that is from the Dutch, perhaps because it travelled better than the French *fromage*. Several of these words show traces in their sound history of an early origin. *Spink* (pin), for instance, is from the French *épingle*, which used to be *espingle*; the *s*, which disappeared from spoken French in about 1600, has been faithfully preserved in Romani.

The final embarkation of the Gypsies is likely to have taken place at French ports, for when they arrived on these shores they spoke of the country as *Anglaterra*, from *Angleterre*, and its capital as *Londra*, from *Londres*. It is not clear when the first phase of the Arrival took place, but it must have been some time before the Reformation, for among the words used in folk tales to describe a wizard is *herimentos*, which is simply the early English term 'heremite' or 'hermit', with the *-os* termination that marks out loanwords. There were no hermits in England after 1536, when they disappeared from the religious landscape at the suppression of the smaller religious houses.

So language is a principal witness – for early centuries, the only witness – to trace the long road of the Romany from the lands of the mango to those of the pear. There was a first diaspora out of the ancestral homeland in north India and Persia, somewhere about the year 1000, which brought the community into the Anatolian and Balkan lands of the Byzantine Empire. Then, in the fourteenth century, just at the beginning of the Renaissance, bands began to travel westwards again, passing through German-speaking lands until they ended at northeast France, on the borders of Flanders. They arrived in England in family groups during the early sixteenth century, until a tighter border discipline on the part of the government prevented any more parties from travelling over. And after that, they were cut off in a strange land, and left to carry on their lives as best as they could.

Speakers of Romani had certainly arrived in Sussex by 1547, for in that year there was a group of Gypsies in the county who shared a few phrases with Andrew Boorde, a scholar writing a handbook on language. This is the kind of thing that Andrew's friends said when they talked Romanes:

> *Lacho tutti dyves!* 'Good day to you!'
> *Keti meila boro foros?* 'How many miles away is the fair?'
> *Mol pies? Levvina? Avava tusa.* 'Are you drinking wine? Or ale?
>   I'll come with you.'
> *Besh taley, ta pi!* 'Sit down and have a drink!'[14]

Evidently, they met in an alehouse, with Andrew supplying more liquid inspiration as the talk rolled out. Nonetheless it is all in good, inflected Romani, with endings for verbs ranging from *pi* (drink!) to *pies* (you drink), and the stem *av-* (come) yielding *avava* (I come; that is, I will come), while the pronoun *tu* has different case endings to express 'to you' (*tutti*) and 'with you' (*tusa*).

What were they like, these strangers at the inn? They had come to a country without much in the way of artistic tradition, so that there are no paintings or drawings of the first English Gypsies. But the regions of France and Flanders, from which people were taking embarkation at the time of the Arrival, had become famous for their representations of ordinary life. Among these is a tapestry, woven in one of the great factories of Tournai in about 1500, which shows us Gypsies meeting gorjers in a woodland glade.[15] A family is arriving from left, with two stocky horses. One of these has been saddled with two wickerwork panniers, which hold the children who are too young to walk. An older boy is sitting in front of them, enthusiastically hitting the long-suffering horse with a branch of a tree. The second horse is for a young woman, who is carrying a little baby at her side in a sort of roper, with another toddler on her lap. Various pans and bottles seem to have been packed on the horses. The father of the family is marching in front of them, with a stout stick over his shoulder. He is dressed like a squire or soldier, with a sword at his belt, but his shaggy hair gives him a foreign look, and so does the velvet cloth thrown over his shoulders like a cloak.

Just to the right, we have the stopping place. There are a few embroidered flames to represent the fire, and beside it a woman is sitting with a baby on her knee, feeding it from a bowl of porridge which is being held for her by a little girl. The woman wears an expensive embroidered dress, covered by a blanket loosely tied at the left shoulder. Like her daughter, and all the other young women, she has her hair bundled up in a kind of turban, tied with a strap under the chin and tilted back so that it shows off her forehead. To the right are three expensively dressed gorjers, gentlefolk who have come to see the Gypsy encampment. An old woman holds the hand of one gorjer girl, obviously dukkering – that is, fortune-telling; but now we can begin to use Gypsy words for Gypsy matters. The old woman is gesturing with her free hand in the manner of someone giving serious advice, while the client looks a little alarmed at the prediction. A young man in a fur-lined coat seems to be saying to his partner 'Look, dear, these are the Gypsies I told you about,' and while she is doubtless exclaiming, 'Darling, how *romantic*!' one of the children has found the delicate red purse hanging down from her girdle, which the enterprising little chavvi is checking for loose change.

Wherever the Gypsies came, they brought a touch of the exotic into otherwise humdrum lives, and this must have made England ripe for colonizing. Here were people who had never seen a dark face, and who would easily credit its possessor with all sorts of powers, hopefully paying them well in return. Of course, it is hard to travel, and impossible to tell fortunes, unless you have a reasonable command of the language. There must have been a time in which members of the community were passing to and fro across the Channel, getting a grasp of English and assessing the natives. The first recorded mention of Gypsies in England describes exactly this.

During an inquest held at Baynard's Castle on the London banks of the Thames, in the spring of 1515, a witness told the lords sitting in judgement that he could bring them to a woman who knew exactly who had done the crime.[16] 'She wolde tell you wonders,' said the man, admitting that he'd heard nothing about the case they were supposed to be discussing, but if someone were to go and ask her she could probably find out, because she was a very clever woman. For instance, if you'd had something stolen, a horse or some other such thing, she could tell who'd taken it, just by looking in your hand.

Therewith the lords laughed and asked what is she? Forsothe my
lords, quod he, an Egypcyan, and she was lodged here at Lambeth,

but she is gone ouer see nowe. Howe be it I trowe she be not in her owne countree yet, for they say it is a grete way hense, and she wente ouer lytell more than a moneth ago.[17]

So there was at least one Gypsy woman coming and going among the lodgings and cheap eating places that stretched along the Thames waterfront to the south of London Bridge. The suburbs, just across the river from London proper, were a refuge for everything that slipped away from the watch of the city authorities: bearpits and theatres, places for men to meet women, and markets for buying and selling unlawful things. Here along the waterfront a few Gypsies first gained some knowledge of England, returning home to their 'owne countree' to discuss the possibilities offered by a new land before returning in larger numbers.

Immigration was never going to be easy, and the records of Gypsy life in sixteenth-century England form a depressing sequence of arrests, apprehensions and deportations. In the summer of 1556 Lawrence Misteldon and his wife Agnes were detained, along with George Roche, John Anthonye and Philip surnamed Lazerdemye. They landed at Sandwich and by June they had got as far as Andover.[18] If they had taken the most direct route, it would have gone inland to Maidstone or Rochester, and then along the North Downs through Surrey to Farnham, before setting off to Alton and the Hampshire towns.

In May of the same year, a much larger party was corralled at Beccles and Lowestoft to prevent them from travelling inland. Among them were Nuscoo and Mary Anthony, James and Elizabeth Vallentyne, and John, Katherine, Onacus and Margaret Peroo; also, a William Demewe. So there were married couples making the journey to England, and the natural interpretation of the list from Beccles is that John and Onacus Peroo were brothers, both travelling with their wives. On both occasions in 1556, members of the Anthony family had made the Channel crossing. There is another family link in the George Roche who arrived at Sandwich in 1556, and who must have been related to the Bridget Roche who was later apprehended at Chilton in 1579. In 1546, orders had been sent that one Philippe Lazar was to be deported on the first convenient ship from London. This suggests that the enigmatic Philip Lazerdemye in the Sandwich group was really a Lazar-Demewe, taking his name from two other families found among these early immigrants.[19]

Most of these surnames sound French; in the standard spelling, they would be Lasser, Demay, Roche, Antoine, Valentin and Perrault (Peroo).

Some are less familiar. Raina Fullesten, who was among the group detained at Beccles, has a Bulgarian first name and a surname that sounds German. Nuscoo and Onacus have no obvious parallels, although they both sound Gypsy. Most people otherwise had first names which were quite ordinary among contemporary Europeans.

The links among their surnames, and the common background to them, suggests that the Gypsies who arrived in England during the early sixteenth century came mostly from close-knit families in the French-speaking hinterland of Calais and Dunkirk. They must have known each other well if they were relying on mutual support in the new country. Immediately on their arrival, they were known as Egyptians; the name is used in 1505 at Stirling, 1510 in London and 1521 near Bristol; in 1530 the government speaks of an 'outlandysshe People callynge themselves Egyptians'.[20] Evidently the immigrants came from a parent community who routinely called themselves the Dukes of Little Egypt when talking to strangers. After all, it helped add a flavour of the exotic.

A family in the Netherlands, *c.* 1660s.

Strangers attract attention, sometimes even admiration. At a banquet held at Westminster in 1510, one of the royal ladies appeared as a Gypsy. Admittedly a rather high-class Gypsy, with a dress of purple and crimson satin picked out with golden pomegranates but topped by an identifiable turban which had been embroidered in more gold. Her arms were bare except for a marvellously thin black lace, intended to give the effect of a dark complexion.[21] Wardrobe masters were expected to have Gypsy costumes in stock, along with other opportunities for the wealthy to dress up as Turks, Moors, Italians, Germans and other interesting foreigners. In 1547 the royal costume collection at Nonsuch Palace included Gypsy dress with sleeved undergarments 'of tawny tilsent', covered by short mantles 'of crymson golde baudkyn, fringed with colen sylver'.[22] The short mantle seems to have been a fashion among Gypsy men during the Arrival. Real examples were unlikely to have been edged with silver from Cologne, but they were probably handsome enough. The aristocratic revellers for whom these costumes were intended had no intention of looking like beggars.

Gypsy style made its way down the social scale. A Leatherhead landlady of the 1520s would go out for the night in her eye-catching red dress topped by an imitation of that familiar turban:

> a whym wham
> Knyt with a trym tram,
> Upon her brayne pan,
> Like an Egyptian,
> Capped about.[23]

She didn't come from very elevated circles, so it's likely that she got her style tips directly from Gypsy customers and not from the nobility.

But a fascination with Gypsy culture did not necessarily mean sympathy with the people themselves, and in 1530 the first of a series of Acts of Parliament was passed against the community. Gypsies were found guilty of travelling 'from Shire to Shire and Place to Place in greate Company', of claiming that 'they by Palmestre coulde telle Menne and Womens Fortunes', and of committing 'many and haynous Felonyes and Robberies'. Henceforward the ports were to be closed to immigrants, and everyone who was already in England had sixteen days to leave, failing which they were to be imprisoned.[24] But the proposed sealing of the borders cannot have been effective, for seventeen years later we find letters being sent to the county administrations of Norfolk, Suffolk, Essex,

Surrey, Kent and Sussex. They were to evict Gypsies and punish 'with extremitie' such as should offend the law.[25] The fact that these orders were sent to counties along the southern and eastern seaboard suggests that fresh parties had been landing there. Certainly, instructions were being sent during these years to Romney Marsh and Dover, telling magistrates to send Gypsies back to wherever it was they came from.[26]

Once people had slipped past the harbourmasters, though, there was very little to stop them travelling unseen. Southeast England was speckled with forests, wastes and extensive commons that the eyes of authority could not easily survey, and open roads which it was nobody's business to patrol. The roads westward from Kent met at Guildford and proceeded along the ridge of the Hog's Back to Farnham. This was a well-governed town, with courts, a prison and other things best avoided; but fortunately it lay at the edge of the great heath which stretched empty and unpoliced from Woking to Windsor.

Gypsies were certainly travelling to the west of Farnham in February 1543, when an urgent message was sent from Westminster to gentlemen at Crondall and Farnborough; they must intercept and evict 'vagabondes going upp and downe in the name of Egiptians'.[27] They hadn't succeeded by March, when the party stopped at Heckfield for three days.[28] It may be that this region was a known rendezvous where small groups would wait for others to catch up, so that they could proceed in a larger troop westwards to Winchester or north to Oxford.

These Gypsies would have included children of the first immigrant generation, perhaps grandchildren. Authority slowly came to realize that the community had naturalized itself in Britain and in 1554 a new Act of Parliament updated the legislation of 1530. The fine for bringing Gypsies into the country was raised to £40. This – or, more plausibly, the loss of Calais by the English in 1558 – seems to have scared captains off bringing in any more immigrants: within ten years, the Arrival was at an end. Any Gypsies who had been landed had to leave within the month, or they would be convicted. The same went for any who were already in the country without plans for getting transported back across the sea, for they too were treated as felons. And the punishment for felony was death.

There were two conciliatory clauses – children under fourteen were exempt, and so was anyone who abandoned the travelling life and put themselves 'in the Service of some honest and able Inhabitant'. But essentially, the Act of 1554 made it punishable by death to be an untransported 'Egyptian'. You could claim – as several people successfully did in a test case at Poole in 1554 – that this only applied to immigrant natives of 'Egypt' (or wherever) and not to those born on English soil.[29] But this loophole was pulled tight in 1562 when an extension of this Act specifically provided for adults who had been born in England: as long as they were found 'disguising themselves by their Apparel, Speech or other Behaviour, like unto ... Egyptians', they were felons. There was no longer any question of deporting anyone. They were to be hanged.

You would have thought that a legal sanction for genocide, imposed by an absolute government on a small and powerless minority, would have swept England bare of Gypsies within a few years. But things are never quite as simple as that. When it came to promoting an official policy such as the extermination of Gypsies, Parliament and the Privy Council had to act through a patchy national network of law-enforcers. None of these were in the direct employment of the state, which meant that everyone from the lord lieutenant of the county to the parish beadle had their own private interests, even if these were merely for a quiet life. Then under these officials came the mass of the population, not easily crushed. Five or six hangings outside the county jail might keep the common people in awe: to see one hundred dead bodies swing would have driven folk to rebellion and despair. And so in practice the Elizabethan statutes had to be applied partially, and not all the time.

When there was a demand for action against the community, it usually reflected a crisis in the government rather than anything the Gypsies themselves had done. In 1569, a year of disturbances in Scotland and Ireland, the Privy Council feared that the wandering people might spread disaffection in the south. They sent letters to Mickleham, Betchworth, East Horsley and Guildford, complaining that officials were winking at the existence of 'vagabonds and sundry beggars commonly called rogues and in some parts Egyptians ... persons whose lives are not only abominable in the sight of Almighty God but very harmful, slanderous and dangerous to the common weal'. The instructions were sent to men living quite near each other, which suggests that arrests were confined to one part of the county – the area south of the Downs between Reigate and Dorking.[30]

Arrests were made, and a body of Gypsies were sent to the county jail in Southwark, which was in fact a converted inn, the White Lion, run by a private contractor. And there they remained, for an unknown period of time, until Sir William More, the deputy lieutenant for Surrey and Sussex, received a message begging him to have pity.

Wee are lick to perrishe for defayet of sustenauncies yf your
wurship faverable and mercyfull hand be not stretched further
… We cann not have no forend nor Kynnesman to helpe us in
this heavy caesse therfor we umble begge your wurship for the
lords sake to release us.[31]

Yes, they confess that they are offenders, but 'we shall be contented to
part home into our contray, be gods grace yf we shall do to the contrary
we will be contented to suffer deathe presently.' And finally, hoping that
Sir William will follow the example of God himself and prefer mercy to
judgement, they promise 'to amend our lyeffes and never to offend in
any thing herrafter'.

It is a heartbreaking and well-composed letter, which suggests that
even in their adversity the Gypsies were able to command the services
of a good lawyer. They had every reason to, for the White Lion was an
appalling place and they needed to get out if they were not to die of infectious disease. That's why they promised so readily to go back to their own
country, although prudently not specifying exactly where this might be.
Nevertheless, the petition doesn't sound like the work of people who were
seriously at risk of judicial murder. It all amounts to 'We're very sorry,
mother die we are. Can we get out now?' And so, no doubt, they did,
because there is no record of anyone being hanged, and the finances of
an Elizabethan county court didn't stretch to keeping people in prison
indefinitely.

Thirty years later, the Privy Council was on the backs of Surrey
magistrates once again, insisting that Gypsies and other rogues were to
be arrested, 'whereby they may be driven by punishment to change that
wicked and dangerous course of life'.[32] This appears to have been part of
a general drive extending into the Midlands, since at the same time eighty
Gypsies were arrested in Northamptonshire and the principal men of the
party sent to London, where they were put in manacles at the reforming
prison of Bridewell in the hope that they would confess to something.[33]

And so the government crackdowns went on, always fierce enough
to terrify and embitter Gypsies, but never thorough enough to eradicate
the community. Repeatedly, magistrates were urged to round people up
and imprison them. But they had no heart to go further and kill those
who they had impounded, so in the end they had to let them go. In other
counties people were sentenced to death under the Egyptians Act of 1562,
but not in Surrey.[34] Of course there were executions of Gypsies who had

broken other, non-racial laws. In 1564 one of the Peter family was hanged at Tyburn. His daughters (Isabell, aged thirteen, and Alice, aged eleven) were taken up by a remedial home for poor children at Christ's Hospital. A few years later they were apprenticed as servants, with Alice sent to a household at Southwark.[35] The aim, as in the 1554 Act, was to assimilate children into the gorjer world, although as the story breaks off there, we don't know how successful it was.

Far from driving people out of the country, the years of persecution seem to have strengthened bonds between Gypsies and other itinerant groups. By the end of the century, the governing classes had ceased to think of Gypsies as foreign nationals at all, and simply regarded them as an extreme case of 'rogues, vagabonds and sturdy beggars', in the words of another Act of Parliament in 1598. This also allowed for the existence of English-born people found in Gypsy encampments, lumping them together with the dark immigrants as 'counterfayte Egipcians'.[36]

So who was who? Throughout the sixteenth and early seventeenth centuries, people in England were taking to the road as never before. Many reasons have been given for this: war and crop failure, the dissolution of the monasteries, the enclosure of fields and the engrossment of farms. But the root cause was that, for perhaps the first time in history, England had a working cash economy. Instead of living off the produce of a family smallholding, as had been the case in the days of peasant cultivation, the ordinary village labourer relied on money wages to purchase food at the local market. When the harvest failed or trade dried up, instead of lying down to starve on their own few acres, people would take to the road and search for somewhere else where they could find money and work. The search was often illusory. In the clunky economy of Tudor England, population often grew faster than the means of employing people. The rootless poor lined the streets and banged on doors, desperately demanding food; they cajoled and lied and stole; they gave birth in porches and died in the fields.[37]

There were so many transient people on the roads of Tudor England that officials at parish level could hardly find words to name them all. They were wayfarers, strollers, trampers or travellers. If they asked for money, they were beggars and mendicants; if they found ways of working for it, they were hawkers and pedlars. Anyone from outside the village went down as a stranger, from the sojourner or alien householder down to the dead sailors who washed up on the beach in maritime parishes. And in the eyes of the law all these people were rogues and vagabonds.

But unlike the Gypsies, these people did not want to wander. Many were economic migrants, displaced from one home and looking for a better one. Some must have done just that, sitting eventually by their own hearthside to reminisce about the wandering days. Others failed utterly. The road is a hard teacher, and it was easy to fall into despair, tramping from handout to handout until disease or exposure cut short an aimless life. But a few survived. Through luck or skill or determination, they learnt how to live on the move. They followed the harvests, worked the fairs and made or mended goods for the settled community. They sang and danced and did tricks, told fortunes, performed wonderful cures. They formed partnerships, bore children, raised and educated them. And for this second generation, the road was home; they were no longer transients but Travellers.[38]

These were the people who would have been closest to Gypsies, for the Gypsies had what other wanderers must have often envied – the strength of a distinct culture and the security that came from numbers and family loyalty. Think what it would be like to encounter a group like this, travelling in the outskirts of London, in 1609. 'The men weare scarfes of Callico . . . hanging their bodies like Morris-dancers, with bels, & other toyes, to intice the country people to flocke about them.' The women wear fine dresses underneath their coarse patched blankets. Patient horses carry the little children in panniers until they are big enough to ride, and then they scramble on horseback all in a line, tied together if necessary. There may be eighty people at a big gathering, but normally 'they forage vp and downe countries, 4. 5. or 6. in a company . . . They sticke vp small boughs in seuerall places, to euery village which they passe; which serue as ensigns to waft on the rest.' At night they gather in a ring on 'some large Heath . . . far from any houses', feasting on some stray goose or livestock. If the parish constable interrupts their gathering, they fob him off with an improvised story; if he insists on asking where the dinner came from, they will blame one of the group and hand them over; but he will be rescued later on, for they are loyal to their own.[39]

This is a colourful account, but it is corroborated by other sources. In 1619 three Gypsies were arrested at Farnham – Henry Mannering, William Poynes and William Clifford. They were accompanied by Walter Hindes, who was singled out for examination by the governor of the House of Correction in Winchester. Walter was a very forthcoming witness; he'd probably had enough of being corrected and was prepared to tell anything

A woman dukkering, 1681.

if it meant he could go free. He confessed that he'd met up with the other men in Hampshire and had agreed to travel up to London with them, carrying some stolen goods. They were going to sell them to William Lasy, their 'unckle' (probably in the Gypsy sense, a respected elder rather than an immediate relative), at the sign of the White Horse. This stood in a yard just off Kent Street, the northern extension of the Old Kent Road. William was a Gypsy who had gone into brick and now received 'Diapre and Dammask' of doubtful provenance. He might just possibly be related to the Lazar family of 1546, although everyone else in this story has taken on a regular English surname.[40]

This was not the first time that Walter had met with the group. He knew that they wintered in London and then set out with their wives and 'ther children and servants . . . to travall the Cuntry all the sommertyme, telling fortunes and deceiving the Cuntry'. The governor listened to all this with great interest and then asked whether the Gypsies had a special language. Indeed they did, said Walter, and proceeded to give more than one hundred examples of words. He got quite chatty – *jukkel*, that's a dog; *motto jukkel*, 'he is a drunken dogg which they call one another in ther drinck' – but this was probably quelled by a look from the governor, who didn't want an insight into Romany table talk. What he wanted was a list of words which could be issued to the *muskro* ('a Constable') so he could understand what the Gypsies were trying to conceal from him.

Nevertheless, the vocabulary gives a useful insight into standards of life among the community at the time.

Gypsies who travel with their own servants are presumably quite prosperous. Certainly this group ate well. There was white bread, *pauno marro*, as well as brown; *mas* meant not just 'meat' but 'beef'; as well as butter, *kil*, and eggs, *yorros*, there was cream, *smentini*; they drank both beer and wine. A fat hen or a cock was a treat, and *shushis* and *matchos*, rabbits and fish, could be caught in the wild. They cooked in a boiler, *pirri*, and ate off dishes, *charros*. At night they slept on straw, but with sheets. And they dressed well. A handsome Gypsy began the day by putting on his *gad*, shirt, and after that his stockings and breeches. The Romani language, not originally intended for Jacobean couture, had some difficulty with these, but settled for *tikno holovas* and *boro holovas*. Next the man put on his ruff (a rather gentlemanly garment), followed by a *chuffa* or *plashta*, coat or cape, and crowned by the *stadi*, his hat. He also carried a *hanro*, his sword.

With outfits like that, you can see why Henry and the two Williams had impressed Walter – so much so that he seems to have been willing to be their patsy and take the risk of carrying stolen goods for them. He had picked up a lot of Romani, including such obscure terms as *tatcho vast* and *bango vast* for 'right' and 'left', a pair of words which suggests some familiarity with the rules of cleanliness and propriety. Nevertheless, Walter was not a Gypsy. He was 'acquaynted with them' and that was all.

He had not acquired a very sound grasp of Old Romani, either. All his plurals are formed in the English style, by adding *-s*, and he obviously had no idea of grammatical gender. *Boro holovas* pairs a masculine adjective with a feminine noun and *nevi chokkas*, 'new shoes', a feminine adjective with a masculine noun. When his lexical knowledge ran out, he improvised in broken language: a pikestaff is *koshti with a saster at the end*. The few phrases which he provided (most of them about crime) are ungrammatical, such as *pogger kair*, to break a house, and *chin kissi*, to cut a purse. In Old Romani, the nouns would have been in the accusative – *phager kheren, čin kisien*. English words seem to have crept into some of these phrases. *Tov yer mui* is 'wash your face' and *kor the gruvni*, 'goe beate the Cow'. Since no man in his senses goes around thumping cows, the phrase was probably a euphemism for domestic abuse, though the Mannering, Poynes and Clifford women might have given as good as they got.

Old Romani, as we have seen, was an inflected language, with a grammar which comes naturally enough if you have grown up speaking it.

But for Englishmen trying to master the tongue, it was difficult to remember all the different forms. The Gypsy world still found a place for these newcomers. 'Euery day the members of it increase, & it gathers new ioints & new forces by Priggers, Anglers, Cheators, Morts . . . and other Seruants both men & maides that haue beene pilferers.'[41] Like Walter Hindes, they lived on the margins of the community, close enough to learn some of the vocabulary, but not sufficiently integrated to become fluent speakers. They solved the problem by speaking a broken language, *poggadi jib*, known to scholars as Anglo-Romani. This combines Romani vocabulary with English grammar to create a kind of halfway house between the two. It is one of a range of Para-Romanis – such as Caló in Spain – which were created at the extreme points of the second wave of migration, where Gypsy met native Traveller. The two tongues, *puri* and *poggadi*, would co-exist in England for the next two centuries, with the ancestral form of the language gradually shrinking to an inner circle of old families; but as both idioms were equally unintelligible to outsiders, it is hard to know which was being spoken at any time. When Margaret Sergeant and her father left Surrey for Somerset in 1656, telling fortunes and sharing secrets in 'that strange language that they spake', was it true inflected Romani or just a series of code-words? We cannot tell.[42]

Gypsies would often have been in contact with the other people of the roads, sharing the same network of tracks and shelters. In cold weather everyone took refuge in large barns, apparently without any objections from the owners.[43] Farmers may have accepted the presence of strangers in winter in the knowledge that they would be back later to help at harvest time. The first migrants had roamed up and down the country in great bands, suspected and suspicious; but their descendants travelled in families rather than clans, making smaller circuits and returning to places where they were already known. It becomes possible to talk of Surrey Gypsies, rather than just Gypsies passing through Surrey.

It might seem constrained to stick to this single county when we are writing the history of a global diaspora, but a tight focus on one territory has its strengths. It makes us hunt out evidence wherever we can – in language, oral history and song, in handfuls of pegs and snares and herbs, in the sheen of golden scrollwork and tombstones: a medley of coconuts, water jacks and hedgehog fat. Gypsy history must be a history of life as it was lived, not just the bleak outlines traced by official documentation, and to do that it helps to view things up close.

Without its casual mention of Guildford, for instance, it would be easy to miss an illuminating episode from a little pamphlet written in 1671. This takes place in one of these barns where itinerant cultures found common space, and where poor Taffie, a Welshman who wishes he'd never left home, has taken shelter.

> He had not been there half an hour,
> Or hardly sate him down,
> But Gypsies came, in number four,
> Who came from Guildford town.

They quickly size up the stranger, and make him an offer:

> Kind friend, quoth they, you shall be one
> Of our fraternity;
> Our secrets to you shall be known,
> And we'll live happily.

All that Taffie needs to do is to climb down the chimney of a nearby house, holding onto a rope. Once he reaches the smoke chamber, where the sides of bacon are hanging, he is to tie one onto the rope, let his new friends pull up rope and bacon together, and then wait for them to throw the rope back down so that he can escape ... Of course, he waits and waits, for the Gypsies have gone, leaving him to face the irate householders alone.[44]

It's a cheap joke from a penny pamphlet, but it tells us something about Gypsies of the time – quite ready to adopt other travellers into their society, but able to recognize a fool when they saw one, and exploit him accordingly. It would take strength of character for a gorjer to win real acceptance in the community, but some passed the test. William Russel of Streatham took up with the Gypsies as a young man in the 1680s; he was a long traveller, visiting most parts of the country, where he mixed with doctors and astrologers, and picked up enough of both their arts to practise them profitably for the rest of his life. At some stage in his travels he adopted female dress, after which he spent his days as a woman, retiring in the end to the village where he was born, and dying there at the age of one hundred or more. Visitors found him – or should it be her? – 'a shrewd sensible person, with a good memory'.[45]

As this may suggest, Gypsies were already beginning to attract attention from the more eccentric sort of gorjer. In the late 1640s there had been another round-up of the community, perhaps out of fear that they might be carrying messages for the Royalist enemy in the Civil War. They were imprisoned, like their grandfathers, at the White Lion in Southwark, where they received a surprise visit from the visionary preacher Abiezer Coppe. 'I sate downe, and eat and drank around on the ground with Gypseys, and clip't, hug'd and kiss'd them, putting my hand in their bosomes, loving the she Gipsies dearly.' Risky behaviour, you might think; but the men of the party seem to have realized that Abiezer wasn't trying to carry on with their wives, but instead acting out a private spiritual vision of freedom from shame. At all events, he got out in one piece to continue his visionary career.[46]

Arresting Gypsies was not always a simple matter. In 1659 Francis Squire was travelling near the county border at Limpsfield with Robert Poole. This was presumably the same Robert who, with his wife Mary, had gone down into Wiltshire the previous year from a home territory on Romney Marsh.[47] Now the two men – without Mary, as far as we can tell – were apprehended and sent up to the House of Correction at Southwark. They were carrying their things on a mare, which was confiscated by the local churchwarden, along with the pack saddle with which she was loaded. Some months passed; Francis and Robert were never prosecuted, and the churchwarden was attempting to recoup the costs of £4 14s 8d which he had spent on hunting them down. The parish constable – who should have been implementing the anti-vagrancy laws, if anyone was – had kept a low profile but was now instructed to levy a special rate on everyone in the village to meet the payment. The sum of £4 was a lot of money – it meant the loss of a day's wages to every taxpayer of Limpsfield – and the zealous churchwarden who ran up this bill is unlikely to have been popular with his neighbours. In future, you suspect, they would let Gypsies pass through unmolested.[48]

Other residents were not so hostile. James Bird, who kept a pub at Ewell, gave lodgings to 'Babylonians otherwise known as Gipsyes' in 1677, and although he was reported for it to the magistrates, his establishment seems to have maintained its reputation as a good place for wanderers. Twelve years later his widow Frances was presented again for harbouring idle people.[49] The same complaint was made about other places at Quarter Sessions, although Gypsies are not specifically mentioned. All travelling people were potentially useful to farmers and anyone else who needed a pool of casual labour, and it was not much trouble for a pub landlord to accommodate them in an outbuilding.

But by this time, life on the roads was changing. The rootless army of unsettled poor, which had troubled the imaginations of so many magistrates since the beginning of the sixteenth century, was beginning to dwindle in numbers. After the convulsions of the Civil War, when many of the wanderers had been recruited as cannon fodder on both sides, there seemed to be fewer of them around, if only because the economy was starting to pick up. And even when population still exceeded the jobs available, people who could not find work or wages in their home village no longer needed to take to the road; instead, they were entitled to support from their own parish, following legislation which culminated in the Settlement Act of 1662.[50] In consequence, the name of 'vagrant', which had once covered throngs of displaced people, was now applied to the much smaller groups who had made itinerancy into a way of life. Chief among these were the Gypsies. No longer a strange people, they were beginning to take their place as the principals among the travelling population of England.

2

Long Travellers:
Georgian Britain

It was a raw, cold day in February 1753, and Mary Squires sat close to the fire, her son George and her eldest daughter Lucy beside her.[1] Like other old Gypsy women, she had endured enough on the road to make her glad of shelter, and she knew she would be welcome at Susannah Wells's house in Enfield. But Mary had not had time to take off her cloak when the door broke open and several men burst in, one of them a constable with a warrant. They blocked the door and told everyone in the house to stay still. Then the Gypsies heard the sound of wheels outside. A carriage stopped in front of the door, and two men came in, supporting a weak, emaciated girl: Elizabeth Canning was her name. They carried Elizabeth into the parlour, seated her by the door and asked if she recognized any of the people there. She looked in turn at Susannah, George and Lucy without recognition, then her gaze turned to Mary, who was still slouched under her outdoor bonnet. Without hesitation she said it was Mary who had first seen her when she was dragged into the house a month ago, who had cut off the stays which laced the bodice of her dress and pushed her upstairs into a dark attic. Throughout January, Elizabeth had remained trapped in this attic, until she was able to pull some boards away from the window and jump to freedom.

Mary stood up, dropping her cloak to show a face that was distorted, with a bulbous nose and swollen upper lip – the effects of untreated scrofula. 'Me rob you!', she shouted. 'I never saw you in my life before. For God Almighty's sake do not swear my life away! Pray, madam, look at this face. If you have seen it before, you must have remembered it: for God Almighty, I think, never made such another.' But Elizabeth stuck to her story. It was the beginning of two lawsuits that would drag on until May and threaten the old woman's life. It wasn't just that she was accused of having the girl beaten up, kidnapped, trafficked for prostitution and incarcerated in an unheated attic for 28 days with only one loaf of bread to eat and a jug of water. Eighteenth-century law could pass over these, which were merely personal assaults. But Mary was also accused of having stolen a set of stays worth 10s, which was theft, and theft was a hanging matter.

Later that February, the case came to trial at the Old Bailey. Elizabeth gave evidence in a courtroom full of her supporters, surrounded by a shouting, cheering mob which discouraged witnesses for the defence. But the crowd did not notice three strangers who were making their way towards the door. They came from the West Country, and they had been brought to the trial by George Squires in a desperate attempt to establish an alibi and prove his mother's innocence. One after the other, they took the stand and testified that in January, when Mary had allegedly been attacking and imprisoning young Elizabeth in the house at Enfield, she was in fact travelling 100 miles away along the Dorset coast. But the jury did not believe them. Mary was sentenced to death.

And yet something about Elizabeth's evidence was not right. In fact, once you stopped thinking of her as the frail innocent victim of an underworld gang, very little of her story made sense. Sir Crisp Gascoyne, who had presided over the trial as the Old Bailey was besieged by the mob, felt some doubts about the verdict. With far more resources at his command than young George, Crisp was able to bring forward further witnesses for the alibi, and to interview others who had been intimidated from giving evidence. At a second trial in May of the next year, Elizabeth was convicted of perjury, and at last Mary – whose life had been preserved by a royal pardon while the dispute ran on – was able to walk free.

The two trials of Mary Squires and Elizabeth Canning generated a mass of pamphlet literature – Accounts, Appeals, Reviews and Refutations. For months London was split into rival factions of Canningites and Egyptians, each one publishing all sorts of squibs and caricatures of the other. But at the heart of all this noisy paper war was the simple question of Mary's alibi. And for that to be reconstructed in any detail, the court would have to identify, and so preserve for us in a written record, the detailed itinerary of a Gypsy family in the winter of 1752/3.

Mary was a widow and had three children living at that time – George and Lucy, who were at Enfield, and young Polly. Polly had a brother-in-law at Southwark who lived among the network of Gypsy lodgings in the Borough and dealt in horses. He, in turn, had a son-in-law, one of

Mary Squires, 1753.

the Martins, the man who would later go down to Dorset at George's request to collect witnesses. There was a Samuel Squires at White Hart Inn Yard 'who belongs to the Customs' – not the most Gypsy of jobs, you might have thought. Then there was another member of the clan, known only as Mrs Squires, in the Borough, and she had a brother-in-law who was travelling in Kent; at the beginning of the troubles, Polly was staying with him, looking after domestic affairs, since his wife was ill. George himself had lodgings to the south at Newington and was 'well known in Norwood and in the towns and villages thereabouts'.[2]

George had left Newington in August 1752 and met up with his mother and sister in Kent. In the last months of the year they began travelling westwards, apparently through Salisbury and Mere.[3] George had some difficulty recalling this part of their route, perhaps for reasons connected with Gypsy business, for his memory suddenly sharpened up around 29 December just after the family had turned off the main route to Honiton and Exeter, and were making their way down through the village of South Perrott.[4] They slept at the Red Lion, and continued south over the hills to Litton Cheney, where a room was made ready for them at the Three Horseshoes. The Squires were on familiar ground; Mary had been travelling this part of the world since before George was born, and everyone knew her. At their next stop, the coastal village of Abbotsbury, the landlord of the Old Ship was waiting for them. It was New Year's Day and a party was arranged with dancing and music. Lucy danced with William Clarke the shoemaker, who was sweet on her and had hoped that someday she would leave the road and marry him.

By this stage their funds were beginning to run low. They had set out with £20 worth of aprons, gowns, handkerchiefs and light expensive fabrics like lace. Mary dukkered a little, and both she and Lucy could mend china, but this did not bring in much money. Nevertheless, they stayed in good rooms at all the pubs and were obviously not poor; indeed, George was generous enough to lend his coat to a shivering exciseman who was sharing rooms with him at Abbotsbury. After a week's stay, the Squires left the village for Upwey, where they stopped the night and then took the road from Weymouth to Dorchester. They crossed the swollen River Frome and followed the highway to Blandford, arriving the following afternoon in the village of Chettle. That was 26 miles in two days: creditable going for an old lady of sixty or upwards, especially one who had disdained the horse which carried her daughter across the Frome, and simply waded through it with the water swirling around her skirts.

There was no money for staying at pubs now, and no goods left to sell at them anyway. Mary would turn into a farmyard as the darkness fell and ask for a night's lodging in the barn; when the farmworkers said yes, George and Lucy would join her out of the shadows. They crossed the Test at Stockbridge and headed up to Basingstoke, arriving on 18 January at the Spread Eagle, where they stopped for a lunch of bread and beer. Lucy asked the landlady to write on her behalf to William Clarke, to make sure he hadn't taken cold after accompanying them all to Upwey. 'Hoping you are all in good health, as I be at present,' said Lucy, who had obviously picked up some Dorset grammar on her travels. 'George and mother give their compliments.'

They continued on the highway to Bagshot, where they spent the night, and then crossed the Thames at Staines, arriving that evening in Brentford, where Lucy had friends and Polly could come out from London to see them. After that it was Tottenham and Edmonton, and so finally to Enfield, their journey's end and the beginning of their troubles.

Then, after the triumphant verdict of May 1754, the Squires returned to the anonymity in which they would have spent their days if the spotlight of the law had not fallen on them. Mary ended up at Farnham, where she died in 1762. She had stopped in the town for six months, under an assumed name; passions still ran high over the mysterious lawsuits of a decade earlier, and she must have been afraid of vengeance from some surviving Canningite. In death she had the recognition which was lacking in life, for one hundred candles burned around her body, and forty Gypsy mourners followed her to the grave.[5]

The trial of Mary Squires shows the level of persecution which people could face in the eighteenth century, but it also shows its limits. Mary was not selected for denunciation because she was a Gypsy; she just happened to be in the wrong place at the wrong time.[6] When the caricaturists made her into a figure of fun, and were indifferent to the possibility of her death, it was not because she was one of the Romany people but just because she was an old, poor member of the underclass, the sort of person who didn't really matter. Fortunately, a number of people around London and in the West of England thought it did matter that someone they knew should not be hanged on a trumped-up charge, and they went to a lot of trouble to save her.

Not that all Gypsies were poor, for we are told that George Powell of Newington was 'in very flourishing circumstances' when he died in 1705, aged 47. Unlike his relative Robert, who we met at Limpsfield, George had gone into brick, since he is described as 'of this Parish' rather than an outsider. He was buried like a gentleman, under a black marble slab in the aisle of Newington church, where he was remembered for many years as King of the Gypsies.[7]

George was not the first to claim this kind of authority. In 1687 the parish church of Camberwell, 2 miles from Newington, had been chosen for the wedding of Robert Hern and Elizabeth Bozwell, 'King and Queen of the Jepsies'.[8] Nothing more is known of this couple, but their wedding must have been quite a grand affair to win a special mention in the parish register. More attention was paid to the funeral, many years later, of Margaret Finch. The Finches and Powells may have been related, since the two families were travelling together in 1658.[9] Margaret was about a generation older than Robert and Elizabeth, if she was really 109, as the report had it, when she died in 1740; but since claims for Gypsy centenarians are usually exaggerated, it's possible that all three were born at roughly the same time in the 1660s.[10] Whenever she was born, it was at Sutton in Kent, and 'after a Course of Traveling the Kingdom, as Queen of the Gypsie Tribe', she settled in the late 1720s at Norwood.

Margaret Finch,
1739.

This was her realm, and it was a good choice. Every weekend brought a stream of day trippers from London, half-sceptical and half-awestruck at being in the presence of the famed Norwood Gypsies and eager to pay for some entertainment as they caught their breath after a walk up the healthy, breezy hills. Here, in what her descendants would call the Wooded Land, Margaret Finch ended her life, and from here her funeral procession made its way to the nearby church at Beckenham.[11] The hearse was accompanied by two coaches and a special funeral sermon was preached, funded by the landlords of local pubs, for whom Margaret had been a profitable tourist attraction. And afterwards? 'This trade was of too profitable a description easily to be given up,' as a later biographer saw it, 'and a new queen was speedily introduced.'[12] This was the niece of Margaret Finch, known as Old Bridget (nobody remembers her surname). She died in 1768 near Dulwich and was buried at the chapel of Dulwich College, since there was no parish church for the village itself.[13] The third in this line of queens was Elizabeth, Margaret's granddaughter and Bridget's niece, who was still living – 'an old woman' – in the 1790s.[14]

But she was not the only claimant to monarchy. Local tradition at Penge remembered 'a celebrated King of the Gypsies' (name not known) who died on the common. After sitting up to watch over him, a great company of richly dressed Gypsies followed him to the grave at Beckenham.[15] In the Mint in Southwark 'Diana Boswell, Queen of the Gypsies' died in 1773. Her funeral, at Newington church, seems to have been even grander than Margaret's. Following the body in a numerous train of coaches, or walking behind them, was a vast gathering of the community, two hundred members in all, with innumerable strangers standing by the roadside and looking on. The ancient lady had a queer sense of humour, and she specified that the usual plumes of dark feathers on the hearse should be replaced by little soot-stained chimney-sweepers' boys, who sat perched around the coffin until the procession was over.[16]

Two years earlier, another Diana Boswell was to be found north of the river, at Isleworth; this was no ancient lady but a young girl, a rakli of 22, 'the King of the Gypsies' daughter', who had just married Joseph Lovell. Forty wedding guests sat down to dine under four elms on Hounslow Heath, with all kinds of food and drink; as they departed, the leftovers were magnanimously distributed among hundreds of gorjer bystanders.[17]

So there seem to have been at least two strains of royalty: one line descending through the Finches and Powells, the other through the Boswells and Hearns. George Powell had a successor of the same name, for the Gypsies of Southwark were still known in 1726 as Powell's gang. There were about fifty of them, meeting up in houses at the top end of Kent Street and at Bird Cage Alley on the west of Borough High Street. In the winter they would split up, some fanning through the streets south of the river, others crossing London Bridge into the City, where they would tell fortunes, 'and thereby cheat and impose upon young People, and the Ignorant and Unwary'; so said a resident of the Mint who for some private reason was eager to have them prosecuted.[18] But this was in March, and within a month or so the gang must have drifted out of town on their summer travels.

Evidently the royal title was worth contending for. But what good was it to anyone? Of Elizabeth, the third in the line of Norwood queens, a contemporary wrote 'her rank seems to be merely titular; I do not find that the Gypsies pay her any particular respect; or that she differs in any other respect, than that of being a householder, from the rest of her tribe.'[19] Respect was certainly shown by the large numbers attending weddings and funerals, and these were events staged by and for the community; the processions, feasts and so on may have caught the eye of outsiders (otherwise we'd never have known about them) but that was a side-effect of their real purpose, which was to affirm the particular place which a few Gypsies had in the esteem of the rest.

Some of that respect was earned by wealth. George Powell evidently left enough money for an expensive tomb. The father of young Diana Boswell declared that he could give his son-in-law £1,000. Old Bridget is said to have 'died worth above 1000*l*', although another source puts it more modestly as a little over £200.[20] At all events an old stocking, found in the wall of Bridget's winter lodgings in Kent Street, contained a further £20 7s 6d and this must have been only a small proportion of her total estate, since nobody had noticed it missing. The Gypsy who discovered the money – she went by the name of Lady Lincoln – evidently felt that it still belonged in some way to Bridget and spent it on a party at Dulwich for twenty people in memory of the old lady.[21] Nobody guessed at the wealth of the elder Diana Boswell, but her clothes alone were worth £50 when they were ritually burnt after her death in Southwark.

The burning, as someone explained to bystanders, was carried out 'according to ancient custom'. The reporter seems to have come away with the idea that it was a special arrangement for Gypsy queens, so that their clothes would not be worn afterwards by commoners, but this is probably a misunderstanding of the deep-rooted aversion that people felt to the reuse of anyone's personal things after death. In the case of Diana, the requirement that such things should be burnt was evidently carried out very publicly, and this gives a clue to what 'king' or 'queen' might have meant in contemporary life. These were exemplary Gypsies – people who had never deviated from the ways of the Romany, and who in consequence had been blessed with worldly success and long life. That surely explains why the tradition of Gypsy royalty began at the end of the seventeenth century, and why it spread from the immediate outskirts of London. This was a time and place where Gypsies faced assimilation into the floating suburban population, and where it became more important than ever to affirm traditions which marked you out as a separate people.

Some of these ethnic markers – the grand funeral, the lavish attitude to wealth – would continue to resonate with Gypsies in subsequent years. In other ways, though, these early kings and queens did not follow all the rules which would later mark out a true Gypsy, a tatcho Romanichal. For instance, they seem to have had no objections to living in houses. Bridget had lodgings at Kent Street, which she occupied 'during the Winter

Season, for nearly thirty Years last past'. Evidently she saw no point in shivering on the windy slopes of Norwood during the dead season when no visitors came. As tents did not seem to have been in use until the end of the eighteenth century, she would have had little alternative to house-dwelling; barns and other outbuildings were the only alternative means of shelter in hard weather, and there must have been a limited supply of these. At Knaphill in the 1760s, families were living in a cave cut into the hillside, its roof supported by planks, and a hole cut into the upper air for a chimney.[22] In the drawing made a year before her death, Margaret Finch squats within a conical structure of branches, apparently clad with bark and brushwood or turf.[23] Later we hear of Thomas Lee, who by this time had married a girl called Eleanor, setting up home in a hut at Brixton Causeway, on the highway north of Streatham.[24]

Margaret was evidently a formidable old lady, although it is not clear whether her hunched posture was really, as claimed, the result of a life spent squatting over the fire, or something forced by arthritis in her last years. They say that she was buried in a square coffin, because nothing could straighten her out, but close inspection at the site of her grave near the church tower revealed nothing that would corroborate this.[25] At all events, she handed down a tradition that any self-respecting ancient Gypsy should be distorted in some way. When Sarah Skemp greeted a visitor to Norwood in 1790, he saw:

> An aged Sybil . . . who from age and infirmity was unable to go otherwise than upon all-fours. Her prominent and large sinews, bones, and muscles, were all perceptible beneath her rigid hide, which hide resembled in hue the smoke-dyed blanket that partially covered her. Nine growling curs, ugly as the monsters depicted in the representations of St Anthony's temptation, formed her body-guard, and prowled around her; and a tame jackdaw hopped upon her finger at command.[26]

That was theatre, if anything was. Who could doubt that such an amazing old lady would be capable of foretelling the future for a silver sixpence? But not everyone went to such extremes. Elizabeth, the third in the line of Norwood queens, lived simply in a small cottage overlooking a green valley where the road ran through the woods. 'On this green, a few families have pitched their tents, for a great number of years, during the summer season' – and this, in 1796, is the first time that tents are mentioned.[27]

Beside Elizabeth's cottage was a pub called the Gipsy House, which in the 1790s had a signpost copying the portrait of old Margaret. It was a stroke of luck for the landlord that she had been drawn with a heavy pewter mug within reach: no doubt the beer helped alleviate pain in those old bent limbs. If early prints are to be trusted, the Gipsy House was a building of some pretensions: two storeys high in weatherboarded white planks, roofed with pantiles and lit by sash windows, it had an overhanging first floor which rested on three wooden pillars to provide a covered area in which visitors could shelter from the sun or rain.[28] It stood, though increasingly rickety, until Hall Green was enclosed in 1808, when its grounds were developed for a small villa which kept the old name.[29]

Enterprises at the Gipsy House seem to have been run, at least in part, by the community itself. Daniel Cooper, of the Windsor Coopers, worked here as a waiter for two years in 1796–7.[30] 'A Person who lately kept a Public-House on Norwood-Hill, and goes by the Name of the Secretary to the Gypsies' was a guest of honour at the party in memory of old Bridget in 1769; his secretarial skills might have been no more than a willingness to read and write letters for people, but at any rate he was clearly a trusted gorjer of some kind. The party itself took place not at the Gipsy House but at another pub near Dulwich, called Allen's in the Wood. Gypsy musicians played until 7.00 p.m. in the evening, and then the company adjourned to Kent Street 4 miles away – which sounds as if they owned or could hire something horse-drawn.[31] There was evidently

The Old Gipsy House, Norwood, 1802.

a network of pubs favourable to Gypsies, like the Rumbo Castle in Chipstead, where little Sarah Wells's mother lay in to give birth to her in 1774.[32] Landlords at these establishments had got to know Gypsies as regulars rather than strangers, and learned to like them. The owner of the Horns at Knight's Hill, half a mile away from the main settlement at Norwood, gave an 'excellent character' for Stephen Lee and his four sons when they were taken up for robbery in 1795, after which all charges were dropped.[33]

By now Norwood was familiar to most Londoners, and in the winter season of 1777, audiences at Covent Garden were treated to the new entertainment of *The Norwood Gypsies*. Most of it was the standard pantomime fare, with Harlequin, Columbine and Pierrot, but the Gypsies provide an opening chorus for the first scene. This is set in a rustic village, from which an angry Justice of the Peace tries to evict them; there is a stage fight with the Justice's men, which the Gypsies win; they then retreat to 'their hutt' and propose, by way of revenge, that Harlequin shall run away with the Judge's daughter. And so he does, in a number of comic adventures which all lead to the big closing number where the Gypsies come back on stage again and persuade the Judge to give his blessing to the union.[34] In that warm, pre-Christmas glow, London audiences were prepared to take the side of the Gypsies against wicked magistrates who tried to move them on.

With this kind of media attention, the Norwood Gypsies had successfully transformed themselves from outcast wanderers into a successful brand. As was said of Margaret, 'the Oddness of her Figure and the Fame of her Fortune telling, drew a vast Concourse of Spectators from the highest Rank of Quality, even to those in the lower Class of Life.' Claims for the highest rank were no exaggeration. In 1750 the settlement was visited by Frederick Prince of Wales, accompanied by his princess and three peers, along with two commoners.[35] The Gypsy queens found themselves courted by the aristocracy of the land. One of the line, presumably old Bridget, was frequently visited by the daughter of an earl, who followed her advice implicitly.[36]

The community now presented themselves as experts in all occult matters, and as new methods of divination were invented, so the Gypsies spread them through the land. Sometime in the early eighteenth century, when coffee was ceasing to be a luxury and becoming affordable for ordinary householders, news went round that the pattern of black specks left in a cup after drinking afforded a glimpse behind the curtain of Fate.

Sarah Chilcock learnt the craft when she was growing up in Newington Butts. In 1720 she married George Kemp, from the same little district, and they set up life on the road together – in summer, at least; it was July 1740 when George and Sarah were picked up by the authorities at Nantwich, he selling hardware and she 'pretending to tell fortunes by coffee grounds'.[37]

Gypsy expertise in this area was commemorated in a painting commissioned in the 1730s, one of a set which decorated the pleasure gardens at Vauxhall. They showed traditional English scenes and pastimes, so the Gypsies were in good company; evidently the management of the gardens had no prejudice against fortune-telling. Three ladies are taking coffee on the lawn outside their house. The silver coffeepot, the ornamental furnishings of the fourth stool, and the supercilious expression of the spaniel who sits there all show that this is a wealthy mansion. The old Gypsy woman, who seems to have slipped out from among the trees around the lawn, is holding a cup and expounding its meaning. Behind the Gypsy a young man rests on the branch of the tree, unseen by the others. We are to understand that he has bribed the Gypsy to discover signs that will further his attempts on the heart of one of the young ladies.[38]

That was alright by the Gypsies, who knew that a little harmless flirtation helps sales. Here is a girl in the meadows at Chessington, ready to charm potential customers on a summer afternoon in 1779:

> Tho her complexion look'd Egyptian her eyes and features were
> so remarkably beautiful that one could scarce look at her without
> surprise. – All her features were elegantly formed, and her eyes and
> whole countenance were animated with an expression that was in
> the highest degree attractive and captivating . . . Her face was oval
> – her nose Grecian and beautiful – her mouth small, and her teeth
> white, regular, lovely – her eyes hazle [sic], brilliant and charming.[39]

She offered to tell fortunes for 1s, but quickly dropped the price to 6d and 'told a great deal of comical nonsense'. She was dealing with a party of two men and four women, too large for a single dukkerer, so her mother came in to help. The older gentleman proved sceptical about the secret enemies whose names and addresses would be revealed for a further 12d, so mother quickly turned to the younger, assuring him that 'he was a Gay Man amongst the Ladies'. This was a misjudgement of a gentleman's character: the young rai quivered, looked embarrassed and refused to hear

Fortune-telling by coffee grounds at Vauxhall Gardens, 1730s.

or pay any more. So she turned to work the ladies. One was married, so there wasn't much to say except that 'she would never have any more husbands than she had now'; but to the spinster it was 'you too have had many suitors, and will have many proffers – but you've fixed your heart on one alone.' And so, in an atmosphere of chatter and laughter and quick repartee, the gorjers are amused and the Gypsies go away a little richer.

A family couldn't make a living by dukkering alone; the men too needed to have occupations. Franes Doe, who was travelling at East Clandon in 1769, was a chimney-sweep and a tinman, while one of his descendants was apprenticed to a basketmaker.[40] Stephen Lee told the magistrates that he 'occasionally lives in the Mint in the borough of Southwark and works in different parts of the Town by driving a Barrow with a Tinning pot, and he works as a Tinker'. Could he have been the same Gypsy tinker who took up a sideline in the scrap business in 1794? This enterprising soul, passing by a derelict pub in Southwark, went back later with two gorjer colleagues and pulled out a cast-iron cooking range with a potcrane, firegrate and fireback, all of which were sold on to a dealer in Mint Street.[41] At all events, Stephen had a son, Adam, who also worked in metal; 'he occasionally lives in the neighbourhood of Wandsworth Putney and Windsor in the Winter working at his Tinkering Business.'[42] A warm brazier must have been a comfort as well as an asset when they were pacing the streets in winter, but during the mellow season the Lees travelled further afield, and they were picked up with seven other people while at the hop harvest in Tonbridge in September 1799. Four years earlier Stephen and his four sons (John, Robert and Thomas as well as Adam) had been apprehended at Norwood; on that occasion they said that they got their living by fortune-telling and horse-dealing.[43] Not that there was anything specifically Gypsy about these trades. Harvesting and hopping, sweeping chimneys, making brooms and mats, mending chairs, tinning and brazing, acting as a pedlar, even fortune-telling: these were crafts practised by transients of all backgrounds.[44] If something brought in a living, it would soon be imitated by other people of the road.

All the same, Gypsies remained distinct from other travelling communities; if you said that someone was a Gypsy, you were not just commenting on their character or lifestyle, but stating an objective fact about their family origins, since every Romanichal was descended from ancestors who had come during the Arrival. But that didn't preclude them being descended from other people as well. It was known that the Gypsy community in England had absorbed a lot of gorjer blood. A writer in the 1740s wrote of how:

This tawny Progeny, either by fair Means or foul (our Annals do not say which) mixing with the British Women . . . propagated their . . . Species, first in the New Forest, then all over Hampshire, Sussex, Surrey, and Kent, and at long-run in almost every County of Great-Britain.[45]

Certainly English Gypsies didn't look as if they had just arrived from Bohemia or the Carpathians. We can tell as much from contemporary art. The eighteenth century was an age of new pictorial forms, one of which was the genre scene of country life. Gypsies were part of this rural scene, and yet tinged with a sense of the exotic, which had an instant appeal in a crowded market, and explains why the walls of art galleries are crowded with canvases called *Gypsy Camp*, *Heath with Gypsies*, *Gypsies by Moonlight* and so on, many of them just copies of other pictures. But an exception should be made for the Gypsy pictures of George Morland. To start with, he was criticized at the time for being *too* realistic in his portrayal of common life. He preferred the company of working-class people to that of his patrons, and he had travelled with Gypsies; he 'lived with them for several days together, adopting their mode of life, and sleeping with them in barns at night'.[46] Furthermore, he was famous for never forgetting a face. All of this suggests that George's portraits of Gypsies are real depictions of the people he mixed with on Hampstead Heath. And they do not look like modern Roma; they look recognizably English.

However, there is no doubt that Gypsies were dark. 'Tawny' and 'swarthy' are the adjectives regularly used, and although these were clichés, a cliché has to come from somewhere. Furthermore, we find that people freely made allusions to their own complexion. The girl at Chessington laughed and compared herself to a blackamoor, then thought of another explanation, and put it down to pre-natal influence: 'Sir, my mother long'd for charcoal.' On Epsom Downs, the boxer Dick Curtis was called out by another fighter. 'Why,' says Dick, 'by the look of your mug, you are what they call a Gipsy? Which set do you belong to?'; and the Gypsy – 'the Browny Index Hero' – proudly replies that he is a Cooper.[47] It was obviously taken for granted by both parties that you could tell a Gypsy apart from other men by his brown complexion.

The survival of the community in a strange land had been made possible by selective intermarriage with other travelling people, which meant that English Gypsies were darker than the natives of England, but lighter than their fellow Romani elsewhere. This is borne out by a report from the centre of Gypsy culture in 1761:

> There have been lately observed, in and about Norwood, a new
> sort of gipsies. They are blacker than those who formerly used
> to be there, and speak very bad English . . . If you ask them any
> questions, they cannot or will not understand you, but are very
> complaisant; and if you give them any thing, they play several
> anticks. They are stout well-made men, and appear very nimble.[48]

These were evidently Continental Gypsies who had recently arrived; their dark faces showed what English Gypsies had been like two hundred years earlier. Like all immigrants, the 'new sort' had picked out the easiest place to make a living in the traditional way. Clearly their English was still imperfect, but that was only a problem when rokkering to the gorjers, since Old Romani continued to be spoken at Norwood well into the nineteenth century.[49] Eventually, no doubt, they merged within the community and contributed a little to the diversity of the Gypsy complexion.

It is not easy to trace this process of integration, because all Gypsy surnames are ultimately derived from gorjer families: in the earliest records, we can trace people of the same name, but cannot feel certain of their ethnicity. How did these surnames come into the community? They might have been adopted at random by Gypsies who had reasons for not wanting to be known under their old name, or they might have derived from a Gypsy girl who, having married a gorjer, was content to let her children carry their father's name rather than her own. Either way, you would expect that people would acquire surnames which were already common in the area where they were travelling, and this is what usually happened.

The one exception to this, at least in southeast England, is the family of the Brazils, for Brazil is not an English surname at all; it is from the Irish clan Uí Breasail.[50] So it is not surprising to find William Brazill, an Irishman and a traveller, christening his son at Penshurst in 1768. William had married Ann, a London girl. They stayed at Penshurst for several years, but their son John felt the call of the travelling life and moved around Kent and Sussex for the next thirty or forty years.[51] After that the record is obscure, until in the late nineteenth century we find the Brazils burying at Chiddingfold with full Gypsy ceremony. Evidently at some point in the intervening years one of William's descendants had married into a Gypsy family and carried his name with him.

As new names were adopted by the community, old ones fell out of use. Though the Gypsies of the Arrival had identified themselves by dozens of surnames, most of them adopted from French or Flemish originals, it is surprising how rapidly these vanished from the English scene. Of the names recorded for actual immigrants, Valentine was the last to disappear; there were still Valentines travelling in the 1620s but after that they were no longer known, at least under that name.[52] And then after a gap of two centuries the name appears again in Kent, with Alexander Vallintine marrying a daughter of Gilderoy Scamp. Is this a coincidence, or had the name survived as a traditional alias? There are other instances of an early surname suddenly appearing after long disuse. In 1579 Philip Bastian was among a company picked up in Berkshire and then in 1791 we find William Bastin stopping on Epsom Common.[53] Similarly, there was a Christopher Stephens travelling with Philip, and Jasper Steevens, 'a poore Traveller', baptized children at Guildford and Godalming before being buried at Woking in 1688. Then, after a gap of centuries, we find Adam Stevens having three of his children christened in 1858 at Hale.[54] But in the absence of any genealogical connection, it is hard to tell whether these are real family links or just newly forged links to names from the settled community.

Surnames come and go. The Powells, Finches and Squires, who once ranked large among the community, are now extinct, at least under that name.[55] But the history of Gypsy names is not one of slow replacement over time. Instead, there is one set of surnames found up until a period sometime in the seventeenth century, after which people went under another, quite different set. The later surnames, which feature with increasing frequency in documents from 1700 onwards, have never disappeared. They are the names of the best Gypsy families today.

We have already seen how Boswell and Hearn were the names of a Gypsy king and queen in 1687. Kemp may be even older as a Gypsy name in Surrey, although the evidence is weak. Mary Kemp, a 'stranger' (which doesn't necessarily mean a travelling woman), was buried at Dorking in 1649. She is down as the daughter of Dordie Kemp, which might possibly mean that a relative, when asked who her father was, answered in surprise 'Dordi! What do you want to know that for?'[56] At any rate there was a George Kemp at Newington in 1720 and a Sarah Skemp at Norwood in 1790. The name must have been current for a while before it split into the two branches of Kemp and Skemp/Scamp, just as the Keets and Sketes were originally one family.[57]

The Lees, like the Boswells, wintered in the warren of small houses around the Borough; in the September of 1735 Elisha and Phillis Lee of Kent Street had gone down to West Malling, no doubt for the hopping.[58] In 1754 Elizabeth Lea, 'child of some gipsies', was buried at Compton just off the Hog's Back, and the funeral of Levina Lee followed the year after at Great Bookham.[59] But the Lees may be much older; at least this is suggested by the code-name Purrum, used when people wanted to refer to the family in Anglo-Romani. Purrum has a range of meanings, from 'onion' to 'wild garlic', but the intended sense here is evidently 'leek'.[60] This would be a good match for the original form of the name, which was Leigh, pronounced with a final consonant. If so, there must have been Gypsy Lees before about 1600, when the name took on its modern pronunciation.

By the time they emerge into genealogical history, at the end of the eighteenth century, the Lees had already branched out into multiple lines and had acquired a certain mystique. This was the say, the family tradition: that they had once been a powerful clan, represented by eight strong brothers, until they were all taken up in one day for sheep-stealing and seven of them were hanged – leaving the youngest, Damon Lee, a broken man. If there is any truth behind this, it must have happened at a very early date. There was a Damon Lee born in 1770, and he had at least five elder brothers, but all of them seem to have escaped the hand of the law. One of these was Edward, who took Elizabeth Lee down the aisle of Binsted church in 1780. Elizabeth was born at Walton on Thames, and her second daughter Keziah was born when the family were at Kingston, but otherwise they mostly travelled in Sussex and Hampshire. She was stopping west of Alton in 1796 when she was taken up for housebreaking with two of her girls and a son, Damon. When interrogated about her life and background, she said that she had borne 23 children, which, if true – *could* it be true? – means that she had been married to Edward for some years before their church wedding, unless he was her second husband. Only twelve of the 23 survived, a chilling illustration of the hardships of life on the road.[61]

But by some mixture of luck and endurance, families did survive and grow. Well-known Gypsy lineages can all be found represented in the eighteenth century; not just the ones we've just seen, but Ayres, Coopers, Lovells, Chilcots and Gregorys. Even the line of Smith – difficult to distinguish from the mass of gorjer Smiths – is represented by Shadrach Smith, who was born at Norwood in the 1700s, although the rest of his life was spent in Oxfordshire. Perhaps his parents had travelled from their usual country to meet up with friends and family, as a later generation would do at Hampton Races and on the Downs at Epsom. Anyway, Shadrach made his living mostly as a rat catcher, although he was suspected of quietly testing the locks on a farm's pigsties and henroosts while he went about his business, and thefts took place not long after he had visited. He was arrested for highway assault in 1738 but released. Finally, in 1761, he attacked a girl on the road near Chalgrove, robbed her of 2s, and pulled a knife on her, but was prevented from cutting her throat by the interposition of his ten-year-old son. On trial in Oxford, he insisted that the boy give evidence, with the inevitable result that he was convicted and sent to the gallows, where he took a large quid of tobacco, protested his innocence, and was launched into eternity.[62]

But, by and large, most Gypsies seem to have earned an honest living, at least by the standards of the eighteenth-century working class. Some pilfering from farmers and wealthy householders was inevitable, given the disparities that existed in income; theft, like parish poor relief, kept life going in a society sharply divided between haves and have-nots.

What frightened authority was not the occasional act of a desperate individual, but the prospect of the whole underclass in revolt at once. The Gordon Riots of 1780 – the last of the really terrifying mob risings – saw London reduced to anarchy over five blazing nights. Two brothers, Joseph and Robert Lovell, were caught up in the violence. Both of them were present when the Southwark jail was broken open and put to the flames. Unfortunately, the energy of the mob was then redirected to the Two Brewers, a nearby pub which was not part of any system of social exploitation but contained a great deal of beer. Robert found an iron bar, smashed in the windows, and helped pass out furniture to the waiting crowd, while Joseph more prudently made his excuses and left. This saved his life, earning him a reprieve after the two men were sentenced to death. There was no such luck for Robert, and he was taken to the gallows in St George's Fields at Lambeth, along with his young gorjer wife Elizabeth Collins. He looked 'uncommon morose'; she was in abject terror, unable to bear having a handkerchief tied over her face as was the custom; at the moment of the drop, she reached up and tore it half away, letting the crowd see what a face looks like in slow strangulation.[63]

The different fates of the two Lovell brothers were typical of a legal system which either killed people or pardoned them completely. It was in reaction to this that the courts had begun to deal in a third alternative: the commutation of a sentence to transportation. At first America was the destination of choice, but the War of Independence put an end to that. For a while potential transportees were piled up on disused ships in the Thames seaway while the government pondered what to do about them. Then, in 1787, the First Fleet sailed to Australia, carrying a cargo of 736 convicts. Among them, on the *Charlotte*, was James Squire.

James was the son of Timothy Squire and Mary Wells, coming from a family who had been travelling for many years in Hertfordshire and Surrey; we have already met his remote kinsman Francis in 1659 at Limpsfield. He was at Kingston in 1774, where he was charged with highway robbery and sentenced to be transported. The American Revolution cut this plan short, and he agreed to serve in the army instead, returning afterwards to Kingston where he ran a pub, married a gorjer girl and had three children. In 1785 he was tried again, for stealing chickens, and although this would not normally have merited such a severe punishment, his old conviction must have told against him since he was sentenced to seven years transportation. Ironically, his brother Timothy Squire was also on the First Fleet, not as a convict but as mate on the *Lady Penrhyn*.

Jemmy Lovell with
his brazier, 1819.

In the starved and brutal atmosphere of New South Wales, James
appears to have been a trusted man. While still a convict, he was armed
and enlisted to accompany the governor, Captain Arthur Phillip, in a
tense encounter with the natives. Later, after his emancipation, Squire
settled on an estate at Ryde and, unlike his neighbours, maintained good
relationships with Aborigines – whether through human decency, self-
preservation or a sense of kinship with the dark wandering people, there
is no way to know. At Ryde he grew hops and brewed the first Australian
beer, drawing on skills carried over from his Kingston pub days.[64]

James may have been entrusted with a gun in Australia because of
his previous time in the army. Many itinerants drifted in and out of military service, especially the young unmarried men, who may have seen it
as a way of getting regular meals and picking up a skill or two. Franes
Doe had served in the Surrey Militia at some point before his marriage
and the birth of his eldest in 1769. Normally militia service was a duty

for householders, but those who didn't feel bellicose enough would often buy in a substitute, and this may be how Franes came to serve. Certainly it was as a substitute that Thomas Lee, who travelled with his brother Adam and father Stephen at Tonbridge, was in the Berkshire Militia from 1791 to 1793.[65] Samuel Ayres from the Hampshire/Surrey borderlands also served in the army, presumably in the 1760s as he was born in 1745, and it may be as a mark of respect for his achievements that the name Major became traditional in the family. The first Major Ayres was travelling in Ewell with his wife Hannah in 1786; three years later they had a church wedding at Hampstead Norris in Berkshire.[66]

Gypsy men certainly looked fit to be soldiers. A patriot, writing to the newspapers about recruiting, paid them that compliment. 'By their habits of life they are inured to hardship; they are a strong, hardy, capable race.' Then came the sting. With all these martial qualities, why should they be allowed to hang around Norwood – 'where they chiefly abound' – and the rest of the country doing nothing, or worse? Instead, they should be collected by magistrates and sent in irons to the nearest seaport to join the Navy, where 'the comforts of warm cabins, and regular meals' would soon convert them to a respectable way of life.[67] It was the latest expression of the old, old dream of authority: its desire to make all the vagrant people vanish forever, thinly cloaked under a pretext of manufacturing good citizens.

But except in fantasies like this, the government was never able to suppress the travelling life. For more than one hundred years the Tudor legislation on vagrants had seemed quite satisfactory, but in 1740 it was updated and clarified in a new Act which, without specifically mentioning Gypsies, introduced a category of 'idle and disorderly persons' to cover all itinerant people not found guilty of anything else. So when George and Sarah Raynes were travelling with Hannah Miles through Worplesdon in 1764, they were picked up for being 'Egyptians and Vagrants lying about in a loose disorderly manner in the open air'.[68] The Act covered a much wider range of people than Gypsies; under its provisions almost anyone could be taken up if their wandering existence annoyed the authorities. This lay behind the instructions issued by parish vestrymen at Wimbledon for apprehending

> all persons collecting alms on pretences of loss by fire or other casualty, all strolling players and jugglers and gypseys, all persons playing and abetting unlawful games, and persons wandering

abroad and lodging in ale-houses, barns, outhouses, or in the open air, not giving a good account of themselves, pretending to be soldiers, mariners, seafaring men, and all other persons wandering abroad and begging.

Each and all of them could be arrested by any respectable citizen who felt so inclined, at a bounty of 10s per head, and sent off to jail in Southwark, where they could lie on the damp floor waiting for the next Quarter Sessions.[69]

The 1662 Act of Settlement and its successors had provided a safety net for the village poor, but this was of little value to people who were not settled and didn't want to be. Everybody, in theory, had a place of settlement. Men might acquire one by owning property or having a regular job; women took their husband's settlement. Mary Squires, who was picked up in London in 1790 under the usual formula of 'lodging in the open Air and not giving a good account of Herself', was asked to give a place of settlement and identified it as Malden, because her late husband James had earned it by working there for a year as a farm labourer.[70]

If the right to relief had not been acquired by a year's hired service or other qualifications, then your legal settlement was the place where you were born. In the case of long travellers, that would have meant a laborious journey home, if it had been performed according to instructions – though it is doubtful if it ever was. We have seen how Sarah Chilcock and George Kemp were picked up in Cheshire and told to return to Newington, 150 miles away. Presumably they left Nantwich on the southeasterly road, took the drom until they were out of sight, and then continued with business as usual.

But although in practice the place of settlement might have little importance for Gypsies, it was always good to have one. If you could show proof of your birth parish, a constable or magistrate would order you to return there, and once out of sight you were free. But if you couldn't present this, you were more likely to be whipped or imprisoned as a vagrant. So, from the 1740s onwards, there was a strong motive for travelling people to get their children baptized. Leaving aside the religious benefits – and they may have mattered just as much – an entry in the parish register would give your child a claim for settlement in later life. This was recognized by the parish authorities, but they took a very different view of the situation, since every poor person claiming settlement in the parish was potentially another mouth to be fed at their expense. Some undignified tussles took place between Gypsies who wanted a birth recorded in the village church, and local magistrates who wanted anything but.

Mary Cooper was travelling with her husband Moses through Merton in 1723. Her time was near, and she gave birth to a baby girl. A week passed; it was Sunday, and the church was full when Mary came and sat in the porch, waiting to have her baby christened. The village constable saw her; he went and whispered to the magistrate, Henry Meriton; and Henry stood up in mid-service and walked out into the porch, where he took Mary by the arm and hustled her across the road, with Moses following after. They were pushed into the courtyard of the magistrate's house, locked in, and forced to swear that they would leave the parish at once, without the child being baptized. Mary was beside herself and, as soon as she was free, she set off to Wimbledon, where Edward Collins lived. He was the minister who had taken the service at Merton before returning to his own village. On Tuesday Mary got access to the vicarage, where she begged Edward to christen her child: and so little Susanna was baptized at last, with her parents standing by, and the village doctor and vicar's wife acting as godparents.[71]

This sort of low-level persecution was part of the travelling life. It was hard, but nothing like the savage pack-hunts being organized at this time against European Gypsies. But even in England there was a risk from vigilante groups of gorjers. The heaths between Chobham and Frimley, with their empty commons and straggling woods, had become a natural refuge for people who had been moved on from more settled regions. Gypsies shared this space with other itinerants, as well as smugglers; when cargo was being smuggled from the Hampshire coast, Bagshot Heath was the last stop before a final night's journey to safe houses in the London suburbs. In 1769 there were supposed to be five hundred men ready to make a last stand in Knaphill Wood, a terrifying confederacy of the enemies of order, although their actual crimes seem to have extended no further than dining on occasional ducks and geese from the nearby farms. However, the local agriculturalists were not taking any risks. Armed with bludgeons, muskets and pistols, they set out from Guildford, marching up cautiously through Worplesdon. At this point the Lord of Bagshot Park was persuaded to join the enterprise, bringing some much-needed expertise – a few years earlier, he had successfully invaded and occupied Cuba – together with the loan of fourteen pieces of cannon. The two columns united to reckon with the forces of anarchy, most of whom promptly made themselves scarce. 'However, after a sharp onset, they took fourteen of them' together with three of their horses, and also five children who had been sheltering from the fight on mattresses stuffed with goose and duck feathers.[72]

This was a rare instance of private warfare; normally in England oppression took place through due form of law, and eighteenth-century law was focused not on people but on property. This, too, could be dangerous; there were rumours of terrible things done in the name of secure ownership. In the 1750s one of the Gregorys was said to have been hanged for horse-stealing at Kingston Assizes, with all his eleven sons strung up beside him as accomplices.[73] But racial prejudice of any kind was alien to the spirit of the age. Even for people who venerated the laws of old England, it was a standing embarrassment that these included something as ridiculous as the 1562 Act which required the capital punishment of Gypsies just because they were Gypsies. In 1783, after many years of lying dormant, the old legislation was repealed 'as an Act of excessive severity'. The path lay open to a better future. Or did it?

3

Lucky for Some:
Regency Days

It was December 1836, a cold season. Snow was threatening and Mary
Cooper needed a sheltered spot to put up the bender tent; luckily,
they had stopped just outside Esher on a bit of ground shielded by
the bank of the Portsmouth Road. Mary was a widow, relying on the
support of her son Matty and his wife Eliza, and her daughter Sarah,
who had also lost her husband. Eliza's time was near; it would be her first
baby, and they needed somewhere secure to stop for the birth. A week
later they had been joined by two more of Mary's sons – Leonard with his
wife Phyllis, and Nelson and his wife Bella. An elderly parent travelling
with her married children was a typical family pattern for large groups.
The men of the company were out most of the day, leaving their wives
and sisters to take care of Eliza and mind the children. And every day,
at 2.30 or 3 p.m., the women noticed that a pair of gorjers would come
walking down the road: a young lady, very quiet but expensively dressed,
and her older companion, for whom she obviously had a high regard.
It was Sarah who broke the ice, by introducing herself, her mother and
her sister-in-law. The young lady needed no introduction, for she was
Princess Victoria, who lived at Claremont House on the crest of the hill
overlooking the road. The daily walks along the road with her governess
Louise Lehzen continued, the princess grew familiar with the Gypsies,
and they with her; so much so that, a week later, Sarah

stepped across the road from the tents, and as we turned and
stopped, came up to us with a whole swarm of children, six I think.
It was a singular, and yet a pretty and picturesque sight. She herself
with nothing on her head, her raven hair hanging untidily about
her fine countenance, and a dingy dark green cloak hung on one

side of her shoulders, while the set of little brats swarming round her, with dark dishevelled hair and dark dresses, all little things and all beautiful children. She spoke to Lehzen and said they were the children of her two brothers, and 'I am aunt to all these'. She . . . then proceeded to name all the children, of which I remember only 5: Dinah, Job, Britannia, Emmeline, and I think Helen. Britannia is a beautiful little large-black-eyed, with a dirty face which was wiped to be shown off. Sarah then pointed to her own boy, called George, her only child, who was carrying another little nephew named Nelson on his back. The pretty sister-in-law is not mother of these children, for she is only 20 and has none as yet.[1]

The daily walks went on, and each time Victoria noticed more things about the Gypsies: how well bred and discreet Sarah was, the good looks of Bella, who 'has a sharp, clever, but good-humoured expression', the 'singular, clever but withered countenance' of Mary, and a glimpse of Matty – 'he has a peculiar, handsome, dark Italian countenance and seems quite young.' By and large, however, the men of the party kept out of sight, perhaps feeling that they might not be quite so welcome as their womenfolk.[2] The Cooper women were all ready to engage in conversation, though it was noticeable that they spoke English with a slight foreign accent and used a number of dialect expressions – 'sad' for 'ill', 'rear' for 'get up'.[3]

Victoria went back to the mansion on the hill and leafed through the only book she could find about these people – it was called *The Gypsies' Advocate*. Yes, the *Advocate* had got it right about the community's family feeling and kindness to the old and weak, and about the dignified way in which people bore themselves. Linen, handkerchiefs and even cloaks were being washed every day, which was a positive sign. How good to know that these wanderers were beginning to take religious instruction![4] By now Eliza's baby had been born. Leonard and Nelson left with their wives and children, but the rest of the party stayed until the young mother was ready to travel. On Christmas Day they received a gift of firewood, soup and blankets, with a little knitted jacket for baby Francis. And then, just after New Year, the Coopers moved on, leaving only scattered wisps of straw where their benders had stood beside the Portsmouth Road.[5]

Long afterwards, when the pale girl in the expensive dress had become Queen Victoria, stories of this encounter were passed down among the Coopers. In the usual way of tradition, details of place and

Sarah Cooper with her nieces and nephews, 1836.

time were altered to suit the audience: Esher became Windsor, because that was where the family usually travelled, and a sock instead of a jacket was passed down through the generations as the very garment knitted by royal hands.[6] For her part, Victoria wrote that 'the place and spot may be forgotten, but the Gypsy family Cooper will never be obliterated from my memory!', which was nice to know, though it doesn't seem to have had much effect on the policies of her government over the next sixty years.

And who was the Gypsies' advocate, and how had he come to be such an authority on the community? That story went back to 1828, when Sarah Stanley, a young woman with three children, was making her way from Dorset towards Farnham, where the hopping season would soon begin. Her road lay through Southampton, where her sister-in-law Patience Proudley was stopping with her aunt, and where the race week was just beginning; good money could be made from dukkering on the racecourse. But one evening, as they were stopping under a hedge on Shirley Common, a gorjer came and joined them. He was dressed neatly, in a clergyman's suit, but was evidently quite at home with Gypsies. It was about 6 p.m., a stew of meat and potatoes had been served from the boiler, and everybody was ready for a cup of tea. Patience introduced the stranger as James Crabb, and he asked Sarah a few questions – Was this her family? Where was she heading to? Was the

Gypsy life a hard one? And then, quite unexpectedly, James said: 'I wish you would let me have your children to provide for and educate.' 'Not I,' she replied sharply. 'Others can give away their children, if they like, but I will never part with mine.' James thought for a moment and then said, very seriously, that being educated would help them greatly, both in this life and the next one; that everyone was responsible for their children before God; and that she knew in her heart that he could do better for her children than she could. Then he left. The stew was still warm, but Sarah didn't have the heart to eat any more. She was so cut up that she couldn't stay, and abandoned her plans for the racecourse, going straight to Farnham and promising to return and reconsider the gorjer's offer when hopping time was over.[7]

The Proudleys and Stanleys had known James Crabb since the Lent Assizes of the previous year, when Francis Proudley, Patience's husband, had been sentenced to death, not just because of his crime (he'd been horse-stealing) but specifically because he was a Gypsy. James saw this, was outraged by the prejudice of the law, and set out to do what he could for the community. He took in Patience's daughter Betsy, along with one of her cousins, and gave them an education; that was why he had made the same offer to Sarah, who eventually took it up. James went on to establish a school for Gypsies at Farnham (not the Surrey Farnham, but a small village in Dorset some 60 miles to the west) and worked, with some success, for better relations with the host population.[8] But his motive was always the saving of souls, for which – as can be seen from the little episode on Shirley Common – he would use any means, including emotional blackmail. He wanted children to live with him and attend his school so that they could learn literacy or useful skills, but with the ultimate goal of de-educating them out of the community.

When William Stanley heard what James Crabb was doing for the Gypsies, he came to Southampton and joined forces with him. William was a remarkable character. Like many Gypsies, he had joined the militia as a young man; after enlisting in Wiltshire, he was posted to Exeter, where he found that his fellow-rankers laughed at him for being illiterate. So he taught himself to read, and looked for a book on which to practise his new skills. Someone sold him a tattered New Testament; he began to read it, and was astounded at the worlds it opened up for him. Soon after this, in about 1799, he joined a Wesleyan chapel and trained as an itinerant preacher. William was one of the first Gypsies to be culturally bilingual; in gorjer society, he could speak and write just like any other Regency clergyman, but back among the tents he would address people in Romanes and be heard with all the respect due to a Stanley and an elder.[9]

That made him an ideal companion for James; he would go ahead and prepare the ground for the arrival of his partner, reassuring people that the minister was not coming to trick them, arrest them, or send their children to Australia. In the autumn of 1830, the two men set out for Farnham, where they gathered a large audience

> after the labours of the day, near one of the hop-grounds, about half an hour after sun-set. A few small candles gave light to a small tenement, used as a lodging place for the hop-gatherers, where the congregation was accommodated. A few of the inhabitants of Farnham, and some of the female Gipsies, who were much delighted to mingle with them in the worship of God, were put inside, and the men, with such women and children as could not get in, stood outside, the place being very much too small for so great a number of people. The preacher stood on the threshold of the door and addressed the people, of whom those without could only be seen now and then, as an adjacent wood fire cast at intervals upon them an intermitting light.[10]

Like most evangelists, William and James may have exaggerated the impact of their message. But this preaching was something new to most people; it stirred up lively discussion, and it introduced a Gospel story which moved the heart. After all, who was this Jesus, if not another traveller? He had nowhere to lay his head; he was harassed by the authorities of his day; in the end, they took him on a false charge and strung him up, like many a good man before him. This was an emotional rather than an intellectual response, but it was one which Methodist and Anglican alike could use as a starting point for more sophisticated understandings of sin, and of confidence in a personal saviour.

Although James Crabb might help Gypsies in practical ways, redemption was his ultimate goal; still, he had enough sense to realize this was hopeless as long as police and magistrates continued their policy of harassment. Unless people were able to remain undisturbed on the outskirts of Southampton, London and the other large towns, it would be impossible for ministers to reach them with news of eternal life. But ironically, James had conceived his project just as these large continuous settlements were in decline. Norwood had been the seat of Gypsy culture in the south of England, and Norwood's days were numbered.

Right down to the 1780s it seemed impossible that this populous wilderness would ever lose its rustic character. That was a time when the roads out of London were packed every fine Sunday, and the hill was so crowded that 'with the greatest difficulty only, could a seat or mug of beer be obtained, at the place generally called the Gipsy-house'.[11] And it was then, when the fun and feasting were at their height, that

> Norwood's prescient tribe appears . . .
> To hear the tidings fate reveals,
> A lovely maiden slily steals . . .
> There the deep Sybil reads her part,
> And frames a case to reach the heart,
> Of faith, unrival'd by the dove,
> Of sighs, tears, vows, – the words of love;
> Of bow'rs of bliss, and lasting joys,
> Not Winter kills, or time destroys:
> Ah credulous! The siren leave,
> For what we wish we soon believe.[12]

These young lovers of picnics and prophecy returned home convinced that Norwood, with its fresh air and distant views, was a very attractive place to go, especially now that the roads were in better repair; but these improvements were the beginning of the end, since they tempted wealthier Londoners to invest in a country residence on the Surrey hills. In this way the Gypsies acquired some unexpected neighbours, such as the Lord High Chancellor, who built a mansion in 1787. Soon after came the news that Norwood was to be enclosed. 'The Lord Chancellor cannot bear the poor Gipsies. Their brows are too dark, and there is somewhat too austere about their countenance.'[13]

For many years Norwood had been saved from this fate by the intricacies of the law. It lay at the junction of several parishes, all with their main centres of population at some distance from the hill, so that the village residents were largely indifferent to what went on up the slopes. It was common ground, in which every parishioner had an interest, however little they might feel it; to extinguish these common rights, turning the land into privately owned plots, required the authority of an Act of Parliament. For many years this was regarded as something impossibly expensive, and anyway of very little use from an agricultural point of view, since each parochial slice of Norwood, even if hedged and fenced, would still have been flanked by the uncultivated waste of other manors.

But times were changing. Landowners in the late eighteenth century had a prejudice against any kind of communal ownership, something which made the cost of an Enclosure Act more acceptable, especially in an area like Norwood where newly appropriated land could be sold not just for farming but to speculative builders. The southern slopes of the hill, in the parish of Croydon, were the first to be enclosed, with the legal process beginning in 1797. The parish of Camberwell, with its daughter settlement at Dulwich, enclosed their Norwood commons in 1805; Lambeth in 1806; and finally in 1827 Penge, which with the last woodland at Anerley had formed a detached part of Battersea.[14]

So the loss of freedom took a generation to take effect, and at first business carried on as usual. They say that the beginning of the end came on a Sunday afternoon when people saw a coach coming up Gipsy Hill. Two gorjers got out, looking like gentlemen of leisure and fashion, since they were beckoning imperiously to a couple of servants dressed in livery. There was evidently going to be a party and the Norwood Gypsies assembled at a discrete distance, ready to supply services in return for the usual small payment. All at once the pretence of a picnic was forgotten as the supposed noblemen and flunkies revealed themselves as police officers, rushing into the crowd and wrestling people to the ground.[15] The next raid, in August 1797, was more brutal. At first light, ten *gavvers* – undisguised, this time – worked their way up to the open space where people were stopping. Everyone was still asleep and since it was a summer night, they had thrown off most of their clothes. Suddenly the officers rushed the tents, ripping away the canvas and blankets, and leaving the Gypsies naked and cold in the chill morning air. Thirty men, women and children were herded, half-asleep, into the three hackney coaches waiting to carry them to jail. In the end, charges were only made against eleven, all of them Lees and coming from a family which had already attracted the interest of police and magistrates. These were the three sons of Stephen Lee – Adam, Robert and Thomas – with their wives Eleanor, Caroline and Jane, together with Adam's son young Thomas, and also four other women – Ann, Elizabeth, Mary and another Mary.[16]

The Gypsies were also under threat from moral organizations. The Society for the Suppression of Vice had been formed to fill a gap in the legal order of the time; although the country had many laws, old and new, to penalize immoral behaviour, there was no machinery for enforcing them. Prosecution was a private business and unless an individual or organization took the initiative in bringing a case, the law was a dead letter. Naturally the society had a great deal of vice to suppress, mostly the sort which was popular among poor people who couldn't afford defence lawyers, and in September 1803 they brought Charlotte Allen before Quarter Sessions with her younger companions Jane Hearn, Mary Ann Hearn and Pentevenny Lovell on a charge of fortune-telling. Girls, it seems, had been setting out for Norwood on a Sunday in the company of well-heeled young men. The couple would share a dinner, with plenty of wine, and then sally forth onto the green where Charlotte or Jane or Mary Ann were waiting. First the women would tell the gentleman's fortune, being careful to pick up any hints about the hopes and background of the girl of his choice; then it was the girl's turn, and she would be told of a future so wonderful, and so closely entwined with the young man's desires, that there was really no point in delaying the matter any longer, and they'd best go and hire a room for the afternoon in one of the nearby inns. This was how South London girls had a good time or, as the society saw it, 'were plunged into inevitable ruin'. When interrogated by the magistrates, the Gypsies expressed profound contrition for their crime,

Euri and Athaliah Shaw being taken by police, 1830s.

and volubly promised never to offend in this way again, at which point they were all freed, apart from Pentevenny, who had rashly left evidence of an agreement with a young man to make a girl 'subservient to all his desires'. She got six months' imprisonment at the Newington House of Correction.[17]

By 1810 appropriation of the Camberwell and Lambeth sections of Norwood was complete and the pressure on stopping places was beginning to mount. In 1815 – once again, on a summer Sunday – the encampment was raided by police, who in the usual way had brought three coaches to carry their captives off to prison. However, the Gypsies were getting wise to this, and before the coaches could lumber away to starripen, a rallying party of forty men and women surrounded them and attempted rescue. They were beaten back by the police, who arrived at the county jail with a mixed group, including an unidentified queen of the Gypsies and her sons Thomas and John. In the end, however, charges were only brought against Robert and Sarah Lee.[18]

After this the Lovells and Hearns seem to have given up on Norwood, for in the final raid, made in August 1823, it was mostly Coopers who were charged under the Vagrancy Act: a married couple, Elisha and Ann, along with Eve, Anne, Anne Maria, Sabraina and young Jane. Mary Ann Lee and Sophia Lee were also charged, but no other men; during raids it seems to have been the menfolk who made the first getaway, knowing that they were liable to be charged for offences much worse than dukkering.[19] Indeed,

> the ban of power was upon them! They were whipped, fettered and imprisoned, but so strong was the predilection they entertained for their sylvan retreats, that in spite of the terrors of the stocks, the strong arm of the law, and the exertions of an *unpaid magistracy* . . . many years elapsed ere they were thoroughly driven into exile.[20]

Within a few years the enclosure of Penge Common and Anerley woods had fenced off the last open spaces, and Norwood was no longer a place where Gypsies could gather freely. This was something of a disappointment for John Hoyland, a bookish old gentleman who visited the area in 1815 and found it still 'a wildly rural spot . . . but having been considerably inclosed of late years, it is not now much frequented by the Gypsies'.[21] On Gipsy Hill, a helpful landlord explained that he had come too late, the summer's raid having happened just two months before. However, a lot of people had already gone into winter lodgings around London, and it might be worth following them there. So John made his way back to town, where a friend kept a grocer's shop in the St Giles district. Word went round that there was an educated gorjer at the shop who'd listen if you came and rokkered to him, an opportunity which the Lovells, Lees, Taylors, Martins and Smiths seem to have followed up, since they and their marriages and the number of their children are all carefully recorded.

There was John Lee, who was living in Tothill Fields and getting work as a chair bottomer; he seems to have been Stephen's John, who (as mentioned above) was arrested in 1795 with his father and three brothers and was then back in court the next year in connection with the burglary of an Essex farmhouse.[22] He got off, again, but they hanged his brother Richard. Mansfield Lee, who was in Shoreditch with a grinding barrow, is likely to have been linked with the Lovells since he later went collecting hay with three of them – Ezekiel, Arthur and John – in 1821.[23] Jemmy Lovell the tinker was nearby and about twenty of his family lodged over the winter in Bowles' Yard.[24] Another Lee, Zachariah the fiddler, used to stop in Norwood as well as Epping Forest. He married twice, the second time to Charlotta Boswell.[25] Charlotte Allen, the leader of the fortune-telling ring in 1803, had moved into the old Gypsy haunt of Kent Street, where she made a living selling earthenware and was supported in widowhood by her seven children. In the same street lived Edward Martin, who hawked fruit, and James Cole, who supplemented the knife-grinding trade by lighting streetlamps in the evenings. And in Tottenham Court Road there was Lusha Cooper, who would return to Norwood and be evicted from it in the final raid of 1823. He and his wife had ten children, but this was exceptional; the average family size was just under four.[26]

Driven from Norwood, the Gypsies had taken lodgings throughout London, intending to stay there until the winter was gone. When demand ran out in the metropolis for bottoming chairs, mending bellows or grinding knives, they would take a long circuit of 20–30 miles round the city to look for trade. Everybody made a living somehow; it was a point of honour never to accept relief from the parish workhouse. Then in summer people might go through Hertfordshire into Suffolk, and cross back through the home counties to Herefordshire and so down to Bristol before returning home. Some had been to Yarmouth, some to Portsmouth, some as far as Cardiff.[27] Zacky and Charlotta were long travellers, often seen around Leeds and Conisbrough.

But travelling was not as easy as it had been a generation before. Land and other resources which had once been held in common were now enclosed and appropriated, while the small freeholders who had welcomed migrant labour in their barns were giving way to a more businesslike class of tenant farmers. Arthur Bowers, when questioned in court, said that he and Joseph Spragg 'when they could not get permission to sleep in the barns or outhouses of the farmers, generally pitched their tent as near a farm-house as they could'.[28]

A new Vagrancy Act was passed in 1822, with revisions in 1824. Like other legislation of the time, it was intended more to tidy up previous rulings than to assert any new principles. In place of the various punishments of the old days, many of which had been too extreme ever to be inflicted, there was now a standard term of three months' imprisonment for anyone found telling fortunes, lodging under a tent or cart, and having no visible means of subsistence. But while the Act may have been passed simply to consolidate existing law, many county magistrates took it as a charter for freshly coordinated attacks on vagrancy. In this they were helped by the Highways Act of 1835, which for the first time made it illegal to stop on the edge of any highway.[29]

Faced with this hostility, people tended to band together and to secure themselves against disturbance, using the kind of precautions seen by two policemen on Peckham Rye Common:

> The tent, which was a tolerably large one, was erected on a slope at one end of a corn field, and its entrance guarded by two strong dogs, who were chained to stakes driven into the ground, one on each side. Two donkeys, chained by the leg, were grazing on the spot. On a sight of the party the dogs showed great violence, barked furiously, and seemed prepared to defend the entrance; it was therefore deemed most prudent to attack in the rear. The stakes to which the tent was fastened were quickly drawn, the tarpaulin removed, and the whole residence exposed.[30]

This had been the home of Sarah Lamb, currently locked up at Southwark on a charge of shoplifting. Since the donkeys' panniers turned out to contain 31 pieces of lace, all of which had gone missing from the Borough shop where she usually made her purchases, Sarah would have found it difficult to mount a convincing defence. Instead, she spent a week testing the weaknesses of her cell, then smashed a hole through the ceiling, got up onto the roof, and climbed down to freedom via the waterspout. Soon afterwards she was stopping on Wimbledon Common, dressed as a man, and flinching from every stranger in case they were a police officer. Then, having purchased a ginger wig, Sarah began a new life in Wiltshire; but the law caught up with her nine years later.[31]

Many features of Sarah's home appear in a sketch of people stopping on Dulwich Common.[32] There is the bridge or pannier lying on the ground – it is a wooden framework able to take the weight of canvas, tent rods and family goods without injuring the donkey's sides. There are two tents, one a bender but the other made on a much larger scale with a V-shaped entrance at the front. Evidently Gypsies were experimenting with all sorts of structures: 'green huts' are mentioned by one author, and a poem of 1793 is set in 'Norwood, where we oft complain/ With many a tear – and many a sigh,/ Of blustering winds and rushing rain . . . Amid our humble sheds.'[33]

Transporting even the most basic of tents would be difficult without a pack-animal. People might bear household goods on their back, or even trading stock – pedlars seem to have carried whole warehouses in miniature – but rods and blankets were another matter. And so, as one observer put it, 'they have asses, which carry themselves, their children, their kettle, and their means of erecting tents, and which tents are precisely like those of the North American savages.'[34] Donkeys were in general use by the 1810s and a grand fete at Vauxhall Gardens in 1811 featured 'a groupe of Gypsies, with their ass grazing, and their fire alight', as if that was the ordinary scene at a stopping place.[35] This was a new development since up until then the only pack animals had been horses. It was horses that were taken as spoils in the Battle of Knaphill Wood, and one hundred years earlier it had been a mare with packsaddle which was confiscated from the two Gypsies at Limpsfield.

Donkeys were cheaper than horses. They ate less, and worse, food, so they could get by on the rough grazing afforded by a common and still be strong enough to carry a load, or pull a two-wheeled spring-cart. But until the end of the eighteenth century they were seldom found in England. They were brought in to support the new industries, which needed a cheap pack animal to transport materials, and this was probably the source from which the Gypsies obtained their animals.

The speed of travel remained much as it had always been, about 10 miles a day. Arthur Bowers and Joseph Spragg made it from Dorking to Sydenham Common in two shifts, stopping near the Half Moon pub.

A family stopping at Dulwich, 1800s.

Another day at the same rate would have taken them to their destination at Greenwich. Other short episodes of travel appear in parish registers which record the journey from babies' birthplaces to the churches where they were baptized. In 1815 William and Eleanor Golbee brought little Elizabeth from Hawkhurst Down in Gomshall to East Hoathly. Journeys from Tandridge through Goudhurst to Etchingham, from Ticehurst to Long Ditton, from Mitcham to Eversley, all appear in registers, as people looked for a sympathetic church to baptize their children.[36] These routes all pass through Surrey into neighbouring regions of Kent, Sussex and Hampshire, a limited horizon confined to counties south of the Thames. Where the successive children of one couple can be traced from register to register, their circuits occupy much the same territory. Stephen Lee married Elizabeth at Betchworth in 1810 and their first son John was baptized down in Hampshire at Bishops Waltham. After that they were back at Betchworth, then South Bersted in Sussex, and finally Ashurst and Bexley in Kent. Sam Cooper married Florinia, their oldest daughter Faurnitty was christened at the family base of Eltham and then the births were at Ewell, Lewisham, Eltham again, Croydon, a second time at Lewisham, and then Croydon once more in 1836.[37]

Sometimes we can learn a little more. It was in October of 1815 that a group of Gypsies approached Dorking, the sort of company you might meet 'on some solitary way, with their dark Indian faces, their scarlet-cloaked women, their troops of little vivacious savages, their asses and horses laden with beds and tents, and, trudging after them, their guardian dogs'.[38] They were a large party, 31 people in all: eight women and five men, with eighteen children and dependents ranging from an unmarried girl of 21 to a beady-eyed eight-month-old. It may have been the size of the group which alarmed the local gorjers, but at any rate, authority descended and arrested them all as vagrants, after which they were sent to the House of Correction at Kingston where, in the absence of anyone wanting to press charges against them, they were asked a great many questions, locked up for a while, and then discharged.[39]

The company was led by Elizabeth Sherlock, born in Shipley near Horsham, who in 1793 had married William from Up Marden near Chichester. Over the next seven years they had three sons – Joseph, Henry and Samuel. Then William had died, and Elizabeth found another husband, by whom she had David and Sarah. She was travelling with all five of her children, and Joseph, the eldest, had himself been married for two years, to Caroline.

The oldest member of the party seems to have been James Deacons, who was born at Cranleigh, presumably at some time in the 1760s since he married in 1788. His family had grown up and moved away, so that he and his wife Caroline were only accompanied now by one daughter, Elizabeth. There were also two single women. Mary Wharton had been married to John from Charlwood in 1789, but he was dead or absent, and there was Ann Willoughby, the young wife of John; he came from Buckland, their church wedding had been in 1811 at Herstmonceaux, and she was looking after little Sally and Patience. John had deserted her in Dorking the previous day, she said – which probably means that he had been out looking for work and had received a signal not to return to the family when authority descended on them.

These families all seem to have been intermarried, and certainly they had all travelled on the same roads, principally the highway that runs along the dip-slope of the Downs. A short stretch of 15 miles along this road connects Dorking (two baptisms) with Betchworth (two marriages and a baptism), Bletchingley and Buckland (three more baptisms) and

Oxted (another marriage). Beyond this, their circuit extended southwest through Burstow, Newdigate and Cranleigh to Rudgwick and Shipley near Horsham, Northchapel and Egdean in the area of Petworth, and then Up Marden on the road leading into Chichester. They also had links with Hadlow in Kent, probably because they went there at hopping time.[40] Ever since the 1760s, this little corridor of Surrey and Sussex had been the world for these connected families.

But not everybody had such narrow horizons. In December 1834, Antonio and Elizabeth Nichols had their daughter Mary baptized in Warlingham. There was, it seems, a small donation forthcoming from the gorjers who stood as godparents to the little stranger with the dark eyes. She took after him, Antonio explained; he was Portuguese by birth, a stranded sailor trying to get back to his ship. As for Elizabeth, she was an Irish traveller who could pass herself off, with a bit of blarney, as someone born in Portugal of English parents. There might even have been a gift of clothes for the little one, since the redemption of a potential Catholic probably played better with clergymen than the baptism of a small Gypsy. If Antonio and Elizabeth seemed at ease with the church ritual, that was hardly surprising since they had already stood as proud parents at the same ceremony four days earlier in East Horley. A month earlier, they had been in Wiltshire, where Mary was christened twice; October saw them in the Midlands (three christenings in Staffordshire alone) and in the summer they'd done Wales. From Warlingham they moved on to London, but someone was getting suspicious, and maybe they had to whisper quickly to each other in 'Portuguese', because six weeks later they were in Cornwall: an impressive rate of travel, even with the convenience of the new turnpike roads. From there they worked their way back up north, and by the close of 1835 little Mary had been to the font once in Lincolnshire, once in Cumberland and twice in Yorkshire. And so the scam went on. Between August 1831 and December 1840, Antonio and Elizabeth arranged upwards of two hundred baptisms for their little Mary – or rather Marys, since there must have been a series of baby girls brought up to do duty at the font. They can't have received the same level of generosity each time, but even with a few duds it was an easy way of living, and they certainly got to see the country.[41]

Few other families seem to have taken up this trick, perhaps because it required such far-ranging travel, but there were other ways in which the credulity of the gorjers could be turned into a source of profit. In 1834 a woman 'of interesting appearance' knew her day was made when a Walworth shopkeeper began hanging on her every word about future events. So she proceeded to impart something truly wonderful to him and his wife. 'I came to London on purpose to tell you both that there is an iron chest filled with treasure secreted in the earth not far from hence, and that it can only be recovered by a charm, of which I am myself in possession, and no soul else in the world.' The charm involved some expense, as charms so often do, but they could split that between them; she'd bring £50 if he could match that sum. No blabbing, mind you! – and the money, hers and theirs, must be wrapped in a Bible, and left well out of sight for three days, with nobody going near it, or the magic would all be undone. Things went according to plan, and on the third day the shopkeeper waited impatiently at the door for his benefactor to come and summon up the gold. But there was no sign of the Gypsy, or of the carefully hidden Bible, or for that matter of the £50.[42]

This was the *boro hokkiben*, a simple but elegant confidence trick that was played, with few variations, at one place or another throughout the nineteenth century.[43] It seems incredible that gorjers should continue to fall for the great deceit when its workings were exposed so often in the popular press – but they did, again and again. Much could be achieved when the Gypsy mystique was brought to play on raw human greed.

Because it began with simple dukkering, this was a woman's trick, but menfolk could do as well through skills that lay somewhere between smart practice and fraud: horse-dealing, for instance. Simon Plunkett was travelling through Mitcham on his way to London when he met with John Glover, a man 'who is very well known in Kent, Sussex, and Middlesex; he serves this country with a great many good colts and horses.' They went into the White Hart and had a pint or two of six-penny ale before John broached the subject of horses. He had a grey gelding and was willing to sell it for ten guineas. Simon beat him down to eight and the deal was done. Within a few days he had exchanged the grey for another horse, with eight guineas thrown in – 'and I thought it was a very good chop'. Too good to be true, in fact, because the grey had been stolen from a field eight days earlier. The rightful owner had to print and paste up advertisements, and send a servant trailing around the country, before he could locate either the horse or Simon; John Glover was not to be found.[44]

Simon's luck held this time, for the court believed him; but three months later, in the spring of 1798, he was found guilty of a fresh offence at Surrey Assizes and hanged. In a countryside which was still largely open, it was not hard to steal livestock. Holmwood Common, on the hills that overlook Dorking, was a popular stopping place. It was also an area where horses were let loose to graze, and the combination was tempting. Early in 1834, when the nights were still long, two Smith brothers strolled around the common on a Sunday afternoon, gazing with a professional eye at the horseflesh around them. They were, as they explained, looking for one that they had lost; but this seemed unconvincing to the locals, who secretly mounted watch. As night fell, one of the Gypsies selected a horse, quickly got astride it and set off at a brisk pace towards Red Lane, with his brother running beside him. This was exactly where the local vigilantes had planted their strongest force, and as the two young men approached the gap which left the common, the elder was knocked off his mount by a series of crushing blows, and both were pinned down and tied. Sent off for trial, they were lucky to escape hanging.[45]

These episodes are typical of Gypsy crime. What began in the ordinary routine of contact with gorjers – dukkering, horse-dealing, the cajoling of gifts at a baptism – became more aggressive and deceitful until it squeezed out all other ways of making a living. But it didn't follow that crime itself was typical of Gypsy life. After all, the string of fraudulent christenings carried out by Antonio and Elizabeth Nichols can be offset against registers which show that other traveller babies in Surrey were

Listening to the preacher, 1820.

79

christened just the once. Other offences are not so capable of statistical analysis but it is noticeable that though Quarter Sessions were quite capable of sending offenders to jail for picking handkerchiefs off washing lines or pulling firewood out of hedges, they seldom passed these verdicts on people with the typical Gypsy names.

The jaundiced view of the farming community – 'they commit acts of murder and theft and arson innumerable' – is not borne out by Surrey court records or the newspaper reports of Union Hall police court.[46] Leaving aside regulatory offences under the Vagrancy Acts, there are not many prosecutions of identifiable Gypsies; indeed, the arrest of the Sherlocks in 1815 is exceptional even as an exercise of the vagrancy laws. The typical response of authority to Gypsies was not to arrest people but to move them on.[47] Police kept a wary eye on stopping places and, following some dreadful murder, they would descend on the encampment and identify suspects – only to report a few days later, with much less noise, that the people arrested did not match the description and were in fact somewhere else at the time of the crime. This happened after murders at Dulwich, Epsom and Fetcham.[48]

The handful of outsiders who got to know the community gave a much less lurid account of Gypsy crime. As Charles Leslie wrote to his sister in 1826, 'it is not that the gipsies are thieves *par excellence*, but as they pilfer only the necessities of life, there is less variety in their stealing.'[49] This was an informed judgement, since Charles had been a guest for many years at Epping Forest and was known to many of the leading figures of the community. Richard Bright, who had spoken to people at Norwood in the last days of the settlement there, was candid in his appraisal:

> For my part, I have not been able to discover all those marks of natural and inherent depravity in the gypsey character which have been so obvious to others . . . Let [a stranger] gain their confidence, and he will find them conversible, amusing, sensible, and shrewd; civil, but without servility; proud of their independence; and able to assign reason for preferring their present condition to any other in civilized society. He will see them strongly attached to each other . . . That they frequently sin against the good order of the countries in which they reside, I freely admit, and that they frequently suffer with justice the rigours of the law; but that the tide of prejudice, which ever flows against them, distresses and overwhelms many unjustly, I have no doubt, and far more criminality

has been ascribed by superstition and credulity to these wanderers than they have in truth deserved.[50]

But Charles and Richard were gentlemen whose Gypsy researches had been a venture, perhaps their only venture, into the world of the poor. How much of what caught their attention was specifically Romany, and how much of it was simply the ordinary culture of the working class? After all, Gypsies were not the only people to treasure strong family bonds, to make their living through an economy of makeshifts or to accept a certain amount of petty theft by the impoverished from the wealthy. It would be more revealing if we had the evidence of someone on the same social level as the Gypsies; someone who would see their distinctive culture from the perspective of the ordinary labouring man. And this is what we find in the notebooks of John Clare.

John was not ordinary, of course; he was one of the great poets of the nineteenth century. But to his fellow villagers at Helpston he was simply another farmworker, even if he was always reading books and had ambitions of writing them. In fact John's life could easily have taken a different turn. In the 1810s he was befriended by the Smiths, whose annual circuit took them from Norwood ('their wood rendezvous . . . where they got sums of money by fiddling & fortune-telling') down into Kent for the hopping and then up to Northamptonshire. They taught him how to play the fiddle 'by the ear and fancy'; how to cook bad meat after washing it in vinegar, cutting it into thin slices, and barbecuing it on a fierce fire; and how to cure scurvy with the plant called burvine, deafness with waspweed, fever and snakebite with furzebind.[51] As the friendship grew, they explained some of the secrets of dukkering:

> In fortune telling they pretend to great skill both by cards & plaster & by the lines on the hand & moles & interpretation of dreams but . . . every lady's fortune was the same that they had false friends and envious neighbours but better luck would come . . . The credulous readily believed them and they extorted money by another method of muttering over the power of revenge which fright the huswife into charity. I have heard them laugh over their evening fire at the dupes they have made in believing their knowledge in foretelling future events & trying each other's wits to see who could make a tale that would succeed best the next day.[52]

On a Sunday they would gather on the common at Langley Bush (this was before Helpston was enclosed), where they played music and danced, although in honour of the holy day they would break off if a clergyman passed by. Then they would brew up tea, men and women would light their pipes, and someone would ask John if he wanted to stay for supper: 'badgers and hedgehogs . . . are far from bad food.' And he was very tempted to join them; after all, one of his friends had married in, and was now on the roads. But then he thought of what a life would be like without books, always in the same unintellectual world ('their common talk is of horses, asses, dogs and sport'). And then there was the cooking, 'done in a slovenly manner', and the thought of shivering through a cold winter. So he decided to stay in the village.

> I never met with a scholar amongst them not with anyone who had a reflecting mind. They are susceptible to insult & even fall into sudden passions without a seeming cause, their friendships are warm & their passions of short duration but their closest friendships are not to be relied on. The men are very hot in their tempers & loose in their discourse delighting to run over smutty ribaldry but the women have not lost the modesty that belongs to them . . . The young girls are reserved & silent-seeming in the company of men . . . They are deceitful generally & have a strong propensity to lying yet they are not such dangerous characters as some in civilised life . . . Their common thefts are trifling depredations, taking anything that huswifes forget to secure at night, killing game in the woods with their dogs, but some are honest.

There was one thing about the Gypsies which caught John's attention, and that was 'the oddness of their names such as Wisdom, Doughty, Lolly, Letice, Rover, Ishmael &c . . . They seem to be names which have descended from generation to generation as their young bear similar names to their parents.' By the 1810s this had evidently become one of the ways in which a Romany identity was passed down the generations.[53]

But they weren't used by everyone. Of the six Lee brothers whom we met in a previous chapter, only Damon the youngest had a distinctively Gypsy name; and turning to their children, born between 1781 and 1804, we find only four distinctive names in a generation of seventeen.[54] It is the same when we turn to parish registers. These are less helpful in identifying ethnicity, but if all the records of 'traveller', 'hawker' and so on are brought together, then the resulting sample must have a high proportion of actual Gypsies; and even so, we find that Henrys and Janes are common while the occasional Neptune or Keziah stands out as an exception.

So the custom of giving Gypsified names was not universal in the community, and it began by following common eighteenth-century trends, though the names soon became more imaginative and distinct. The increased importance of the Bible is reflected in the baptism of Levi Cooper (New Malden, 1827) and Reuben Gregory (Farnham, 1864), and in the name of Solomon Lee (buried at Chertsey, 1840). Zacky Lee from Norwood passed on the biblical tradition to a second generation by calling his daughter Vashti, after the Persian queen in the Book of Esther.[55] The churchgoing tradition also promoted names from virtues and good qualities; John Clare had met a Wisdom among the Smiths, and there was a Golden Hope travelling at Chertsey in 1861.

Another category, that of names from the classics, marked aristocratic status among gorjers, but Gypsies felt themselves to be natural aristocrats and made free use of it. 'Caesars and Catos are quite common,' said Charles Leslie, from his knowledge of the Norwood community; Damon Lee was named after a famous exemplar of ancient friendship and a philosophical Plato Taylor was travelling at Claygate in 1853.

The creation of first names from surnames had begun among the landed classes, as a way of remembering their ancestors in the female line, but was then adopted by Gypsies for the commemoration of any admired person. There was a Nelson Cooper at Epsom in 1835, and as he was already the father of a son at that date, he must have been christened himself not long after the death of Admiral Nelson at Trafalgar. That sounds like a consciously patriotic gesture, which would also be true for Brittania Hughes, baptized in 1853 at Ham, and her namesake two years later at Farnham. Belcher Lee, baptized at East Molesey in 1859, took his name from another warrior, though not a military one; this was Jem Belcher, the bare-knuckle hero, whose last fight took place against Tom Crib on Epsom Downs in 1809. A more elevated patron was Lord Derby; there was already a Derby Equal travelling through Cobham in 1782.[56]

At Epsom races in 1832 there was an Onslow, just as there was a Vanzloe Cooper christened at Ewell in 1825.[57] Ultimately the name derives from Wenceslas, the saintly Czech king of Christmas carol fame, and as this might suggest it is not usually an English name. Neither is Jasper, which comes from one of the Three Kings and was most popular around their shrine at Cologne; in 1747 Jasper Wood was travelling at Clandon, where he christened his son, 'born in a barn'. Another name of apparently Continental origin was given to Perryn Smith, baptized at Beddington in 1816.[58]

Foreign influences also lay behind Councelletta Walker, who brought her baby to the font at Banstead in 1830, and Gentila Cooper, baptized in 1852 during race week at West Molesey. One of these names is Spanish – *consuelo*, 'comfort', with a feminine ending – while the other is Italian. Menanatti Cooper, another West Molesey baptism in 1860, took her name from the French Mignonette, although this might have been mediated through the popular flower of the same name. Certainly Gerania and Florinia Cooper both had floral names; they baptized children at Banstead in 1832 and Ewell in 1825. Women typically had names that were longer than those given to men, with a more flowing sound, often beginning with the sound s-, as shown by the baptisms of Celendra Smith (1846, Alford), Cinnamunti Stevens (1854, Farnham), Sindamia Lee (1855, Farnham) and Centinia Smith (1869, Barnes).

Gypsies might not read or write but they were never cut off from the world of literature. Sabraina Cooper, who was caught up in the raid at Norwood in 1823, took her name from the water nymph in Milton's *Comus*, while storytelling based on books is the only way to account for the name of Cinderella Cooper, baptized at Ham in 1858.[59] Lazarus Hiller, who christened a son at Ash in 1798, must have owed his name to foreign chapbooks: it was on the Continent, and not in England, that Lazarus, the beggar of the Gospel story, had given his name to stories about vagrants and wanderers.[60]

So the tradition of colourful Gypsy names grew from the mideighteenth century onwards. It drew on many different countries and traditions for its materials, but appropriated them culturally in subtle ways, remodelling many of the women's names with the Romani female ending -i. We have already met with Pentevenny, Menanatti and Cinnamunti, and other examples include Limpady Lovell and Mazally Cooper, christened at Banstead in 1825 and at Norwood in 1854.

As this might suggest, the Romani language retained much of its integrity among Gypsies in the early years of the nineteenth century.[61] By now it was generally known that this was an Indic language; soldiers who had campaigned at Plassey or Nagpur would come home with a little knowledge of the local dialects, and set out in search of Gypsies with whom they could talk.[62] This was all very well, as long as they paid. In 1798 a woman and her children at Norwood were accosted by gorjers who asked about the names of things in the encampment. Forty Romani

Summer afternoon on Reigate Heath, 1845.

words seemed to match their Bengali equivalents, 26 of them exactly, a recital which earned her half a crown.[63] These exchanges were not always complimentary. Another old Gypsy at Norwood, perhaps the same one, understood much of the Hindi which was addressed to her by an old India hand, who later turned to a girl and said, slowly and carefully, *tu – boro – chor*. 'I'm no thief,' she said hotly, 'It was all got honestly by fortune-telling.'[64]

Prices reflect demand, and by 1817 the going rate for an introduction to Romani was just over 1s a word; at least this was the price quoted by some of the Lees at Kew to a passing gentleman, who declined the offer, simply recording his overall impression of 'a language somewhat resembling Irish, but it had tones more shrill'. Evidently its phonetics were still quite distinct; in fact when the family spoke English, they did so with a slight accent. There were twelve people in the group, stopping at Mortlake Road, where they had put up three tents – not benders, but V-shaped tents with a ridgepole and sides pegged down. They had two donkeys with them, four dogs, some blankets and assorted bags and boxes. Apart from the children, there were three married couples, one of them with an old mother, who was famous for dukkering. 'I've known her get five or six guineas on a wedding-day,' said her son-in-law, 'part from the lady, and part from the gentleman; and she never wants a shilling, and a meal's victuals, when she passes many houses.' He himself was a gorjer by birth, a tinker from Shoreditch who had married in. He looked different from his relatives, who had slighter features and darker complexions; but he spoke Romani as fluently as the rest and was completely assimilated.[65]

The boundaries of the community were more porous than might have been expected. In the 1830s Florinia Cooper was walking down Camberwell Road when she met with a girl, evidently lost and staring at the houses as she gnawed on a piece of bread. It turned out that she was a little gorjer who had been sent by her parents from their home outside Hungerford, so that she could get a job near London. They left it up to her to find lodgings, which was quite a lot to expect of a ten-year-old. Florinia invited the girl to supper on the green nearby and while she tucked into pudding, there was a long family argument; at last Florinia and her husband Sam decided that if no one else was going to look after her, they would. Two years later her birth family caught up with her; she was given the option of going home, but by that time she'd had a taste of Gypsy life, and she knew which was better. She grew up in the community, married the Coopers' son and lived to a great age – telling fortunes, driving donkeys and rokkering Romanes with the best of them.[66]

Not all stories of adoption ended so happily. A couple who were passing over Kennington Common in the summer of 1802 met with a twelve-year-old girl, cold and hungry, who begged to be allowed to join them. They already had six chavvies, and thought that another wouldn't be too much of a burden, so they let the girl come down with them to Wandsworth. After a week in the encampment, she ran away, and was next picked up by some charitable gorjers at Southend, where she identified herself as Elizabeth, the daughter of Captain Kellen, and told a long story of how she had been kidnapped from her home in Plymouth by Gypsies who had stripped her of all her fine clothing and made her into their slave, dragging her across the country. There was an outcry; the family who had originally supported her were put in jail, and over the next few days, fifty Gypsies travelling in and about London were arrested, more or less at random, and brought before the magistrates in twos and threes in case Elizabeth would accuse them of being involved in the kidnapping. She didn't, and they were discharged; meanwhile her story gradually unravelled. Her real father arrived and explained that she had run away from home that January, while the manager of Rotherhithe Workhouse identified her as the girl who had boarded there from March to May, and then absconded. The family who had helped her were let out of prison, with expenses paid, and an additional collection made for them by local gentlemen.[67]

As Elizabeth's escapade shows, Gypsies were frighteningly vulnerable to accusations of child theft. Mary Oxford, just arrived from Hampshire in the Mint, was arrested in 1835 simply because she had made friends with a runaway girl who helped on a walnut stall in Covent Garden and was going to accompany her down to the hopping. The girl made no complaint but Mary was sent down for two weeks.[68] This was an age when working-class children were self-reliant from an early age, and family ties were loose: the adoption of a young teenager made economic sense, since they would earn enough to support their keep. That couldn't be said for the taking of a baby or toddler, and yet this was something that Gypsies were accused of, over and over again. It would have been a pointless thing to do – as people said, in what rapidly became a cliché, 'Why should we steal children when we generally have more of our own than we know what to do with?' But the gorjers could never be persuaded, and were haunted by a secret fear that occasionally flared up in attacks on encampments.[69]

In real life, it was not kidnapping that bridged the ethnic barrier, but love. At Norwood, Nancy Cooper, 'the celebrated beautiful Gipsy of Hope-cottage', married John Sharpe, a young farmer, in 1827. It was a dream wedding: dressed in white satin and lace, she was carried to church in a carriage drawn by four Arab horses, distributing white gloves and ribbons to girls on either side of the road, while the day ended with sumptuous catering.[70] A few weeks later, Nancy's sister Mary was working the crowd at the Woodman; her brother supplied the music while she danced, and then, bringing out a mandolin, she sang: 'Merry Gipsies all are we/ And from Norwood do we come/ Oft with cheerful song and glee/ Thus we wander far from home.' Carefully memorized from somebody's reading of popular sheet music, these verses weren't exactly the voice of the people, but they went down well with the Sunday afternoon crowd. Running in and out of the inn, Mary found a foreign gentleman who wanted to know about English Gypsies, and after some not very successful dukkering (she was only fifteen and mistook his German accent for an American one) she told him all the news. Yes, her mother lived at Norwood – she was telling fortunes in the parlour right now. She had five elder brothers, but they were all travelling on their own now, in other parts of the country. Her sister Nancy – wasn't it wonderful! – was being educated for free by her new husband and would soon be able to read and write.[71]

There were other, similar marriages. Liti Smith, descended from Smiths on her father's side and Chilcotts on her mother's, married a farmer's son from Kingston called Robert Palmer. Then their daughter Genty married back into the community, to Oliver Cooper, but he was too free with his fists and after several years of bad treatment she left him and settled down with the keeper of Battersea Bridge.[72] The romance of Jem Chewbacca Matthews and Liddy Gowan had a happier ending. According to the say among her family:

> Jem . . . was a prize-fighter . . . And someone would collect money for him. You know, they'd go all round with a purse and ask: Money for the Champ. And then the local bully, he'd try to claim that money – but no – he couldn't have it – not 'less first he defeat the champion – and that were Chewbacca. Well, it was Ewell Fair, and there's Chewbacca punishing this local feller when Lydia Gowan she sets eyes on him and knowed straightaway – that's the one she'd marry – and, you know, no matter her father being a preacher and that and her being a fine Latin scholar and all – she'd have her way. And, do you know, she made this kushti lace – on a pillow – and used to show it off on the stalls at fairs. And the book-learning, that was kushti too, and she taught one of her chavvies to read from the Bible at her knee . . . And that were Liddy.[73]

Liddy lived long and happily with her prizefighter, raising seven children and setting the family on the road to prosperity. Chewbacca may have been grateful for her skills, since reading and writing was often seen as women's business. When a man who did a little fiddle and tambourine playing at Norwood was asked 'Can you read?' he said 'No; my wife can,' as if that was the natural order of things.[74]

Education had a particular appeal to young women, because it gave them something they could call their own before the long years of family responsibility set in. In 1811 two of the Coopers, Elisha and Tryphena, were wintering in a street between Clapham and Brixton. Elisha – Lusha to the family – was the brother of Henry, husband of the Mary Cooper who would meet Princess Victoria on the Portsmouth road some twenty years later. He and Tryphena had eight children; one of them was Daniel, whom we met earlier as a waiter at the Old Gipsy House; another was thirteen-year-old Trinity, or Finetti in the Romani form. Opposite the Coopers' house there was a little school run by a lady who taught poor children. Trinity was fascinated by this, and presented herself as a pupil, but she hadn't allowed for gorjer prejudice; the school was prepared to teach paupers and industrial workers but drew the line at Gypsies. Trinity stuck to it, however, and was eventually admitted, along with two of her brothers. School was very different from home – you had to sit still all the time and you couldn't shout out or say what you thought. The children felt like singing birds that have been taken and put in a cage, beating their wings against the bars, wanting to get out into the open air again; but they mastered their feelings, and learned to listen attentively. When April came, the Coopers set out on the drom, and Trinity was upset to leave the school behind.[75]

The Coopers were a remarkable family. Trinity's determined pursuit of an education, like her cousin Sarah's unselfconscious dealing with royalty, reflects the confidence born of a long tradition of dealing with the gorjers. True, the powers of law enforcement were still arrayed against the Romany, but most prosecutions were reserved for serious crime and government otherwise featured only distantly in the lives of the marginal classes. Much more present, and profitable, was the growing leisure market created by the expansion of London, with its crowds eager for Gypsy entertainment, and the string of opportunities for making a living, honest or otherwise. Every era looks back with nostalgia on its predecessor, but there may have been some truth in the later memories which saw early nineteenth-century England as a golden age for Gypsies.

4

Test Your Strength:
Early Victorian Times

Jack Cooper was walking down Leadenhall Street, just one among the anonymous London crowd. He saw a huddle of strangers around an omnibus, and in the middle of them a woman, grabbing and yelling at a young girl – shouting 'You have picked my pocket, you have taken my purse.' The girl broke out of the crowd and ran down the street, brushing against Jack as she did so. His hand reached out, hers clutched against it, and a green silk purse passed between them. The girl was cornered and gave herself up, protesting that she was innocent, they could take her before the police for all she cared, they'd find nothing. But not everyone was so easily fooled. Jack was turning away when a smartly dressed man came up and told him to hand over the purse. One blow from Jack's fist and he was knocked down, like many others before him; and then the Gypsy ran.[1]

But it was not as easy to run and hide in London as it had once been. Jack was taken and brought to trial in the Old Bailey in 1840. He was forty; his lover and accomplice, the little gorjer girl Mary Ann Hart, was only nineteen. They were both sentenced to transportation for ten years and were shipped to New South Wales, he on the *Eden*, she on the *Surrey*.[2] And that was the last that England saw of Fighting Jack Cooper.

Why did they call him that? His parents were Lusha and Tryphena Cooper, who we have already met; Jack, born in 1799, was the third of their eight children, followed in 1801 by Tom, who would also make a reputation in the same business.[3] In their short time of glory – half a dozen years at most – these two men were the most famous Gypsies in England. They owed it to that peculiarly English institution, the prize-ring.

Crowds will always gather to watch a fight, especially when it matches two men of equal strength and takes place under some sort of rules. By the eighteenth century these were beginning to attract attention from outside the immediate neighbourhood. New ideas of spectator sport were in the air, which meant that an audience would gather quickly, especially if they could put their bets on some kind of contest. It might be a race between horses or pedestrians, a struggle between gamecocks or best of all a fight between men. If you had two strong fists, and knew how to use them, it didn't matter what class you were, or whether you were Black, Jewish or Romany – you could be the hero of the Fancy, and gentlemen, maybe even nobility, would want to shake your bruised hand.

Prizefights were staged in the open air away from towns, because there were doubts about the legality of two men hitting each other until one of them couldn't get up anymore. Despite this, the ring enjoyed enough upper-class support to prevent the magistrates putting it down, and anyway it could be combined with other sports until the assembled crowd was large enough to defy the law. On the Hill at Epsom, there was an area within the racecourse kept aside for Gipseying and Pugilism, and it was here that Jack gave the first real demonstration of what he could do.[4] It was 1820, two days before the Derby, and the gathering crowd had already seen a couple of matches, but they still weren't satisfied. Jack stripped off; he was a welterweight, 5 feet 5 in height, and obviously fit. 'These sort of wandering coves are always in training,' wrote an admiring journalist, 'and have a better chance of winning a turn-up than most other men.'[5] Jack was already a seasoned fighter (there had been a previous match, also at Epsom, with the Jewish lightweight Little Gadzee) and now, given his choice of an opponent, he chose one of the professionals: Richard West, whom they called 'West Country Dick'.

The fight lasted for half an hour, with 29 rounds; it took only a minute or two for a man to go down, since the prizefighter's style in those days included grappling holds as well as punches. Jack was all motion, going for his opponent's head with great slashing blows. Dick dodged and sparred, but every time he planted a facer, Jack took it unconcerned and kept on coming. By the twentieth round, both men looked battered; they were hitting wildly and falling heavily, but Jack got second wind while Dick began to fall to his knees, taking blows to the face without resistance, and finally having to be carried off in a terrible state. Jack's people went wild. Trinity led her brother at the head of the Coopers across the Downs; he was still just about able to walk at her side, with blood on his face and thirteen guineas in his pocket.[6]

More fights followed and in October Jack faced Dan O'Leary at Molesey Hurst. This was a popular location for the Fancy, partly through

Jack Cooper, 1824.

its racing connection, and partly because it lay at the very edge of Surrey, with Middlesex just over the Thames. If magistrates should interfere, then the company – contenders, seconds, crowd and all – would be ferried over within minutes into another jurisdiction. Though Dan lost, he inflicted some sharp punishment on Jack. There was unfinished business between the two men, and it came to a head in August 1821, back on Epsom Downs. Jack went in eagerly, hammering with his right, but he hadn't allowed for Dan's defence. Finally, in the 31st round, he managed to land one of his lunging right hits. Seven rounds on, he fetched his adversary a heavy blow on the temple. Dan sank onto the knee of his second and didn't get up. He was carried off to the Cock at Sutton, where the doctors put him to bed, but he didn't get up there either. He was dead.[7]

Within weeks, Jack was on trial for his life. The case became a test of prize-fighting itself; nobody disputed that the match had been orderly, or that the two men were fighting as champions, not out of personal animosity, but Dan had nevertheless been killed as a result of illegal activity. The judge summed up with a strong suggestion of murder, but the jury had a more sporting attitude, and Jack was convicted only of manslaughter, which carried a sentence of six months.

In the summer of 1823, he was back and facing Stephen Strong, the Iron-Arm Cabbage, at Twickenham. The odds were on Jack, five to four, and this time both men were fit, determined and able to take sustained punishment. Cabbage made the mistake of trying to outlast Jack in a waiting game, but after one hour and 51 rounds, a blow to the throat finished him off. The prize money was £50, though Jack immediately handed £10 of it to his opponent for gallant fighting.

That was Jack's last golden moment. A string of defeats followed, and the gaze of the Fancy turned to his brother Tom, who was matched in 1826 with a comparative newcomer to the ring: Samuel Elias, known as Young Dutch Sam. They met on the banks of the Thames, at Grays near Tilbury; both alert, both cautious. Within five or six rounds, it was obvious that Tom had no chance:

> The courage and resolution of the Gypsey was admired by every one present; but his mode of fighting is wildness instead of science. He trusts too much to desperation – he slashes out without looking at his opponent; in a word, he is not a marksman. In the hands of a scientific boxer, like Young Dutchy, he stands no chance.[8]

After half an hour, Tom was lying on the ground, unconscious of the voices calling time, while Sam walked out of the ring with nothing worse than swollen hands. Now family honour was at stake, and Jack called out Young Dutch Sam. The fight was finally organized a year later, at Andover, with predictable results. Jack ran at his opponent like a bull; Sam sidestepped him and kept up a run of cruel left jabs. At the end of nine long rounds, Jack was receiving blow after blow without any power to return them. His career in the ring was over.[9]

No longer was he the famous slashing Gypsy, who had sat at a bull-baiting between the Earl of Uxbridge and Whiteheaded Bob, one a coal porter and the other a son of the heir to the throne. The Fancy made for some queer friendships, but no doubt Jack did well out of it.[10] The loss of fame must have left him and his brother short of money, and Tom began acquiring it by more direct methods. At Chelmsford races in 1833 he was part of a gang that waited in the refreshment booths; one customer was hustled and had 32s in silver taken out of his pockets; another was knocked down as he left the tent, with Tom holding his hand over the victim's mouth to stifle cries of 'Murder!' while others lifted his silver watch, penknife and small change.[11] It was a clear case and Tom was sentenced to transportation for fourteen years. But tradition didn't like to remember his exit in such an undignified way. Instead, the say among the Coopers was that Jack and Tom had gone together to a ball, where Jack had picked up a silver snuffbox and dropped it in his brother's pocket. Next day some gavvers were sent round to the tan, and one of them cunningly offered Tom a pinch of snuff; about to sneeze, he tugged on his handkerchief, and out popped the snuffbox, much to Tom's surprise; so he was taken off for trial, despite the (quite true) protestations from both him and his brother that he had nothing to do with the theft.[12]

With a background like this, it is not surprising that Jack ended up acting as the heavy for a London pickpocket, although it wasn't for lack of steadying influences. Shortly before his first big match, he had married Charlotte, the daughter of David Lee and Sophia Stanley.[13] They called her the Rinkeni because she was the most beautiful of her generation among the Romany.[14] Charles Leslie met her shortly before her marriage; he had seen plenty of Gypsy belles at Norwood and Epping, but was awestruck by this one:

> I thought her the finest specimen I had ever seen of a gipsy
> young lady of high rank. Her glossy black hair was arranged with

surpassing taste, and adorned with a silver filigree comb of curious form and workmanship. She had a variety of rings on each hand. Her cloak, of the brightest scarlet, hung gracefully folded over one arm – her bonnet of black velvet, with its crimson silk lining, and its deep black lace edging, was thrown back from her face, as if to give her fine features the full benefit of the sun and air.[15]

Charlotte was well-matched with Jack the welterweight, since she stood just over 5 foot 1.[16] Born in 1796, she was three years older than him and could hold her own in a sparring match; when they got bored with talking and laughing under the trees of Epping Forest, they'd get up and trade punches. They had a church wedding – 'what a nice man the clergyman was,' she remembered, 'and what funny things he said' – and at the beginning of 1820 a baby boy was born at Egham, named Oliver after Jack's loyal second, the gorjer Tom Oliver.[17]

The fine costume was put away, the silver comb sold and Charlotte dressed like an honest Gypsy wife. Jack spent most of the time away with his expensive friends, and often when he returned he was drunk. The blows came hard and fast, and this time it was not a game. Then his prizering winnings dried up, money ran short, and everything was sold that could fetch a price, even the blankets from the tent. At last Charlotte caught smallpox, and lay shivering with disease on the matted straw. She recovered, but her beauty was gone. Soon Jack became infatuated with his young pickpocket, and before long he was gone too.

Yet a golden light still lingered around the memory of Fighting Jack Cooper. He had been a hero, among a people who couldn't lay claim to many heroes, and so all the blame for his fall was pinned not on him but on the stranger woman.[18] It was for that painted Jezebel that he had thrown his fights and lost the confidence of his backers; it was out of misplaced loyalty to her that he gallantly stepped forward and claimed responsibility for thefts which were all her own. This wasn't literally true, but it was the story that Charlotte needed to tell herself again and again in the long years when she was scraping a living in Wandsworth Flats and waiting for a husband who had long since served his term of transportation on the other side of the world, but who would never return. And so she lived until everything that she knew had died away, and she was the sole survivor:

As we sat in the tent by the smoldering fire, whose smoke gave a delicate chiaro-oscuro [*sic*] to the scene, and I looked at the old woman, so unlike anybody whom I meet in ordinary life, my mind wandered to the strange people and scenes which she must have lived amongst long, long ago. She had known the chiefs of her people in the days when they were really fierce and law-defying men who died on the gallows-tree, or in some form of violent death, – the days when the Rom was a leader in the prize-ring, or noted as a highwayman, and wore hunting-boots, and green coats with spade-guineas for buttons, and always carried the tremendous *chukni* or jockey-whip, characteristic of his people.[19]

Those coats with coins for buttons were a must-have for any ambitious man; Adam Lee, the Norwood fiddler, wore one fastened with gold guineas, while his brother Richard had a fustian coat set with silver dollars.[20] Unlike other forms of conspicuous display, coin-studded jackets had the advantage of retaining their cash value if times turned hard. But they were also easily recognized by the detectives, which would explain why they fell out of use in the 1830s, as Londonside Gypsies came under increasing observation from the law.

Portable wealth certainly made sense, and if you had it, why not flaunt it? At Fairlop Fair and Hampton Races,

> I have seen young gipsy girls – gloriously beautiful some of them were, too – literally draped from shoulders to ankles in silk handkerchiefs of the most costly description, great gold bangles on their wrists, heavy jewelled ornaments in their ears, and flashing rings on their fingers ... With them would walk their chosen gipsy swains, clad in shining velveteen, spangled with buttons of gold, silver, and pearl. Buckles of silver and glittering paste adorned their clog shoes, and peeping from the black, well-oiled locks that hung under the broad felt hats to their shoulders might be seen enormously thick gold ear-rings.[21]

That was to be expected at the great annual gatherings, when young people wanted to show off to friends and score points off rivals. But the taste for colour influenced ordinary wear as well. On the streets of Esher in 1837 a man was wearing a green jacket and a grey hat, with a red diklo tied round his throat.[22] For women, scarlet cloaks had become a standard item of wear in the eighteenth century; they replaced the loosely tied blanket which had been traditional since the Arrival, and were just as useful

Charlotte Lee, 1826.

for protecting a dress from work and weather. Many years before, these cloaks had been the usual wear for gorjer women; then fashion changed, and they were found only among country folk and in outlying regions; finally, they became a cultural marker of the Romany. Charlotte Lee wore a cloak of the finest scarlet, and about ten years later, at Sittingbourne in 1829, the Ramsgate coach overturned when its horses took fright at a party of Gypsy women in red cloaks; evidently this was something they didn't see every day.[23]

By the 1830s the range of costume had widened. Sarah Cooper and her sisters-in-law had cloaks in a variety of colours – green, black, grey and red chequered with black – fitted with shoulder-length capes. Mary, the grandmother, habitually wore a bonnet, while Eliza had a broad straw hat, and Phyllis went out once in a long poke bonnet, but Sarah was proud of her raven-black hair and wore it under a contrasting crimson handkerchief.[24] A Gypsy girl at Cobham would wear 'a handkerchief tied over her head . . . upon it a large flapping bonnet with lace trimming, or black beaver hat'.[25] The glossy sheen of beaver hair contrasted well with a bright cloak; there were several styles, but Gypsy women preferred low round hats with wide brims. At the 1851 Derby, women could be distinguished from a distance by the red or yellow handkerchiefs round their head, as they strode through the crowd promising fortunes (or rather, the same fortune) to anyone who would lend an ear.[26] Behind all this bright display, there may have been a sense that red was a lucky colour; certainly Mignonette Lee of Wimbledon was fiercely attached to her coral necklaces, and refused to come to church unless she was allowed to wear them.[27]

These gay and colourful ensembles only extended down to the ankle, for most Gypsy women wore practical footwear. They had to, if they were to earn a living by going out calling each day. At Cobham, where a girl was 'typically strapping, tall, and strong', we are told that 'she has her lower limbs arrayed in black stockings and stout shoes that would do for a wagoner.'[28] All of Sarah Cooper's nieces and nephews, young as they were, had good shoes. From time to time an artist would portray a Gypsy belle with her lovely feet stretched bare on the greensward, but this sort of thing aroused polite incredulity in the community.[29]

So a Gypsy girl from a respected breed would have at least two sets of clothes – one for everyday, one for best – not to mention the necessary changes of underclothing. And she would be only one among many sisters and brothers with similar needs, for families were growing larger. In the early nineteenth century the Hearns, an old lineage who occasionally strayed into Putney and Barnes, averaged about six children in each generation.[30] A hamper would be needed for all the family's clothes, and that meant finding a way to travel with it. The same was true for blankets, tools, the washtub and the cooking things. Then there was the silver teapot, produced with a flourish from its cloth wrappings for special guests, and the fragile fine china.[31] Gypsies might live simply, but that didn't exclude participation in the national rise in living standards as English manufacturers began to produce quality goods at affordable prices.

Large groups were often seen travelling with carts, the best way to carry all these accessories. In 1832 some of the Penfolds made their way to Kingston from Normandy near Ash, transporting their goods in three carts, and accompanied by a string of seven or eight horses, at least one of which was thought to have been relocated from a nearby farm.[32] The Norwood Coopers lived in tents and carts on a small piece of land, later supplemented by a thatched cottage, until it was requisitioned by the Crystal Palace railway.[33]

At the same time, we begin to hear of caravans, although it is not clear exactly what these were. 'Caravan' was a word from the exotic East taken up in eighteenth-century English to describe almost any sealed unit on wheels, from a shepherd's hut to a horsebox. Already in 1818 we hear of a man in Epsom who 'travels with a caravan drawn by a donkey'.[34] Unless he had a particularly heroic donkey, this can hardly have been more than a two-wheeled spring-cart with a tilt. At the other extreme, Gypsies of the Midlands were travelling ten years later in 'a caravan drawn by two excellent horses'. This must be the sort of vehicle which the papers of 1833 describe, with a touch of exaggeration, as 'capacious machines larger than a Paddington omnibus, drawn by two or more horses', evidently the same as the 'pair-horse vans' which attended Hampton Races in 1845.[35]

None of these descriptions are particularly revealing. We know that the vehicles were living-vans, not just places for storage, for Thomas Hearn was stopping in a van on Wimbledon Common in 1831. At the Derby of 1850 waggons could be seen on the Hill, 'each tiny chimney sending forth its smoky evidence of the cooking operations progressing within'.[36] There must have been several variant designs, large and small, but by 1858 a sketch of the Gypsy quarter at the Derby shows a recognizable kite waggon, of the sort that was rapidly becoming standard; it already shows signs of decoration, in the form of ornamental brackets.[37]

The word 'caravan', in all its senses, was soon shortened to van; the long form disappeared from ordinary English and would not be heard again for many years. The homes of Gypsies were distinguished from the other sorts of van by being called living-vans, or in Romani, *kair vardo*, 'a house cart'.[38] By the late 1850s these were easily available. One man boasted that he had been known to lose up to £75 in a day's gambling at Epsom races, where he had often arrived in his waggon, flush with money, and left after losing the money, the van and some of his clothes into the bargain.[39] Evidently he had found no difficulty in buying a new vehicle when his luck turned for the better.

In the South London area, they seem to have formed a halfway stage between tent life and bricks and mortar. As the built-up area grew, it had become more difficult to take lodgings for the winter months after a summer's travelling. Instead, once the rainy season had set in and the opportunities for farm work or fairground trade came to an end, people would return to the outskirts of London and find some little patch of unwanted ground, make an agreement with the landowner if there was one, and then move in.

In 1851 Hills' Yard at Wandsworth was occupied by a row of waggons, each with its family.[40] Thirteen years later a settlement to the north of Wandsworth Common was visited by George Borrow, the childhood friend of Ambrose Smith and himself a man of the roads for many years. He had criss-crossed his way through Europe and was known to Gypsies from Spain to Russia. Rumoured to talk better Romanes than any gorjer living, George had written bestsellers and then outlived their fame. He had lived in caves and castles and jails, and now he was in Brompton.[41] For such a man, a day's trip to a Londonside settlement must have seemed a bit mundane, but his powers of observation remained strong. George saw some waggons – 'not numerous', though evidently bought by people with money and ambition, since the best ones were equipped with handsome stoves and mirror-glass against the sides. But it was tents which filled the ground.

He describes in some detail the bender tents.[42] They were made of rods, 4–5 feet long, set in the ground at 20-inch intervals to create a rectangular outline. At the far end, three or four rods were set in a half-circle; the entrance was left as an arch, facing downwind. At first, each rod would be pulled over and tied to the opposite one to make an arch, but later it became usual to fix them into a long roof piece with holes bored in it at the right places. Then cloths or blankets were stretched over the framework and pinned together with long skewers. At the bottom, they were pegged into the ground; and finally, a little gulley could be cut all around, with the earth piled up on the inside, to keep water from running in when it rained. A bender was typically 5 or 6 feet wide, and the length could vary from about 8 to 12 feet, as the needs of the family required.[43]

At the far end, a bank of straw was held in place by blankets to form the main bed, with more straw and blankets along either side for the children. The clothes hamper and water bucket stood here. During the day, the main bed could be covered with a sheet or green cloth to form a kind of couch, the best seat in the tent; this is the one where visitors would be invited to sit. Since the bender was no more than 4 feet high, there was no room for standing; you clambered in from the front, and sat cross-legged. A family of six to nine people would fill all available space, but everybody knew how to fit in, and with so many people close together, the bender kept warm in winter.[44] Heat came from the fire pan, a big three-legged cauldron pierced with little eyes all round to draw in the air. This was filled with coke, which burnt steadily and didn't smoke as much as coal. Wood was not easy to come by on the outskirts of London, where every hedge and tree must have been picked over a hundred times. Later on, when the old-fashioned cauldrons were no longer made, people made holes in a bucket and used that instead.

Encampments were noisy places. Fifteen or twenty benders, each guarded by a barking, aggressive dog tied to the front rod, home to some half a dozen shouting, playing children: that was something which could be heard from a distance. Most of these places had been set up in defiance of authority, so order had to be maintained by the residents themselves. In 1850, on a summer Sunday night in Battersea Fields, screams were heard as a man struggled to get into a tent, pulling up the blankets on the far end. The bender belonged to Bobby Cooper; his son Joseph was there, with his niece Sarah Taylor, and Sarah's sister-in-law Philadelphia Jones, who had come over for the night from her usual stopping place on Barnes Common. The gorjer was being robbed by a couple who dragged him back out of the tent, pushed him down into the ditch, and threatened to knock his brains out with a livett. (This was a long stick or truncheon, used for throwing at the targets in cock-shies and coconut-shies; evidently there were piles of them on site, waiting for the next fair day.) There was uproar. The Coopers called to the man to come into the front of the tent; small boys ran around getting their fathers to intervene; the robbers ran off but were accosted soon afterwards in the pub by Bobby Cooper, who knocked one of them down because he wouldn't hand back the money he had stolen. Following the intervention of a policeman the case came to court, but it is clear that some sort of rough justice was already being maintained by the Gypsies themselves.[45]

These large settlements flourished wherever there was a no man's land missed by development; the smaller yards were typically next to railway lines, which by cutting across the existing urban landscape had left small triangular areas too awkward for housing. They were both part of the ragged expansion of London's built-up area and were regarded by the authorities as quite acceptable accommodation. When Barbara Lee died in her bender in 1864, the coroner asserted that 'a gipsy's tent is a palace to some of the overcrowded and pestilential dwellings at this part of the great metropolis'. Barbara had left Wandsworth Common, where her late husband Benjamin used to stop when he was not on the road with Aunt Sallys and cock-shies. She had come to see her daughter-in-law Keziah at Bethnal Green, walking across London without any trouble; after that she ate a hearty supper, and talked to Charlotte Lee, who arrived from Kingston that afternoon for a gossip by the fire; then at eight in the morning she died in her tent, of mere old age. Keziah, speaking as a Gypsy (or, as she put it, a Traveller), said that tents were the healthiest places possible – if her mother-in-law had gone into the workhouse, she would have died years before – and the coroner and jury agreed.[46]

Barbara Lee was said never to have had a day's illness in her life, but then she was also said to be a Gypsy Queen and to have been ninety going on one hundred at the time of her death; that was what you always said at the death of a respected old lady. A more realistic assessment of health among the community came from Benjamin Richardson, a doctor who practised near Barnes Common and first began ministering to Gypsies when he was called in after an accident:

> One day a youth at the back of one of the tents attempted to harness a donkey to a little cart. By mere accident the donkey, meaning no ill, made a start before its time, ran the shaft of the cart into the back of the boy, and broke his spine. I reached the tent a little time afterwards, and there on the straw lay the half-dead lad, his legs insensible to pain. He knew everybody, could swallow everything administered to him, tasted everything, spoke about everything he knew, told the story of the accident, and, to my great delight, prayed that the poor donkey, who had done no intentional wrong, should not be punished . . . [I] attended to his injury, put him in the right position, made up his rough bed, and saw him take his food. The lower half of his body was as dead as it could be.[47]

Though he could do nothing for the paralysed boy, Benjamin had gained people's trust, and from 1851 onwards his services were regularly called on, usually for women in childbirth.[48] The services of a doctor were much appreciated in difficult births – if one would come. Doctors in Dorking objected to attending confinements on Leith Hill Common, complaining about the 'terrible conditions'.[49]

Custom and social expectation laid heavy burdens on mothers-to-be when their time came. Young and frightened girls, trying to avoid bringing uncleanliness on their tent or waggon, could end up giving birth in the most unexpected places. At Abinger Hammer a young woman left her family on the common and crawled under the timber piled up in a woodyard. The village midwife crawled in after her to deliver the baby, then tied the cord with a lily leaf, as she usually did, and fetched a cloth to clean and wrap the newborn. Holding her precious burden, the mother stood up and returned at once to the road.[50] This sort of resilience was expected of women, whatever the personal cost. At Chobham a mother gave birth in her bender on a bitter winter's night, without a midwife, and was out calling the next morning to get money for the baby clothes.[51] Phoebe Lambert was near her time when she set off from Croydon to see her parents at Ewhurst, 30 miles away; on arrival she went into labour and bore a son. It was mid-December. Her father, finding that she was sitting up in bed, gave her a pile of greenstuff and told her to make herself useful twisting holly wreaths for the Christmas trade.[52]

Not all these children lived. Little Methuselah Lee died in 1853 when his parents had come up from Folkestone to Epsom for the Derby; he was two years old, just one of many infant burials, and remarkable only for the irony of his name.[53] Growing up was full of hazards. There was the fire to burn, and the cauldron of boiling water to scald; animals to bite and kick, and wheels to run over a little body.[54] After the years of babyhood, children would have to be left unattended for much of the day, when their father had to ride away on Gypsy business and their mother was out calling. That was one reason why people travelled in extended family groups, since a Granny Elizabeth or an Aunt Sarah could look after an extended string of brothers, sisters and cousins while the rest of the family searched for the work that would put bread in their mouths. And so on a typical day 'the children have been left to look out for themselves or to the care of the eldest, and have tumbled around the van, rolled around with the dog, and fought or frolicked as they chose.'[55] Under such a regime those children who survived the hazards of infancy were likely to grow up sturdy, independent, competitive and uncontrolled; the kind of chavvies seen by one observer in the 1860s at Box Hill:

Many children, quick to scan
A new thing coming; swarthy cheeks, white teeth:
In many-coloured rags they ran,
Like iron runlets of the heath.
Dispersed lay broth-pot, sticks and drinking-can.
Three girls, with shoulders like a boat at sea
Tipped sideways by the wave (their clothing slid
From either ridge unequally),
Lean, swift and voluble, bestrid
A starting-point, unfrocked to the bent knee.
They raced; their brothers yelled them on, and broke
In act to follow, but as one they snuffed
Wood-fumes . . .
Soon on the dark edge of a ruddier gleam,
The mother-pot perusing, all, stretched flat,
Paused for its bubbling-up supreme.[56]

These children had food and air and exercise, which was more than many of their gorjer contemporaries could hope for. It was a healthy life, and once infants had survived the risky years of childhood, they could expect many years of travelling. Reported instances of extreme old age, especially those for women, owe more to storytelling than arithmetic, but a realistic assessment of about fifty life histories suggests that over the course of the nineteenth century, a twenty-year-old Gypsy could expect on average to live to be sixty.[57]

By the end of his own long life, Benjamin Richardson knew more than most about the health of the community. 'Gypsies were constitutionally a very healthy race,' he thought, if you made allowance for the rheumatism that came from sleeping so close to the damp ground, although those who began to mix and live with gorjers would naturally pick up their diseases. Infectious disease was less serious among Gypsies, because encampments were at a remove from new infections, and too small to contain a reservoir of old ones. Benjamin had never seen small-pox on Barnes Common, and the one local outbreak of scarlet fever in 1850 left the tents untouched.[58]

In fact smallpox had only recently diminished, having previously been just as lethal among Gypsies as gorjers. We have already seen how Charlotte Lee suffered from the disease, although she survived, like most of those infected; the mortality rate was about one in seven.[59]

James Stanley 'was suffering dreadfully under the small-pox' when he was arrested for stealing a horse in 1827; several witnesses remembered seeing him at work that day in a market garden at Kingston, 50 miles away from the scene of the supposed theft, but he was condemned to death anyway.[60] Job Cooper, the son of Leonard and Phyllis, whom we met as a mop-headed boy in a white smock on the Portsmouth Road at Esher, died of smallpox at the Derby in the 1860s; Jephthah Curder died of the same disease at Wisley in 1845.[61] And then, as the nineteenth century progressed, these deaths became rarer, either because the disease had become less virulent, or because it was beginning to be controlled by vaccines. That couldn't have affected its incidence among Gypsies, however, since they were seldom approached during vaccination schemes. When they were, as at Putney in 1865, they viewed them with great suspicion.[62]

But as one disease lost its vigour, others were on the rise. The global reach of Victorian commerce meant that epidemics could easily leap from one continent to another; cholera had arrived in this way from India to London, and it showed no signs of going away. In 1866 Edward Cherry from the Wandsworth encampment was out begging, trying to support the family. Back in the bender, his father was lying weak with the disease, while his sister tried to nurse him; their mother was already dead; there was another child in the tent stretched out stiff and cold.[63] More prosperous travellers were equally vulnerable; in the same year John Smith, toy hawker and fairground man, died of cholera in his waggon on Ripley Green.[64] Cholera, though nobody knew it as yet, was communicated through the water supply; so was typhoid, which at Windsor in 1862 took the life of Liddy Matthews, nursed to the end by Chewbacca, the husband who had caught her eye so many years before at Ewell Fair.[65] Two of Liddy's granddaughters died ten years later of scarlet fever, another of the new epidemics, and one which was particularly threatening to children.[66]

Infection was something that spread from gorjers to Gypsies; the settled community, with its overwhelming population, dense conurbations and endlessly reused and reinfected water sources, formed a breeding ground for infections. The typhoid which carried off Liddy was endemic in Windsor, where it had claimed the life of Prince Albert in the previous year. It was a tragic reminder of how much Gypsies were caught up, for good or bad, in the fate of mainstream society.

This was particularly true for the Matthews family, who had concentrated more and more on providing fairground entertainment for the Victorian crowds. Chewbacca and Liddy had raised five sons – young

Jemmy, John, William (Redshirt), Chorley and Joseph (Harelip). Their eldest followed the Gypsy life of his father, combining chair-mending and other crafts with small prizes as a bare-knuckle man. After marriage he and his parents made two roads of it, and Jemmy moved out of the family story; so did his brother John; but the youngest three stuck together, and formed a tightknit clan as they worked the fairground circuit. Looking back in later years, Redshirt dated the decisive moment to the summer of 1856, when as a thirteen-year-old he helped amuse soldiers at the review in Frimley:

> My father came to that district because he saw business ahead in his line. The troops were returning from the Crimea, and our show proceeded to Chobham Ridge and took its share in providing entertainment for those poor chaps who had gone through months of hell. I can recall that Queen Victoria, with the Prince Consort, held a great review on the Ridges . . . Yes, there was plenty of money when the troops came home.[67]

To be in the right place at the right time for entertainment, it helped to have something ready to charm the crowds. That was why the fiddle was a natural instrument for Travellers – lightweight, small and secure in its case, it could be practised at odd hours around the fireside. Old Adam Lee, who was hanged on false charges in 1812, had played the fiddle at farmhouses round Norwood and Streatham.[68] In the Southampton area there was a Gypsy Tom who 'attended fairs, wakes, private parties, and houses notorious for immorality and vice'. He took the children with him, so that they could learn the business through practical experience; there was no risk of them contracting either vice or immorality, as they were kept too busy; at one party Tom played the whole night through, until in the small hours he was the only sober man left in the house.[69] Others were less abstemious. In the 1850s London pubs were paying Gypsy musicians 2s a night, with as much beer and spirits as they could drink: an open temptation. One fiddler put away a pint of rum and uncounted pints of beer during a session; another sank 2¾ pints of rum in an hour and a half.[70]

The effects this had on his music can be imagined, but the audience were probably too drunk to notice. All they wanted was a good tune that they could dance to. The next step was for the Gypsies to cut out the middleman and themselves provide customers with everything they needed. This was taken by John Stevens in the 1830s. He bought a booth large enough to accommodate several dancing couples, supplied refreshments, and set up the whole arrangement at one fair after another, hanging out a green branch in the traditional way to advertise what was on offer. At first his core market lay in other Gypsies, who came to the tent to socialize after a day working the fair; then gorjer visitors got curious and made a special visit to his booths just for the experience of being among the Romany, especially John's wife – he had married Trinity Cooper in 1817 – and their two dark-eyed daughters.[71]

John was a quiet, well-conducted man, except during his fits of mindless rage.[72] One of these came in 1832 at Harlow Bush Fair, the big September celebration to the north of Epping Forest. Among the company in the dancing booth was Elijah Buckley, who was suspected (rightly or wrongly) of being too close to Trinity.[73] John grabbed hold of a tent-pole and threatened him – Elijah's people backed him up – and a fight broke out. Two or three blows with the pole were too much for Elijah, who took to his bed and died.

This was not forgotten, and some people wanted revenge. Three years later John set his tent up for the Derby, and at nightfall a cry of 'Murder!' was heard from the booth; a policeman ran to the scene (the new Metropolitan Police were now on duty at Epsom races) and saw a man standing over John's motionless body, with a heavy hedge stake in his hand. The stake proved equally useful for battering the policeman, who persisted in making an arrest. This led to a running battle in which two policemen were stabbed, though they got away with their man. He was identified as Trinity's brother, for the Coopers had now been drawn into the feud.[74]

John recovered quickly enough. A certain amount of violence was to be expected in the fairground trade, and it doesn't seem to have harmed his business. By 1844 he had acquired a base at the Mulberry Tree in Stepney and was appearing at Wandsworth fair with a 'monster booth', which seems to have deserved the name since it was nearly 400 feet long.[75] These were the days of longways sets in country dancing, 'for as many couples as wish', though with a line this long, he may have staged his fiddlers in relays. Running the monster booth would have required a considerable investment in materials alone, since dancing took place on sections of plank flooring which had to be laid and fitted before each fair.

But the family was beginning to suffer from John's inability to keep his temper. Late one night in 1846, a passer-by heard screams coming from the Mulberry Tree, and raced into the building and up the stairs, where he found John knocking Trinity down with the fender from the hearthside. He then knelt on her chest and continued to beat her. She was rescued and sent to hospital, while he was committed to prison. At the trial, however, Trinity explained that her would-be rescuer had completely misunderstood the situation. She had in fact fallen accidentally, knocking her head against the fender as wives often do, and John had not touched her at all. The magistrate thought that this was an unlikely story, given that her husband had to be dragged off her after he had been seen repeatedly hammering her head against the floorboards; Trinity stuck to it, however, and as she declined to press charges, the case was dropped.[76]

Despite her husband's attentions, Trinity lived until 1870, surviving him by sixteen years, while the business was taken over by their son, Thomas (Bishop) Stevens. Bishop was at the races near Molesey in 1856 when he was stung by a bent fiver. Two gorjers, gentlemen of the turf, had struck up an acquaintance with a third party, whom they invited to dinner in the refreshment booth. Having nothing smaller than a £5 note, they wondered if their new friend could take it to the counter and get it changed, which Bishop gladly did for him, charging his usual fee of 1s in the £1. Clutching his £4 15s, the new racegoer rejoined his companions, who shortly afterwards disappeared into the crowd. Bishop, who probably wasn't as gullible as the friendly young sportsman, promptly disposed of the fiver to another Gypsy, Mary White, in payment of an earlier loan. Mary looked at the note thoughtfully and tried palming it off on a Southwark clothes dealer two days later, but he wasn't having any of it and the case ended up in court.[77]

There had been racing at Molesey Hurst since 1815; the course was run in June on flat meadow land beside the Thames, on the same ground that had been used for prize-fighting. The village of Hampton lay just across the river, easily accessed by ferry, and so the event was known as Hampton Races. At first, like most racecourses, it was just a meeting for owners, trainers and horsey men; but Molesey was so easily accessible from Kingston, and therefore from London, that by mid-century Hampton Races were attracting a huge Cockney crowd.[78] That was an unmissable opportunity for anyone providing entertainment: 'a greater number of gipsies attend these races than even the Derby.'[79] The Matthews were at Molesey in 1861; after the races were over, when there was time to dress up and look smart, Redshirt married Mary Ann (Polly), the daughter of Bennie and Annie Bushnell. Meshach and Alice Hearn had baptized their little Kezia Ann here in 1840. Matty and Eliza Cooper were here as well, christening three of their children in race month – Vanselo in 1854, Perron in 1856 and Oliver in 1858.

All races had originally been run in this way, on a stretch of open land near a town. Whoever was interested could attend, and they attracted all the sideshows of a fairground. But from 1875 new courses, like Kempton and Sandown Park, were laid out within enclosures that charged for admission. They recouped their costs from the entrance fees of dedicated racegoers, so casual entertainers were not welcome, and certainly not Gypsies. One by one, the traditional open courses found themselves unable to pay their way, and stopped racing – even Hampton Races, which were last run in 1887. There were only three exceptions to this rule in the southeast: Goodwood, Ascot and Epsom. To stop running the Derby was unthinkable, and the Derby course lay on common land of the Manor of Epsom, which could be not fenced, walled or blocked off to the public. An easy day's journey from London, Epsom became the favourite day out for thousands, and as the race crowds grew, so did the number of Gypsies looking to profit from them.

There had been racing on the Downs before the first Derby in 1780, and even at that early date there were stallholders to sell them drinks, and

Waggons and benders at the Derby, 1858.

gambling dens to take advantage of the drunk and reckless. But those races were run largely for aristocrats, the sort of people who arrived on the Downs in a carriage and viewed the course from horseback. It is not until the 1820s that the Derby became a popular festival:

> Caravans, carts, & waggons were seen approaching from most parts of the compass, heavily laden with the 'materiel' for erecting booths, and providing accommodation for the expected crowds; and in a short time the green turf was covered with edifices of various characters, calculated for the reception of every order of visitors, from the Peer to the peasant . . . As some little pastime was necessary before the sports began, two Gypsies, in order to earn 'an honest penny', proposed to gratify the spectators by a fight. The offer was hailed with satisfaction, and in a short time a purse was collected . . . The course was completely covered with pedestrians, who as they promenaded backwards and forwards, were amused in various ways. Ballad singers, puppet shows, gambling tables of the minor class, Gypsies telling fortunes, beggars fighting for the occasional offerings of the charitable, tumblers, grimaciers, and musicians all claimed attention in turn, and contributed towards the general fund of good humour.[80]

In 1851 the numbers attending the Derby were estimated at something like 250,000; after that the management simply gave up counting.[81] A grandstand had been built, by private enterprise – the Lord of the Manor remained neutral – and the business of racing was run more professionally, but the throngs of those who provided the crowd with entertainment were unregulated as before. People arrived over the days leading up to the big race, pitching out wherever they could on the bleak expanse of the Downs. A journalist, taking the chance to accompany a policeman on his rounds for the night before the Derby, saw all the sights: trampers crouched round their fire and ready to sleep in the open; a shed full of vocal, laughing Irish; a neat warm booth for a family of showfolk; and then the Gypsies at rest in their benders, each one guarded by a fierce dog. Over one thousand people, all told, lay sleeping, ready to work the crowd the next day. In the morning, the Gypsies have lit a fire to boil their kettle, with grandmother gathering branches, father sitting against the donkey cart to smoke his first pipe and the children already at play. Catching sight of the day's first customer, the young mother sets to at

The Gregorys in their bender at Mitcham, 1879.

once – 'Noble gentleman, leave us a little sixpence. Do, my Sir, and you'll have luck to-day. You were born under a lucky star, Sir. Do, my Sir – one sixpence from the rich gentleman for the poor gipsy . . .' – but the journalist flees before any more can be revealed.[82] Never mind: another 249,999 punters are on their way.

The Gypsies were in turn a draw for evangelists, who arrived early, experience having shown that it was best to preach the Gospel to people before they started work or found their way to the beer tent. In 1859 a missionary went round some 75 families in a single morning, handing out two hundred tracts. In the afternoon interest in his message waned; the women were dressing up, so that they would look their best while dukkering, and avoided catching his eye. 'The gypsies seem to think me in the way when I meet them at these places,' the good man sadly recorded. 'They say "We must get a living, Sir."'[83]

Among the evangelists, though not very typical of them, was George Borrow; for much of his wandering career he had been the agent of the Bible Society, and old habits die hard. At the 1865 Derby he met with Clara Boss, whom he had seen years before under very different circumstances.

Clara was the sister of Riley Boss, a hard-riding madman who dressed in golden buttons. As a teenager she had spent a month in the house of a friendly gorjer, and since she was a polite, outgoing girl, good at making and mending things, she got on well with the family. She taught them how to make a hedgehog whistle and sing, by squeezing his toes; in return, they taught her something about Christianity. Then came a thunder of knocks on the door, and there stood Riley, calling to his sister in Romanes. She was terrified at the thought of going with him, but go she must, and that night she was carried in a cart across England to Norfolk, which is where George met up with her. Three women looked after her night and day; they were afraid to disobey Riley's orders, and he had told them to make his sister back into a Gypsy.[84] They seem to have been successful, for when she next saw George on the Downs she was

> a full-blown Egyptian matron, with two very handsome daugh-
> ters flaringly dressed in genuine Gypsy fashion, to whom she was
> giving motherly counsels as to the best means to hok and dukker
> the gentlefolks. All her Christianity she appeared to have flung to
> the dogs, for when the writer spoke to her on that very important
> subject, she made no answer save by an indescribable Gypsy look
> . . . She had been twice married, and both times very well, for that
> her first husband, by whom she had the two daughters whom
> the writer 'kept staring at', was a man every inch of him, and
> her second, who was then on the Downs grinding knives with a
> machine he had, though he had not much manhood, being nearly
> eighty years old, had something much better, namely a mint of
> money, which she hoped shortly to have in her own possession.[85]

But Gypsies formed only a small proportion, perhaps a tenth, of the great amorphous throng who provided services and entertainment.[86] And the boundary between Gypsies and other travellers was not immutable. John Stevens traded on his identity as Gypsy Stevens; his son did not, presenting himself simply as an innkeeper who ran a sideline in dance tents. The Matthews family changed their identity more gradually. Chewbacca was never described as anything but a Gypsy. His daughter-in-law Polly was the centre of an animated crowd at Cobham Fair in 1873, at which all conversation was in Romanes. 'As if we weren't all alike to God,' she said to a bilingual gorjer. 'Doesn't his sun shine the same on a Romany as on my Lord Duke?'[87] But although the English spoken by the next generation was still rich in Anglo-Romani expressions, they had come to identify themselves as showfolk, not as Gypsies. Chewbacca died in 1890, and Redshirt became the head of the clan; in 1921 he told the revised story of his ancestry to the newspapers, beginning 'I was born at Shackleford, Godalming, in a caravan. I am the son of James Matthews, a Sussex showman.'[88] The decisive moment seems to have come in 1883, when he bought a loud, bright, steam-driven roundabout, with 24 Dobby horses, from Savages of King's Lynn.[89] It was a good investment for a man whose life was now spent entirely on the fairground circuit, but with its heavy footings and blaring organ, it also led to many conflicts with local councils and deafened residents. The last thing that Redshirt needed for his litigation was to be identified with a people mostly found on the wrong side of the law, so it was as a showman that he conducted his disputes. Not that this stopped him living in a waggon, drinking out of the best Crown Derby, carrying all accounts in his head, laying patrins as he took the road from fair to fair, and relying on his horse whip to settle any little difficulties in business.[90]

A rift was developing between Gypsies and showfolk. When Lord George Sanger looked back on the rough early years of a career which had led up to his becoming the country's leading circus master, he was careful to emphasize the separate character of the two communities. 'The gipsies, it is true, went from fair to fair, but it was as horse-dealers, hawkers of baskets and tinware, workers of the lucky-bag swindle, fortune-tellers, and owners of knife and snuff-box shies.'[91] Their tents were pitched in one part of the ground, while the showfolk pulled their vans elsewhere; not that this stopped individuals crossing the line from one group to another. Plato Smith, for example, must have been born a Gypsy, although he was on record as a Show Traveller when wintering at Battersea, and nearby was a woman with the impeccably Gypsy name of Concelleta who had married James Washington Durant, Contortionist and Acrobatic Performer.[92]

Underlying the ethnic divide was a difference in occupations. Showfolk had invested in equipment which needed to pay its way, so they were committed to the whole circuit of fairs from Candlemas to Bonfire Night. Gypsies could find other seasonal labour at harvest and hopping time, which meant that their fairground season was more limited. Unless they were stopping near a town or village at its local fair time, a family would only expect to work the big regional gatherings in May, June and July, and then they made the most of the occasion. At the Derby:

The wild-eyed gipsy is, indeed, everywhere. When the first wag-
onettes and brakes arrived we found him with bare arms, swarthy
face, and eager looks, ready to unharness horses and drag the
vehicles into a good place; now he is engaged in a thousand occupations. With cries and blows he urges on the half-dozen sleepy
donkeys on which are sitting half a dozen girls and matrons, their
cotton gowns tucked up, their faces flushed with the wild delight
of the ride. Regardless of hurling missiles he serves the patrons of
'Aunt Sally' – snatches up the sticks that have been thrown while
the air appears to be thick with those that are being thrown; and
very rarely is he compelled to yield up the small (and probably
empty) cocoa-nut which is the reward of exceptional skill.[93]

Since the season for fairs and races was so short, people did not want
to carry much in the way of equipment, which is why cock-shies were
popular for fairground pitches. All you needed were some livetts, which
could be whittled from hard wood during the winter; pole stands, which
were easily made from hazel rods; and a back-cloth, which might have
done service overnight as the blanket over a bender, and was now pinned
up to prevent stray livetts from braining some passer-by. At first the targets were cheap knives, tobacco containers or iron snuffboxes, which were
balanced on the rods, looking ready to fall at any minute. It was not until
the 1860s that coconuts became cheap enough to be used as targets. At
two or three shies a penny, a punter might hand over a fair sum of money
before giving up in disgust, for winning at a cock-shy wasn't as simple
as it looked. You could set the distance of the throw to confuse people,
or arrange things so that the goods always fell outside the magic circle.[94]
Generally the public took this with a good grace, although soldiers were
always a high risk; they were less inclined to accept defeat, and more likely
to swap notes and take collective action. On more than one occasion,
troops combined to attack Gypsies on the fairground.[95]

Not all the violence at fairs came from disappointed punters. The
national tradition of prize-fighting had been driven underground in the
1840s but its code of honour was still respected by Gypsies, as it was by
other working-class communities.[96] When two men had a dispute, they
would settle it in a good, stand-up fight – fair play, no favour and the best
to win. If other people wanted to watch, then so much the better. And
that was why the fairground suddenly grew quiet after the Hampton
Races of 1845, as the crowd began moving down towards the river, where

a ring had been made for Jimmy Lee to take on Tommy Rossiter.[97] There had been bad blood between the Rossiters and the Lees since Fairlop Fair, and now it was to be settled between man and man. It was 8 p.m. on a June evening, still light enough for young George Sanger to pick out everything from his pitch on the hill above. 'I saw a quick flash of sinewy arms, two jumping, dodging bodies, now close together, now apart again, and knew that the big fight had begun.' But before the men had gone five rounds, the crowd swayed in and closed the ring. A small body of police were pushing forwards to break up the fight. They squeezed their way right into the centre and caught onto one of the fighters. But that was just the beginning, for the only way out from Molesey Hurst lay across the Thames, by ferry, and that was where the police were going to have to take their captive. They retreated towards the river, and hundreds of Gypsies followed them in a sudden terrible rage. Perched on the hillside, the Sanger family looked down on it all.

> 'My God, boy! There will be murder done this day! said my father, who had climbed on the roundabout to my side, and it certainly looked like it. We saw the police with many of the frightened spectators scrambling towards the two big ferry-boats. Behind them pressed the gipsies with those terrible livetts, beneath which men went down like pole-axed oxen. Still forms were distinguishable here and there on the river-bank stretched out dead or insensible. It was like a battlefield for its action and its clamour, and I shall never forget the scene or the white faces of that other crowd that, deathly still, watched it with ourselves from the vantage point of the showground.[98]

The police fell back, releasing their captive. 'Give it to them,' roared George Lee. Damon, Perrin and Robert hurried after him, and the Lees were joined by Uriah Cooper and Zachariah Boswell. For a moment it looked as if the constables would all be pinned down and thrown into the river, but then suddenly the crowd wavered and pulled back. A runner had arrived with the news that more gavvers were on their way from Kingston, and these were armed. At once everyone retreated up the hill, ready instantly to pull up tents, load carts and leave the ground. The roads to Walton and Esher were clogged for more than a mile by the retreating force.[99]

Never again would Gypsies be able to take on the agents of the state in such force. Up to this time, fairgrounds and popular gatherings had

Providing entertainments at the Derby, 1863.

been almost free from control. They were usually held on common or waste ground and attracted numbers so great that they could defy the authority of local constables. In 1844 a party took on ten policemen at the Derby and would have won the day if the landlord of the Rubbing House hadn't joined forces with the law and opened fire on the Gypsies from his window, his wife loading one pistol while he blazed away with the other.[100] But those wild days were at an end.

Open spaces were gradually coming under official management, a change which began nearest to London at Battersea Fields. Like Epsom Downs and Molesey Hurst, this became a venue for popular entertainment in the early nineteenth century. The Fields were so easily accessible from the Chelsea side of the river that they could support a fair every Sunday, with dogfighting, badger-baiting and hare-coursing among other country sports. Pubs and tea gardens did a good trade, and so did the dance booths and portable theatres.[101]

Clearly, despite the presence of pimps and pickpockets, Battersea Fields was far from anarchy; in fact, it was this combination of raffishness with order which made them a good place for Gypsies, since it put potential customers at their ease. Fifty or sixty people stopped here over the summer to provide entertainment.[102] As one visitor wrote:

What a novelty it was then for a smoke-dried Londoner to walk two miles along the road, or land at the Red House from a two-penny boat, and plunge suddenly amongst this mysterious eastern people, and tranquilly to observe their ethnological distinctiveness in the comfortable assurance that there was a police-station within easy distance . . . Here a young girl with an eye sparkling like a stray sunbeam from the south over our dull northern morass, tranquilly watching a combat between two walnut tinted lovers; and here her elder relatives, harnessing donkeys for the little boys, or tempting their cupidity and enterprise by vociferous invitations to the ancient game of 'Three shies a penny'.[103]

But by the 1840s official attitudes had changed. Reformers, for whom the fair was 'an institution around which concentrated every evil under the sun', suppressed it through the patriotic strategy of making the Fields into a Royal Park. By 1858 the grounds of the Red House and the old stopping places had been transformed into 300 acres of bleak parkland, and the Gypsies were evicted.

At the opening of the nineteenth century, London had been ringed by commons and open spaces, from Richmond through Sheen and Barnes to Putney and Wimbledon, and then onwards to Wandsworth, Clapham, Streatham, Dulwich and Peckham Rye. These all had stopping places and wintering grounds, where people could pitch a tent knowing that family and allies were to be found nearby, and there were ample opportunities for making a living. But the growth of the capital was taking these places from the Romany. It was not that the commons themselves were disappearing, since development usually took place on former agricultural land, but the lines of villas favoured by the speculative developer were tenanted by a class of people unlikely to be sympathetic to Gypsies – or to most other users of common land.

The conflict of old and new came to a head at Wimbledon, which was the largest of the commons, with a considerable Gypsy population. Seventy people stopped here over the winter of 1831.[104] Earlier that year, part of the common had been occupied by a group including Jeremiah Taylor, who specialized in making baskets, accompanied by his wife Sarah Fisher and their children, apart from Alice, the eldest of the family, who was with her husband Meshach Hearn. Meshach's father Thomas, another basket maker, was on the common, and so was William Faulkner, who made mostly pegs and skewers. Everyone was in tents apart from

Thomas Hearn, who had his waggon. Will came back drunk from selling his skewers in Wandsworth, and called Jeremiah out, saying he could beat his master's master. Jeremiah tried to calm him down, but a direct challenge like that couldn't be ignored. Although the family attempted to get them apart, the fight went on for twenty minutes until Jeremiah, who was 47, collapsed with a ruptured blood vessel. He died soon afterwards.[105]

The Taylors and Hearns had pitched their tents on Jerry's Hill in the northern part of the common, overlooking the Kingston Road. Nearby, just to the east of Queensmere, a circuit of land was called the Ring or the Gypsy Ring.[106] The hill had a sinister reputation: it was named after the highwayman Jerry Abershaw, who was hung here in chains at the end of his career. But, more usefully, it was the point where the boundaries of Putney, Wandsworth and Wimbledon met. When authority arrived to chase Gypsies away, people only needed to up sticks and move their benders a few yards into another parish, and at once the duty of harassment fell to another constable, and one less bothered about it. Later the manorial rights over Putney Heath and Wimbledon Common were combined, so that a single keeper of the commons could take action on both sides of the border; but this underestimated local support for the Gypsies. James Roberts, 'a great stickler for privileges' and a market gardener who may have relied on Gypsy workers, was certainly happy to let people stop on his land whenever they were evicted. Meanwhile the common continued to supply them with wood for fires and grazing for horses and donkeys, whether their tents were pitched on it or not.[107]

This live-and-let-live attitude was not endorsed at higher levels. In 1864 a public meeting was convened by John Spencer, who was the fifth Earl Spencer and owned joint manorial rights to Putney and Wimbledon. He began by outlining the problems, as he saw them: the common was too wet, all sorts of people were taking gravel and wood from it and to cap it all there were the Gypsies – 'not desirable neighbours to the houses that are now found near here'. He was thinking of the newly built villas along Wimbledon Park Side. In order to make the common acceptable to this class of residents, it would have to be drained, fenced and made more like a park; and to pay for these works, John proposed to enclose the western part and sell it off for housing.[108]

Certainly the Gypsy population of Wimbledon seemed to have increased in the last generation. There was now a community of up to 130 in encampments scattered around the common, one of them containing forty people.[109] The common was a popular transit point: it was easy to head eastwards across the London hinterland to Kent, or to take the road westwards to Kingston, and so up the Thames valley, with another route heading southwest to Guildford and Farnham. People who usually travelled in Kent could be found here, like the twin brothers John and Robert Pateman. Robert's daughter Alice was born on the common in 1842; John's first child, Esther, was also born there in 1844.[110]

John Spencer had been contemplating action against the Gypsies since the late 1850s, although opinion was divided, even among the wealthier residents. There were some who wanted to see people prosecuted, others who were keen to move them on, and a few who hoped to get families settled, at least long enough for the children to go to school.[111] To complicate things further, the common was often used by tramps, regarded by some of the settled community as indistinguishable from the Gypsies, though others indignantly distinguished them as a separate class entirely. There were also homeless prostitutes soliciting for custom among the young men of the neighbourhood. This was resented by Gypsy women just as much as by the respectable householders; one of these girls was set on by a group of vigilante van dwellers, who wanted to throw her in a pond.[112]

One of the residents remembered with gratitude the time that Gypsies came to help put out a heath fire, caused by a careless villager. Others made a point of dropping in on an encampment during their morning walks or Sunday excursions.[113] Among these was George Borrow, now in his sixties but still a tireless walker in wild places. There were Smiths stopping on the common, presumably distant relatives of Ambrose and his clan, but George did not have much time for them, brusquely dismissing them as kipsiengros rather than graiengros.[114] This seems a little unfair; baskets may have been a less honourable trade than horses, and certainly not as profitable, but horse-dealing had been associated for so many years with theft and sharp dealing that it was not a wise occupation to follow when you were under almost continual surveillance.

The Gypsies of Wimbledon kept to small crafts: mending pots, bottoming rush chairs, and making brooms of heather.[115] The Smiths, like the Taylors and Hearns, were known for their baskets – not an easy skill to master, for you needed a quick eye in identifying the different sorts of osier (it was just as well that the common had so many pools and bogs) and a knowledge of the different styles and strengths of container employed by various trades. When the family were at work, it was the father who was making a basket, while his son had the less intricate job of creating wooden flowers.[116] It is hard to see how any of this could cause friction with the gorjers. John Spencer himself admitted that the Gypsies had not committed any depredations worse than taking hedge stakes for firewood, which led to horses and donkeys straying into market gardens. The children ran out in old clothes and barefoot to beg from passing carriages and some boys once climbed on top of a waggon and shouted at the mourners during a funeral at Putney Vale Cemetery.[117] This was about as bad as things got. And yet the vicar of Holy Trinity in Roehampton stood up in 1864 to tell his parishioners that the Gypsies were guilty of 'things so atrocious that it had been impossible to put them on paper'.[118]

To many of the prosperous new residents of Wimbledon, Putney and Roehampton, Gypsies were the wrong sort of people in the wrong place, and that was that. When asked exactly what grounds a common keeper might have for proceeding against Gypsies, one witness was baffled by the question. 'It is generally supposed to be the normal state of a gipsy to make a nuisance of himself.'[119] When pressed, the advocates for clearances spoke vaguely of vagrants being liable to spread disease, but this was little more than a metaphor: to them, Gypsies *were* a disease, from which society should be cleansed.

The Wimbledon campaign was not a success: too many local residents had a romantic attraction to the unenclosed and unimproved common and, in 1871, after years of dispute, John Spencer was persuaded to convey the whole space to a body of conservators. The Gypsies carried on making baskets from its willow trees, for a while. But following the dispute, which threatened to repeat itself wherever the enclosure of commons pitted a lord of the manor against public interest groups, Parliament began an inquiry which ended in the 1866 Metropolitan Commons Act. The open spaces which ringed London were now free from the threat of enclosure, but they were also subject to rules and bye-laws designed to cripple the lives of travelling people. 'I am willing to adopt any effectual way of putting down the gypsies,' John had written.[120] A new kind of prejudice had arrived, and it wasn't going to go away.

5

Waggons Roll:
The Victorian Age

How were they to live? asked Mary White. It was pitiful, they were headed for ruin. George was an innocent man – everyone knew that. Nobody had a word to say against her husband, except for that bengtail who had told some gavvers about the horse. And he never stole the horse, it was all a pack of lies; they'd fetched a lawyer with a package of papers who proved all that. But lawyers cost money – beautiful golden money! – and now it was gone, all gone, to save her husband's name, and they were *ruined*.

She paused for effect. The red light of sunset glanced off the rippling Thames, coloured the stones of Walton Bridge and shone on the bearded face of the gentleman who was ignoring all her appeals for money. He strolled over to her waggon and looked at it with an appraising eye. 'That's a nice one,' he said. 'I hear George has it insured for a hundred pound.' Mary got ready for a final, impassioned tale of woe – she had her self-respect to think of and couldn't give up without getting something from the man – but he ignored her, climbed up onto the footboard, and sat down inside. That made him a guest, and you couldn't mong from guests. Besides, both the Whites knew about Charles Leland from Matty, their uncle: George was Sarah Cooper's son, and Mary was his cousin, the daughter of Leonard and Phyllis.[1] They'd heard that the bearded American could be generous enough when the mood took him; only it was a quirk of his to give away money recklessly of his own accord, but to clam up as soon as you tried to get anything from him.

George joined them in the waggon, taking the other chair. A fire had been lit in the stove, just on the left as you went in; a waggon travels with the door facing forwards, so left is the off-side, and it is prudent to have the stove on that side because its chimney will then stick out towards

William Hampton's
waggon at Battersea,
1877.

the middle of the road, where it can't be knocked about by low-hanging
branches. A dark-eyed young cousin was baking apples on the grate, and
a kettle was on the boil; the Whites offered tea or coffee to Charles, but
he preferred beer. Mary was rather proud of her waggon and welcomed
the opportunity to show it off. Look, here was their table, next to the
stove; it hung on hinges, so you could drop it down when you needed
more room. And here, between the two chairs on the near side, was their
chest of drawers; and there, at the end, was the bed, raised up, with a
space under it for keeping old clothes and other oddments. The bed was
6 feet long, with a mattress and covers. Feel it, my rai! – wasn't that better
than anything you ever slept on? And Charles admitted that, yes, it was.[2]

Waggon makers had to satisfy a discerning market. By 1874, about the
time that the Whites were stopping at Walton, a basic working design had
been achieved, as seen in the photograph of William Hampton's waggon
in one of the Battersea yards.[3] The bodywork is 6 feet wide and a little
over 10 feet long. It is built from 6-inch boards, beaded at the top edge,
and joined by tongue and groove; the boards run along the length of the
waggon, and are held firm by upright ribs, at a spacing of about 8 inches.

The roof of the waggon extends over the footboard, where the driver will sit when it is on the road, and is held steady by porch brackets, pierced and carved to add a decorative element.

The body of the waggon stands between 3 and 4 feet off the ground. Not much can be glimpsed of the underworks, though they look sturdy and the iron tyres are worn: evidently William had just come back to Battersea after a summer on the road. The structure, unseen as it is, would follow the ordinary pattern. The hind carriage is framed on the bed of the waggon, while the swivelling fore carriage or lock is built separately.

When a waggon was on the road it steered easily since the front wheels were little more than 3 feet high and could turn right underneath the body. This enabled the waggon to take sharp corners and get in and out of fields easily, but there was a price to be paid: it was impossible, if the waggon was to respond well to handling, for the wheels to be much more than 6 feet apart on the axle. At the same time, stability required that the back wheels should be larger than the front – about 4 feet in diameter. The bed of the waggon therefore had to be sunk between the back wheels, and the only way to gain extra living space in the body was to make its sides slope outwards, so that the roof was wider than the floor, ending up with a kind of kite shape.

Throughout the 1860s and '70s the kite waggon was the only kind used by Gypsies, though wheelwrights were also developing an alternative design, particularly sought after by showfolk.[4] This differed mainly in the underworks, where the back wheels were only a few inches larger than the front, so that the waggon stood over the wheels and not between them. In consequence the body could be framed wider at the bed, and its walls stood upright instead of sloping. On good roads and level fields, a waggon whose wheels ran under the body could handle as well as one where they ran outside; but on rough ground it swayed and might even overturn. But this was of little concern to showfolk, who rarely went off-road.

A showman's waggon was typically framed in post and panel, rather than rib and matchboard. Instead of having a window on each side, it had two at one side with a blank face at the other – allegedly to deter curious visitors to the fairground from staring in. The other difference lay in the door, which opened into the waggon, not out onto the footboard. Tradition (at least among showfolk) said that doors turning outwards were a necessary concession to domestic disputes among the Gypsies, in which all sorts of things might be hurled out of the waggon, usually ending up with the husband or wife.[5]

As this story might suggest, there was little love lost between the two communities of travellers; but just as Gypsies and showfolk intermarried and took up each other's vocations, so they would chop waggons. By the end of the century, designs had become increasingly codified and waggon makers from different regions were specializing in their own styles. The traditional kite waggon became known as the Reading, in homage to Alfred Dunton and his sons who traded at that town from at least 1874. The showman's favourite style was called the Burton, after Burton-on-Trent in Staffordshire where waggons were built by several proprietors including George Orton. Hybrid styles were also on offer: it was possible to combine the underworks of a Burton with a body framed along the sides and back in rib and matchboard, the panels being limited to an elaborate display at the front. Other waggons were made with a body entirely in rib and board and one window on each side, the characteristic framing of a Reading, but set on a carriage with the wheels running under. And a new style, the ledge waggon, was developed to overcome the awkward structure of the Reading body with its sloping walls. The ledge had the same large hind wheels, set close together with a narrow body between them; then, 1½ feet above the bed, the bodywork expanded sideways, with upright walls forming the ledge over the wheels, and allowing more room for the bed and furniture inside.

At fairs and festivals, where all kinds of travelling people were brought together, the different styles of waggon would appear side by side. Mitcham Fair in the 1880s hosted a mixed population of Burton and Reading waggons, along with other vehicles improvised out of a cart sheltered by some kind of canvas tilt. One family turned up in a rough-and-ready ledge waggon, framed out of wide boards with no sign of any ribs to hold them. At the edge of the common, just where passers-by could see them, there were brush waggons. These had a structural design all of their own, owing something to the horse bus as well as the living-van, but their most obvious features were the rows of tubs, chairs, baskets, rugs, mats, brooms, brushes and other saleable things which hung from racks and hooks on the outside.[6]

Waggons were built to order, each one taking up to six months to complete after the wood had been thoroughly seasoned. That left a great deal of time for other tasks, and most of the wheelwrights worked on related trades. Henry Thomas, who began trading at Chertsey in the 1870s, built swing boats and other fairground accessories as well as Burton waggons. His son Freddie ('F. J. Thomas' on the brass hubcaps) continued the tradition from the 1890s, expanding into works which extended from 15 to 19 Guildford Street. In addition to the completed waggons, he supplied underworks to other wheelwrights; Duntons of Reading and Leonard of Soham both built on Freddie Thomas unders.[7]

A good set of underworks needed more craftsmanship than any other part of a waggon, but they were not expensive: Freddie charged £18 for a set. A well-framed body and fittings cost much more, and Charles Leland's estimate of a total £100 is backed up by other contemporary prices.[8] But as a woman in Battersea explained: 'It's like buying a house; you can pay 15*l.*, 20*l.*, or 60*l.* for one; if you have enough money to buy a superior van so much the better, if not you must put up.' She'd known a waggon change hands for £1, although the condition of a vehicle that cheap was left to the imagination.[9]

Waggons, like horses, were always for sale, for people felt no particular attachment to any one model and would trade up when they could. The plan and internal fittings were standardized, which made it easy for a family to move their goods out of one and into another, although it was the custom that outgoing families should always leave net curtains in the window.[10] Remembering that a waggon might be chopped at any minute, people took some care to keep them in good condition. If a vehicle stood still too long over the winter, its wheels would flatten out; in summer, they would get dry and loosen at the joints, while movement over rough ground opened up cracks between the boarding and direct sun blistered the paintwork. Wheels could be protected by throwing a coat or wet cloth over them, and the bodywork could be sheltered from sunshine by canvas ducking, but even so a waggon needed a yearly overhaul.[11]

This usually took place in March or April, in preparation for summer travel. At Lock's Fields in Walworth, an extended family – 33 people in all – were ready in the spring of 1875 to 'be off and get a sniff at the wholesome green leaves and daisies', and so they had divided up the tasks between generations:

> There was a tremendous bustle amongst them. There were houses on wheels and a cart; and turning the corner to reach the 'bit of waste' where the vehicles found standing room, the wind came at me so powerfully impregnated with paint and turpentine as nearly to take my breath away. All the adults of the party were literally up to their eyes in brilliant colours – grinding and mixing and laying on first coats and second coats, and picking out wheel-spokes and

panels; while the great-grandmother was the proud custodian of the three brass knockers, which she had splendidly polished, and which, as I was informed, she wrapped in a flannel petti-coat, and took to bed with her of a night, to preserve them from marauding fingers.[12]

Cans of paint had probably been picked up wherever they were cheap; certainly the colours were varied. At the yards in Battersea wag-gons were painted 'red, blue, yellow, and all the colours of the rainbow, not to speak of black decorated with moresque carving and scarlet cur-tains, and others of the smart wasp-like combination of dark brown and gold'. The road to the Derby in the 1890s was brightened by waggons that had been 'gorgeously painted', mostly in yellow.[13] As a rule waggons were painted in a single overcoat, but a more artistic owner might apply one tint for the body and another to pick out the waistboards, weatherboards, porch brackets and shutters. Red and green was a popular combination for this.[14]

Only the better-off could afford this kind of display. A bright waggon was one of the assets that marked out the flash traveller from his more indigent relatives, much more visible than old china or silver tea things. Already in 1863 a visitor to the Derby could tell the 'well appointed van of the prosperous hawker' from 'the tents of . . . ragged gipsies'. Over the next thirty years, as cheap second-hand models came on the market, van ownership became more common; at Bisley they were first seen in 1866 and 1867, then appeared six more times over the next two decades.[15] In the crowded Londonside yards, waggons had become the normal accom-modation, but wherever land was available they were still outnumbered by tents. Of the 231 people stopping on Mitcham Common over census night in 1881, only 35 were in waggons.[16]

In the yards, where people were packed close together, waggons made it possible to keep things clean and neat in a way that had not been so easy in benders. They stood 4 feet off the ground, above the mud of the path-ways, and they could be emptied out in fine weather and cleaned, much more easily than a tent. The provision of chintz chair covers and muslin curtains made sense, in a way that it had not done before.[17] That in turn meant a great deal more cleaning. On a sunny afternoon at Donovan's Yard, with the men out on business, women sat on the steps of the wag-gons, mending clothes and gossiping, while others got down to the wash. 'Bent over tubs and buckets in close proximity to a fire, on which clothes

Donovan's Yard at Battersea, 1903.

are boiling briskly, they are rubbing and rinsing with a will, now and again going off for more water to a tap at one end of the ground.'[18]

This was possible at the Battersea yards, where water was laid on as part of the site services. That couldn't be counted on further out; the settlement at Wandsworth Common had no water, so women had to use the ponds for laundry. When the menfolk were away, they stripped down to wash their clothes, which scandalized the gorjers.[19] The supply of water, like the need for firewood and grazing, was a flashpoint for disputes with house dwellers. At Irons Bottom, where the road from Reigate to Horley crosses the Mole, there was a good stopping place where fourteen waggons might be strung out along the verge. Here the local villagers were friendly enough, and supplied water, so that the hedges were festooned with half-dried washing.[20] But in areas of limited supply, relations with gorjers were more strained. At Kingswood a house dweller complained wearily in 1898 that 'gipsies make frequent requests, not to say demands, for water, boiling water for preference, and if refused, as they sometimes must be at homes whose supply of water is entirely dependent upon the rainfall, they become insolent and abusive.'[21] Epsom Downs had the same problems of water supply, but during Derby week people used to collect water from the cattle troughs in Epsom High Street and the Horse Pond in Ewell.[22]

Given the problems of fetching and carrying water, even when it was readily available, Gypsies treated it economically. Admittedly Bruce Boswell had a bath installed in his sumptuous tent at the 1885 Derby; but he had been in America for three years, and they have strange ideas about these things over there.[23] As a rule people washed themselves from a basin when and where necessary, and otherwise relied on regular changes of underclothing for personal cleanliness. Provided that a family had enough shirts and shifts and so on, and could wash and dry their laundry, this worked well enough. To be a Gypsy was to smell of woodsmoke, of tobacco fumes, and of weather-beaten working clothes; it was not a dirty smell, but it was distinctive, and marked people out.

It was difficult, even with a regular wash, to keep fleas, lice and bugs away; in a large encampment, they would spread from poorer families to the rest, and a bender with its fabric covers, blankets and piles of clothes gave them too many places of refuge to ever be thoroughly cleaned out. Emissaries of the London City Mission often left tents with 'a sad cargo of live stock', much to the annoyance of their wives back home.[24] Burning or abandoning the straw and peg shavings which stuffed a mattress must have kept the bedbugs down, but Gypsies, like most working-class people, accepted vermin as just another of life's problems, to be accepted philosophically:

> Now it's brother had a lice, sister had a flea,
> Brother had the bottle and uncle had the tea.
> We had some scratches from the jub, some bites from the flea,
> Some drink from the cup and he's gone and lost the tea.[25]

It was women who bore the brunt of the endless battle against dirt, damp and pests. On a wet September day in hopping time at Bagshot, a family were sitting round for supper. After getting the hop bines down, they were all drenched and covered in mud, and it was just then that the missionary gentleman appeared. The mother of the family looked up and said resignedly, 'Though we is like pigs, Sir, we ain't pigs.'[26]

That was one of the attractions of a waggon: even if most family life still went on outside, it provided a place where things could be neat and bright and dry. Like a house dweller's parlour, it was a sacrosanct space for displaying best china and family photographs: you could be photographed for 1s at the Derby, and then send copies to all your family.[27] And it was warm. A Colchester stove, of the sort that Mary White showed off to her guest at Walton Bridge, burned wood, or coal if you could get it. The original design of sheet metal was superseded towards the end of the century by the Hostess stove in cast iron, which, if it was well built up with the door and windows closed, could heat the brass rails above the range until they were too hot to touch.[28] This was extreme, but a snug heat could be easily achieved, even if it didn't last – for waggons had poor insulation and after a long winter's night the temperature would be close to its level outside.[29] The older children, who would be sleeping in a bender alongside the waggon, had the better deal, for with the larger numbers in a smaller space, these kept warm: 'sometimes a good deal too warm', as one lad said after a stuffy winter's night.[30]

Still, winter could be hard, as Matty Cooper knew in 1873 when he improvised his Bokalo Gilli, the song of hunger. Matty was no longer the dark, handsome young figure glimpsed by Princess Victoria on the Esher Road: he was in his mid-sixties now, a mop of pale hair where the glossy black curls had been, and years of watchfulness weighing down his shoulders. But he was still a tatcho Rom, who had never stooped to sleep under a roof or claim a dole. Now he stopped in the middle of the road and broke into Romani verses, which in English would have been something like this:

> My children are hungry,
> They are dying of cold –
> They have no food,
> They are poor and destitute.
> My little tent is beaten,
> It is all in rags –
> The cold wind blows through the holes.
> All night I hear the wicked wind howl,
> All night we mourn, faint on the ground for lack of bread.
> My children have no mother!
> Diddle dum dum.[31]

That 'diddle dum dum' does rather dispel the heartrending effect, and in fact Matty was neither poor, cold nor hungry: he was just coming to the end of a 25-mile hike with the hospitable Charles Leland. They'd met up at Oatlands Park and walked down through Ripley, with Matty pointing out all the places where Leonard and Nelson and Lusha had stopped in years gone by. Though it was a November day, the weather was warm, and he offered to carry Charles's coat for him. Of course, carrying a velveteen coat is hard work and – dordi! wasn't that a pub there, on the road ahead? So they stopped and had a drink. By the time they arrived in Woking it was time for lunch and Charles, being a rai, booked a private room with table service. Matty rather enjoyed being waited on, but once the door had closed behind them, he put the plate quietly on his knees and tucked in as if he was beside his own fire: he was a Gypsy, and he would eat like a Gypsy.[32]

They cut north to Virginia Water (more pubs), crossed the river to Staines (some more pubs) and so down through Laleham to Walton Bridge, where Matty danced a little jig and sang the song of hunger. At the ending – 'Mande'd die if 'twasn't for miro kushti rai!' – he looked benignly at Charles, who never gave money to anyone who asked for it: but singing was different, so he sighed and pulled half a crown out of his pocket. And Matty went off smiling into the dusk.

It had been two years since he first met Charles. Gentilla, the youngest of Henry and Mary Cooper's children, had an informal franchise on the Devil's Dyke at Brighton, dukkering for ladies and gentlemen when they came to see the beauty spot on their Sunday excursions from Brighton.[33] Matty had been visiting his sister, at her cottage – for she had married a gorjer and gone into brick. And there was Charles, listening to stories of Gypsy life and writing them all down in a pocketbook, so he could remember the language. Now Matty had been picking up rare and unusual Romani words for many years, so he agreed to come and teach what he knew: 3s a session, with drink and a smoke thrown in. This went on for weeks, with Charles pulling out one dictionary after another to test for words, and Matty weaving them into quirky little fables and stories as the fancy came to him.

But the conversations which took place in the study at Brighton, and later in the lanes and fields, were not just about words. Matty – 'that reprobate old amiable cosmopolite', in the amused judgement of his friend – knew what gorjers were like and how little they understood of Gypsy ways, so he was always ready to explain.[34] He might launch into a song:

Mande latched a hotchiwitchi
A boro hotchiwitchi
A tulo hotchiwitchi
A-jelling 'drey the vesh.[35]

But this was not just a jolly rhyme about a big fat hedgehog found in the woods; it gave him a chance to explain the Gypsy fondness for these little creatures. For their size, hedgehogs were rich in meat and fat (when you live outdoors in the cold, you appreciate a bit of fat) and they were not owned or protected at all. But, just as importantly, they were not eaten by anyone else; that made them a kind of Gypsy national dish.[36] People would walk from Donovan's Yard as far as Wimbledon just to catch a bag of prickly balls on the common. 'All agreed that outsiders had no appreciation of the value of hedgehog. Not only was its flesh far richer and more delicate than rabbit, but its fat was a very efficacious cure for deafness.'[37] The bodies were gutted, skinned and spitted on stakes to roast by the fire. In the old days they had been cased in clay – gutted or not – and set to bake in the embers; but this method was dying out by the end of the nineteenth century, and in time it would be dismissed as a myth put about by ignorant gorjers.[38]

You could hunt down hedgehogs by kicking through the dry leaves in which they nested; but it was quicker to use a terrier. In fact, dogs were the easiest way to take any kind of wild meat, and the better trained, the more valuable. Looks didn't count. The ugliest lurcher was shown off one year at Molesey Hurst with the boast 'He's very clever, but he'd never a-been worth seven pounds if I hadn't teached him how to steal rabbits.'[39] A Gypsy dog knew when to be silent, and when to be unseen. He and his master might go out for a stroll, with the dog running in and out of the hedges; suppose a gavver came walking down the road, he'd see nothing but the Gypsy, maybe whistling a little soft tune; the dog would have dropped down in the long grass, waiting for the sound of heavy boots to thump away before he slipped out again with a hare in his jaws.[40] It was a dog like this that was glimpsed in the early morning light in the Thames by Walton Bridge, swimming back across the river with a rabbit in his mouth. He dropped the little body down by the nearest bender and went back to catch the next one. Of course he would receive his reward at breakfast, but that was nothing: the dog had become Gypsified, and poached for the sheer fun of it. Nobody could serve a summons on *him*.[41]

Besides, there were other less risky ways to garner food from the surrounding countryside. At Oxshott, girls would round up the cattle grazing in nearby fields and drive them under the shade of the silver birches, then place a bunch of kex for them to graze on, while the boys milked them – a cup from each cow. This might have attracted the presence of the law, but the stopping place lay where Oxshott Heath adjoined Esher Common: two waste grounds sharing a parish boundary with a third one in Claygate. On the arrival of a gavver from one parish, people would shift to the next one, and as three constables never arrived at once, they could remain undisturbed.[42]

Birds' eggs from the hedgerows, mushrooms, rabbit stew – these wild things were very important to people's sense of self. If only the Romany could be like this forever, living freely off the woods and fields! In practice, however, most food came from the shops. After a day tramping the streets, selling small things and doing a little dukkering, the mother of the family would return with her basket full of loaves, while other goods were stowed away in her monging apron. Ballovas and yorros – the bacon and eggs which provide a refrain to many old songs – would sizzle in the frying pan, while slices of bread soaked up the fat. Preserved goods were not despised, either; the sites around Newlands Corner were ringed with discarded cans and empty bottles.[43]

The three essentials for cookery were a frying pan for quick meals, a boiler for stews and puddings and a kettle for tea. The old people used to hang their boilers or cauldrons from a tripod of three green sticks, tied together over the fire, and no doubt thrown away whenever people moved on; but in waggontime, when it was easier to carry domestic things around, this arrangement was replaced by the kettle iron, a solid bar with a hook at one end, driven into the ground at an angle. This was a handy all-round tool, good to make holes for the bender rods, and a compelling argument in a fight.[44] A few people stuck to tripods, now in the form of a wrought-iron chitti fitted with rings and hooks to hang different things over the fire.[45]

When morning came, the waggon would set out with the boiler and kettle swinging underneath, and all other cooking things stashed away with food in the pan-box, along with knives and tools and a plug-chain for the horse.[46] Blankets for the bender were folded up and slung in the cratch, while tent rods were strapped alongside the vehicle. The family were ready to move on again, as they had done every few weeks since March and April, when the annual travelling cycle began.[47] At Hindhead in 1895, locals knew that

No business is stirring in the way of osier or heather cutting or an occasional bit of poaching while snow lies on the ground; but when open weather comes again, the gipsy leaves the town he never really loves, and returns once more to the breadth and freedom of his beloved uplands. My friend of this morning was busily engaged in cutting up gorse-branches with a sort of long-handled meat-chopper in a wooden box as fodder for his mare. She, poor creature, lean and skinny, a mere machine for slowly dragging the dead-weight of a van, stood by expectant, sniffing the air from time to time . . . The children had hacked off the green branches with a cutlass from the bushes, and the father was chopping them up fine.[48]

Before waggontime, the care and feeding of horses had not been a priority.[49] Now travel required more planning: a good stopping place would need water and grazing, as well as a hard surface so that the vehicle did not get stuck in the mud. A waggon travelled at walking speed, 3 or 4 miles an hour, and a day's trip was about 10 miles, though longer distances could be covered in an emergency; so stopping places remained spaced out at much the same distances as they had been in the days of donkeys and tents.[50]

There were still long travellers. One family kept a diary recording how, over about a year, they had stopped in 41 different towns throughout the country, ending at Kingston.[51] But for Londonside Gypsies, the months of travel were fewer than they had been, and the distance covered was less. Most people from Wandsworth and Battersea spent only six months on the road, and some were out for less than that.[52] Latchmere School, which had a large intake of Gypsy children from Mills', Manley's and Donovan's Yards, kept enrolling and de-enrolling them as their parents went on the road. This would be at some date between March and May, but a few delayed departure until after the Derby; mostly they came back after hopping was over, so that while some families were travelling for half the year, others were away for no more than the three summer months.[53]

On the whole, short travellers tended to be less well off than long ones. Many of the people at Chobham were miserably poor: at Christmas 1884 James Lamb and Ann Lynch of West End sat round the fire cooking Christmas dinner in a bucket for want of anything better, and the children were digging their naked feet in the ashes for warmth.[54] They were both Surrey-born, from Farnham and Guildford, and had never been out of this small patch of country.[55] Thomas Gobey worked his way round a circuit which was little more than 4 miles across. He was born in Mayfield but moved up to Dorking after his marriage. His second son Henry married a girl from Charlwood in the 1860s and for several years they travelled around her country, sometimes returning north to Capel.[56] These were the singing Gobeys: at Christmas they would go in twos and threes to the big houses of the neighbourhood, playing the fiddle or singing unaccompanied. 'The Moon Shines Bright' was a favourite, with a simple moral message of redemption and repentance; if you skipped the bit about 'a happy New Year', it would do just as well for May Day house visits.[57] 'King Pharim Sat A-Musing' is a much stranger carol, with vivid disjointed images – of a roasted cock that comes to life on the table and sits up to crow three times, and of the Virgin Mary sitting by the roadside and watching a husbandman who sows his corn and reaps the ripened harvest, all in one day.[58] These fragments make sense if you know the stories told about Christ's infancy in the Middle Ages, but of course the Gobeys didn't. There was no way that they could have heard legends which had dropped out of the life of the Church hundreds of years earlier. But the songs had been passed down.

It was the cycle of agricultural work which took people further afield. Born in 1869, Albert Doe grew up in the New Forest, where his family wintered in benders around Minstead while the women hawked their wares through the streets of Southampton. In summer they would all travel over for pea-picking at Pyrford, and then return to Hampshire for hopping at Binsted. But when Albert was a young man, his father Nehemiah had led the extended family into Surrey, so that in 1900 there were twenty Does stopping at the Warren, close to Walsham Lock on the River Wey. Nehemiah and his wife eventually returned to the New Forest, but Albert remained behind, working as a road sweeper in Pyrford until he was 85. Here he is, as remembered by his grandson Terry Doe:

> He had clear blue eyes, sharp features, a large moustache. He dressed in woollen trousers and jacket, a waistcoat with a Smith's pocket watch tied by a chain from a button-hole to a small pocket, a collarless shirt, shiny black boots, and a cap which he always wore when out of doors . . . On summer days he would sit in the garden and play his accordion, on winter days he would sit by the fire diddling tunes whilst beating time with his fingers on the arm of the wooden chair . . . During the autumn he would come home

with pockets full of chestnuts which I would put on the top of the stove to roast. There were always sweets somewhere in his pockets and he would delve and come up with an extra-strong mint tasting faintly of pipe tobacco.[59]

For those who were able to move long distances, and knew how to do the work, there could be four harvests in the year. The sequence began by going up the country to Middlesex for peas-hacking in the market gardens; then down to Chichester for wheat-fagging; then up to the northern parts of Hampshire, where the harvest was a little later, for a second round of wheat-fagging; and finally over to the hop gardens at Farnham, where some relatives would have secured a bin in one of the better locations.[60] At Chobham, where the travelling circuit was much smaller, people were away for four or five months each summer, beginning in the last weeks of May with pea-picking, then hay-making and bringing in the harvest, and finally hopping.[61]

Hop-picking was the crown of the year. Here the Gypsies were used to the work, knew all the dodges and, most importantly, could keep themselves warm and well-fed each day. A correspondent from *The Times*, walking through Weybourne and Hale to Farnham, passed by the barns and barracks in which thousands of London gorjers were trying to sleep. Everything was dirty and smelly and dangerous, until he came to the Gypsy quarter:

> The gipsies are the best workers in the hop-gardens. Their hands are not hardened and their touch coarsened by constant labour, and in hop-picking delicacy of touch counts for much . . . There are aristocrats amongst them who come in state in the covered vans which serve them as house and home, and are seen at races and fairs. The tents of other gipsies whiten a whole field. Hop-poles, ranged like rifles in piling arms, make an airy sort of tent, under which a fire is burning and the pot boiling, while gipsy men and women hold cheerful talk there . . . 'Does your tent turn the rain?' I ask in passing, and the answer comes at once in no rustic drawl, 'Yes, every drop.' Yet it is nothing but coarse canvas stretched over a few rounded sticks. These people are merry, and an appetising smell from their *pot-au-feu* shows that they live well and mean to wind up the day with a good supper.[62]

Getting supper at the Derby, 1913.

For the people stopping on the Hurtwood, hopping was one of the three best times of the year. After this they would return to Peaslake and Shamley Green for the holly season, when the winter greenery was cut to make wreaths for the London market.[63] Then in July and August came the whorts – or, spelt phonetically, hurts.[64] These grew prolifically on little bushes all over the heathy greens and slopes, but because they were so small and fiddly to pick, no one tried to cultivate them commercially; instead they were a wild crop. You picked them with a berry comb or rake, which was quicker than fingers; these combs could be narrow (and more likely to snag on a branch) or wide (and liable to pick up leaves as well as the whorts). Gypsies used wide rakes, the women often taking the bright combs out of their hair for the work; locals preferred narrow ones. Dark Liza was a famous picker on the Hurtwood, and she always wore a black pinna over her white one, so that the stains from the whorts didn't show.[65]

Stooping to pick the whorts was backbreaking, but you had the satisfaction of knowing that you were working for yourself, not as wage labour; every quart measured and sent off to the towns was pure profit.

All the most popular Gypsy crafts had this in common: they took some wild resource which could be gathered for free and turned it into a saleable item. The commonest of these manufactures was making clothes pegs from sticks of hazel wood. This was an old tradition, but in the 1860s it suddenly became more common – perhaps because the older rural practice of leaving cloths to dry on hedges had died out, or perhaps someone had realized that clothes pegs, unlike other household equipment, will wear out and need replacing on a regular basis. Whatever the reason, peg-making soon became a craft at which whole families could work. People at Lower Kingswood would pull on by the lane where they would 'build huge fires, set their children to collect hazel wood, the women then stripped back the bark and the men then cut up old tins to bind the clothes pegs together, which they could then sell'.[66] At Mitcham Common in 1879 a family of six children were at work, under the command of the eldest girl, who could not have been more than ten, while they waited for their parents to come back to the tent. It was a winter day, and they were sitting around the fire, on which a pan of water was simmering. One of them chopped the sticks into lengths and threw them into the hot water, which loosened the bark; another took out the lengths, and (not having a knife) peeled the bark off with her teeth; another split and mouthed the pegs; and finally came the boy who ran the strip of tin around the peg and nailed it firm.[67]

Skewers were another woodland product for which there seemed an inexhaustible demand; an enthusiastic reviewer claimed that 'the millions of skewers in use at the London meat-stalls are every one whittled out by busy gipsy hands.'[68] Since these were usually thrown away after use, the supply could be kept up indefinitely, although more durable goods – mats, baskets and coarse brushes – were being sold along with them in 1896. At Sutton skewers were one of several craft items, together with the ubiquitous clothes pegs and birch brooms, fancy flowers made from the pith of rushes and mysterious 'cunningly devised articles made from thin wood slats'. One family of Smiths made only skewers; they would go travelling in the spring, but always returned in their waggon to pull on at Forest Road, just off Sutton Common. Since other aspects of their family life were equally regular, the mother of the family was able to boast that she had born nineteen children in the same lane.[69]

The level of skill in these crafts was fairly low. Children who had watched their parents whittling skewers or going through the stages of peg-making could do it themselves from a young age, and with practice came the dexterity necessary to turn out very large numbers. Work was ceaseless, because the rewards even for five or six hours of non-stop effort were low. A man stopping on Holmwood Common reported wearily:

> I can make about a thousand a day, but the butchers get so mean we can't git more'n half a crown for a thousand, and only 1s 6d for the smaller'ns. Only last week I tried to sell some in the town, but could get no more'n 1s 6d for 'em, so I tramped to Reigate and got three bob.[70]

But there were other manufactures which required a proper course of training, such as basket-making. A kipsiengro, like Henry James, whom Charles Leland met at Walton in 1872, usually made baskets and nothing else. The pair's encounter did not begin promisingly. 'He greeted me civilly enough, but worked away with his osiers most industriously, while his comrades, less busy, employed themselves vigorously in looking virtuous.' This was understandable, since everyone had taken Charles for a gavver, patrolling the riverside in search of offenders. But once they heard him start talking in Romanes, everything was suddenly put on a different footing, especially when he suggested that they might like to share a beer. Someone was sent to borrow a 2-gallon jar, and someone else to find a chair, for gorjers were notoriously inept at sitting on the ground. And they sat, and drank, and passed on the latest news of the road, as Henry, slipping a new withy into his basket, 'deftly twined it like a serpent to right and left, and almost as rapidly'.[71]

In the large settlements, it paid to have as much variety as possible in the crafts, otherwise the surrounding urban market would have been saturated. At Battersea you could see families 'hard at work under the vans or arches making basket flower stands, pegs, mats, and caning chairs, while others walk far into the country for primroses and violets in order to sell them'. Everyone said that they didn't mind work; the problem was to sell their goods once they were made.[72] At Bramley people made clotheslines, pegs and baskets; created flowers out of shavings, and dyed them in different colours; made more flowers from bulrushes, with the pith stripped off; cut bark off the trees, and worked it into flowerpot hangers; turned out crosses and wreaths of holly for the Christmas market; and then, when the warmer weather came round again, gathered bunches of the little daffodils or Lent Lilies, as well as primroses and bluebells.[73]

Finding the customers was the difficult part, whether you were selling goods or marketing a service. James Baker at Chobham swept chimneys, and his wife Eleanor made beehives; they were both poor, but they found the time to attend the Gospel meetings run by Stanley Alder in the kitchen of Frees Farm. In the autumn of 1882 James took up the preacher's offer of a cottage at Lucas Green. He and his wife had more children than furniture when they first went into brick. They carried in the butter tub which Eleanor had used to sit on in her tent, and some straw to sleep on, and that was about it. Their seven chavvies had never seen stairs before and were having a grand time racing up and down them; doors, too, were unfamiliar and young George was crying because he'd just pinched his finger in the jambs. Stanley raised £1 12s 6d for furniture and a change of clothing, and within a few months the family had acquired chairs and a table, and were sitting round it at teatime, while four of the children were going to Sunday School. James traded up his donkey cart for a pony and trap, so he could travel out further with his bags and brushes, and look smarter; this evidently put him in a better line of business, and in the evenings he would come home well content, pick up the fiddle and play a few of Sankey's hymn tunes. He also knew some rather more scurrilous songs, but he didn't play these when Stanley was visiting.[74]

Sweeping chimneys was a good door-to-door service, with an opportunity for repeat custom; so were tinsmithing and knife-grinding. In 1865 Clara Boss had been proud of her man with a grinding barrow, as if it was something rather rare, but as the years passed, they grew more common. For Sampson Tarrant, born on Epsom Common in 1868, his grinding barrow was only one among many ways of earning a living. When he married Amelia White in 1892 they were both set down in the marriage register as hawkers, and so was Sampson's father, but that hardly does justice to their range of achievements. After they'd settled at Redhill in 1900, they were making and repairing copper kettles, mending china, sharpening tools and caning chairs.[75]

And then there was rat-catching, another of those trades, like chimney-sweeping, where you could charge a year's fee for a day's work; and a chance, perhaps, to strike a fresh blow in the endless war between the people of the tents and the hengtails. Matty Cooper had his own recipe for dealing with rats, which involved long hours stewing yew branches over the fire. The dark liquor which resulted must have been irresistible as well as lethal, for he did a lot of trade at houses around Windsor, including the grandest house of all. Once, so the say goes, after he had taken two whole bushels of the little horrors from all around the castle, he rolled them out on the carpet for inspection by the Queen herself. The silence was broken by loud chuckles from Prince Edward, who put his hand in his pocket and pulled out a half-sovereign – paying for the entertainment as much as the rodent control.[76]

This was not an isolated incident; the future Edward VII was good to the Romany, especially if you were female, pretty and young. In times to come, almost fifty years after the king had been laid to rest, Granny Walters would remember how he called her and her sisters to perform for him in front of the royal box at Epsom Grandstand, and how they had dressed in their brightest clothes and danced to the beating of a tambourine, as the coins showered down on them. Sovereigns and everything: the Walters sisters took £50 that day.[77] And the royal generosity was indiscriminate. Two or three dozen Gypsy children would scramble for the money he threw, and Matty's grandson Vanselo remembered picking up many a half-crown from the king on Derby Day.[78]

Faced with so much diversity, you begin to suspect that a talented Gypsy could turn his hand to just about anything, but people did specialize. At Mitcham in 1881, for instance, there were sixteen basket makers, five tinsmiths, four knife grinders, four chair bottomers and three peg makers.[79] These skilled men were a minority, though; two-thirds of Gypsies classed themselves as hawkers. Some were selling pegs, skewers and other cheap things that they had made by harvesting the woodland, but others kept up the tradition of the country pedlar, bringing small cheap goods to the front doors of those who did not have easy access to shops. They went to specialist dealers for the wholesale supplies – even of things which Gypsies might be expected to make themselves, such as brooms. When John Greenway the brush maker was visited at his Wandsworth shop by Caroline Penfold and Mary Hearne, he was only too happy to let them view his stock, until he found after they had left that there was one less broom in the shop than before they came. This was all a great mistake, as Caroline explained to the magistrate. 'We had some brooms, baskets, and other things, and when we went into the shop we laid them down close to the gentleman's brooms. When we came out we took up our brooms, and with it the gentleman's broom.' Really, said the magistrate, dismissing both parties with the suggestion that they should be careful about making these mistakes in future.[80]

The Kent Street dealer who wholesaled 'wares, brushes, mats, and tin things' to the waggon trade was more prudent: he insisted on cash in advance before the goods were handed over.[81] A Gypsy family had to transport themselves and their home as well as the stock, which must have limited the quantity that could be carried. This had led to the development of the brush waggon, able to carry a whole shop's worth of goods.[82] There were some, like the Hawkins family, who used to make a journey each year to London, where they would stock up at a wholesale warehouse. In 1882, when the young John Hawkins was about ten years old, they had come in through Staines, crossed the river, and made the long haul up Richmond Hill, hitching a sider horse alongside the vanner to help with the climb. Now their spare horse was tethered behind the waggon, and young John was in charge of him while his father stopped at the pub. He thought that the horse, like his master, might appreciate a drink, and so he got ready to lead him to the water; but a cob is stronger than a ten-year-old boy, and this one took off, wrenching the rope out of the small fist, and clattering down the road. John heard him go, and saw his father rushing out of the pub, racing after the runaway horse, and only stopping for a moment to yell 'You wait till I come back – I'll break your neck!'

Listening to the teacher, Epsom Downs, 1910.

Now this may perhaps have been an exaggeration, but John didn't wait to find out. He sprinted in the other direction and didn't stop until he got to Richmond Station. He had the morning's takings still in his pocket – 2s. That got him to Waterloo, and then he had no idea what to do next; but he was a Gypsy boy and could take care of himself. Working as a shoeblack, and resting at nights in a home for destitutes, he came to hear about Christ, and young as he was he began first to give witness, and later to preach. Under the name of Gipsy Hawkins he became a travelling evangelist, but he never found his family again.[83]

Most families left totting to the womenfolk, who were better at persuading gorjers to be generous, and less likely to take a pub break at lunchtime.[84] At Barnes in the 1880s, after the common had been drained and put in the hands of keepers, people moved to a series of wooden shacks called Uncle Tom's Cabins, from which they continued to go calling in the village. 'Mignonette Lovell, a very handsome clean woman, used to go about hawking laces, cottons and clothes pegs . . . Sometimes the gipsies sold little brooms – "buy-a-brooms" as we called them – and little baskets made of peeled rushes from the Common.' Mignonette's niece was Lemonelia Smith, 'a very big dark gipsy with a stentorian voice', who sold flowers at East Sheen.[85]

Flowers were a good line of business, since in the nature of things they had to be gathered or purchased in small quantities and then retailed almost immediately – the favoured Gypsy way of doing things. Besides, the best flowers were grown near London, on the dry, sun-facing soils which ran from Croydon to Cheam. After Mitcham Fair ended on 14 August, people would stay on to work in the physic gardens there, picking rose buds and chamomile heads, and cutting the peppermint and lavender.[86] The lavender season lasted from the end of July to the end of August. Being a small, wiry plant, it would stand being carried all day through the streets without wilting, if you cut it early in the day. Janet Penfold got up at four in the morning to walk from Battersea to Mitcham, where she collected the fresh flowers. Her walk took her through Chelsea and Pimlico to the heart of London, holding out a bunch of sixteen stems in one hand, in the other a bundle or basket of the unsold flowers. This is the 'Lavender Song', as remembered by her and her daughter Florrie:

Won't you buy my sweet blooming lavender?
There are sixteen blue branches a penny, all in full bloom.

You buy them once, you buy them twice,
It makes your clothes smell sweet and nice.
Come all you young ladies and make no delay
My lavender's fresh from Mitcham and we're round once a day . . .
'Twas early this morning, when the dew was a-falling
I gathered my sweet lavender from the valley, all in full bloom.[87]

The second line of the song was traditional and never changed, though girls sang it with some discreet businesslike slurring of the words; it had been a long time since bunches had been sold as cheaply as that. Even so, there wasn't much gain from selling the flowers themselves, but they formed an introduction and once people had bought the lavender you could trade laces, pins and other little things. Mothers would carry their baby in a roper, and kindly gorjer ladies would usually give something extra for the little one after buying the flowers – though young women who didn't actually have a baby might have to make do with a slumbering bundle of clothes. Real babies grew up into small ragged children who would accept the lady's coin with a shy smile and then (after some training) hand it loyally to their mother once the pair were out of sight round a corner.[88]

The days were long and the work was hard, but it was made a little more tolerable by company. Little groups would come in from Mitcham, split up for work, and then reunite when the day was over:

The women of these families were amazingly tough, and would cover many miles daily, hawking their small wares around. Pins, pencils, ribbons, elastic, collar studs, and cottons made the bulk of their stock, but quite a few also carried brushes or home-made kettle- and iron-holders and wool mats. These sold for a few pence each . . . The profits on these small sales were not great but these raklies were adept in cozening cast-off clothing, boots and other articles, which later could be disposed of to swell their earnings. Generally at the end of the day they had disposed of little actual stock but had accumulated quite a load of garments, without cost to themselves, and not a little food also that sympathising gorjer women had given to the older chavvies. Beyond the town they would choose a piece of waste land, or even the grass verges of suburban roads, and sort out their gains. This was when they relaxed and lit their clay pipes, and it was quite common to see a row of raklies sitting along the kerb enjoying a well-earned smoke at the end of the day's bikkining.[89]

Hawkers, said the Kent Street dealer, 'live wonderful hard, almost starve, unless food comes cheap . . . But most of them, when they get flush of money, have a regular go, and drink for weeks; then after that they are all for saving.'[90] This was part of the Gypsy character and even Matty, that respectable old mush, confided to his friend about the time when for two whole months he hadn't seen three nights when he wasn't as drunk as four fiddlers.[91]

With these unpredictable swings between good and bad fortune, it is hard to estimate an average income. The profits of hawking were not a simple balance sheet – so much paid out on goods, so much taken for them. As we have seen, the profits on a bunch of lavender, even if it was going for more than the traditional penny, really lay in the chance for selling other goods, monging and picking up unwanted items for resale. Besides, a Gypsy woman was ready at any point to drop what she was doing and begin telling fortunes, at a price which she graded according to the gorjer's ability to pay and not the accuracy, or even originality, of her predictions.[92] The retail price of other standard goods varied widely: a dozen pegs sold for 1s at one place, 1½d in another.[93] No doubt it depended on where you were in the streets of London, rich or poor, and what other plans you had for the day.

Wage labour was more predictable. Of the five yards in which people over-wintered in Battersea and Wandsworth, the most respectable was occupied by wage earners, who brought in about 4s 8d a day.[94] One of the Stanleys sang a song about farm work, when they were stopping beside the Wey somewhere between Pyrford and Byfleet in the 1880s. 'Mande'll del pansh kollas the divvus,' the farmer says: 'I'll give you five shillings a day.'[95] Certainly Matty thought that 3s a day was a reasonable recompense for the time he took off work to teach Romani to Charles Leland, and it is clear from the family tradition about his work at Windsor that 10s was an extravagantly royal payment for a day or so spent catching rats.

As a rule, people preferred piecework to being paid by the day, since it gave you a chance to do well through hard work. Many crops were paid by measure. Whorts fetched 1s the quart, and since in a summer day even children could pick four quarts, the daily income was 4s.[96] The rate for hops was 2½d to 3d a bushel, and pickers could take between ten and twenty bushels a day, which works out at daily takings of between 2s and 5s. At Farnham in 1874 a father and his three children were picking 61 bushels of hops in a day at 3d a bushel, which is 15s a day, and over the three weeks of the hopping season they reckoned that they would take £15.[97] The larger the family, the more they could earn as a combined team. In 1879 five adults together earned £42 at harvest, and they expected more from hopping.[98] That was a lot of vonga.

We hear less about the income to be expected from basket-making, tinsmithing, knife-grinding, chimney-sweeping and so on. 'When I feels like it I sometimes makes a pound a day a-making baskets,' said George White, but this may have an element of exaggeration.[99] He got his osiers for nothing, so it was all profit, anyway; typically, he didn't factor in his time as a cost. A Gypsy man would always be doing or making something, come what may.

Matching up the different accounts, it seems that 3s or 4s a day was regarded as a reasonable income in good times, through a season that lasted most of the year from April to October. But this steady income, based on long hours of repetitive work, was interrupted by the occasional windfalls that rewarded Gypsy initiative. The £50 scattered from the royal balcony over the Walters sisters was very much a one-off, but women could often achieve smaller triumphs by dukkering. In 1872 Drusilla Skarratt called on a house in Wandsworth and got chatting to the maid-servant. For 6d, the Gypsy said, she would reveal the secrets of the future. This was not very hard, as the girl was obviously getting ready to leave her employment, so Drusilla told her as much and then added significantly that she was leaving because of a man who had come there. She could summon up more knowledge but to do this she needed the magnetic power of gold. How much did young Jane have? £3 16s in life savings? That would do nicely, and Drusilla took it away in a bundle, promising to return with the necessary information at 5 p.m. That time came and went; then a policeman was called, who ran Drusilla to ground in the tent settlement at the Waterside. They gave her three months with hard labour, and she was sent down, shouting 'If there [were] no fools there would be no living!'[100]

For men, the equivalent chances came in horse-dealing, one of the few trades where a mark-up of 50 or 100 per cent was possible. A worn-out old horse fetched about £5, a better one could sell for £10, while a good vanner, capable of pulling a cart or light waggon, was £15; and in the flurry of the fairground, it was sometimes hard to tell the difference.[101] At Farnham there were attempts to grade the horses by their position along the High Street – the worst ones near the Castle Street turning, where 'a gypsy hostler would trot out a succession of the weediest old screws that ever kept out of the kennels', while better ponies and cobs were to be found further up the borough and West Street, where they ran up and down through the swaying crowd, with the dealer holding onto the halter as he shouted out the merits, real or assumed, of his animal.[102]

It was not just the profit in horse-dealing that appealed to people; it was the skill that it demanded, the pitting of wits, man against man. At Cobham Fair in the winter of 1873 you could see Sam Smith in action. Sam was a respected man, the second husband of Athaliah Taylor (Matty's daughter-in-law by her first marriage), and normally a bit of a dandy – indeed, his final quarrel with Athaliah was over a new suit of clothes in which he was to appear at Kingston Fair.[103] But now he had dressed down carefully. To all appearances, here was the owner of a smallholding, perhaps, or a little farm, the sort of honest man who (bless him!) is not very quick at keeping up. And here, at the edge of the crowd, are five or six others, also small farmers by the look of them, each dressed in shabby rustic clothes with the sad look of a man who must sell his horse that same day, be the price as low as it will. They all speak to each other quietly, in Romanes, and go about their business. Of course none of these horse-dealers actually initiated any business. That was done by the spruce-looking agent, who then introduced the potential purchaser to Sam or one of his compatriots; only it turned out that the horse was already sold – no, that deal's called off, and here he is again. All this time, of course, the purchaser's mind is on anything but the actual quality of the horse, which is probably just as well, for Sam could curry and clip and beautify £5-worth of horseflesh until it looked worth a great deal more. And then he sold it for just a little less than it wasn't worth, and that was horse-dealing.[104]

You didn't have to be a rogue to sell a horse – provided you bought cheap and sold dear, it didn't really matter how the mark-up was achieved. You could bring a string of New Forest ponies into Surrey, or Welsh ones over to the East Midlands; you could take some exhausted animal and carefully nurture it back to health with mallow and comfrey for its sores, coltsfoot for the cough and green broom tips for the worms; or you could artfully disguise the most obvious defects and hope for a quick sale.[105] As they said at Wimbledon, 'Horse dealing is horse stealing in a way . . . It's all square in gambling, and nobody has any cause to complain.'[106]

Money which came so easily was likely to flow out again just as fast – either in drink or in gambling. Since a man's gambling partners would be his fellow Gypsies, the cash stayed in the community, but that cannot always have been much consolation, and not everyone was as lucky as young Charlie Lee, who turned his luck around at pitch and toss:

> I knew a little fellow once that lost all his money in the toss-ring. Then he went home to his father's sacks and took five pounds out. After a little while he saw his father and told him he'd taken five pounds from his bags. But his father said, 'Go on, spend it and win some more money!'. So he went again to the toss-ring and got all his money back, and five pounds more. And going home, he saw his father sitting by the side of the tent, and his father said, 'How did you do, my son?' 'Very well, Dad. I got all my money back; and here's your money now, and a pound for you and four pounds for myself.'[107]

This suggests that an ordinary Gypsy would, as a rule, have several pounds available in ready cash; and, as we have seen, average daily takings through most of the year would be between 3s and 4s – say £1 a week.[108] How does this compare with incomes in the gorjer working class? A Surrey labourer in the late nineteenth century earned 12s to 15s a week, which is significantly less; besides, the labourer had no chance of making any of those sudden profits which brightened up the travelling life.

Many Gypsies were rumoured to have large sums stashed away, and sometimes the rumours were true. The Davis family at Godalming had £200 in sovereigns.[109] Another hoard was found after Mary Ann Doe died at Frimley. They were breaking up the framing of her waggon, ready to set fire to it, when someone noticed a shiny line along the edge of the planks. First one, then another was found to consist of two thin boards nailed together, with gold sovereigns between them: in all, a hoard of over £400.[110] On the whole, it seems that a Gypsy family could do nicely for themselves, if things went well.

But things did not always go well. In the autumn of 1884 John Matthews went hopping with his wife and two small children, accompanied by his old parents. They all worked fiercely in the hop gardens, planning to invest the money straightaway in goods that could be hawked over the winter months when there was no other source of income. After hopping, they came down to Guildford for St Catherine's Fair, where the family would run a coconut shy. Louisa Matthews was near her time, and it would cost money to get a doctor or a midwife; besides, there was the loss of her earnings to be considered. But they would get by, or so they thought, until John fell ill. Four days after the fair, he died, and Louisa was left with two small children, a newborn baby and no source of income. Yet enough was gathered to bury John respectably in Guildford Cemetery, with forty mourners. 'He won't want for anything,' said the people who had been at the fair. 'We are all relations here – brothers and sisters. Some are better off than others; what one hasn't got another has, and we help one another.'[111]

As if the natural hazards of sickness and accidents were not enough, people had to reckon all the time with the costs of police harassment. The penalties on fortune-telling imposed by the 1824 Vagrancy Act were applied by magistrates on a sliding scale; even if there was no complaint by the client, a woman could be imprisoned. Emily Lee of Woolwich was sent down for a month after a detective listened from the corridor as she spun a line ('You will not remain long where you are and your prospects are very bright'); the same punishment was given to Ann Smith of Wandsworth. There was no question of predatory fraud in either case, the women charging only 3d and 1s 6d.[112]

Where families worked together as an economic unit, the cost of a month's imprisonment was much higher than a fine would have been, since the wife could no longer sell what her husband had made. And there was a string of regulatory offences, none of them specifying Gypsies or even itinerants, but all passed at one time or another to criminalize the travelling life. You could be fined 10s or imprisoned for sleeping out, making a hole in the grass, leaving your waggon, having no water, having no loo, having a waggon without lights, having a waggon without a name-board, having a dog without a licence, having a gun without a licence, hawking without a licence, wooding, monging and 'neglecting' your children (that is, raising them as Gypsies).[113]

It is hard to estimate the cumulative effect of these prosecutions. Clearly there were warrants in law for the harassment of Gypsies every-where, all the time – and since the County Police Act of 1856, the whole of Surrey, urban and rural, had been under systematic policing. But mag-istrates did not want to spend all their time on prosecutions for regulatory crime, and policemen usually had better things to do than annoy Gypsies; it might be their duty, but they only reported carrying it out once or twice a year.[114] In 1909 Surrey Gypsies were found to have committed a total of 227 regulatory offences, and no serious crimes at all: that would be about one prosecution a year for every head of a family in the county.[115] Fines

Face-off with the Surrey Anti-Vagrants Association, 1909.

and imprisonment were not always enforced, being used more as threats to make people move on somewhere else.

But between 1870 and 1900 relations between Gypsy and gorjer deteriorated almost everywhere in the Surrey countryside, though even the worst enemies of the Gypsies, if they could control their rage long enough to be specific, did not accuse the community of large-scale robbery or fraud, but of . . . well, being *difficult*. When the respectable residents of Holmbury St Mary complained about people living on the Hurtwood, it was because their horses wandered loose, and woke up villagers at night; because their children did not go to school, but ran up and down the roads monging, or offering little things for sale; because, if a Gypsy was seen, women did not like to walk across the common, or children to go gathering nuts. Most serious of all, for a village on the tourist trail, these people were frightening the summer visitors.[116] As another petition explained, the activity – indeed, the mere presence – of Gypsies in the countryside was likely to 'deprive the inhabitants of some of their enjoyment of this beautiful district'.[117]

'Their life amongst us has a degrading influence,' said the good folk of Holmbury, and this explained more than they liked to admit; it was not that Gypsies were strangers, but that they were, in uncomfortable ways, too close to what villagers might be or had once been. After all, Holmbury sat at the heart of a belt of woodland stretching 8 miles from Madgehole to Blackbrook; an isolated place, famous in days gone by for petty crime and smuggling.[118] At Peaslake, a mile to the west, local youth used to descend from the hills onto the relative civility of Shere, yelling 'Hear all the mothers shout,/ "Don't let your daughters out!"/ Here come the Pizlick boys!'[119] To be a Gypsy was to live in this world of raucous insubordination, or so the good people thought, and they wanted a clean break from it.

But this attitude was by no means universal; it never found a home in Epsom Common, which had for many years been a stopping place on the way to and from the Derby. From the 1860s people were invited to attend an annual tea here, held in a barn during the week before the races, in which bread and butter was distributed along with plum cake and more spiritual nourishment from travelling preachers.[120] The Bowers and the Coopers and the Matthews had their children christened beneath the tall tower of Christ Church, rebuilt in 1876 to civilize the surrounding cottages.[121] Several families stayed for most of the year in the area; the Marneys, who ran a coconut shy at Fair Green on the outskirts of Epsom, were well known locally, and a road was named after their yard. There does not appear to have been any serious friction with the gorjers, as there was elsewhere. Perhaps that was because the common was already seen as the rough fringe of Epsom, and the locals had no desire to give it a more elevated status. Perhaps, also, it had something to do with personality. The resident bailiff, George Oakshott, made sure that people did not stay for too long, or in too large numbers, and luckily 'he had a gift for this sort of negotiation and was positively liked by the gipsies, as well as by the residents on the Common.'[122]

At the Hurtwood, by contrast, bailiffs were ineffective: 'the ranger of the Shere Manor would chase the gypsies off the common and they would go through the larches and be safe on the Albury side. The Albury ranger would chase them away and they would move their camp back through the larches to the Shere side.'[123] But the real problem lay in numbers, with upwards of one hundred people stopping in a barren wood where there were few resources for making things and only small villages in which to sell them.[124] 'The real objection of the Surrey people to the gipsies is, not that the tribes are dishonest, or paupers, or immoral, or carriers of disease, but that there is not room for more than a few of them in any county, and that Surrey gets far more than its share.'[125]

It is not easy to trace the social history of prejudice, but all the evidence suggests that, until the late nineteenth century, little animosity was felt against Gypsies by working-class gorjers. At the beginning of the century there had certainly been harsh laws against vagrancy, but there were others just as stern against poaching, fighting, brutal sports and the other pleasures of the common man. Magistrates might take action against Gypsies in the name of 'society', but by that they meant the society of the better-off and respectable, which was forever safeguarding itself against the mutinous mass of the poor. Gradually, through the reform years of the 1830s and 1840s, the number of those who thought themselves decent and respectable grew and grew, until it stretched well beyond the middle classes and struck roots among ordinary agricultural workers.

Significantly, one of the earliest reports of ordinary country children being prejudiced against Gypsies comes from a group of self-improvers, the Sunday School class in Dorking; when an enthusiastic teacher invited some Gypsy boys to join in 1876, there was a great deal of foot-dragging and muttered comment from her regular pupils.[126] The soothing powers of religion did not always work, and Stanley Alder's work with the people stopping at Chobham came to a sudden end in 1892, when a group of young gorjers descended on the encampment, ripped up the benders and sent everyone packing.[127]

These vigilante groups would never have been formed if the police had been more active in evicting people themselves, but then persecution was not carried out by a united front. At Chelsham, Jack Smith, who had been providing entertainments over many years for the Foresters' summer fair, was moved on in 1889 after being objected to by a local gentleman; during the process he was beaten up by the police and his wife cut around the face before their waggon was put on the road. This did not go unnoticed. 'The village was in an uproar for several hours, and the villagers cried shame on the proceedings.'[128] Villagers disagreed with gentry, and gentry with farmers, about the right way to deal with Gypsies; the police did not necessarily hold the same view as the bench of magistrates; highway, health and education authorities had different priorities; and over them all was the government, which cared nothing for Gypsies as such, but required its subjects to respect the principle of equality before the law.

Conflicts of this kind brought an end to the ambitious plans of Reginald Bray, whose family estates included the Hurtwood.[129] In February 1909 he joined up with William Onslow for a meeting of landowners and lords of manors who wanted to prevent Gypsies stopping on their woods and fields. By April they had banded together under the name of the Surrey Anti-Vagrants Association, although in practice members were all from the area between Guildford and Dorking. And then, within two months, the association was disbanded, having hit an insuperable problem. By stopping on land which was someone else's property, the Gypsies were trespassing, which was a civil offence but not a crime. The landowner could lawfully move people off his land, but that was all; and it was his responsibility, not anyone else's, to move them.[130] Reginald wanted a more robust response from the government, or the county council, or the police, or indeed anyone who would evict the Gypsies without him and his fellow landowners having to pay the bill. But Mowbray Sant, the Chief Constable of Surrey, put his foot down politely but firmly. His men were there to deal with crimes, not civil disputes. If the Gypsies – or, for that matter, the bailiffs – were guilty of assault in the course of an eviction, then of course the police would act, but not otherwise.

At the same time, Surrey County Council (which was itself largely made up of rural landowners) was pressing for something to be done. In 1897 a conference was held at Kingston to coordinate action with other counties, though these did not provide the expected support. It was clear that the presence of travelling people vexed the authorities in Surrey much more than elsewhere. Furthermore, local authorities could only act to enforce the law, and there was no law specifically against Gypsies. By 1906 the county councillors felt that they had collected enough complaints and objections to campaign for an Act of Parliament which would give them more powers. Reginald Bray and his colleagues threw their weight behind this as well, and it was considered in 1909 as the Moveable Dwellings Bill.

Evidence for the relationships between Gypsy and gorjer came from Abinger, Seale, Gomshall and Netley Heath as well as the Hurtwood: some witnesses painted a picture of a terrorized countryside, others reported a state of reasonable co-existence. But this was irrelevant: to the extent that the Gypsies committed acts against the law, they could be dealt with by the courts. What Surrey County Council wanted was power over Gypsies as such, and that was not something which would be countenanced by Parliament. Instead, as the title of their bill suggests, they pressed for power to register and control people's homes. However, as the more perceptive witnesses pointed out, Gypsies – even those from families with waggons – were mostly sleeping in benders. You couldn't register twelve sticks and some blankets as a 'dwelling'. Furthermore the bill, by using the category of van and tent dwellers as a euphemism for Gypsies, gave local government powers over any gorjer who happened to be sleeping under canvas, including holidaymakers and the British Army. In 1911 the bill failed to pass through Parliament. It was presented again in 1912 and 1914, again without success. After that, the country had more important things to worry about.

6

Between Two Fires:
The Early Twentieth Century

When news of war came in 1914, many were thrilled: here was a chance to get caught up in great events, to support right against wrong, and – especially for young men – to show what you were made of. Abraham Ripley enlisted with the 7th Battalion, Royal Fusiliers (City of London Regiment); his nephew and best friend, also Abraham Ripley, signed up with the 4th Battalion, Duke of Cambridge's Own (Middlesex Regiment). The family were stopping at Weybridge when they left:

> Everyone went out of the yard to see them off. The two young Abrahams laughed as they waved and walked away into their uncertain future. The family stood in silence until the two had disappeared, then they went back to the yard until only my mother stood looking down the empty lane, even after the sound of their boots and their laughter had died away.[1]

They never came back. Young Abraham died on the first day of the Battle of Passchendaele, his body torn up by shells, or slipping unnoticed into the treacherous mud, and all that remains is a name on the Menin Gate. His uncle fought on until 1918 and then, only six weeks before the Armistice, he too was killed, and rests in the Quarry Wood Cemetery at Sains-les-Marquion, east of Arras.[2]

They were not the only Gypsies caught up in the remorseless machinery of war. Frederick Parker was born at Malden Rushett, the son of Henry and Viletta. The family stopped at Horton Lane in Epsom, and Frederick was working as a general labourer when he joined the 18th Middlesex, a pioneer division. He was 36 when he was killed at the Somme in December 1916, a month after the great battle had formally ended; but there were continual minor offensive actions up and down the Western Front, and it was one of these – a trench raid to gather intelligence, or an attempt to silence a troublesome machine gun – which accounted for Frederick. He is buried in Delville Wood Cemetery.[3] Swailes Lawrence was born in a tent at Epsom in 1893; Job Lawrence and Annie Taylor were his parents. He worked at flower-selling in Leytonstone before being called up in 1916 and died at Ypres the next year.[4] Albert Williams from Kingfield in Old Woking fought with both the East and West Surreys until his end at the Battle of Polygon Wood in September 1917.[5] Henry Ayres, the son of Neptune and Talitha, was a married man with seven children when he answered the call, soon after war broke out. He left his wife Louisa Harris at home in Chertsey, said goodbye to his mates in the Hatch Farm brickfield, and sailed with the Leicestershires to Mesopotamia, where he died in March 1917.[6] Samuel Brazil was born in Ash, the son of James Brazil. He served in the 12th Battalion, King's Royal Rifle Brigade, and died in the German advance of May 1918. He is buried in the Military Cemetery at St Pol-sur-Ternoise.[7]

Sidney Harris saw the war almost from beginning to end as a Lance Corporal in the Royal Berkshire Regiment. He was born at Knaphill, the son of George Harris and Keziah Gregory; afterwards the family moved towards Esher, where they occupied two waggons in the settlement of West End, between Claremont and the River Mole. Sidney was either a trained soldier or a very early volunteer, for he entered the war in November 1914, towards the end of the First Battle of Ypres, and continued serving with the Royal Berkshires through Loos, the Somme, Arras and Cambrai. He was wounded in March 1915 and October 1916, and carried on, a weathered old soldier at the age of 24; but his luck ran out when the Royal Berkshires tried to stem the major German offensive at the beginning of 1918, and he died in March. His final pay, £13 7s 4d, was sent to his stepmother, now living in brick at Hodgson's Cottages in West End, and a year later this was followed by a war gratuity of £21.[8]

Sidney, Samuel, Swailes, Frederick, Henry, Albert, the two Abrahams: they were the unlucky ones, men who by the random trajectory of bullet or shell became names on a war memorial. There were many more who served and lived, though they were changed forever by what they had gone through. Apart from anything else, there was the sheer strangeness of the experience: in 1914 the boundaries of the known world were very small for most Gypsies, and Flanders lay well outside them. 'None of us have ever been out of Surrey in our lives except our men who fought in the war,' said a group of people stopping on Epsom Downs in 1927, adding loyally that 'many of them enlisted immediately at the outbreak of war.'[9] Dark eyes look out of old photos, proud to find themselves in uniform but bemused at the same time: Ted Baker came from an old Kentish breed, and his wife was granddaughter of the charismatic Gilderoy Scamp who bore his white top hat like a ragged crown, but what did any of this mean to the British Army? Pitched into a completely new environment, Gypsy recruits could not even keep in touch with home, for the tale-telling of an oral culture had no place in modern industrialized communications. At Hindhead, mothers stopping in the Devil's Punch Bowl would crowd round the postman, asking him eagerly to read the postcards which their sons had written, or dictated, from the trenches, since they themselves were illiterate and could not write back.[10]

Gypsy skills had their uses at the home front. On the outbreak of war, Daniel Cooper – nephew of Matty Cooper – had two sons of military age. Walter was stopping in a waggon next to his father on Lambert's Ground, by Arthurs Bridge in Woking, while his older brother Mattie had gone into brick and was living at Abbey Road in Horsell. When Mattie enlisted in 1915, the officers noted 'a good nagsman', and 'would make a good horsedealer's man'; so he went to the Remounts Service, which was based outside Southampton. Walter, who seems to have preferred tinkering with metal to dealing in horseflesh, ended up in the Tank Corps of the Middlesex Regiment, although his military papers record that he was occasionally absent from duty.[11]

Walter/Wally Doe, Albert's son, was only fifteen when he signed up for the Navy; it was 1917, and the shortage of manpower was beginning to tell. Wally had been in school right up to his teenage years, so he had the education to train as a signaller. He saw active service as part of the blockade of Turkish ports in the Red Sea and remained in the Navy until 1920.[12] Joseph Penfold of Croydon, however, was 32, comparatively old for a soldier, when he enlisted in the Suffolk regiment in the same year. He didn't take kindly to military discipline – on several occasions he went AWOL, and ended up spending time in the Glasshouse, or military prison.[13]

As the years pass, disreputable incidents like this fade away, and all that remains is a memory of heroism long ago. 'Me granddad Sam Ripley was a soldier in the 1914 war, he never talked about his time but he was always known to be a brave man.'[14] Fred Wood, who like his son Fred was a good man with a horse, was employed to carry messages. 'Once

Ted Baker in
wartime, *c.* 1914.

he was with a party in No-Man's-Land – they were all killed, but he was behind the enemy lines with a horse, and he kept himself and the horse alive until he could finally make his way back to our lines.' For this he was mentioned in despatches.[15] They say that Jesse Frankham was awarded the Croix de Guerre after he, too, went behind enemy lines on horseback, dressed as a German officer – and maybe he was, but it sounds like a tale that has grown in the telling.[16] These brave legends overlook the appalling consequences of the war, not just for families that lost their sons, but for the young men who faced a crippled future. David Matthews, the son of Job Matthews from the settlement at Hollywater, was only twenty when the war ended but his wounds meant he would be disabled for the rest of his life. His girlfriend Susan Ridley stood by him, and they were married at Headley in 1919.[17] Eli Smith was sent to Woburn Abbey to be treated for his injured leg, and to the day of his death had to wear one shoe made higher than the other before he could walk straight.[18] And not all the injuries were physical:

> Grandad's brother Jo fought in the First World War, he was at the fighting on the Somme. Jo was a man's man: he'd walk away from trouble, someone would have to actually take hold of him before he'd react, but then he'd let them know what he was made of! When he came back from the fighting he never talked, he'd just sit by the fire all quiet, but when you looked at him there'd be tears running down his face, he just couldn't forget what he'd seen.[19]

The upheavals of war made strange friendships. In 1916 Marshall Ripley was out totting when he heard a noise in the street. There was a boy dressed in rags, and the gorjers were throwing stones at him and yelling. Marshall stopped and looked, and the boy ran up to him, whimpering that they wanted to kill him because he was German. Now Marshall was as patriotic as the next man – Abraham Ripley, serving with the City of London Regiment, was his brother-in-law – but he knew what it was like to be hated without a cause, and he pulled the boy up onto the cart and took him home, where they adopted him. His name was Frank Deach, and the oldest boy of the family, young Marshall, loved him like a brother. But one day a stranger found the Ripleys, said he was Frank's uncle, and took him away. They never saw him again: such sudden disappearances were part of life in wartime. Many years later someone took the family photo, where Frank was holding the horse for Marshall's cart in the street near the old Weybridge Hospital. They rubbed him off the print, because they said he spoiled the picture with his rags and everything.[20]

Gypsy sympathy could be extended further than this, perhaps further than was wise. People on the Hurtwood had often hidden those who were wanted by the police, and after 1916 they began sheltering deserters. Young men who wanted to evade the Military Service Act relied on the support of their families and the ease of concealment, but neither of these were infallible. At Limpsfield warning signals were given by children who had been stationed round the encampment, so that young Henry Collins could run into the brushwood, but the police sprinted after him and hauled him off to Redhill recruiting office.[21] At another encampment, a police raid uncovered two young men who had deserted; they were promptly dragged all the way to the station for London, followed by a long line of wailing women and children.[22]

But this was unusual, for normally Gypsies supported the war. So did the rest of the country, of course; young men of all classes and backgrounds were pressing round the recruitment posters, all motivated by patriotism, some also by the prospect of regular food and guaranteed pay. Conscription, which became law between March and May 1916, superseded all other arguments, but Gypsies did not wait to be ordered into uniform. Of the men listed above, eight (a little more than half) enlisted or served at dates leading up to the Battle of the Somme, which was the last engagement to feature only volunteers. The Romany did their bit, no better or worse than their gorjer brothers-in-arms.[23] And sometimes, when the war was over, a normally ungrateful world remembered this.

Aaron Hoadley, who stopped in 1923 off Snaky Alley between Ewell and Epsom, was at the Derby wearing his medals when someone bet him that he couldn't borrow £1 off George V – but he did, because he was an ex-serviceman. They say he also got a pass which allowed him to stop anywhere he liked in the country. When he died, they buried him with all his medals on.[24]

Such acts of generosity were exceptional. At the end of the war, Gypsies had the same position as when it began: a beleaguered and mistrusted minority. But how large a minority? And how embedded in the host society? These were difficult questions to which, for the first time, the records provide an answer.

Nobody ever counted the Romany as an ethnic group, for that was a concept quite alien to the official mind. But the level of detail in the 1911 census is good enough for us today to assess how many people would have ranked in this way among their peers. A meticulous examination of the records finds 1,042 people who were fairly certainly Gypsies living in administrative Surrey – exclusive of Battersea, Wandsworth and the Southwark area, which had passed to the new London County Council.[25] Of these, 107 families were in waggons, 77 in tents only and 29 in housing. The last category was of no interest to the government, which only wanted to measure vagrancy. That was easier to do, and in 1911 the authorities reported some 1,210 van and tent dwellers in Surrey, the figure being

Aaron Hoadley in peacetime, 1920.

a little uncertain since it is taken from a total which also lumped in the tramps sleeping in barns.[26] It seems, then, that the recognizable Romany population, whether on the road or in brick, was rather less than the total number of itinerants: about 85 per cent of it.

Numbers, especially those in official reports, sometimes take on a life of their own, but you might ask how reliable those 1911 figures are. After all, the previous census had found only 649 van and tent dwellers, about half the number that were counted ten years later. Had there been some great migration of the people of the road into Surrey? Unlikely; the spike in figures seems rather to reflect concerns felt by the administrators. Spurred on by the fuss which Surrey County Council was making about Gypsies, census enumerators trekked up and down the fields looking for encampments which they would not otherwise have noticed. Two independent surveys bear this out. In 1907, and again in 1913, the council instructed Mowbray Sant, as Chief Constable, to count the Travellers in Surrey. These exercises were to be carried out in the summer months, later than the census, when all seasonal travellers would be on the road. They were made at midnight, so there was no likelihood of people escaping observation. You might have thought that people who could be woken up in the middle of the night by a single constable, and would then patiently give him all their family details in the dark and cold, were less of a threat than the councillors imagined; and Mowbray, who was a decent sort of gavver, did point this out, but no one listened to him.[27] Anyway, the conclusion was that in 1907 there were 1,231 itinerants in the Surrey police district, and in 1913 1,424.[28] The fact that the police, who of all people would have known where the Gypsies were, produced figures which corroborate the 1911 census suggests that this was an accurate record.

In that case there cannot have been much more than one thousand Gypsies in administrative Surrey, with a further two hundred itinerants and temporary migrants. This seems a rather small body of people when you consider all the uproar that was being made about them, and in fact the county landowners routinely overestimated the number of Gypsies, sometimes by a factor of ten.[29]

There was some excuse for exaggeration, for Gypsies were highly visible. By 1900 waggons had superseded tents as the normal accommodation for a family. Whereas a bender could have been pitched out of site behind a hedge, a waggon would be pulled visibly near the gate, or on the roadside if there was no field where people could stop. Large gatherings could be seen for miles: in Ascot week there were sixty waggons stopping on Chobham Common, with an estimated 150 people in them.[30] Next year there were fifty, all of them eventually moved onto the road by one sweating labourer and his horse, acting on behalf of a bailiff and watched by twelve constables, a sergeant, an inspector and the Chief Constable himself, just in case the Gypsies should cut up rough, which they didn't. Once in the middle of the road they ceased to be the responsibility of the Lord of the Manor, and became that of the police, who moved them on.[31]

People got together in readiness for race days and other economic opportunities, but they also gathered as a response to harassment: there was safety in numbers, especially if you could meet up on common ground where the bailiffs were weak or tolerant. Sometimes, as on the Hurtwood, this led to overcrowding and bad relations with the gorjers, but not always. In 1911 the largest concentrations of Gypsies were to be found in the parishes of Croydon, Ash, Chobham, Shere (the Hurtwood), West Horsley, Woking and Farnham (Hale): between them, these places accounted for almost half of the people stopping in the county.[32] While the villagers at Chobham and Shere were certainly unhappy with their local travellers, no such complaints are reported from the other parishes.

But then on the heathlands and other thinly settled areas, the boundaries between Gypsy and gorjer seemed less significant. Frederick Grover of The Bourne knew all the families around Farnham: those in tents and those in houses, the horse-traders and the basket makers, those that had taught him cures and those that had hired him for building work, with all their ways and family quarrels – 'an' then the best of it was, they'd come round after they'd done, an' ask you what you thought! An' you didn't know *what* to say. 'Cause if you said anything, you'd be like enough to be in the wrong.'[33] He had his own views on 'they gyps', which weren't always complimentary, but at least they were based on encounters with people he knew, not on a fear of anonymous strangers.

Frederick's uncle had in fact taken to the travelling life, while several other families in The Bourne originated with a Gypsy who had settled down. Exchanges of this kind were being made throughout Surrey. Goldie Lovett, who married a cow-keeper at Oxted, used to work as a cook on the farm, and never said much about her Gypsy origins. If someone asked how, unlike the other village girls, she had never been taught to read or write, 'she will reply that when she was a child, she lived with her old granny at the bottom of a wood' – which was true, but not the whole truth. Her cousin married a gorjer labourer, and for a while they kept up a Gypsy life in a waggon, but when their little Rosie fell into the fire one night when her mother was busy cooking, the family moved into a dilapidated cottage by the pub.[34]

And the exchange could just as easily be the other way, with a man or woman marrying into the community. Anyone seeing Bill Beaney in the pub, with his long thick grey hair and a silver-topped whip never out of his hand, would take him for one of the old families, especially when he was talking ten to the dozen about chopping horses. Not so. 'I'm a gorjer,' he would say, amused at your ignorance. 'Born in Croydon, if you want to know. But my old mort's a proper Romany – one of the Lees.'[35] And it was another Lee – Ithal, son of Drui Lee and Darkus Price – who took on a gorjer girl as his adoptive daughter. Her name was Kathleen, and she was cared for by his family after her mother had died. Later on she would go dukkering at the Derby with her adoptive sister Melanie and their cousin Rosie Price.[36]

Among the Londonside Gypsies, family lines become even more complex, since these people were making a living and finding partners among an urban population all involved in related trades. Lemonelia Smith, the flower seller of East Sheen, was born on Barnes Common, and that's where she lived with her husband, George (Feathers) Smith from Mitcham. All their children were raised on the common until the last, Patience/Paisha, who was born in 1911 after Lemonelia and Feathers went into brick at Westfields. Paisha used to sell flowers on the Upper Richmond Road south of Mortlake Station, and she married a gorjer called Tom Parsons, who had been a general dealer and coal merchant at Richmond. Paisha and Tom had a son, Ivor, and a daughter, Janet; Ivor married a woman who numbered among her grandparents a Spanish Gypsy who had come back to England after the Peninsular War, while Janet married the son of a general dealer from Westfields. So within three generations the Romany line branches out into a web of relatives of whom it could be said 'that if they were not actually "Gypsy", they were somehow "mixed up" with them'; and this was true of many other families in the London area.[37]

Who, for instance, was Charlotte Birch? Her mother was a Gypsy, Harriet Orchard, who had married out to a timber merchant called Robert Birch. Charlotte ran a boxing booth, for which her younger brother Jack provided some of the muscle. She married three times, first to Samuel Frankham, who was a basket maker before he got taken into the family business. Her second marriage was to the showman Joseph

Darkus Price with her grandchildren on Epsom Downs, 1931.

Beckett, sometimes known as Joseph Boyce as he liked to have an alternative surname when authority became demanding. The third marriage, to William Gilham, produced a single son to go with the two Beckett/ Boyce children and the five Frankhams. George and John, sons of the first marriage, were boxers, and so was their Beckett half-brother Joseph. When Joe went professional, he found it prudent to identify with his father the showman, and not his mother the Gypsy, so in the interests of family solidarity his two half-brothers went under the same gorjer name of Beckett and not their father's name of Frankham.[38]

There were a lot of children from mixed marriages, so many that they came to have a name of their own, the didikais. The origins of this word are something of a mystery; it is often said to be a joke at the expense of those too ignorant to pronounce *dik adoi*, saying *did akoi* instead, but this is simply a piece of ingenious wordplay. Until the 1930s it was simply another word for 'Gypsy', in Surrey at least, but after that it developed a harsher meaning of 'half-breed'. No doubt this was because Londonside Gypsies had more gorjer blood in their lineage than people from further north and west.[39]

In the first known use of the word, a fragment of lullaby sung on Epsom Downs in 1910, it does not seem to be pejorative at all. A mother would sing:

Ushitel, didikai!
Your father's gone to poov the grai
Near the tober skai
Six o'clock in the morning.[40]

This is so scrambled linguistically that it would puzzle anyone apart from a baby. 'Ushitel' is a survival from Old Romani *ustela*, 'he gets up'; 'poov the grai' is standard Anglo-Romani; but 'tober skai' is not Romani at all. It comes from Shelta, the language of the Irish Travellers, and began as back-slang for *bóthar uisge*, 'the way of the water', and therefore 'river'.[41] A mixed language is probably the consequence of a mixed background. In the 1930s, Surrey Gypsies were increasingly likely to use words from Cant, the idiom of native English Travellers: they said *mort* instead of *juvvel* or *romni*, *gatter* instead of *levvina*, *scran* instead of *hawben*, and *kennick* instead of *kairengro*. They might even refer to themselves as 'needies', although that was a Shelta word, another bit of back-slang from *daoine*, 'people'.[42]

These borrowings suggest contact with Irish culture, though that could take many forms. There was Patrick Stanley, for instance, who travelled around Shere with a handcart, mending chairs and killing rats. He had travelled the length and breadth of Ireland, though he was born an English Gypsy, and had ended up speaking in a rich Irish accent liberally sprinkled with Romani words. He had run his own roundabout and swings, but spent all the profits on drink; he had worked as a travelling photographer, with the same result; and then as a crocus, or quack doctor:

It were a good trade, prala, for I could earn as much as three bars ivery day of me loife. But it were the dhrink again that was me ruination, bad cess to it. I got meself lit up one night an' fell on all me bottles an' busted the bloody lot. I'd spint all me money on booze an' 'ad none left for new bottles, so that were the end of me as a crocus.[43]

It was the drink, too, that ruined his one and only chance of photographing a leprechaun; but despite this promising background, Patrick claimed not to have a drop of Irish blood in him. Other traditions suggest intermarriage, however. There are the Marneys, first recorded at Epsom towards the end of the nineteenth century, whose name must be an Anglicized form of Mahoney; Susan Marney was described in 1920 as 'a sun-browned Irish gipsy woman'.[44] Two large framed portraits passed down in a Gypsy family, one of Robert Emmet and the other of Charles Stewart Parnell, must have descended from some Irish patriot who had to leave the country long before the War of Independence; and another family passed down the tune and title of 'The Song That Was Sung Was Old Ireland Free'.[45]

So it is not surprising that a visitor to the Derby in about 1910 found the people there 'ruddy, fair-haired, and poorly-clad', by contrast with the darker Romany of the North.[46] But Londonside Gypsies, whatever their connections with showfolk, Irish, native Travellers and other allied groups, remained part of the community and there were many marriages with the older families. Ted Scamp used to talk about one of his relatives, who had branched off from the Kentish family years before, when he escaped from the gavvers and had to move to another part of the country. He got as far as Wales, where he married a local girl, and his son took after the mother's side:

> Old Jack Scamp speaks like a Welshman, but he knew more
> Romanes than any man I've ever known. And dark? You ought've
> seen him. Like an Injun. He comes up this way now'n'again, to
> Epsom very often. Travels with about five vardos – and every man
> in his fam'ly's a good bosh-player. Every man.[47]

You might think that being compared to the wild men of North America was a bit harsh, but people took it as a compliment. Frank Cooper, Matty's son, said one day at Walton that 'he had been often puzzled by Indians in America and their great resemblance to Gypsies'.[48] The Romany quarter in Mitcham was called Redskin Village, while Indians Wood at Burrows Cross, south of Gomshall, was where the Gypsies lived.[49] And at the Victory Derby of 1919, a family were stopping in a tipi – an authentic-looking structure with tree-trunk poles and flaps. Buffalo Bill had come with his Wild West Show to Earls Court before the war, and this piece of transatlantic imitation suggests that some Romany visitors had made careful observations of the Indian village there. Wigwams were set up at subsequent Derbies, sometimes decorated round the sides with picture-writing worthy of the Sioux or the Cree.[50]

There were stranger sights than this to be seen on the roads. In the halcyon days before the Great War, the jealously guarded borders of Europe seemed to be easing up at last, and many Roma set out from the old homelands to see what could be achieved in the West. Gustevan Teodorovicks and his family left Serbia to arrive, after many adventures, at London Bridge in June 1907. They were travelling with two perform-ing bears and a couple of waggons, one marked *Animaux Ambulants*, but despite this advertisement they got a cool reception in England. Ten days later they had got as far as Cobham, where the seven Gypsies were escorted by a flotilla of policemen, each standing by his bicycle and keep-ing a judicious distance from the bears. The party were escorted through the suspicious countryside to Folkestone, where they re-embarked for Boulogne.[51]

Onlookers certainly got their fill of the exotic when Nikóla and Míloš Tšóron and their families stopped in a timber yard at Battersea. The group, numbering about 150 in all, were Kalderash from Galicia, to the south of Poland, which they had left for a tour through Europe, eventually winding up at Liverpool and working their way south through England in the hope of a music-hall booking to supplement the money they made from copper and silver vases, trays and trinkets.[52] In September 1911 they were turned out from Battersea but moved a short distance to the Gypsy stronghold of Garratt Lane in Wandsworth, and then to Beddington Corner in Mitcham. There were six or seven families in the group, each with a high triangular tent, made colourful inside with thick rugs and draped with curtains and icons, for the Galicians kept to the reli-gion of their homeland.[53] They welcomed visitors, as long as these were a paying proposition, and the gorjers went away with souvenirs and mem-ories of strange, bright, colourful people: the men with beards hanging down over their blue and scarlet shirts, wearing baggy trousers stuffed into high boots, and the women in skirts of many colours topped by embroi-dered blouses, silk handkerchiefs on their heads, and everything shaking and tinkling with golden ornaments. In October Nikóla's daughter Zâža, the wife of Adam Kírpatš, died after childbirth and was buried with full ritual: she was dressed all in new clothes, with a necklace of gold coins round her neck, and the coffin left open on its journey to Mitcham Old Church, with the women of the family wailing and lamenting along the road. Not long after that the group split up to continue on their travels, some going overseas to Ireland and Spain, others returning to the north of England.

The Galicians were quite happy to be the subjects of ethnological investigation – they were here, after all, to go on show – but other visitors were more mysterious in their ways. Who were the 'wild outlandish people . . . making their way slowly along while stopping here and there to pass the hat round' at the Derby in the years before the First World War? 'Tall, dark, nonchalant and superb, some beat on enormous tambourines, others led gigantic monkeys or rather apes, and all joined, when they felt like it, in the chant.' Augustus John, who was fluent in the puri jib, spoke to them in words that should have been understood by any Continental Gypsy, but they gazed at him without comprehension.[54]

Two groups of Kalderash began moving into England in the years following 1929, claiming some kinship to the Tšórons, though they claimed many other things as well; usually they said they were from Greece. A visitor to Epsom in 1937 found

> the 'Greeks', on the Monday before Derby Day, comfortably settled on 'The Hill' with two tents and a dukkering tan . . . old Mārya Yevanovič, with Yōsi Stīrio and her granddaughter Elēna and children . . . the whole family now called themselves Mitchell! A little later these 'Greek' Gypsies also visited Mitcham Fair and Ascot Races, where . . . the Stīrios were on quite friendly terms with English Romanichals on the field, and seemed to be travelling with a gorjer from Sunderland, who might have been acting as an interpreter for them. A small girl of the Yevanovič clan was trotting round happily with a couple of English Gypsy children, teaching them how to mong in true Coppersmith fashion from the grand ladies on the race-course.[55]

Views on the Balkan Gypsies were mixed: the Boswells and Hernes, who were rather proud of their own lineages, stayed aloof from these interlopers out of the old Romani world, but the Surrey and Londonside families were fascinated by their dark faces and gold ornaments, not to mention the magnificent cars. The admiration was not returned: Spīro Stīrio, talking to a bilingual member of the Gypsy Lore Society, said indignantly, 'Why don't those mongrels down by the rails speak good Romani like you do? When I talk to them as I am talking to you the fools say I am not speaking Romani at all!'

And once again there was a funeral, this time of old Mārya, who was buried at the Greek Orthodox Cemetery in West Norwood after a funeral conducted at St Sophia in Bayswater. The service followed the usual lines, except for the loud crying and weeping of the family as they stood around Mārya's coffin.[56] But there were some Gypsy rites after the burial, as remembered by Petra Lazarovič, who had travelled with the Yevanovičes before she married Andrew Ryley, a grandson of Drui Lee and Darkus Price, and began a new life in Epping Forest. Three times in the course of the year following the death, a great feast was laid out on fine tablecloths in a field, lit up by candles and the headlights of the expensive motors. Nothing was eaten: each time, the food was given away. The family wanted to give their friend a special dress, too – one which had been made for old Mārya after she died. But Petra looked at Andrew, and he looked at her: neither of them wanted to have such a mullerdi thing, so they quietly got into their motor and left before the ceremony was over.[57]

Their hosts do not seem to have been offended by this, and they soon found someone else to give the dress to. It is surprising how well the Greek and Galician Gypsies seem to have understood their English compatriots, and to have been understood by them. These groups were, to all outward appearance, quite separate – divided by almost five hundred years of cultural isolation – and yet each quickly recognized the other's adherence to Gypsy norms; a proper funeral, for instance.

Big funerals were part of English working-class culture as well, but Gypsies had other rites, such as destruction of the property of the dead, which seemed strange to gorjers. There were usually newspaper reporters in the crowd when the waggon of some respected figure was burnt, since the ceremony was not a common one. Three women, each in her time a familiar figure on Epsom Downs, received this mark of respect. Sentenia (Henty) Smith, who came down each year to the Derby to tell fortunes in a richly decorated tent, died and was buried in her home territory of the Black Patch at Birmingham. Two hundred children, grandchildren and great-grandchildren attended the funeral and afterwards the waggon was burned 'to prevent any dispute in her family'.[58] Urania/Reni Buckland was a reputed centenarian when she died at Reading in 1912; she was one of many to have received the haphazard silver thrown by Edward VII from the Royal Box at Epsom. Her waggon, too, went up in flames.[59] And there was Lilo Smith, who used to come from Buckinghamshire to dukker the crowd each year, returning to keep order over her descendants on Iver Common: when she died, her waggon was burnt, along with her shawls, her feathers and beads, and even her gold earrings, because no one could decide who should inherit them.[60]

This burning of the waggon was not carried out at every death; it would be unworkable if the deceased had left behind a husband or wife, so that normally it marked the funerals of the very old. In fact there are only three recorded instances of it being practised in Surrey during the first half of the twentieth century. The leader of a group at Ockham – her name was Morella – died in about 1920, and after her waggon had been burnt, the family moved on.[61] In the 1940s a 'Gypsy king' was buried at Ash, with families coming from as far away as Newcastle, and his waggon burnt afterwards.[62] And when Ada Todd died at Chobham, people gathered from miles around for the funeral, followed by the burning of her waggon on the common, even though Ada, at forty, was comparatively young.[63]

Though the burning of waggons was usually reserved for the old, there was one exception. Among the people who stopped in The Dip above Langley Vale in the 1930s, 'if a gypsy woman died in childbirth, the whole caravan was burned and all the china smashed.'[64] It seems that the local midwife was delivering babies in the waggons, and not in a birth tent, so that if death and childbirth both happened there at once, the vehicle became *mogadi* and had to be destroyed.[65] Otherwise, though, people gave a much more practical reason for waggon-burning: it was to avoid squabbles among the living over the property of the dead. These two justifications, the superstitious and the pragmatic, had more in common than might at first appear, since they both respected the need to draw the line under a life – to declare it finished, with nothing carried awkwardly over into the business of the living. And the longer and more celebrated a life had been, the more fitting it was to bring it to a fiery close.

Not that Gypsies were any strangers to superstition. Alice Emma (Totty) Matthews of Leatherhead had one for every occasion. 'I was there one day when a dog kept howling, and Gran said "Oh dear, that will be old Mrs. Boswell". Soon after there was a knock at the door, and Gran went out with her old biscuit tin. I later learned she used to lay out the dead. I never did find out what was in the tin.'[66] She was not the only old lady to know unfathomable things. Living in one of the South London yards, Mrs Lee was famous for her dukkering – not the usual flim-flam, but the proper art, which could see what was true, though it came at a terrible price. She lived in her own waggon, where she had a good many hundred pounds put away, but they say she died hard:

Just when she was at her last gasp, a face looked in at the door from above it, downwards and inwards, like as if somebody was lying on his stomach on the mollycroft roof and bending over the top half of the door, the part that was open. They like to have it open when they're dying. It was certainly a sort of a man's face, and it said to her 'I've got all the money I gave you, and now I've got *you*.' At that she died.[67]

It was unusual for the *Beng* to come in person to carry you off, but many an old lady was rumoured to know something about his business, and accusations of witchcraft were sometimes made in the course of family quarrels.[68] Claiming supernatural powers was a risky business, but it had its temptations for a woman who wanted to be able to intimidate her relatives, especially the menfolk: for the two sexes were often in conflict. 'The men!' said an old grandmother from Oxted. 'They drive you out to work all day, selling clothes pegs and begging on the roads, and when you get back at last they beat you 'cause you haven't brought more money.'[69] Lilo Smith, when asked why she had a broken nose, said succinctly 'Me 'usband – twice'.[70] When Poll Ayres went down limping into Farnham, Fred Grover asked what was up and she said 'Why, my Fred, the blackman have kicked me on the leg, an' hit me on the nose'; and that was before he went for her with the handle of his whip.[71]

Money was the root of these quarrels: money which was usually in the wife's hands, for 'the women always keeps it all,' as Fred Grover said in surprise after seeing how much Poll had tucked away. 'She put in her hand an' drew it out of her bosom – a purse half's long's a stockin' – an' all full! She 'ad purty well a hundred pound in there!' Leaving money with the women was the obvious thing to do. Firstly, a woman's body was sacrosanct: once something had disappeared under her pinna, it was out of reach, whereas a man might be robbed.[72] One of the early settlers at the Quadrant in Ash was found to have £71 hidden in her underclothing.[73] And then a woman would remain with the waggon, minding the family's assets, where a man might go down the pub and venture everything in a bet or a deal. 'We women hold all the money – it's safer in our hands,' as girls at the Derby told the artist Laura Knight in the 1930s. Later, Mary Smith confided in her:

I'm saving to get a decent wagon instead of the awful old leaky tent me 'usband 'as landed us with. All men's the same – allus in the pub choppin' everything they can lay their hands on. When I married I brought three hundred pounds with me – working hard

with a crystal at an old woman's back door. It took me two years
to earn that money – not all of us have the gift and can tell the tale!
All a man's got to do is sit at a pub gawpin' at nowt.[74]

We don't hear the men's side, of course. A man might sit in the pub
for six days, and on the seventh make a chop, or hear about some opportunity, which brought in more money than he could have gained in a
week of routine labour. It was the difference in income strategies which
put a marriage under stress – the contrast between steady reliable earnings made by one partner, and large unpredictable takings hoped for by
the other. Every now and then men did vent their exasperation at the
way women did things, as in the song, popular on the Downs at Epsom:

All through mi rakli,
Kicking up a gudli –
Like me dear old dadus, boy,
I'll leave her in the tan.

Like many Gypsy songs, this is a kaleidoscope of images rather than a
straightforward narrative, but the general sense is that the singer's girl
has been making a fuss about something ('kicking up a gudli') which has
attracted the attention of authority, for when the singer goes to the wood
to chin a bit of kosh, a gavver comes up and tries to arrest him for cutting
the sticks. Naturally, there's a fight, and someone, perhaps the girl, ends
up saying 'Like me dear old dadus, boy/ You can kor well!'[75]

In the end, the two sexes needed each other; travelling alone was very
difficult, and people who had grown up among a milling crowd of relatives had no taste for solitude. When someone talked of being on my
kokkero, or by their lonesome, it was a sign that they were frightened and
sad. So most Gypsy marriages endured. From the day when the girl first
threw a coin-studded cake over the hedge where the young man was waiting, to the time when, after having run away together, they returned to
face the parental wrath, the couple knew that they were going to have to
work together. Indeed, they would be growing up together: analysis of
the 1891 census suggests that most marriages took place when a girl was
just out of her teens, and her husband was only two or three years older.[76]

It is not easy to arrive at definite figures, but the age of girls at marriage
seems to have dropped during the nineteenth century. People had always
married younger than gorjers, who delayed their weddings until the bride

was 26 or so, but that was in response to the shortage of resources in village life. Gypsies by contrast could live off the land and their wits, and once they had these skills there was nothing to stop them leaving their families and starting a new life together. As the twentieth century progresses, we hear more often of teenage marriages. Mayday Smith eloped when she was fourteen and bore her first child at sixteen, in a field down Kent during strawberry picking. Li'l Bill the baby slept in a peg basket and spent the day slung in a roper, covered with a shawl, while his mother went about her business. And how she loved him!

> Sweet as a lark her voice would cry to him: 'Oh my Li'l Bill, Li'l Bill, my wonderful chavvi'. And her brilliant lips would kiss the white face. 'Ain't he a li'l prince now; ain't he the rinkeno krallis?'. Answering her own question, she would promptly inform her son triumphantly: 'They sez you is like a krallis. They all sez you is'. 'They' were the nodding trees and grasses.[77]

Cosseted children have golden memories. Phoebe Barney grew up sitting on the footboard, listening to her father as he named the flowers and told stories about the stopping places around Chertsey and the Hampshire border. She loved Dolly the white horse and Patsy the mongrel dog, and she loved the long days spent playing with her sister in the fields. 'Louie and I would keep ourselves amused with a ball or spinning top and whip . . . Sometimes, if there wasn't any hard ground for our tops, we would see who could make the longest daisy chains – oh what happy days they were!' But not all children were cosseted. Phoebe's aunt Ena died young, leaving three children, and her husband married again. One day cousin Willy came to call, and it was obvious that the palms of his hands were burned: his stepmother had burnt them. He stayed until his father called to collect him, and then left quietly enough but with a 10s note sewn down into the lining of his cap, so that as soon as he could run off to a railway station and buy a ticket, he was back again. Not long after, it was seen that Willy's two sisters weren't being looked after either, and they were taken away and added to the families of two aunts. In this way the wider family regrouped to minimize the damage of bereavement and neglect.[78]

The duty of relatives to support each other was understood very early in life. At the yards in Battersea, where the children were 'wretchedly clothed, but . . . bright and interesting', it was obvious how 'the boys take great care of their sisters, and it is pretty to see the protecting air they extend towards them.' If their parents fell sick, the young ones would labour all day at anything they could do to get bread for the family.[79] Gypsy children, more than most, understood that it is work that puts food on the table, and they started from a young age. Sammy and Phoebe Ayres of Upper Hale made a living out of troops-hawking; whenever the soldiers came to a halt after a particularly exhausting route march, there would be the Ayres, waiting for them with trays of sweets, chocolate, fruit, home-baked cakes and patent lemonade. As soon as their little Annie could walk, she was sent running behind the lines to sell refreshment. By the time of the Great War she was eight, and able to follow the army up to York and down to Salisbury.[80]

It wasn't hard for a sweet-looking girl to sell refreshments to dashing young men in uniform, and it can't have been too unpleasant either. Some work was dull, like helping in the family production line for making pegs, but some of it was a challenge, a chance to show adult skills: because Gypsy kids grew up with adult role models always around them, their manner was more grown-up than that of their gorjer contemporaries. On Esher Common, in the unseasonal return of winter weather in April 1908:

> The snow lay in blue shadows unmelted under the gorse bushes, and amongst the gorse and sodden bracken twenty ponies snuffed for grass. Three gypsy boys shuffled through the fern near them. What did they do with the ponies? I asked, and the eldest told me they sold them; they were good ponies; he was voluble in suburban English. What did they fetch? That depended. What was that one worth? – it was a small chestnut creature with a child's pink pinafore for a halter. 'Ah! That one,' he began, and his eyes became inscrutable. He would have sold it well.[81]

On a first encounter with strangers, children often seemed struck dumb, like the Lovells who stopped at Leatherhead with 'the children standing in silence, listening with interest to all that was spoken, and gazing at me steadfastly with their bright eyes, examining every detail of me'.[82] But once they had weighed people up, all reserve vanished. There was a wood above Gincox Farm, south of Oxted, where families usually got a sympathetic welcome from Marjorie Dixon, the farmer's wife. Derby Smith's daughter Minty would stop there sometimes, with her husband Frank Smith; then her younger sister Amy, with her husband

Nelson (Lightfoot) Smith; and finally, in around 1937, when news had got round that this was a good place, a whole throng of Smiths – all the rest of Derby's children. Eliza Cooper was their mother, but she was dead, so they had to look after each other. 'They found my kitchen uninhabited, and so started buzzing round my back door like a lot of wasps around the jam cupboard, all anxious to talk, to tell me about themselves and their relationships, under the pretext of fetching water.'

Levi, at sixteen, was the eldest, but Levi 'laid about him too much with those fine eyes of his. He was too plausible.' It was Levi who, hearing that Marjorie was after Gypsy tunes, sang her an old traditional ballad about a broken-down vardo, waiting patiently while she picked out the notes on the piano, only for her to find later on, showing off her knowledge of the music of the roads, that she'd been taught the latest Country and Western number 'The Wheel of the Waggon is Broken'.

Next came Jasper, just turned fourteen. 'His looks were arresting, mainly I think on account of his expression, which was at once sensitive and bold . . . a shyer bird than the others.' Rachel, aged twelve, 'has amber-brown eyes and a mass of thick, almost blue-black hair that just clears her shoulder-tops as she moves in the dance that is her passion': she and the two Stockin girls would form a circle outside the door to dance the Cockadilly, which the books call Cock o' the North. Little Reuben and Aaron filled up the numbers of the family.[83]

Confident, outgoing and inquisitive, the Smiths seemed ready to take on any challenge. And yet these same qualities were crushed out of Gypsy children as soon as they set foot in school. By the time they found their way into the educational system, they would be older than the infants, but only just beginning to learn their letters, so they either sat with the little children and felt insulted, or with the older ones and felt left out. Used to an outdoor life, they found it hard to sit down and stay at a desk. They were quick enough with tools, but had never tried handling a pencil, and had to learn the knack of this before they could begin with anything else. And they were quick with their fists, too; it took time to learn that disputes could not be settled at school in the same rough and ready way that they were in the field.[84]

Section 118 of the Children's Act of 1908 had made provisions for Gypsy children attending school. Next year, the Home Office printed a leaflet, 'Warning to Parents', to be distributed to all itinerants as a reminder of their duties under this Act. Some of the gavvers had evidently backed up these meaningless bits of paper with an explanation of the new law, for in the spring of 1910 several families arrived at school, only to be excluded 'in fairness to the other children'. What this meant, as is evident from petitions coming from Shere and Kingston, was that gorjer parents refused to let their offspring associate with Gypsies, and were forcing the hand of the school boards.[85] At Holmbury St Mary the parents crowded into a managers' meeting, demanding that the Gypsies be turned away from school – law or no law.[86] In the autumn of 1910, after hopping time, three girls turned up for school at Ewell. After some dithering their names were put down in the register. Next year they were back again, but this time the headmaster had been told by the school managers to exclude them, and although the girls' parents turned up and demanded admittance for them, they were sent away.[87]

In districts where there were large numbers of children to be accommodated, the managers might provide separate schooling. This was done at Send School in 1910, when Ethel Read was appointed Supplementary Teacher in charge of the Gypsies. She ran a separate class for 31 children in the old Technical Room, a galvanized shed on the far side of the playground. The standard curriculum of reading, writing and arithmetic was supplemented by history and scripture, drill and organized games: a programme which, they hoped, would turn unruly chavvies into little citizens.[88]

The problem of educational provision was at its most acute where relations between Gypsy and gorjer were bad, and they were very bad on the Hurtwood. The community had settled there in large numbers, and there was no love lost between them and the locals. Whenever pheasants had been poached, landowners would send round police to rip down the benders and throw people out into the cold. In return, the Gypsies would retaliate by strewing the path of the gentlemen's motor cars with broken bottles. Only a few people tried to build up some trust between the opposing sides, among them a Nonconformist minister who used to come up the hill from Cranleigh on Sundays, with a pocketful of sweets and oranges to tempt out the children, saying 'Jesus loves you.' He said it over and over again, which was rather limited from an educational point of view, but it broke the ice.[89]

As the summer of 1921 drew to an end, the people on the Hurtwood held a meeting, evidently planned in advance since it was attended by someone who could write the sort of wording that local authorities like. At the end of it they had drafted a formal resolution, duly sent to Hambledon Rural Council: 'That this meeting of gipsies will welcome legislation to provide properly arranged encampments, with water and sanitary arrangements, and, in addition, to provide for the education of our children.'[90]

The proposal came at the right time: now that the war was over, the county council was trapped once again between the national demand to educate traveller children, and the sullen local resistance against it. An independent Gypsy school would show that something was being done. Besides, Reginald Bray was prepared to give them his backing. As lord of the manor of Shere, he had spent a dozen years opposing the people who stopped on his land, with so little success that he was now prepared to try anything, even benevolence. For the first time, he gave some security to the settlement, allowing up to one hundred families to stay on payment of a 5s licence, as long as they behaved themselves and left no rubbish. At the edge of Winterfold Heath, in the heart of the wild land, builders were paid £240 to fit up a long schoolhouse of galvanized sheet metal.[91]

Now Surrey Education Committee advertised for a schoolmaster. They were looking for someone unconventional who wanted a job free of red tape, and Stanley Milner was just the man. A former member of Lord George Sanger's circus, he was now in Tolworth but was ready to move on site if the council could supply him with a waggon. A representative was hastily dispatched to Winchester, where they picked one up for £174. Stanley spent the winter months tramping up to the Hurtwood to meet people. It was not a good time to make contact: the police had just moved on 27 waggons from the woods, and men were ready to set their dogs on any suspicious stranger. Stanley bought a pair of dog-proof gaiters and

Hurtwood Gypsy
School, 1926.

carried on.[92] Meanwhile the school building was being prepared for use, and the managers needed a caretaker. By luck or judgement they chose a Gypsy woman, Phoebe Fagence. Phoebe was the daughter of Philip Roberts and Annie Hoadley, had grown up in a bender off North Park Lane in Godstone, and was well-known on the Hurtwood.[93]

And then, in January 1926, came the first day of school. The children clustered in twos and threes behind the trees that skirted the clearing, uncertain what was going to happen. First one and then another came closer, until only a few stragglers were left. Standing at the door, Phoebe gave the Romany *jota*, and as she finished whistling the last few ran inside. She had dressed up for the occasion, in a white starched pinna and the heavy jewellery she wore on fair days. The children relaxed when they saw she was around; and while she made tea, cut bread and butter, and chainsmoked, Stanley began talking to them. It wasn't easy to understand him, because he spoke posh, but he was learning to rokker. There were 25 boys and 12 girls in all, and after a tussle with letters and numbers, the children settled down to drawing, which they were good at, and plaiting reed baskets, which must have been familiar enough.[94]

By Easter the roll had built up to sixty or seventy children. They were smart enough – they could tell anyone what the change was from a £1 note at once – but it was getting them to put figures down on paper that was the challenge. When it came to nature study, they were well ahead of their teacher; they knew the names of every animal, and how to catch it too, but they had never before articulated what they knew. The children loved having something to do, and new things to learn, for until now the Hurtwood had been their whole world, and everything outside it was news to them. As they got used to school, they fought less and played more, although it took a while to get the hang of football. At the first match, Stanley lined up the boys and threw in the ball, only to see it disappear from view in a huge scrimmage. A few minutes later one boy emerged from the mass, his face scratched, his clothes even more torn than usual. 'There it is, Sir,' he said, running up with the flattened ball, 'I got it.'[95]

The school was to be a place for everyone, not just for children, and socials were held on Saturday nights. At the first of these the community turned up in force:

There were swarthy grandfathers smoking clay pipes, with grandsons of eight or nine years old puffing at cigarettes. Young girls came in hats and costumes fashionable 20 years ago. All the children under six months old were tied with string to chairs round the stove and exhorted to keep quiet while their mothers sang duets and danced to the accompaniment of an accordion. Romany songs and quaint step dances of the gipsies were sandwiched in between classical songs by London artists. The star turn of the evening was Mrs. Fageance, the caretaker of the school, who did some whirlwind dancing to the accompaniment of bones and a great stamping of feet.[96]

That was a special occasion, but the regular evening classes attracted almost as many people, with about sixty adults attending in the first few months. They took place on four nights a week, with reading, writing and maths on Monday, and on Tuesday the crafts – woodwork, basket-weaving and rug-making. On Friday the women came for needlework. And Thursday was for geography, history and citizenship. This part of the curriculum, unlike the rest, was dictated by the outside sponsors of the project, who had their own agenda. One topic was the work of the policeman, something about which the Gypsies were no doubt better informed than their teachers; and Stanley was required to explain the regulations imposed on people by a local committee of landowners, the bluntly named Hurtwood Control.

For, in the end, however popular and inspiring he might be, Stanley was on the side of the gorjers. He wanted the Gypsies to live in houses, to follow rules, to send their children to ordinary schools; the education which he had done so much to promote was not intended to make them more competent in their own world, but to bring them as subordinates into the mainstream. Eight girls had left the settlement and gone into domestic service, and that was the kind of thing he counted as success.

In 1932 the school was still going strong, and there were plans to add tinsmithing to the range of crafts. About 35 children were on the roll, with one class of infants and one of the older children. Frank Smith liked school better than holidays, because it opened up new worlds to him; at eleven, he was getting the hang of reading. There were lessons in woodcarving and fretwork, useful stuff which would earn the respect of a Gypsy boy. William Fagence had painted a rocking horse and then cut and shaped a leather saddle for him.[97]

But the days of the school were numbered. Local landowners, banded together as the Gypsy Nuisance Committee, had welcomed its arrival with enthusiasm, not because they thought that children would come to it, but because they were sure that they would not. When it turned out that, far from fleeing the district to get away from education, the community were taking every advantage of it, the committee changed its tune. Some sixty families had applied for one of the new licences, so they could stop in the area and have their children taught, and 58 of them were turned away. In 1926 there had been 260 Gypsies on the Hurtwood; in 1933 there were 60, and the school roll was down to 19. It was no longer viable.[98]

Around this time the county council was developing a school at Walton on Thames, and although this was 16 miles from the Hurtwood and in a quite different kind of country, it made sense to the bureaucratic mind to transfer the children there. The galvanized building went first; Stanley took up the headmastership of East Walton School; and the families were to follow. Six bungalows were built for them by charitable subscription, and the whole community was resettled there, like it or not. At least, the sixty adults with dependent children were; a further twenty adults were simply thrown out. On the night of their departure, they held a symbolic funeral in which the old tents were set on fire, blazing against the black silhouettes of the pines and the darkening night sky. Shrewdly, the Gypsies had invited a film crew to record the last moments of the settlement.[99]

During the years of comparative stability, people on the Hurtwood had pioneered a kind of tent not seen elsewhere, using a house-shaped frame with upright walls and a pitched roof made of pallets. These stood about 10 feet high, and were clad with fabric and blankets in the usual way. This was one of many new styles which had become available after 1918, when the market was flooded with surplus military tents. Traditional benders were still common, but they were no longer the standard form of accommodation. And many more people now had waggons of their own.

This was because new vehicles were being made faster than old ones were lost; with care, a waggon would last a generation, but the big wheelwrights were turning out three or four a year. That left a lot of second-hand vans making their way down the chain of supply. The waggons seen at the 1921 Derby (about one hundred of them) 'ranged from quite luxurious homes, in which were snowy white curtains and elegant parlour furniture and up-to-date cooking utensils, to lumbering old vehicles with leaking roofs and scanty fittings'.[100]

And the continual dealing and chopping of old vehicles had begun to create a national market, in which the styles of north and south were

Families on Arbrook Common, *c.* 1910.

mingled together. Traditionally, Gypsies of the south and east had travelled in wooden-roofed waggons of the two main types, Reading and
Burton. People in the north country favoured a quite different design,
the bowtop; this dispensed with side walls and roof altogether, replacing
them with canvas stretched over curved ribs. It was a design well suited to
steep hills and rough roads. A canvas waggon was safer than a wooden one
if it overturned, and it was less likely to spill anyway because the centre of
gravity was lower. Because it was lighter, it could be pulled by a smaller,
cheaper horse; whereas a medium-size wooden-roofed van would require a
vanner of 15½ hands, a small bowtop could get by with one of 14 hands.[101]

The first appearance of a bowtop in Surrey seems to have been on
Arbrook Common in 1904, and by 1929 they were quite common on
Epsom Downs.[102] Later they were supplemented by a cheaper version,
the openlot, which dispensed with the front wall and door. Instead, it
had a rounded opening braced by two upright poles and left open in the
daytime, being closed up by a canvas sheet at night. The openlot may
originally have been an Irish design, and certainly with its lack of insulation it seems suited to a country of mild winters. The first one to be

seen at Epsom arrived in 1936, and was lined out in scrollwork.[103] This was distinctive at a time when very little painted decoration was to be seen on wooden-roofed waggons, which relied instead on a richness of carved ornament.

The range of cheap waggons was completed by the square bow or Dorset type, which was built like a bowtop except that the canvas was tacked around a square frame, so that there were upright walls and a roof. The square bow had its defects, principally in the roof, which tended to sag until it collected a pool of rainwater that eventually made its way inside. Some of these waggons were sturdily made, but they were never worth ornamenting.[104] And some were very scruffy indeed. However limited his experience, a country carpenter would be asked to frame together something that would stand on the underworks of a trolley. Others look like peg-knife waggons, knocked up by Gypsies themselves from whatever was cheap and available.

The different grades of status and substance among the community were as important as ever, and they were increasingly likely to be expressed in vehicles and outfit. It was in the 1930s, during Derby week, that one of the Smiths ran away with a Mitchell boy, and the two fathers came together to sort things out. It was suggested, in a friendly way to be sure, that the Smiths were a bit of a poverty breed and had no business to be associating with older and better families. Just then some new waggons came up over the hill to the stopping place. Three Readings, one after the other: heavy vans, each one carved and decorated, bright with paint, shining with gold trim. Both men stopped to look at them, and then the father of the Smith girl turned back. 'That's my foki,' he said. 'And you tell me we're not fit to marry in with you?' The argument was over.[105]

Competing to have the best waggon, people commissioned new designs and ornaments. The first and most obvious of these features was the mollicroft, a raised section for clerestory windows in the roof, which was first seen in 1900, and generally adopted within a few years.[106] Soon every new van had one of these, and the Reading, Burton and ledge styles became collectively known as skylight waggons. The design was already familiar from the roofs of Pullman railway cars, which had been running since the 1860s; like many innovations in Gypsy design, it may have come by way of the showfolk, who adopted mollicrofts some decades earlier.[107]

More distinctively Romany was the use of boarding on waggons, rather than the panels seen on Burtons of the original style. At first the strips had been 6 inches wide, but these were superseded by penny-farthing boards 2 inches wide, or the even narrower penny boarding. There does not seem to have been any structural advantage to this, but the repeated close parallel lines gave a good effect. They were accentuated by inter-rib carvings of leaf sprays and birds. Pierced porch brackets, one of the oldest decorative features of the Gypsy waggon, were emphasized with volutes and sunflower heads or acanthus scrolls. The crown board, supporting the roof above the waggon door, was another favourite place for display. Its carving would consist of leaf scrolls on either side of a central motif, usually a horse's head.[108]

Even those who could not afford these elaborate carvings wanted to keep up. A waggon on Epsom Downs was occupied by the 'only original famous Gypsy Lee' – so she said – who shared it with two sisters, Pashey Cooper and Uni Pidgley. They had improved the crown board with decorative motifs made out of a sort of putty called bomanteek, half-dried and then sculpted into shells and whorls and horseshoes.[109] But then Epsom was a place where people wanted to be seen at their best, where families would meet up and cast an appraising eye on how their relatives had prospered since the last year – or not. For four years from 1915, this tradition was interrupted, since racing was suppressed, and people could no longer stop on the Downs while they were being used for military training.[110] But with the return of peace came the Gypsies.

In April 1919, at the first Spring Meeting since the war, Bill Wingfield – Moocher Wingfield, they called him – was on the Downs. It was a chance to get back to business after the troubled times, and he was pleased to spot a face he knew. This was Alfred Munnings the painter, who had met up with the Wingfields and Gregorys during the hopping season at Binsted and Froyle, six or seven years before, when Moocher was only a lad. Alfred was worth remembering; he paid 2s 6d a session to his models and would stand a round of drinks afterwards. Besides, he was good company; he had an eye for a horse and had lived in his own waggon for a few years among the East Anglian Grays.[111]

They headed over to the Hill, where the waggons had pulled. Moocher's sister Fanny was there, with her husband Alfred Gregory and his sisters Ocean and Comfort. They were joined by Thomas Stevens, who was Comfort's husband, and his sister Clementina, who had married a Loveridge. The men clustered round Alfred, eager to talk horses. Did he want to paint the white mare? Wasn't she a fine animal?[112] All in good time, said the artist: first he needed to prepare some figure sketches.

For the next six years the family saw him, on and off; in September he might be at Binsted, and at Epsom in June. They liked him well enough, although he was always called 'Mr Money' in a half-joking reminder that this was a commercial relationship. He didn't interfere with work, usually doing his sketching in the evening, when the day was over and everyone could relax in the last of the sun. People accepted his presence and tolerated his occasional trips behind a furze bush to take a quick gulp of whisky from his hip flask.[113]

Most of the time, though, he sat and watched, catching people on canvas as they went about their business. Here are Moocher Wingfield and his brother-in-law, graiengros both, leading in a horse with a light, graceful step, or standing in front of one with legs astride and one hand lightly resting on a whip. They stretch out on the grass, resting on one elbow, watching as the younger men put a yearling through its paces. The men are wearing waistcoats and jackets over their white shirts, with a red or black diklo at the neck, and smart wide-brimmed hats.[114] But it was the women who stood out, unforgettable in their race-day splendour. Alfred came away with a confused impression of 'large, black, ostrich-plumed hats, black ringlets, big ear-rings', and a friend of his, cajoled into a visit to the Downs, confirmed it. 'Not Solomon in all his glory was arrayed like some of the old gypsy ladies I saw on Derby Day . . . Such yellows and purples, red and greens, festoons of beads and braids, I have never seen better bestowed.'[115] The most patient among Alfred's models was Comfort Gregory, who stood again and again in a favourite pose, hands on hip, her left profile seen under the tall, plumed hat. Her bodice might be pink or blue, always in a bright colour, with a matching skirt under a black pinna, or sometimes a black skirt belted under a pinna that matched the blouse. She liked shawls, at first slender black ones that matched the ostrich-feather hat, and later an elaborate rose pattern with long yellow fringe, tied at the neck with a round gold brooch. Comfort's sister Ocean preferred much larger shawls or blankets with floral patterns. The younger women wore the same colourful combinations of blouse and skirt but had given up the grand hats of the older generation, sometimes tying a handkerchief around their heads in a style which looked convincingly Gypsy but was also favoured by their gorjer contemporaries.[116]

Unmarried girls often went without hats, the better to show off their sleek black hair. Elizabeth, Clementina Loveridge's girl, strode onto the Downs in an orange skirt fringed with black, a white blouse and a scarf round her neck to match the dress. Like most of his models, she kept in touch with Alfred and wrote to him, many years later:

> Thank you very much for the ten shillings, and I bought myself a blouse. In the remembrance of you it's an orange colour, what you said always suited my colour, but I have not got my hair bobbed, as the women nowadays you can't tell from men. Dear Mr. Money, do you paint now, as if ever I go to London I should like to see your drawings as the colourings looks very nice on our little one . . . With all good wishes and good luck from your friend, Gipsy Nell – X (Please excuse the kiss, that's only my way).[117]

Alfred had painted people as they wanted to be seen – colourful, confident, standing among their gilded waggons with fine horses and lean dogs. But other gorjers did not view things in quite that way. Even in this golden summer of Gypsy culture at Epsom, there were plans to banish people entirely from the Downs. From 1929 to 1937, the authorities on the racecourse would mount a campaign intended to clear stopping places which had been used before even the first Derby was run. They would not have been able to do this if it had not been for a major development of the inter-war years: the growing obsession of officialdom with the harassment of Gypsies.

7

The End of the Road:
Post-War Britain

The road through Salfords was familiar to anyone travelling out of Surrey into Sussex: not the main highway down from Reigate, but the quiet lane which ran past familiar stopping places at Nunlands and Masons Bridge Road, Picketts Lane and Horley Arches and Tapners Barn. At each of these places there was a slip of land, not much but enough for a few waggons to pull on, places where you might peg the horses out to graze and gather wood for the fire while the children slept.

That was if you could avoid the attentions of PC Bluenose. This was not his real name, of course, but a nickname given to him by the Gypsies who passed through his district, because he was so often drunk. When tanked up, he would go out to find a family who had pulled on in his district. Maybe they would be just beginning to boil something for supper, but so much the worse; he'd go up to the fire and kick the pot over, and as it dribbled onto the sodden wood, he'd call the men out to a fight. If they won, they got to stay. If they lost, they had to move on. Bluenose, who had little else to occupy his time, kept a diary which records that, between 1934 and 1936, during the 26 months that he was at Salfords, he dealt on 114 occasions with 68 different Gypsies passing through. His actions can't have been much of a deterrent, since the same people kept coming back again, sometimes as often as twelve times. Derby Smith was there with his daughter Minty; Patsy Chapman and his wife Pacie Sandhurst; Fred Fuller from Mitcham with Daniel Jones and Jack Eastwood; Tom Harber with his son young Tom, accompanied by Jack Harber from Reigate; and Bill Whitehair Smith.[1] They all came and went down the lanes as part of a circuit which could take them as far west as Ash and Guildford, and eastwards into Kent.

Each time they took the road down to Crawley, they were at risk of police harassment, but that was routine. To see a pot of food kicked over before the eyes of hungry children, to watch as rods and cloths of a bender were ripped apart, to have your waggon broken into at night and be thrown out of bed: these had become part of the normal hardships of the travelling life. It took a lot to rouse Gypsy resistance, like that of Minty's husband Frank:

> Me granddad was sitting around the yog and the gavver run there and kicked the fire so the firebrands went all over me granddad Frank and burnt him. Me granddad jumped up, even though he was in pain he had it in he's mind to hit the gavver so rushed at the gavver, but me granny rushed in front of him and so did a couple of the older boys (me dad's brothers), as they were holding him the gavver was tormenting me granddad saying 'Come on gyppo hit me, then you will go down for a very long time' to which me granddad shouted back 'I'd do life for you, my mother's cunt', me granny was screaming and the chavvies was crying, and me granny was begging to me granddad to stop cus he would be took away.[2]

This growing aggression by police was a new development of the 1930s. It was not based on any new laws – the canon of anti-Gypsy legislation had been substantially completed by the beginning of the twentieth century – but on consistent, grinding enforcement of those which already existed. Fines were graded by the length of time that a family had stopped in some forbidden place. A gavver would watch the arrival of a Gypsy family, leaving them alone for days, perhaps weeks, until the accumulated fine had reached £10 or more, and then he would serve his summons. They were just like herons, White Will Smith said, when they stand motionless by the waterside waiting for the fattest fish, and then pounce.[3] At Salfords, a small village with no noticeable criminal tendencies, the harassment of Gypsies was the main justification for having a police officer at all. This was exactly the situation that Mowbray Sant had resisted until his retirement as Chief Constable in 1930. The police force was not being allowed to concentrate on crime in the ordinary sense of the word; instead, it had been co-opted as the agent of a policy aimed at wiping the land clean of Gypsies altogether.

As soon as people came into contact with authority, they were at risk. The Devalls were making their way through Croydon in 1939 when they lost touch with each other. Dora had gone out with the two younger children while George rode ahead with the eldest boy; he turned a corner, and when she looked for signs of his passage, they had all blown away. Dora, left on her own, had nothing to sell and no food on her, so she picked up the little one and started to mong for money to get them all supper. But her luck was out; the only bystander to take any notice was a plain-clothes officer, and she was marched off to the police station and committed for begging. After a night in the cells, they took her to a magistrate and set a fine of £2, with the threat of a month's imprisonment if she didn't pay: which, having no money, she couldn't. Dora burst into tears and asked to be allowed to go to her husband and collect the money. It took a while for the court to realize that she would have to do this on her own, as no one else would be able to trace his path, but in the end they trusted her. The police took her out of town past Addington and she picked up the patrins that George had left. Here was a clump of grass thrown down on one side at a fork in the road; there was a mark in the verge. She set off at a brisk walk, and in about half an hour she had caught up with him at Tatsfield. The next day he drove her back in the town and paid the fine, to the surprise of the magistrates, who had not expected Gypsy honesty. It sounds like a happy ending (less the £2) but the court thought otherwise. They took away Dora's little girl and put her into care; and they sent the eldest son off to a farm school, to turn him into a gorjer; so that out of all the Devalls' family, only one child survived.[4]

Hostility to Gypsies began with changes in local government, as power passed from landowners and lords of manors to elected county and district councils. Landowners had at least been a mixed group, some hostile to travelling people and others more tolerant, while a few such as Reginald Bray were capable of reversing their policy in the light of experience and common sense. But councils were elected on a programme of social reform in planning, education and public health. Since Gypsies often offended against one of these ideals, and usually all of them at once, harassment of the community was the cheapest short-term solution. No doubt they would eventually go somewhere else.

But what if there was nowhere to go? Commons, which had been the preferred stopping places for previous generations, were gradually being closed off as their management passed from manorial bailiffs to local committees. In 1929 a total of 642 vans and 283 benders were moved off Horsell Common, just outside Woking, along with 718 horses (and seven donkeys, for the more traditionally minded).[5] So many evictions took place – over 3,000 people, or about fifteen families a week – that they must have repeatedly targetted the same individuals, as at Salfords. Gypsies were not camping on the roadside out of choice, but because all other open spaces were being systematically closed off.

There were problems even at Chobham Common, where people had always gathered in the weeks before Ascot. They would pull on, tether the horses out to graze, and go picking bundles of white heather to take on the course and sell to racegoers who needed a charm to turn around their chances. After a good day's trading everyone would come back and celebrate in Chobham pubs. This was all received in good humour by the locals who, like most heath dwellers, could understand the Gypsy lifestyle, and felt there was room on the common for all.[6] But Chobham Parish Council was less tolerant, and in 1935 they took action against the seventeen or so waggons which had remained on the common through-out the winter. One family was keeping kannies in a long poultry run, another had planted a vegetable patch; several installed wireless masts so that they could listen to dance music from the Light Programme. What with that, and the stories told round the fire, and the excitement of prac-tice fights, life was good, but it ended in March when the gavvers arrived and told everyone to leave within 24 hours. Only Richelda Bagley defied their order, sitting beside her battered trolley in a ring of dying fires.[7]

Next year the Chobham Commons Preservation Committee voted on whether to allow pitches during Ascot week. After a heated argument as to whether it was either prudent or ethical to evict people from their customary site, they took advice from the police, who reported that they now had the powers to deal with unauthorized encampments; so in June the committee decided unanimously to prohibit Gypsies from stopping on the common at any time.[8]

At Epsom things remained under the even-handed administration of George Oakshott until 1926, when the Epsom Grand Stand Association bought the manorial rights over the Downs. The association had little sympathy with Gypsies. It was a commercial body, run for those who wanted to view the racing from a privileged enclosure, and not for the wider interest; as seen from the grandstand, the teeming life of crowds on the Hill was little more than a nuisance. In 1929 the association made its first move against anyone pulling onto the Downs. They had hired one of the new motorized tractors, which proved very effective at haul-ing waggons off the Bushes and onto the road. Then it became clear that the Gypsies' horses were just as good at pulling them back again. Some

Threatened off
Epsom Downs, 1929.

people took the wheels off their waggons, and one bold spirit lay down under the shafts and shouted, 'Now move it, if you like.' Five people were brought before the magistrates, but the association had a weak case in law, and the defendants were simply bound over to keep the peace.[9] William Shoebridge and young William, William Vinson, William Stacey and Dolly Smith returned to a hero's welcome on the Downs. 'This is our home,' said William Shoebridge. 'We belong here.'[10]

If Gypsies had rights at law, then it was time for the law to be changed. The association worked slowly with parliamentary draftsmen to prepare an Epsom and Walton Downs Regulation Act, which was passed in 1936 and became law the next year. The Act scrupulously refrained from using the word 'Gypsy' but since it prohibited vans, tents, fires and sleeping out on the Downs, there was not much doubt about who was meant. A body of conservators, established under the provisions of the Act, announced that they would prevent people from occupying the Downs for the Spring Meeting in April.[11] The tractor was brought back out of retirement and a team of sweating employees spent the day moving waggons. Each one was taken exactly 3 feet over the bounds of the conservators' land before they turned to the next; then people would move them back; and this went on all day until at last the meeting was over.[12]

As the Derby approached, it was clear that there was going to be a confrontation. The Gypsies were gathering in increasing numbers, while the conservators stuck to their policy. Lord Derby asked them to back down a little, as did Lord Ebbisham, Lady Eleanor Smith, the vicar of Epsom, and fifty academics from the Gypsy Lore Society, but this roll call of the respectable had no effect.[13] The Epsom Grand Stand Association had spent ten years planning for this moment, and they were not going to lose their victory. Then, at the last minute, a solution was found. Lady Sybil Grant, the owner of the Durdans estate on the Epsom side of the Downs, opened a field and invited people to pull on.

> Within five minutes the gaily painted caravans had joyfully rum-
> bled in. Children swarmed about, dogs were unleashed, horses
> rolled in the deep grass, and great-great-grandmother Collins,
> with her gold earrings, gold brooch and a thick gold ring on every
> finger, was squatting on a bundle in the sun. 'God will reward
> her ladyship.'[14]

For eleven days, the Paddock served as an improvised Gypsy site. Some 83 waggons made use of it, with 115 horses at graze. On Sunday the company finally pulled off, after gathering up all the rubbish and putting it on a fire under the eyes of the police. At the gate each waggon was handed a card, signed by Lady Sybil, to thank them for keeping the site in an orderly fashion. The numbers leaving were larger than those who arrived, for Lena Cooper had a new baby, and so did one of the Matthews.[15]

Gypsies would remember Lady Sybil with gratitude for years to come, but her bold action had not solved the problem. Indeed, it showed how little could be achieved any longer through the politics of patronage, even in traditional-minded Surrey: she was a prime minister's daughter, but her intercession had counted for nothing with the professionals who ran the association. Next year a group of twelve Gypsies took up the challenge; they had all stopped at the Paddock in 1937 and now, with Sybil as an intermediary, they briefed a solicitor to present their case. Bill Smith, Alf Hoadley, Will Marney, Fred Baker, Joe Fuller and Henry Harber, with other Smiths, Hoadleys and a Vinson, all agreed to pay £1 for twelve days' pitch on the Downs, exclusive of horse grazing. They would give details of names and trades, place themselves under police supervision and offer an undertaking of good conduct. That seemed fair, but not to the conservators, who turned them down.[16] People turned up anyway, with up to a hundred vehicles lodged at stopping places a mile or two from the

Gathering in Lady Sybil's field, 1937.

Downs. The mood was rebellious, and one spokesman announced plans for a protest march which would stop the day altogether. 'We shall go in procession past the grandstand with our horses, our trailers and our vans, a mile and a half of us. If we start at 10am we shall be moving slowly right through the race traffic until 4pm.'[17] Nothing came of this, but it showed the way in which things were developing. Far from banishing the Gypsies, the conservators' hostility had aroused a new sense of purpose among the community. In future people would not rely on luck or the caprice of the well-to-do to protect their interests at the one great meeting of the year: the Romany were beginning to organize themselves.

But effective combination lay a long way in the future, and meanwhile everyone, Gypsy and gorjer, faced a more pressing threat. The 1939 Derby was run in the last summer of peace, and for the next six years there would be no time for such frivolities as horse-racing. Britain entered the Second World War with a policy of total mobilization in which civilians, and not just soldiers, were to be counted and sorted and set to whatever work was needed for the war effort. Public support for this policy was enlisted by posters, songs, films and broadcasts, all of them reminding people that this was a united cause, that hardships and burdens were fairly shared, and that anyone who relapsed into selfishness or idleness was betraying the efforts made by everybody else.

This was all very well for house dwellers, who were literate enough to read the posters, knew how to tune in to the broadcasts and had grown up thinking of themselves as part of the national 'we'. But the view from the road was less indulgent. Suddenly, after twenty years of intensified harassment, the gorjer State had changed its tune and was asking Gypsies to join the labour force in order to bring Britain to victory. Could it be trusted?

In practice there was no alternative. The government had carried out a national registration of all citizens in September 1939, undertaken by the team who usually did the census, and who were therefore used to counting Gypsies. This latest interference by authority was not welcome:

> The gorjers are a-trying to drive we Romanies off the drom and
> off the face of the earth. Pushing we here, a-driving we off there,
> plaguing we with identity cards and ration books, but this I knows
> and all we travellers knows, there's bin travellers since the beginning
> of the world and there'll still be travellers at the world ending.[18]

Other impositions were equally unpopular. At Ash, where the school had a high population of Gypsy children, gas masks were issued in the usual way to all pupils, with extra steel helmets for the teachers. The chavvies were impatient at the routine of air raid drill and nearly went berserk when forced to wear the gas masks; they were not used to restraint of any kind.[19]

But for all the muttering and resistance, families had to accept war-time regulations, for life was impossible without them. 'We've got enough to eat,' said Dora Devall, 'and, what's more, we've got ration cards too.'[20] The registration scheme had uses beyond the food supply, since it formed a clear base for conscription. The government knew who its young men were, and where and when they could be issued with call-up papers. The last war was still fresh in memory, and some men were enlisting for the second time. Walter Doe, who had been a boy signaller with the Royal Navy in 1918, returned to war, this time as a soldier.[21] For others, going into uniform was part of growing up. Jasper Smith, no longer one of the crowd of Gypsy children but a tall young man of eighteen, called in at the back door of Gincox Farm to say goodbye as he left to join the army.[22]

As the conflict spread, it swept up whole families and scattered them across the world. 'I had nine in the war,' said Ada Smith of Croydon, 'and they all came home . . . They used to write to me and the lady in the post office, she was kind and kept my letters. Sometimes I walked nine and ten miles to get them.' Distance had its advantages. One of Ada's boys was posted to India, and when they told him he could go home for a holiday, he said no, if he went back the temptation to desert would be too strong and he knew well enough how to hide; he was better staying where he was.[23]

The war took young men away from everything they had known, but it also gave them access to education and a new kind of self-respect. And, perhaps for the first time, those skills were being brought back on furlough by men who were proud of being Gypsies and had earned the right to say so. 'I am a full-blooded Romany who has followed my people's way of life since my birth,' wrote Isaac Pinder, Sgt A/G, RAF, from his stopping place at West Byfleet, in protest against some racist letter to the newspapers. 'The vast majority of young Romanies are serving in the armed forces of the nation – as would be expected of a people noted for its sturdy independence – in the fight against Hitlerite slavery.'[24]

As yet, the full truth about Nazism was not suspected, because it was hardly believable. Vanslow Cooper, Matty's great-grandson, was in the Royal Engineers during the Dunkirk evacuation. He was detailed to drive to bridges and set explosives under them; then after letting any civilians cross, he would blow up the bridge to impede the advancing German army. On one occasion he noticed that the last group to cross the bridge were dark people, so he went and spoke to them. '*Romani tu shan?*' Yes, they were Gypsies; he and they could just about understand each other. The old mother of the group waved in the distance – did he know who was coming? 'Watch out!' she said – Germans – Gypsies – and then, eloquently, ran two fingers across her throat.[25] But knowledge of the Nazi genocide of the Roma had hardly grazed the consciousness of anyone in England. Gypsies enlisted as part of a national struggle for British freedom, not to save their own people overseas.

Military service was the easy part. Once a young man was in the army, his future was mapped out for him, while civilians needed continual chivvying and encouragement if they were to take their place on the home front. Bureaucracy was not the answer, since Gypsies had a well-earned mistrust of anyone who arrived at an encampment with clipboard and regulations; instead, the gap was filled by cultural intermediaries, who understood what the government wanted and were prepared to put it over to people in their own terms. This was a role that came naturally to lay preachers. They had a double fluency in the literate and oral worlds, and their mission gave them the sort of moral authority which did not always grace policemen or planning officers.

Ernest Williams was an evangelist at Marden, preaching under the conventional soubriquet of Gypsy Williams; but unlike his precursors Rodney Smith or John Hawkins, he was bringing the gospel to other Gypsies and not to gorjers.[26] At the outbreak of war, Ernest was put down for fire-spotting on a factory roof, but he wanted something more demanding than that; a trip to London brought him to the attention of the Minister of Labour, who liked the young man's enthusiasm and in 1943 had him issued with a bicycle and a roving commission to enlist the Romany. He rode everywhere on that treader, 370 miles a month, stopping wherever he saw a wisp of smoke, talking to people about the crisis of the nation.

> Williams found one family who didn't even know there was a war on. 'Do you not see the papers?' Williams asked. They explained they were unable to read. 'Have you not noticed anything un-usual?' The head of the family said that they never went near the towns but that they had noticed a lot of flying machines and some loud noises. At the end of the conversation, four sons volunteered for the forces and subsequently went into the Commandos.[27]

More importantly, Ernest brought whole families into the war effort by enlisting them as casual labour on the land. He knew where people were, and he was in touch with the agricultural committees who needed help in gathering the crops. 'Farmers need have no fears of being burdened with Gypsies when the work is completed,' he added brightly. 'They just notify me, and I can arrange for the Gypsies to go on to someone else.'[28]

As this suggests, wartime conditions had not abolished the mistrust felt by gorjers for Gypsies. It was simply pushed out of sight by the need for hands to bring in the harvest, pick fruit and vegetables, fell and thin and transport timber. To be fair, some employers had a legacy of mutual respect. Heath Farm in Send supplied peas, raspberries and other perishable produce to Covent Garden, and the farmer had always employed Gypsies. When the war came, he helped by building huts as makeshift accommodation, from which people set out to work in the fields alongside land girls and prisoners of war.[29] Women, foreigners, Gypsies, deserters – farmers and foresters would accept pretty much anyone who would turn up and lend a hand, no questions asked.

This put the community in a good bargaining position. Patriotism aside, the war was like a year-long harvest, with continuous demand for semi-skilled casual labour. Deft Gypsy fingers, used to working all day at hop-picking, quickly adjusted to making munitions. Emily Smith, Jasper's younger sister, worked in the factory at the Royal Arsenal in Woolwich.[30] 'In Britain our Gypsies were to be found in all the fighting Services, working in munition factories and on the road, and generally playing their part in the national effort. Few were left to travel the roads.'[31]

No doubt the recruitment that Ernest Williams promised to the Ministry of Labour would have happened anyway, as people took advantage of the opportunities for work opened up by the war. But the real effect of his mission lay elsewhere. He was doing what comes naturally to a preacher: telling a story, or rather, since he was bilingual, two stories. To the Gypsies, he gave reassurance that they were not just enduring the war like any other calamity but participating in a national work of effort and sacrifice. And at the same time, he was telling the gorjers that Gypsies had done their bit in the great struggle, that the community were helping victory and should, when it came, be treated with the same fairness as other citizens.

That seemed a long way off, and meanwhile everyone had to struggle with the hardships of wartime life: blackouts, shortages and air raids.

Ernest Williams
spreading the
message, 1944.

Frank and Minty Smith were asleep one night, snug in the bed of the waggon with the girls and little Levy. Jasper was on leave then, and had come to see his sister, so he was sleeping under the waggon with the boys.

> When the sirens started to go off, they all jumped up and started to run to the shelter, me granddad and Jasper carrying some of the smaller children and me granny carrying me dad in his blanket. As they were running me granny dropped me dad out of the blanket but was so afraid she just kept running. When she reached the shelter and me uncle Jasper asked her where me dad was, me granny started screaming he was outside. By this time bombs were dropping and they could hear them going off, but me uncle Jasper, without a second thought of his own safety, run out to get me dad and bring him back to the shelter . . . Next morning when they came out of the shelter, right where my dad had lay, a bomb had hit.[32]

But when peace came, these memories of brave deeds carried very little weight. Newly demobbed, Jasper spoke to a stranger as he walked by his horse down a lane at Lingfield. 'I fights for this country, Sir, in the war, and what does I return to? Sure as God's in heaven, it's always "Move along!" from the gavver.' And even as he was speaking, a police car slowed down beside the waggon and shouted at its occupants to shift.[33]

When Nelson Doe returned from the war, he and his wife Dorcas Gregory stopped with their children on land by the Coombe Hill canal in Gloucestershire. This stretch was owned by a decent gorjer woman who let people stay for as long as they needed, but the local authority had them thrown off. Then when Nelson died, Dorcas moved to be with her mother and brother at the Quadrant in Ash Vale. Her waggon was neat and clean, the tent beside it was large and new, there always were strings of washing hung to dry, and the youngest three children were in school, but none of this counted for anything with the rural district council, who didn't like the Quadrant and were determined to clear everyone off it. Then they might go anywhere that they could: that wasn't the council's problem. But to the surprise of the local authority, this ruling was overturned in 1949 by the local magistrate, Robert Haining, who reminded them that the Does had human rights like everyone else, that 'prosecution may nearly approach persecution', and that a decision to evict would incur the responsibility to find new accommodation, not in bricks and mortar, but on a proper site with hard standing, a water pipe and a sanitary block. The news spread like wildfire among people in Ash and all the surrounding district, that a gorjer – and a magistrate, at that – had spoken up for a Gypsy woman's right to live her own life.[34]

That was the exception, though; the war ended, just as it had begun, with Gypsies on the roadside, no nearer being accepted into the nation than before. And six years of shortages had left their mark:

Some folk think a travellers' life is peaches and honey
But they've never known the needies' own way.[35]

White Will Smith and his people were in a hard way when they stopped on Banstead Downs in the 1940s, in a winter so wet it was a desperate business to keep the fire going in frost and rain. You wrapped straw round your legs for insulation, and draped sacks round your shoulders, or newspaper if there were no sacks. The family had been moved on, so there was no stock of dry wood, but a fire could be got going by thrusting sticks wiped with grease into an old car tyre. Rubber stank horribly, but the fierce heat was enough to dry out kindling and clothes. 'Their clothing was true raggle-taggle, their faces pallid and their bodies over-lean from lack of nourishment; their waggons miserable living-places, mostly carts converted into caravans by their own carpentry.'[36] The golden days of waggontime were past, and surviving Burtons or Readings now shared the road with much rougher vehicles rigged up out of tea-chests on trolley underworks.[37]

With wartime restrictions on timber and labour, the big firms could no longer build new waggons, or even maintain those which were in use. If spokes snapped in a wheel, it was hard to find a wheelwright who was competent to replace them, and many people went over to wheels with rubber tyres instead. At least these had some grip, whereas metal tyres tended to slip on the much-used surfaces of the new main roads. The increase in road traffic was a threat to slow-moving convoys of waggons, and a car might easily smack into one simply because the driver couldn't register how slow it was. Things were made worse by the increasing hostility of villagers. Many farriers refused to shoe Gypsy horses, so people had to do it themselves, and take the risk: bad shoeing could lame a horse. And when a family had been forced onto the verge, beside one of the new trunk roads, there was a risk of accidents, like the one that drove Minty Smith into an improvised, passionate lament:

Me brother's horse was killed on the A2 . . .
And that's when the car hit him
And he was all me brother had to make his living with;
He was a smart horse, a real good cart horse –
God, I wish he hadn't tried to cross the road!
Oh dordi, dordi – dik at the gavver, dik at the gavver . . .
Come on chavvies, we'll have to shav off a wavver drom or
    we'll be lelled.[38]

The grai had been a quiet companion of the Romany for so long that it was hard to imagine horsedrawn transport coming to an end. But novelty had its charms. They say that Tenant Buckland was the first to use motorized transport, appearing on Epsom Downs with an American Overland before the First World War, though there was nothing for it to pull except his Reading waggon.[39] Already in the 1920s, families had flirted with the idea of travelling in a converted motor bus.[40] These were soon replaced by the two- or four-wheeled units manufactured by gorjers for the holiday trade. The obsolete word 'caravan' had been revived to describe these, so that there would be no risk of middle-class tourists having their new acquisition confused with a Gypsy van. The Gypsies, just as anxious to avoid getting mixed up with the wrong sort, took to using the alternative name of 'trailer' for their new homes. Anyway, trailer or caravan, these vehicles were first observed at the 1933 Derby. The next year, there were more of them, brightly painted, some costing as much as £250. And 1935 saw 'smart motor caravans rapidly superseding the old-fashioned shoddy horse vehicles'.[41]

The war brought an end to these improvements, as to so much else, but the next generation was primed to give up the horse in favour of something mechanical. When Edmund Brazil married Mary Hilden in 1953, they needed an outfit for travelling together.[42] Money was not in short supply, for Edmund was a good hand at lopping trees, road-mending and gardening, and both of them were young and strong enough for long days of farm work. They needed to cover a wide stretch of country – from Guildford down into Sussex, over to Kent for the hopping, and sometimes up north of the river – and so although they both had been born and raised in waggons, Edmund and Mary bought a trailer. Edmund couldn't read, but he already had a driving licence, most likely arranged for him by a literate relative who knew how to go through the formalities. So they got a motor, with space at the back for an extra table and chairs, the pram, and things like spare tyres which needed to be carried some-where that wouldn't show the dirt. The trailer, by contrast, was gleaming – every surface dressed with polished copper kettles, Crown Derby cups and saucers, and framed photos of the family and their wedding day.

There were many who welcomed the change. Fred Lee of Kingston went over from vans to trailers about the same time, and his daughter Shirley remembered this as a great improvement:

> We could get along the road faster, and leave all our troubles
> behind with the horses. We leave all our worries behind. We'd get
> along quicker. Same places, but we'd get along the road faster.
> And we could park on the car parks in towns, where we'd be in the
> country with the horses, down the road and down the lane sides
> and on pieces of waste commons. But we could go anywhere with
> these. People told us we could park in the car parks in towns, see
> more of the towns.[43]

By 1965 waggons had almost gone out of use in the south of England; there were none to be seen at the 1968 Derby.[44] Prestige had passed from the sleek horse and gilded waggon to their mechanical equivalents, which could be equally ornate. Daisy Boswell, who dukkered on the South Shore at Blackpool, went everywhere in a magnificent Napier saloon and matching trailer, with DB laid out in a gold monogram on each door. She didn't drive it herself, of course – she had a man for that, although every now and then she'd tap him on the shoulder and tell him to stop the car while she levelled her double-barrelled shotgun at some passing pheasant. She was a Romany of the Romany, and on the one occasion that she came down to Epsom, the locals took her for a strange royal lady and didn't recognize her at all as one of their own. One girl even took her hand and began to tell a fortune, artfully dropping in a few words of the old language to add to the mystique. Daisy put up with it for a bit, and then when the poor mort's invention began to flag, she snatched her hand back and cursed the girl, her parents and every relative for five minutes solid in effortlessly fluent Romani.[45]

But Daisy was exceptional: most people ran a motor, not a car. What was the point in having a vehicle which did nothing but move people around? A motor would replace both horse and trolley, since you could load up the back with scrap for trading, heavy tools for work, garden waste for the dump, a crowd of mixed relatives or anything else that needed to be fetched and carried. You had to learn to drive, of course, and to maintain a vehicle; these mechanical skills were more easily picked up by young men, especially those who had seen military service. Often the son learnt to drive, while his father didn't, which meant a subtle shift in the balance of power between generations. Gone were the comfortable days of Leonard Smith:

> He used to stop with his waggon at the bottom of Worldham Hill and wake up about 12 noon. He would get washed and changed into his silk shirt and go into Alton and into the pubs. Leonard would wheel and deal with the other Gypsy men and always had a good deal. Very often he got so drunk the men would throw him into the back of his trolley or cart and his faithful horse would carry him all the way home back to his Gypsy waggon.[46]

That was one old habit that had to be shaken off, but others were carried over into the machine age with little modification. Where a good horse, combed and trimmed, might have been paraded as a sign of his owner's self-confidence, he was now replaced by a gleaming motor. As Jim Penfold said at Battersea:

> The boys like to have a good lorry because it's a good front, you know. When you go to a factory wanting scrap or a job or what- ever it is, it's always good to have a good moulder, a good lorry. The governor comes out and he looks at your lorry and he looks you over and he thinks to himself: Well, at least the boy's got some money in his pocket because he's got a good lorry.[47]

And only the right kind would impress. From 1959 to the 1970s, everyone aspired to a Bedford J-type; when one of these rolled up to the 1965 Derby, it was the envy of those whose opinion was worth having. 'Old Mosey, spruce in panama hat, fall-front trousers, and red braces, a coloured hand-kerchief at his throat, inspected my little Bedford with both admiration and pleasure, noting each and every detail.'[48] Paintwork was an important part of this effect, as it would have been on a waggon, and many decorative motifs were perpetuated from tradition. Bunches of fruit, flowers, horses' heads in a horseshoe were transfer-printed; mascots of horses' heads, or greyhounds, or Native American warriors were fixed at the front; the sides of the motor would be lined out, waggon-style. The fashion for chroming up motors reached its peak in 1961, when one flash traveller had an entire cab made from chrome. It fitted like a hood over the real cab and impressed everyone until 'this magnificent piece of "one-upmanship" led to his being prosecuted. The expanse of chrome was considered dangerous when it dazzled oncoming motorists in sunny weather.'[49]

When Wisdom Penfold pulled on at Chobham Common in the early 1950s, he was the last of his extended family to keep a horse. The efforts of the Preservation Committee to keep this stopping place free of Gypsies had long since been abandoned, and the Penfolds, who had just gone over to motorized transport, arrived with seven trailers. On the far side of the furze bushes were some old-fashioned waggons, and on the opposite side a square bow, with a young man sitting by the fire brewing up. Wisdom got talking to the stranger, who introduced himself as Dominic Reeve: he was born a gorjer, but had just taken to the travelling life, and there was a lucky look about him. So for the next few days they went partners, taking Wisdom's horse and trolley down the back streets of Woking to collect scrap. Two iron bedsteads and an old mangle made a good start; at the end of the day they had thirty hundredweight. Come Saturday, they loaded the week's collection onto the back of a motor, driven by one of Wisdom's brothers, and drove to the scrap yard at Guildford, where the proprietor paid cash out of a black velvet bag, and there was enough left over for a drink at the Rowbarge.[50]

Scrap didn't sell as well as it had during the war, when demand led to the exploitation of some unexpected sources. In 1941 Joby Chapman at Outwood was handed a hacksaw by his father and told to cut up a lion's cage which had been bought the day before at the auction of Sanger's Circus.[51] Several families in the area joined up to buy land at Green Lane, each plot being owned independently. The standings rapidly filled up with old vans, buses which had lost their roadworthiness and various sorts of shed. It formed a useful base for scrap metal collection and log dealing, with piles of materials stacked around the site where the owners could keep an eye on them.[52]

Similar settlements could be found nearer London. At Mitcham, the Victorian terraces north of Homewood Road were neglected after the war, with little attempt to repair the damage caused by air raids. The area went downmarket and the Gypsies moved in. 'Caravans were everywhere, either in licensed yards, where a semblance of order was maintained, or on patches of waste ground.'[53] Wherever there was an odd corner, it would be used by totters to dump scrap metal or rags for sorting. This abundant open land helped people accumulate a stock-in-trade, and there was little risk of it being cleared away. After dark, so it was said, the gavvers would only go in pairs – though given their history of encounters with police, this probably helped residents feel more secure.

Outside Capel the Pharos set up a scrap yard at their house in Marshlands Cottage, but the noise they made hammering and cutting up the metal was too much for the gorjer neighbours, and they were forcibly moved into a council house.[54] Others were more successful, escaping the notice of authority in the general chaos of post-war life. At Send the Roberts family moved into an empty bomb crater, with a mix of vans and shacks to accommodate their growing numbers. The men cut logs and made pegs; the women sold these, and collected rags, but this division of labour was not always respected. Young Mary was a strong girl, and by the time she was fifteen she could heave a sack of logs onto the trolley as easily as her brothers.[55]

But the travelling life continued to be harassed, with people driven off the drom into some kind of settlement. Job Matthews (who was sometimes Job Cooper) married Celia (Ceni) Smith, Jasper's cousin; their summers were spent doing farm work and the winter cutting and splitting logs. They would go up to Wisbech for the fruit harvest and then return to Surrey, but this was increasingly difficult in the post-war years, with the county council evicting people from every place where they stopped. 'The Coopers and Smiths continued to travel the old routes and were constantly fined for camping on waste ground that was serving no useful purpose whatsoever.' In 1951 Job and Ceni sold their waggon and went into brick, in a three-roomed cottage at Ripley. But she couldn't abide the house – it gave her headaches – and they wanted to get back into a waggon again.[56]

The world of new opportunities divided those who had bought motors from those who kept to horses and waggons. The new-style generation had the resources to deal in scrap, tarmacing, roof works and landscaping; those who kept to the old ways were more likely to stick to the traditional crafts. Bill Smith, White Will's son, specialized in making wooden flowers. This skill had been developed over the last generation or two until it became a mark of competence in any Gypsy man who claimed to be handy with a knife. Bill used willow, although it was more common to make them out of elder. Putting a cloth on his knee, and holding a knife steady in his right hand, he pulled the stick back against it so that the bark came off in long strips. Then he carried on using the same action, but this time taking off curls of wood, which bunched up like the petals of a chrysanthemum. Once made, the flowers were dyed in different colours, made from whatever was handy. You could use apple bark for pink, waterlily roots for black, or fern for green, though a little disc of fabric dye would give colours that were brighter and more commercial.[57]

In the autumn, there were sweet chestnuts to roast and sell; in winter, rows of Christmas trees could be taken into the towns.[58] Just after the war, when times were hard, Vanslow Cooper and his brother-in-law Les Costa tried to break into this trade; they didn't actually have any trees, but they'd seen lots of them growing out Ripley way, and were sure that a lorry-load more or less wouldn't be missed. The gavvers who flagged down their motor saw it differently, Les and Vanslow were put on a charge, and it was porridge for Christmas.[59] It was safer to trade in wildflowers, which Eiza Cooper sold throughout the year, starting with the first snowdrops and progressing through primroses, cowslips and Lent Lilies to the bluebells and sweet violets of summer, until in June her basket was heaped high with bunched briar roses. Sitting with the family in the old railway carriage which served them as home, she took off the thorns first, so that customers wouldn't get scratched, and bound the bunches neatly with green wool. Then with her daughter Caroline she would take baskets out onto the streets. Caroline was a fine girl, plump and dark-eyed, full of laughter. Her sisters, more plain-looking, stayed at home where they wouldn't interfere with sales.[60]

As the old hawkers say, first you sell yourself, then you sell the goods. This meant that a child could have as much success as an adult, and sometimes more, like Shirley Lee, who began when she was seven, when her mother

> learnt me to sell pegs and tea strainers, combs, and little bits of things, needles and cottons and threads, you know. And then I used to say to me Mam, 'Let me come.' . . . 'No,' she'd say, 'stay in and do a bit of work, and help to look after your handicapped brother and another little un.' I kept saying, 'Let me come out to get some clothes for Christmas. Let me come, won't you Mam.' So my Granny used to say to her, 'She's a good little hawker. Can take money, Shirley can. She can charm the flowers off the trees.' And so she took me out, and then I was given the wages, and she never let me stop home any more . . . They used to like me, the people in the houses. They'd buy to look at me.[61]

Like other chavvies, Shirley loved working and contributing to the family. For a girl, this could mean going out calling, or it could involve learning homely skills beyond the usual domestic routine. Many women still treated their families in the traditional way; everyone knew a few hedgerow remedies, but some people had gone further and built up a practice out of the oral lore. 'My old aunt couldn't tell A from a bull's foot, but there wasn't an illness that she couldn't cure, more'n the doctors.'[62] In 1947 the Coopers and the Kings were stopping at Little Egypt, down in the meadows below Leatherhead. There was a gorjer woman living nearby, Juliette de Baïracli Levy, who was known to the Gypsies as an animal doctor and herbalist, and she persuaded Emily to tell a little of what she knew about herbs. Cuts and bruises were to be treated with the leaves of mallow, plantain and dock; liver complaints were dosed with dandelion and toadflax, fevers with yarrow and sorrel. You smoked colts-foot for coughs and took nettles and cress in spring to clear the blood. Cowslip made a good tea, and so did marigold, elderflower and wild rose, while a special infusion could be made by mixing primrose and cowslip flowers with the tart leaves of wood sorrel.[63]

No doubt people talked about these teas more than they drank them, but that didn't matter; they were still a potent reminder that the Romany inherited a wisdom that let them live off the land, even if in practice most people preferred to brew up an ordinary cup of meski. But there were times when floral drinks were just what was needed. Keziah Cooper's family used to brew their own hedgerow beer when they were hopping. Boil five pints of water with a handful of dog rose petals and (of course) a handful of hops; infuse twenty elderflower heads; then melt in 2 pounds of sugar, plus a half-cup of white wine vinegar. The wild yeast on the elderflowers started fermentation, and after two days it could be bottled as a refreshing fizzy drink. Sometimes there was wild honey instead of sugar, if grandfather had been able to track down a nest of bees on the heath. He would smoke them into quietness by burning the roots of heather and old man's beard, then whisk the honey away before they could recover their senses. This meant that it tasted of smoke as well as furze and heather blossom, but that was all part of the flavour.[64]

Other herbal remedies had a darker side. 'I tell you what we do, my dearie,' said Ada Smith when asked about the right way to quieten a teething baby. 'We pick thirteen deadly berries and thread them on a cotton, and if it's a boy a woman ties it round his little neck, where he can't eat them, and if it's a girl a man does it.' There would be no trouble after that, either because the right magic had been carried out, or because the baby was completely stupefied.[65] It's not for nothing that *drab* means poison as well as medicine. But these strange remedies had often proved their worth. Louie Smith, White Will's daughter, was sinking with pneumonia. Though the doctor shrugged his shoulders and gave up, the family were determined to make a last effort to save her. Hot cow dung was the traditional treatment, as fresh as possible, made into a poultice on the chest. So evening turned into night as the Smiths chased a herd of cows around a field, scooping up the jank and slapping it on Louie's chest, front and back. By sunrise she was getting her strength back, and when the doctor came to fill in the death certificate, he found her sitting up on her mother's lap and tucking into bread and milk.[66]

It seemed as if remedies, like people, might be rank and rough on the outside but full of goodness within. In the Cooper family, 'Mam and Grandmam used to give me crusts of bread which were green with mould to feed to the grais. They were kept especially for this purpose to cure any infection.' Keziah adds that 'I developed a great liking for this revolting bread myself and, as a consequence, rarely ailed.' And her family knew how to treat burns by an immediate application of cold water, followed by a layer of honey; after two days of lying under this sticky mess, the skin healed without a mark or blister.[67]

Burns were all too common among people whose life still centred round the fire. The new trailers, like waggons before them, were heated by woodburning stoves, too small to cook on, so that for any domestic business you had to light a fire outside. And this had a cultural value well beyond its immediate practical use: the thinnest wisp of woodsmoke carried with it a feeling of home. When two or three families were stopping at the same place, each would be expect to light their own fire, however scarce fuel might be. Someone might saunter over to another family's yog, and stand chatting for a while, but not sit down unless a sawn-off chair had been pulled out specially for them. Children soon learnt manners: not to get between an adult and the fire, not to throw things that were unclean onto the flames.[68] Even the inconveniences of damp firewood had secret benefits, if Jim Smith – Muggy Smith – was to be trusted. 'Dad believed that the smoke from the fire was good for your eyes. It smoked all the shit and dirt out of them, he said, and that was what his dad had told him.'[69]

A fire was part of Gypsy identity, not just in sight and smell but in taste. As Jim Penfold said:

Cooking over an open fire is something that's not so easy as it looks or it sounds. It makes things very tasty. This is in the wood. Burn a bit of kosh, chuck a bit of green kosh on and a bit of smoke will turn up into the food and this is what gives the flavour to the food.[70]

There was more than smoke in Emily Cooper's Gypsy cake, made from flour and water with an egg and some fat, mixed with salt and pounded into a lump. She would bank up the hazel shavings and off-cuts from peg-making, make a hole in the heart of the fire, and drop in the cake, covering it with ashes. When it started to smell done, she hooked it out with the kettle iron, cut away the burnt crust and divided up the golden core among everyone sitting round the fire. The dogs ate the burnt bits and thrived on them.[71] This was made when times were hard, by a family that didn't have a Dutch oven, but even they would have carried a frying pan and a boiler. Frying was the quickest and cheapest way to cook, it only needed a stick fire and would have a meal ready in minutes; that was how a man travelling on his own would usually prepare dinner. The classic dish was Joe Gray. You sliced up some onions and put them to fry with the meat, which could be bacon, sausages or rabbit. When this was brown, you covered it with water and threw in potatoes and carrots, simmering for ten minutes. Then you added some flavour – tinned soup or Oxo cubes, with tomatoes and mushrooms – and a bit more water, so that it served up as a kind of runny stew.[72]

Meals for a whole family would be cooked in the boiler, each course wrapped separately in a cloth or teatowel. In good times, this would be the afternoon meal, but when food was scarce it was reserved for Sunday dinner. For bacon pudding, you rolled out a lump of suet pastry to about a foot long, laid out strips of bacon and onion, then rolled up the whole gui, pinched the ends together and tied it into the bag, to be boiled for two or three hours depending on size. Vegetables could be added straight into the boiling water after a while, and a sweet pudding beside the main one; this had the same base of a suet pastry, only instead of making it with just flour and water, you added black treacle to the mix. Because everything was tied carefully at both ends in a cloth, the meat and sweet flavours were kept separate.

The suet stuck to your ribs to keep you warm through a winter's night, but real nourishment lay in the meat. Gypsies could afford to be generous with this, since they always knew where more could be found.

One season Levy Smith – Frank and Minty's son – was picking cherries down in Kent with his cousin Wally (Buddy) Smith. They had eight casuals working for them, and food had run out. So he took his ferret up to a place where he knew there would be rabbits; Buddy came with the nets, and soon enough they were back with four shushis. They gutted them, cut their heads off, skinned the bodies and diced the meat. With some wild mushrooms, carrots, potatoes and onions they made a stew that fed ten men for two days.[73]

Fred Wood spelled out the poacher's creed:

> We all believed that three things belonged naturally to all men:
> the wood that lies on the ground, the birds and beasts that live in
> the forest and on the heath and the fish in the water. These were all
> free for the taking and no man had any right to deny another the
> privilege of the taking.[74]

And that privilege was underwritten by a sort of moral code – no taking game in the breeding season, no picking out animals under a certain size, and no more hunting after there was enough for the pot. Or, as Fred adds carelessly, 'for our customers', which puts things in a rather different light. The odd hare or rabbit might be snared for an evening meal, but real serious poaching was done for the market. Jasper Smith was a lot less idealistic in his song about the craft:

> Mande has a jukkel, and a kushti jukkel, too,
> Mande kers him for his pleasure,
> For to muller some game in the middle of the rati
> While the yoggers lay sleeping.
>
> Up jumps a kanengro and away he shavs,
> Right down through some plantation.
> Mande kers him up then poggers his crown,
> Then he puts him in his putsi . . .
>
> Mande kers this old man to some sea-port
> To see what kanengros were fetching.
> 'Five joes a brace', said my bonny chavvi,
> 'That's if you can ker mande plenty.'[75]

The best lurchers were fast as greyhounds and smart as collies; quiet when working a field for rabbits, loud when protecting the stopping place against intruders. A few men were able to make a trade out of their dogs. Johnnie Hilden from Wandsworth was famous for his lurchers, and so was Peter Copper. They would take them up to the Derby each year and make a sale.[76]

The jukkel is a man's eyes when he is at work and a man's ears when he is asleep. A good one would guard the trailer and protect the children as well. The Coopers had Waxie, a true Gypsy dog, picked out from a litter that had been pupped under an old waggon in Kent. Vanslow's boy Keith took a shine to her, and one day boy and dog were out walking when a crowd of gorjer children passed by on their way to school. They all began to yell 'Gypsy!' at him, and some of them threw stones. Waxie didn't like that at all and later in the day, when the children were coming out of school, she saw that they were getting ready to do the same again. Cheered on by Keith, Waxie began to chase them, and none of those kids had ever run so fast; there was one of the teachers that was running with them too. After that there were no more cries of 'Gypsy!'[77]

Any dog would be cherished, if it was fierce and loyal and clever. Among the people that Juliette knew in the 1940s, the Coopers and the Kings travelled with a great black deerhound, two lurchers and four terriers; White Will Smith had two lurchers and a terrier; and Clara Lee, stopping at Leatherhead, had a large brindled greyhound bitch – 'her eyes were big and topaz-hued and shone brilliantly' – who was suckling seven pups. Young as they were, they all had names: Ruby, Brick, Queen, Lark, Lassie, Dream and little Sorry, who was the runt of the litter.[78]

Somehow this bitch had got into one of the carts and had her pups there; it seems that in their excitement, the Lees had let standards slip, for dogs, however loved or valuable, were still unclean. It would be repulsive to let one into the waggon where it could jump up on the seats or sprawl out on the bed. These rules were not enforced so strictly on puppies or lapdogs, which like children could come and go without offending against the decencies. But things used for feeding dogs were kept well away from the washing-up bowl, and if a dog managed to lick a plate or cup or bowl, the offending item would be smashed.[79]

That was part of the web of unspoken rules to which people kept, even in rough times when they could keep very little else. Once, when he was a boy, Jasper went from door to door with his father Derby, looking for work. They hadn't had much luck, and it must have showed on their faces, for there was one gorjer woman who decided to take pity on them. She'd just been baking and had a batch of little cakes fresh out of the oven, so she bundled some of them together and brought them to the door. *In her apron*: holding them out in her apron, and smiling, as if it was the most natural thing in the world. The Smiths were very polite, they took the cakes with all the gratitude they could muster, and then Jasper looked at Derby, and as soon as they were out of sight, they threw the mogadi things into a hedge. Times were hard then – 'they can talk all they like about property', said Jasper in later life, 'but they'd talk something different if they'd been walking for three days without eating.' But nothing would persuade a decent Gypsy to take food that had touched a woman's clothes.[80]

This kind of self-respect was strongest in those who, like Louie Taylor, had generations of Gypsy values behind them. The granddaughter of Mattie Cooper, she lived to a great age and eventually went into brick in a house near Kingston.

> As she got older Louie would sit at her door, smoking her clay pipe, and keeping an eye on what was happening. On day she heard a neighbour refer to 'dirty old Gypos'. She rose from her chair, and her son Albert, who lived with her and looked after her, gave a smile, knowing that this was going to be good. She pulled up her long black skirt to show her crisp and clean white petticoat. Looking straight at the neighbour she said, proudly and unanswerably, *'I'm* a Gypsy, and *I'm* not dirty,' and ruffled her petticoat.[81]

This was how values were passed down, in a story; this was how children learned the right ways. Rosie Smith remembered all her father's stories; 'as chavvies at night me and me brothers and sister would lay in bed and listen to him tell stories that would have us straining our ears to listen.' Levi would tell the tales that his father Frank had told him; 'although he would tell us the same stories over and over again we never seemed to get sick of hearing them, even though we all knew the words he was going to say before he said them.' It was the same at the cherry-picking down in Kent: at night when work was done 'we would all sit round the yog and rokker, joke, or listen to the older ones tell stories and some nights me dad would play his accordion and we'd all have a sing song.' Rosie would dance around with her cousins until at last her mother got frightened

White Will Smith and family at Banstead, 1952.

that she would trip over and fall into the fire, so with a smack round the ear she was sent away from the embers.[82]

White Will Smith loved music, and so did his sons; young Bill could play the squeezebox, and George could step-dance. Will talked fondly to Juliette of the autumn nights after hopping, when boards used to be spread out on the grass and the young men and women would step to the accompaniment of mouth organ and fiddle. Afterwards there would be a jig or a country dance for the young people.[83] These memories offered some comfort in 1952 when the extended family gathered on Banstead Downs. They had come to sit up for a five-year-old girl who had just died in hospital. A great fire of brushwood spat and roared on the hill, warming the crowd – fifty people or more. One of the family had made a coffin and in it the little mullo was laid out with her toys: a ragged clothes-peg doll and the horse carved from tough holly wood by her father in happier days. Candles were lit, stuck into jam jars and placed on the coffin. First one man, then another, sang for the comfort of the dead. A fiddle had been sent for, and Bill Smith began to play in the moonlight. It was a hard frost, but the men took no notice of that; their backs were white with rime, and locks of hair stuck down under their caps. For three nights they sat up, and then it was time for her to go, on a trolley garlanded with strings of red bryony berries, down to the gates of the cemetery, into an early grave.[84]

People might boast of secret potions and herbal cures, but children still died young, and so did many adults. By the 1960s life expectancy for Gypsies had slipped behind that of gorjers by as much as ten or fifteen years. Perhaps things were no worse than they had been for the grandparents' generation, but they were no better, either; the post-war revolution in healthcare had passed the community by. This was hardly surprising for travelling people who found it difficult to follow up any long-term course of treatment as they moved around their country, or to register with a doctor, or even to get treatment as human beings. 'Once,' Christine Smith remembered, 'when I thought my children had chicken-pox I went to a doctor in Egham and he told me to take them to a vet.'[85] As the good stopping places were gradually boarded up, people found themselves shunted to the side of roads, filled with the new roar of traffic, which put children and elders at risk every time they ventured out of the trailer. There were lead fumes in the air and filth in the water.

And that was before you factored in the continual stress and uncertainty caused by harassment. Women who were carrying needed rest and good food, but instead they were faced with continual evictions, leading to the loss of their child or an enfeebled birth; if, indeed, they were able to bear the child in peace at all. Minty Smith was down in Kent when:

> I was expecting one of my children, you know, one of my babies, and my husband's sent for the midwife and in the time he was going after the midwife the policeman come along. Come on, he says, get a move on. Shift on, he says, don't want you on here, on my beat. So my husband says: Look, he says, sir, let me stay, he says, my wife is going to have a baby. No, don't matter about that, he says, you get off. They made my husband move, and my baby was born going along and my husband's stayed in the van and my baby was born on the crossroads in my caravan. The horse was in harness and we was travelling along and the policeman was following behind, drumming us off and the child was born, born at the crossroads.[86]

Get along, move along, *shift*. The pressure was relentless. Shirley Lee's people would travel all day, pull on in the evening, and then be moved as soon as they stopped. Anywhere near a village was risky; even if there were only a few houses in sight, it was only a matter of time before residents would phone their local police station, the gavvers would come and everyone was back on the road again. With such continual interruptions, they couldn't earn anything. 'We never had no money. We'd only have enough money for one day's food. We'd have none the next. We had to get stopping somewhere to make a living.'[87] Jim Penfold was summonsed 27 times in a week for obstruction, and that was what forced him to move into Battersea and get himself a house. Yes, he could earn good money without losing it all in fines; yes, the children had the schooling which he never knew; but it was not the life that a Gypsy was meant to live. For years afterwards, he would wake up in his neat, terraced house from a dream of the road, wanting to get into his motor and just drive and drive and drive until he had left the gorjer world behind him.[88] 'Some folk may say: Why does he have to put up with it?' said one of the Smiths at Bookham. 'Why don't they come off the road and live in houses and work in a factory? Well, it would be like taking a wild bird and putting it in a cage.'[89]

Of course, there had always been persecution, but there had also been ways of dealing with it. Children grew up watching as mother moodied a difficult gavver to get a bit of a laugh out of him, and father hid the carriage lamps so that the waggon was without lights and the family couldn't be moved on until morning; you learnt how to do these things yourself, as part of the ordinary business of Gypsy life. But with the increased scale of harassment these old tricks were no use, along with all the inherited skills of moving and staying and making a life on the road. It was easy to lose hope.

On a wet spring day in 1964 Jim Vincent was running his trolley through the lanes south of Dorking. The shafts were split and bound together with twine, patchwork boards had replaced the sides and, after the reins snapped, he had been making do with string. There was a car coming the other way, but luckily the old cob was steady, and Jim was not much worried until he saw what the driver was doing: he'd pulled out a big camera and was snapping away with it. Clickety-click it went, while Jim, weary and frustrated, yelled out at the stupid dinilo and told him where he could stuff his camera.[90]

A fortnight later he was stopping at Charlwood when a car pulled up, and out stepped the gorjer, holding a photograph this time, and apologizing for having been so ignorant. His name was Tony, he said, and he liked to take photos for a hobby. Here, have a fag. And so, cautiously but with a growing set of pride, Jim and his Louisa and their children let a stranger record their lives, in the last year before everything fell apart. Jim had always lived according to the old ways. Twenty years before, he

Overtaken by the modern world, Epsom Downs, 1940s.

and his brother had been respected horse-traders; in between deals, they had made ends meet by selling pegs and flowers, muck-hawking and selling firewood, while their womenfolk dukkered the servants at the big house.[91] But that was no longer enough to support a family. When he next saw Tony, down at a farm in Penshurst, Jim had to tell him that the horse had died. Waggontime was literally over – the two cheap vehicles which housed the family were falling apart, and they moved into a bender. Ironically, it was the photos of their travelling life which got them accommodation, after an exhibition put their troubles on display, and someone found a cheap cottage for the family. But they did not take easily to life in four walls, and it was not a happy ending.[92]

There was another side to the story, though. Not all Gypsies were trapped in this dilemma – a life of constant victimization on the one hand, a loss of identity on the other. In walled yards and on sheltered pitches owned by relatives, you would find quality trailers: the Berkeley and the Bluebird, the Lunedale and the Westmorland Star. They weren't cheap, even in the standard models – and Harry Vickers would provide any accessory that his customer wanted, at a price. More strips of stainless steel on the bodywork? More glass undercut with grapes and vineleaves?

Uplights in the china cabinets? All the walls in Formica? Yes, and yes, he would say, notebook in hand, adding £100 to the cost for each accessory: but nobody wanted to be left behind when it came to showing what they were worth.

These were the vehicles that pulled every year onto Epsom Downs, where there was no shortage of prosperous travellers. Dominic Reeve, who had learned to make good if intermittent money out of trading up his vehicles – waggons at first, and then trailers – could be seen with his wife Beshlie, casting an approving eye over the luxurious fittings, flash outfits and exquisite Crown Derby. Muggy Smith was there for Show Out Sunday with his sons Wally and Jimmy freshly washed and scrubbed and wearing their new suits. It was a time for showing off. 'The best china would be on display inside the trailer,' Jimmy remembered, 'visible through the windows, because the lace curtains would be drawn back. The trailers themselves would be gleaming, the polished-up chrome reflecting the sun.'[93]

Muggy was a gambling man whose life seemed to revolve around games of head'n'ems in the Ring. Sometimes he won, sometimes he lost; one year, the coins carried on falling the wrong way until he had lost all his money, then the motor, then the trailer itself. Not wanting to leave Betsy and the children homeless, the extended family clubbed together and bought him an old Escort van so that at least he could drive away at the end of the week. Next year he was back again and won £12,000. This time, he pulled off with the show trailer that had been brought on site by its maker as an advertisement, too good to be sold.[94]

It seemed he had a charmed life – until one wet Wednesday, at the horse market in Southall, an argument blew up over someone's gambling debt. Wally and Jimmy laid in a few blows to stand up for their dad's interest, the whole thing died down, and the boys went round to the boxing club. They came back to find their father killed by a blow from a hammer. Later there was a trial at the Old Bailey, but the case against Muggy's murderers was dropped.[95]

Hundreds of people came to join the funeral procession, which stretched all the way from Epsom town to the Grandstand. When they came to the place where the Ring would usually be set up, everything stopped, his sons got out the funeral car and spun two pennies high in the air for the last time. Then they buried Muggy, the King of the Ring, at the top of the cemetery, nearest to the Downs.

8

New Ways:
The Modern World

'No Gypsies Served', said the sign on the pub door, but Jasper Smith pushed it open anyway and stepped into the front bar. He knew he would not be alone in the Bull's function room – a rather grand name for a garden shed, but that was where the others had agreed to meet. Jim Penfold was there, and Fred Wood, together with other men he knew: Solly Brown from Corke's Pit, Nelson Fenner and more Smiths and Coopers. There were darker faces from France and Romania; Irish Travellers, too; and a slim young gorjer, declaiming and persuading, the man who had first invited Jasper to come to the pub in St Paul's Cray. His name was Grattan Puxon, and he had a reputation for making things happen. In Ireland he had organized the Travellers so effectively that the Church called him a public enemy, Dublin Council sent its employees to burn his school and gunmen proposed taking him off to be shot in the mountains. It was time to move to England, where he pulled on some waste land in Kent and spent the summer of 1966 getting to know people, including Jasper, who was at Edenbridge. Grattan was a quick learner. Jasper took him rabbiting and introduced him to people in Kent and Surrey and the London outskirts. As soon as he'd made the first contacts, Grattan began to organize Gypsies and gorjers together in combined resistance to the harassment suffered by travellers.[1]

This was something new. There had been Gypsy politics before, of a kind, but it had followed the path of respectability: letters to bishops, appeals to the Queen, petitions to Parliament. Even the campaigning of Norman Dodds, though he kept it up from the passing of the 1947 Planning Act until his death in 1965, seemed to begin and end with asking questions in Parliament. Norman was Labour MP for Dartford and was on site when people were evicted from Darenth Woods. He worked with a representative body of Gypsies, including Ernest Williams from Marden, and drew up a charter of everything necessary for the ending of harassment – proper transit sites, facilities for education, opportunities for work, an end to prejudice.[2] But Parliament listened without doing much, and the local authorities took no notice of Parliament. They all paid attention to Grattan, though, because he was in the thick of the action. 'At the first sign of a bailiff arriving to evict from an unofficial site a Gypsy would run to the nearest public telephone and a mixture of housewives, pastors and students would assemble with the Gypsies, making a human barrier.'[3]

The new politics brought an end to the old passivity in the face of gorjer aggression, and this was nowhere more true than at Epsom, where resignation had become a way of life. On the night before the Derby, at about five in the morning, uniformed security guards would go round to dislodge people. They pulled out tent-pegs and rods, shook the ropes and let the canvas flop on top of the sleepers, who crawled out as best they could. Anyone in a trailer was woken up and told to get in their lorry and pull it off, which they did. Two or three hundred yards down the hill, a brother or cousin would move over into the driver's seat, turn the motor round and drive back up onto the same pitch; as soon as the guards stopped him, he would protest volubly that he had only just come onto the Downs, hadn't seen anybody, knew nothing about it. When ordered to shift, he would turn round and drive until he was far away enough for another relative to take over at the wheel, and this went on and on while the sun rose and the men in uniform grew hot and tired. So, after hours of this charade, the day went ahead just as if it hadn't happened at all.[4]

But the combined weight of the Downs Conservators and Grand Stand Association was no longer enough to victimize people like this. In the summer of 1967 Fred Wood used the backing of the Gypsy Council to challenge their ban. He had a twofold strategy: there were threats of direct action, in which the race would be stopped by everyone dragging their vehicles onto the course, and these were backed up by a legal challenge in the courts.[5] Two hundred trailers pulled on at the beginning of Derby week, with one hundred more following over the next few days. Both sides geared up for a confrontation, but in the end the race went ahead. 'We did not stop the Derby,' said Fred, 'because we have won. We are on the Downs.' That saved face, at any rate; and on their side, the association proceeded with 27 summonses, bringing in £3 each. The police were indifferent to the whole business, and the conservators could not afford to pay for privatized policing on a scale which would have any effect, so it was stalemate.[6]

The Grand Stand Association gave in first. They had already broken rank with their colleagues the year before by leasing pitches to Gypsies, and finally in 1970 they gained a legal ruling overriding the objections of the conservators. Some 12 acres at the Rubbing House were set aside and finally in 1974 the Gypsy Council was brought into discussions. Ironically, just when it became legitimate to stop at the Derby, there were fewer who arrived there. In 1977, 430 bookings were registered for the site, but numbers had fallen to 278 by 1980. The days when there was a shining wall of chrome along the hillside, when you couldn't pin the door of your trailer open without almost banging someone else's . . . they didn't last.[7]

Not that people didn't want to travel to the Derby, as they always had; only it was becoming more and more difficult to get off-pitch from a recognized site, spend a week at the races and then have somewhere that you could return to. The Gypsy Council's activism had finally stirred government into passing the Caravan Sites Act of 1968 but this had results that were less benign than expected.

When the Act came into force in 1970, campaigners hoped that the new legislation would provide a stable background for their lives – a cross between the half-remembered days when heath and common had been freely open to Gypsies, and the modern world of hard standings, piped water and plumbing. It could have provided a new network of transit sites which would have replaced the old geography of stopping places, but in practice it did nothing of the kind. The Act failed because the construction of sites was in the hands of local authorities, and they wanted something quite different from the people that the sites were being built for.

The implementation of the Act was allocated to county councils, which were looking for somewhere to put away all the Gypsies, and to districts, which showed no enthusiasm for having any Gypsies at all. For sixty years their automatic response had been to move travellers on, and they were in no hurry to change. This soon led to absurd confrontations: in 1972 Surrey opened a site at Tupwood Lane, only to be immediately prosecuted for so doing by the urban district of Caterham and Warlingham.[8] Even when it was not cut short in this way, the creation of sites was a protracted business. The land would be purchased by the county, with the approval of the district, and then run by a local warden. The costs of infrastructure and the warden's wage were managed by the district and if there was a shortfall, the county made it up. But first the county had to find land which was on the market, and then announce its intention of purchase – and that was not something that the neighbours took quietly. Christine Smith was prepared to leave the road, as official policy required:

> I had tried to buy land near Guildford but the locals objected to us being there. We got threatening letters, and the police came out. While they were there someone shot at us and just missed my grandson's head. I invited people round to see how we lived – they were welcome to have a cup of tea and a chat. But no one came and we were evicted. We were given a site near an open sewage pit and I went down from eleven stone to nine stone living there. I worried about diseases and the children and made such a fuss that the site was closed down. They gave me another one next to the motorway and I had to tie my children to the trailer – I was frightened they'd get run over. This is what we've had to settle for.[9]

In the summer of 1978, the borough of Reigate needed a new Gypsy site, and the town clerk was charged with finding it. A farm in Lower Kingswood, already owned by the county council, looked suitable until 1,261 residents complained that this would mean housing Gypsies in an attractive area. Why couldn't they put the site somewhere else? 'We don't want to see Gipsies all over the place,' a concerned local wrote. 'It is not unreasonable to ask that they be put out of view . . . That is why we pay our rates.' The Rookery Farm option was discussed in a council meeting, at which law-abiding ratepayers caused so much havoc that it took 25 minutes to clear them out of the public gallery. So the council looked instead at land adjoining Park Lane. But that was turned down as well because it was in the Green Belt. 'It is intolerable that the owners of highly priced property should have this situation inflicted on them,' wrote another concerned local. 'The value of their property must inevitably be lowered.' And then there was Mogador Road, which was at least owned by the borough council, but not otherwise suitable. A year had gone by, and Reigate and Surrey couldn't agree where to build a site, or what to build there. Ernest Chapman wrote in asking for a pitch, as he didn't want to continue stopping on Whitebushes Common; all the cottagers flanking the green space were hostile. Could he move onto Three Arch Road? No, there weren't any places. Could he have a pitch on a new site? No, because it hadn't been built yet. And so it went on.[10]

To keep this kind of struggle to a minimum, council officials tended to propose large sites, of fifteen pitches or more, hoping that this would let them fulfil their quotas with as little disruption as possible. In the 1970s there were about 224 families on the road in Surrey, and the administrative county had eleven districts, so in theory one site in every district could have accommodated them all.[11] But sites of this size would have ended up taking people who had no family links and might not get on with each other. This sort of friction had never been a problem when the road was free, and you could solve any difficulties by hitching on your trailer and moving somewhere else. But now there was nowhere to move to: the number of pitches was inadequate, only about a fifth of the total needed. At the same time, county councils were all seeking the prized status of 'designation' – an official endorsement of their claim that they had laid out enough pitches, which would then enable them to go back to the old practice of harassing everyone who stopped anywhere else.

In the battle of Rose Hill, Sutton Council spent two hours with heavy machinery unsuccessfully trying to evict people from behind a barricade of overturned lorries. By 1971 fifteen families had been living in the settlement for eighteen months because there was nowhere else for them to go, but Sutton, having already fulfilled its quota of pitches, was under no obligation to find a stopping place. Roy Wells from Garratt Lane, later to be London chairman of the Gypsy Council, was in charge of the defence until a bulldozer knocked him down and he was taken off to hospital. And while the fight went on, Grattan was struggling to coordinate delegates from all over Europe in the First World Romani Congress. Gypsy politics turned out to be more complicated than anyone had expected.[12]

The old stopping places were disappearing one by one. An unofficial site at Journey's End Café outside Hookwood had already been closed by Dorking and Horley Rural District Council in 1970.[13] The Hog's Back between Guildford and Farnham had long been a stopping place for people going to and from the Derby, with fields just off the ridge where a trailer could pull on without causing any disruption, but in 1974 the whole line of the road was lined with poles and crossbars to prevent people from stopping.[14] When the new road bridge sank under freak rainstorms, rumours of a Gypsy curse began to circulate and an enterprising reporter found Jasper Smith happy to oblige with a story or two – oh yes, Granny Charlotte had often told him about the wicked luck that fell on anyone tampering with the Hog's Back, ever since the raids in old times, when many innocent men were sent to starripen. No use repairing that bridge: 'after five years or so, it will go wrong again.'[15] And so it did, and it did again five years afterwards, but that was poor consolation for the people who had lost green fields and resting places.

The fencing of all other stopping places made it impossible for the new sites to act as transit points, as had originally been intended. Unable to move freely due to the shortage of places, people had to stay put where they were. So, consciously or not, officials began to see Gypsy sites as a means to assimilate the Romany to the gorjer way of life. Their management was modelled on council housing estates, not stopping places; tenants were caught in a web of rules and regulations. By 1980 there were only seven official sites in Surrey outside London: Elm Farm in Lyne near Chertsey, Cox Lane in Ewell, Kiln Lane in Epsom, Green Lane in Outwood, Tupwood Lane in Caterham, Cobbetts Close in Worplesdon, and the Willows at Runfold.[16] There were also two sites in Spelthorne, which was part of Middlesex but had been administered by Surrey after the break-up of that county in 1974.

And even these sites had to be fought for. Cox Lane in Ewell began as an informal settlement in the 1960s and grew as people who had stopped at the Derby found there was nowhere for them to go afterwards. Jasper had moved there from Edenbridge but was disgusted at the prevarication of Epsom and Ewell Council when, after taking over the site in 1971, they decided to close it down so that they could develop another area for Gypsies. In the end he built his Rocket to the Moon, a 30-foot-high contraption of packing cases fastened to a telegraph pole. We might as well go to the moon, he said, because they won't let us stay anywhere down here. It was a shrewd publicity coup, and brought Epsom and Ewell to the negotiating table. So did the threat that if official standings were not provided for locals, the area would be flooded again by refugees from the Derby. By 1978 there were thirty families accommodated, and Jasper was warden, a good practical man to have in charge. After some trouble with young hotheads in their motors, arrangements were made to install two sleeping policemen, but on the next visit the Gypsy Liaison Officer was surprised to find them already laid. Oh, I wanted it done, said Jasper: cost me £25 the pair. The town clerk went off to write a chilly letter to the gorjer contractor who had quoted £100 each.[17]

Sometimes there was a living link with the past, as at Little Egypt, south of Leatherhead, which had been known for generations as a good stopping place. Nobody seemed to care who owned it; a railway

Jasper Smith, 1999.

embankment kept the wind at bay, and so did the rough hedges of oak and ash. There were willows and rich grazing by the water, with fields spotted in gold by coltsfoot flowers in the spring and all the colours of foxglove, rosebay and yellow flags through the summer. That's how it had always been, and how it was until 1953, when Surrey County Council put up a large notice prohibiting the 'Parking of Caravans'. Shortly afterwards, by one of those unfortunate accidents that happen in the dark, the board and its promise of £5 and £10 fines was knocked down by a waggon led by the Coopers; but it returned again and again, until some twenty years later the bridge over the Mole fell in, and during consolidation works the track that led down to Little Egypt was destroyed.[18] Then the highway authority decided that the road past Bocketts Farm should be upgraded, to give Leatherhead a new bypass, so a four-lane bridge was built across the river, with all the land on either side hacked down to white chalk. A bit of ground was scraped flat for the construction vehicles, and when these moved on people began to stop there once again.

Jimmy and Mary Wilson at Little Egypt, 1976.

The Wilsons, who had come down from the North, were there in force: Tommy Wilson and his sons Tommy, Jimmy and Michael. Jimmy married Mary, the daughter of Mary Lee and granddaughter of Ceni Smith; and in the same year, Michael married Ann Smith, whose father Henry was Mary's cousin as well as Jasper's. 'We had an Astral then,' Ann remembered, 'I was so proud of it because I'd just got married and it was my own. Then I found out it had 110 mirrors and they all needed cleaning.'[19]

After a while, the county agreed to make the stopping place into an official site, with ten pitches, each with a wash house and utilities and electricity. There were rent books, and a man from the council to stamp them every week – a retired army man, turned Gypsy Liaison Officer. 'He don't seem a bad sort of feller, proper rai, you can see that,' was the judgement of Ambrose Smith, who stopped on the site for a while.[20] But then the officer's task had been made a little easier by changes on the site, changes which transformed the reputation of the people there – not just the routine of semi-sedentary life, though that may have had something to do with it, but a deeper influence. God had come to the banks of the River Mole, and Little Egypt was now Salvation Place.

It all began in the early 1980s when Davey Jones pulled on the site. Davey had made his own commitment to Christ some years earlier; he had learnt about salvation from gorjer missionaries, but although conversion had made a different man of him, he was still a Gypsy through and through. Unlike the converts of previous centuries, he was not going to leave the Romany world behind: instead, he would take it to salvation with him. Since Davey was a man who knew about persuasion and organization as well as faith, the Light and Life Church gradually kindled around him. Here he was, stepping out of his motor at the bottom of Young Street and announcing that he would hold a gospel meeting. At first no one was impressed, and then slowly everyone was, first the women and then the men. Only young Tommy Wilson stood out. He had seen the workings of grace in his sisters-in-law, the first to give their lives to Jesus, and then in his own wife, but that was not enough to change his heart. Until one morning he felt compelled to walk to the top of Box Hill.

> When he reached the top he fell on his knees. 'I couldn't cope with the way I was living any more,' he explains. 'I'd watched Mary for all these months and heard Davey's preaching and I knew my life wasn't right. I just called out to God on the top of that hill and said to him that I wanted to know him in the way that Mary did.' While Tommy remained on his knees he felt that God was speaking to him. 'It was like it was in my mind,' he said, 'this voice said "Tommy, you're a sinner." After that I had a picture of all the sins I had done in my life, it was like they had been recorded on a video camera.' At this point, Tommy remembers, he broke down and wept. He recalls that it was the first time in his life he had ever cried. [21]

He ran down the hill, a changed man, and the conversion of the site was complete. Tommy went on to train as a pastor. Now prayer meetings were so large that they could no longer be fitted onto the site, but people set to and built a church, made with usual Gypsy efficiency in three days. It filled a long rectangular pitch – all of wood and very plain, for Light and Life, being a Pentecostal church, preferred to focus entirely on the Word and did not want decoration or ornament. [22] When building was finished, Mole Valley Council agreed to have the site officially renamed Salvation Place.

But every site had a different history of management, or mismanagement. Green Lane in Outwood began as an independent settlement, like Cox Lane and Salvation Place. The land was bought just after the war by several families, who divided up ownership in the traditional way so that notice could not be served on all of them at once. Within a few years it was a scruffy, lively place, with people living in old buses, reused prefabs and anything else that was available. There were piles of scrap and a steady trade in logs and firewood. Then in 1960 a man from the Godstone Rural District Council visited and didn't like what he saw. The newly passed Caravan Sites Act gave the council powers to acquire the site, which they did. They cleared up and threw away people's stock-in-trade and then divided the area in two, with a high chainlink fence down the middle in case anyone tried to reoccupy their own land. Residents were then told that they 'would be allowed to stay, provided they could equip themselves with a satisfactory type of caravans'; they could even continue logging, as long as they paid extra for the privilege. The remains of the settlement were laid out in 51 pitches, many of them occupied by the old families, although the council moved in others and added a number of gorjers who needed to be accommodated somewhere. Outwood was no longer a very pleasant place to live; 'full and constant supervision is difficult,' sighed the officials, not least because newcomers were siphoning petrol out of the motors of old residents and stripping them of moveable parts. This wouldn't have happened if everyone was parked next to their own trailer, but that of course would have been against the rules.[23]

In the 1970s Tandridge Council, successor to the old rural district, responded to these problems by cutting down the number of pitches first to 25 and then to 18, but there was a lot of triple and quadruple occupancy, so some 72 families were still present. The site now had a reputation for ringing cars – buying insurance write-offs, then doing them up with parts cannibalized from fresh cars of unknown origin so that the vehicle could be relicensed and sold as good as new, which most of it was. This was not the sort of business which welcomed close inspection, and the Green Lane residents discouraged it by blocking the lane from time to time with felled trees or burning cars. A tall bank had been raised alongside the road, so that passing motorists wouldn't be offended by the sight of Gypsies going about their business: the chavvies used to climb on this and throw concrete blocks at anyone they suspected of interfering. In 1988 the police called to look for stolen cars, though they didn't find any. But they confiscated all the best things from people's trailers, in case these had been stolen too. The gavvers got back in their cars and prepared to drive off. One boy threw a stone. Then fifty riot police from all over Surrey and Sussex stormed the camp, where they arrested anyone they could.[24]

Which went to prove that the project of settling Gypsies in little civic ghettoes, whatever else it might achieve, was not integrating the residents into mainstream society. A site might become a stairway to Heaven, or it might turn into a no-go criminal zone, but no amount of mains electricity and rent books would turn it into an extension of the settled world. There were boundaries, the worst ones invisible. Once, Gypsies had been targeted because of the antipathy between settled and nomad; now, people were increasingly tied down to the sites, but the gorjers remained hostile, because of race and race alone.

It only took a flick of prejudice to turn the course of a life, especially when you were young and headstrong, like Joe Smith. Joe was the grandson of Rymer, brother of Muggy, King of the Ring. He'd learnt a lot from his grandfather. He knew how to handle himself properly in a fight, because Rymer had worked the fairground booths and even turned professional under the name of Jack Daley, but he'd learnt other important things too. 'The best man is the one that walks away,' old Rymer said, and Joe would nod because he idolized his grandfather even though he was too young to understand him. And Rymer taught the boy something less usual: how to play golf. Back in the 1930s, when golf courses were being laid out over heaths and commons throughout the country, he and his cousin Nelson had pulled next to one and spent a summer afternoon watching the gorjers at practice. It didn't look that hard, and they thought they'd have a go, breaking a couple of branches off the trees and knocking around a ball in the evening when the course was empty. Then they got a couple of clubs and practised some more. By the time they were caught, Nelson was sinking a hole in one, and this earned some grudging respect from the club committee: they let him and his cousin play on, as long as they did it after hours when no one could see them.

It would have been out of the question for them to become members: in those days golf clubs were social centres for a certain class of people, a class which certainly didn't include Gypsies. But surely things would be different in 1985, when Joe and his family drove up to the gates of Home Park in Kingston. And, for a while, they were: he was a keen young lad, the sort that wants to be as good as he can. Too good, in fact. Steps were taken to make sure he didn't collect the Grand Challenge Cup. And not long afterwards, a reason was found to expel him from the club.[25]

Joe was only sixteen when the bottom fell out of his world. Like most chavvies, he'd been protected from the hostility outside; the only gorjers he'd known had been fine men like Grattan Puxton, or Jim Needle who came on site to teach him how to read, or his mentor the golf pro at Home Park. Now he knew a bit more about the world, he was angry, and he threw over golf for fighting. That might not have lasted, if he hadn't been so good at it. There was a fight on the Cranford site with his uncle Ruffey's son Champ: one of those family disputes that flare up over nothing between cousins who will be best of friends afterwards, but honour matters, and besides a large crowd had gathered to watch. Champ was older and stronger; he got through Joe's guard and cut his eye, but quickly, before it swelled too much, Joe landed so many body shots that Champ gave him best. And afterwards, in the pub, a north London man who had done very well out of the fight slipped Joe an envelope. He opened it and counted £5,000. If that was what you got for being a hard man, he would be one of the hardest.

> I could walk into a pub alone and people went quiet and moved
> away for me to get to the bar. Sometimes when I was served
> my drink the landlord would wave his hand as I delved into my
> pocket to pay. 'On the house, Joe.' It wasn't because of the fight so
> much that changed the way people reacted to me, it was because
> of the people I was wrapped around and were wrapped around
> me ... Serious criminals are by necessity a fairly close network
> and although you can be on nodding and first-name terms they
> are wary who they allow into their network ... After the fight
> there was a shift in their attitude and I stepped enthusiastically
> into that circle. I couldn't see it at first, but I had embarked on a
> criminal career.[26]

From swaggering to debt collecting with threats, from that to protection rackets, from that to a gang stand-off involving a machete, chainsaw and (ironically) several golf clubs: it could have gone on, and worse, if Joe hadn't been brought up short on a charge. The isolation made him think hard about himself and by the time his case came up – an acquittal – he had turned his life around.

He still fought, now and again, though his heart was really set on winning the British Open. Two different worlds, but related in spirit when golf, like bare-knuckle, became a straight contest of ability, man against man, with a crowd of bystanders watching and applauding (or otherwise) the results of every move. In both cases, the individual reputation was what mattered; that was why team games never really caught on among Gypsies. If it was a case of putting your money down on a favoured contender, then you wanted a contest in which one protagonist – man or animal – brought everything to the wager: breeding, training, skill. That was true of many gorjer sports, but they lacked the added frisson of violence. Only when everything was to play for, when pain, physical integrity, life itself was at stake, could a competitor show what they were made of.

In chicken-fighting, for instance, there are no runners-up. One cock wins and the other one dies. This is how things are when the birds fight each other naturally, although in the wild, or in the farmyard, the loser has a chance to run away, and this wasn't always provided in the ring. Fights between cocks had been made illegal in 1835, but a lot of things that weren't legal carried on in the quiet places of the Victorian countryside, and the tradition survived in a small way into the twentieth century. The overhang of a ledge waggon or a bowtop could be provided with a platform and rails to make a portable coop for bantams, to be matched with each other when families met up; but serious investment in breeding and training twenty or thirty birds was not compatible with the travelling life. It was the enforced sedentarization of the 1970s which made possible the revival of chicken-fighting; that, and the new-found status of Gypsy sites as no-go areas. They were, or they were thought to be, the sort of place where authority did not venture without good reason: no one was going to rush a site with fifty police in riot gear to rescue a few cockerels. So the business of breeding and training went ahead, especially in Kent, which was well placed to import fresh blood from other countries where the sport had never been banned.

'The birds are trained carefully,' said Jimmy Stockin, no stranger to fighting himself, 'by throwing them into the air to strengthen their wings and by pushing down on their bodies so the bird reacts by pushing upward. It is a form of press-up, you could say, and builds the bird's muscles up.' The owner treated his charges as carefully as a trainer preparing his champ for the big fight. 'Finally, you present the chicken with a mirror, where it will perfect its technique and learn aggression by attacking its own reflection. By the time he meets the real thing, the cock is raring to go.'[27]

The betting on these cocks was high, and so were the prices: Johnny Love, the top man for the sport in Kent, paid £600 for a bird in the 1980s. It lost, which Johnny accepted philosophically, knowing that a gambler who could take a big hit to his wallet and not complain would be as admired as a fighter who took body blows and didn't give best.

If chickens proved unlucky, there was the other competitive animal sport of hare coursing with dogs. This remained legal for many years, although it had to be organized among the community as formal matches were in the hands of the National Coursing Club.[28] It needed little preparation, just an open bit of land in an area where hares could be found and beaters would gather. They would drive the hares forward, the flankers would keep them in and, as one ran by, the slipper would loose a dog alone, if it was a time trial, or two if they were matched against each other, wearing white and red collars to tell them apart. Then came the real test of skill. As the dogs gained on her, the kanengro would dart sideways and run on a fresh trail, so that the dogs had to twist and lose the advantage of speed and then, as they got closer, once more she would jink again. The dogs had to be intelligent enough to see this coming, and agile enough not to fall over themselves, but even so the hare usually got away. If not, she was dead in a moment, with the dogs snapping the neck in one strike, for they could waste no time when running at speed.

To win three out of three – running a dog three times, and a strike every time – was no easy matter; greyhounds had the speed for a single run, but not the endurance to keep it up, while other breeds had the strength and intelligence but not the quick run. Different men would swear by different breeding strategies for their lurchers, usually agreeing on some sort of greyhound-saluki cross. Family tradition accounted for much, because everyone had grown up with dogs from the days when a good jukkel was a necessity to keep the family supplied with rabbits and the odd pheasant. He guarded the waggon by day and slept by it at night. Once, when the Bagleys stopped at Shepherd and Flock roundabout at Farnham, there was no bender for the boys and the waggon was full of girls, so Bluey and Ruffey slept under the shafts. They had a tarpaulin to keep off the rain, but that didn't do much to keep out the cold, so they were glad when the dog lay down between them; not so glad the next day, when they found they'd got mange.[29] There was common sense behind the rule that dogs, however admired, should be kept out of trailers, away from food and off people.

In the gorjer world, a pet had a quite different status, as a sort of honorary family member: they treated animals as people, which would have been more tolerable if they hadn't been so ready to treat people as animals. 'I was a boy then,' Ambrose Cooper recalled, 'and it was always me that got sent round with the bucket to get water from the houses, but I learned that I had to say it was for the horse, they'd give you water for that; they wouldn't give you any if you said it was your family that needed it.'[30] When Jim Vincent pulled at Capel, his grai was near the end of its working life. The knacker was offering him £15, which shocked local house dwellers who clubbed together to send it instead to a rest home on the Isle of Wight. Part of the deal was to provide funds for a new strong horse to pull the waggon, though it is not clear that this ever happened: certainly, the good people of Capel were much more concerned about Dobbin the Gypsy horse than they ever were about Jim, Louisa, Jimmy, Louise, Nelson, Janie, Valentine and Daphne the Gypsy Gypsies.[31]

If the pragmatic Gypsy attitude to animals disturbed gorjers, it was probably because this had once been part of their own culture; animals were treated without sentiment in Victorian times, and this approach survived among the working class until well into the twentieth century. But with changing times, even working men had grown unfamiliar with violence – among animals or people. Before the First World War the average man in pub or alehouse accepted without question that he should settle questions of reputation with his fists. By the 1960s it would have been rare to find any young gorjer brought up according to this code, and even rarer if he actually knew how to fight. But among the Gypsies it was still essential that one man should be able to stand up to another. There were no institutions within the community to mediate disputes, and recourse to the police or law was unthinkable, so arguments could only be brought to a clean, mutually accepted end if the two men had them out before a ring of onlookers, the larger the better. At least, that was the theory behind the fights which went on day after day in Derby week, although a lot of them were stoked by nothing more than hot tempers and tender egos. Wally Stockin took on Johnny Docherty after they'd been playing pitch and toss. 'He didn't know the man from Adam but carried on arguing because he felt strongly that he was in the right and the man was not being straight. It was all over a £5 note, but the two men were shouting in each other's faces, and it was obvious that a fight would have to be had.'[32]

After all this raised temper and shouting, the fight itself was serious and almost orderly; not only was it in everyone's interest to keep disputes from spilling over into a general riot, there could also be good money hanging on the match, so it was important to have a clear outcome with winner and loser. The ring might be kept by a known bare-knuckle man – Mark Ripley or Johnny Frankham or Jimmy Stockin himself – if they had no family connection or stake in the game; otherwise, order depended on a sherro rom, someone who had earned enough respect for their word to be accepted on this occasion as law. In 1980 Jasper Smith was called on to act as ringmaster in this way at the Derby. Obviously the fight would have to take place out of sight of the gavvers at the Grandstand and Rubbing House, so the crowd had spilled over onto the far side of the hill, where the ground slopes down towards Walton. No one had realized that this was also the start point for the mile-and-a-half race, until a police car drew up and a sergeant stepped out briskly towards the fight, which was already underway. The crowd parted and then closed around him, all alone; this did not look good. Then Jasper seized the moment and shouted, 'Is that my friend Mr Crowhurst, what was good to my Aaron?' – young Aaron Smith had made a business at his site in Croydon of accepting gangsters' used motors and burning them out, but he had been treated tactfully on arrest and the free curries at the police station were not forgotten. Yes, the lone figure was Sergeant Crowhurst, and now he was here on behalf of the Queen Mother, who was about to race one of her horses, and would appreciate it very much if horse and jockey could get to the starting gate. Jasper turned to the crowd. 'Everyone off the course for Her Royal Highness and my good friend Mr Crowhurst *right now*,' he roared, and a thousand men swarmed obediently down into the valley, where the fighters had found their feet and were trading blows again.[33]

Nobody, it seemed, had money on a runner in the race; no one appeared to be interested in it at all. But Gypsies were not indifferent to the strength and speed of horses; it was just that this was reserved for another time and place, away from the familiar Downs. Just as Gypsy churches had learnt to present the faith and hope of Christianity in ways acceptable for the community, so there were races which were specifically for Gypsies. These took place well away from gorjer eyes, and they were won or lost by trotting horses.

For a trotting race, you needed a long straight road, preferably on a Sunday morning when there was no traffic to get in the way: for many years the Hog's Back was the track of choice.[34] Each horse was fastened to a sulkie or spinner, the lightest of two-wheel carts that lets a man control his animal while adding as little as possible to the weight. Someone measured the road, set up a winning post and off they went; up to 4 miles was possible, but a mile and a half was best for racing; full-breds were the natural choice, but any horse could be entered, as long as it had been trained to run with the sulkie, and they could quickly pick up speed to about 30 miles per hour. Up to four drivers could fit onto a road (provided there was nothing coming the other way) but the real excitement came when two men went head to head.[35] That and the bets . . .

'My mush, dik at him goin'!' shouted a lined-featured London man, smoking a cigar and wearing a camel coat. A few diamonds glittered from a heavy gold ring on his left hand. 'I'd a-thought Davey's would've beat that any day . . .' On closer inspection I saw the winning pony to be driven by a man called Levi, a London traveller long since settled down, with his own prospering car-front. His thin face was taut with achievement and excitement as he reined the pony to a halt and ran round to its head . . . 'I tell you what, boys', challenged Levi: 'I bet five hundred pounds I can win the next one too – how about it?'[36]

Trotting with a sulkie was a competitive, slimmed-down variation of ordinary working routines, when young men went calling with a pony and light two-wheeled cart. Now and again they must have challenged each other for speed, but this would have been reckless at a time when a horse's strength was needed for work and for pulling the waggon. So it was not until the end of waggontime in the 1950s that trotting became a sport, and gradually it was organized: by 1978 a Surrey family were heading up to Tuxford in Nottinghamshire where a stretch of the Great North Road had been appropriated for the race.[37] There was big money in trotting – £3,500 was offered for the winner at Tuxford – and any man who could manage his horse well was worth respect. David Stacey of Chessington

David Stacey's funeral, Epsom, 2000.

was the best, a respected contestant and a member of the British Driving Association. He died suddenly, outside his home, and a London trolley driven by fellow horseman Dave Hilden bore the coffin from the funeral, past Horton Country Park where other men held their horses with heads bowed in respect, and so through Epsom High Street. The mourners' cars were crowned with horseshoes of white flowers, and after them friends and fellow competitors came on black sulkies to accompany David to burial upon the Downs he loved.[38]

A funeral was a time for complex emotions: for grief and loss among the family, of course, but also for others to stress the good Gypsy life of the deceased. Because gorjers could not decently interfere with the burial of the dead, funerals allowed people to get together in hundreds and affirm their Romany identity without being challenged or censored. By the close of the twentieth century, a proper way of dealing with funerals and the dead had been established, drawing on ancient custom, the lavish ceremonies of the Victorian age, and adaptations made for the contemporary world.

So, despite the fact that in modern times people usually die in hospital, they were brought back home as if they had breathed their last in the family circle. Once, there would have been a special death tent; now the undertakers provided a trailer so that visitors could come and view the body, paying their respects. Other people from the site or the street might come and go, but close family kept vigil all night. With easy communications, the news of the death rippled out instantly, giving everyone time to prepare tributes for the funeral.

When Jasper Smith died in 2003, the funeral was everything that was fitting for a Romany elder. Jasper was 82, the former site warden and unquestioned head man of the site at Cox Lane, where most of the residents were his relatives anyway. He had fought for his country in the war and he had fought for his people on the Gypsy Council. He had advised the 1977 Cripps Report on accommodation for Gypsies, and beaten Epsom and Ewell Council to a standstill, forcing them to make Cox Lane into a permanent site. Along with his sister and brother Minty and Levi, he had been photographed under the whitethorn blossom for a special issue of Topic Records devoted to Gypsy singers; Peter Kennedy and Ewan McColl had travelled to hear him; he had been on the BBC's *Folkweave*. To the end he had carried himself with dignity and a natural authority, and now he was dead. More than one hundred cars clogged the road leading from Cox Lane to Christ Church on Epsom Common, with the family in limousines followed by a string of flatbed trucks carrying the floral arrangements – first among them the Chair of Flowers, for if anyone had earned the right to rest it was Jasper. The church was crowded and spilling over. The coffin was light oak, carved with panels of the Last Supper, and as it was carried down the nave people wept and reached out to touch it for a last remembrance. Then the service and funeral address from the vicar (Christ Church had always been good to Gypsies) and a crackling guitar chord over the sound system announced Levi's song, 'Will There Be Any Gypsies in Heaven?' Always the same sad anxieties – will they let us stay; will we be shifted and moved on, as we were again and again in life? – but to chase away those feelings the next song was Jasper's favourite from when he was courting, 'The Blue-Eyed Blonde Next Door', pure George Formby and not folk at all. And so to the interment in Ashley Road cemetery, looking out over green fields and blue sky.[39]

Gypsies kept together in death, as in life. Ashley Road had its own cluster of graves kept bright with renewed flowers, as did Lingfield with its Smiths Corner. Large, sculpted and shining in the sun, these monuments were easily distinguishable from the gorjer graves around them, although this had not always been the case. When Jasper's father Derby was buried at Lingfield, a simple grey headstone sufficed but, in the following twenty or thirty years, monuments became much more elaborate, each trying to do credit to the deceased: competitive self-respect, of the sort that had played out in life with a trailer full of chrome and cut-glass mirrors, found a final home in glossy white marble and Jersey granite. And every surface carried golden letters of poetry, telling and perhaps helping soften the sorrow of loss:

We sit and talk about you Dad
And often think about you too
We have all these lovely memories Dad
But none compare with having you

If tears could built a stairway
And memories a lane
I'd walk right up to Heaven
And bring you back again

Memory is the golden chain
That binds us till we meet again[40]

This came from the hearts of the mourning family, still aching from the loss of someone loved. The theme was universal, which is why the poetic tags were often repeated. Outside that innermost circle, other people could show respect with their floral tributes, brought to the graveside after the funeral was over. In the 1970s these had been mostly sprays and wreaths but as time passed the florists were called on for more and more elaborate work: not just structures like the Chair of Rest and the Gates of Heaven, but horseshoes and framed photos, models of trucks and trailers and a favourite pub, a packet of cigarettes beside the dartboard, a waggon and its horse. If you had known the deceased well, you would soon recognize their favourite drink or hobby; if not, it was the more generalized symbols that caught the eye, as they would on the monument when that was built. Here the dogs and horses reappeared in black or gilded outline, a new motor on one side balanced by an old waggon on the other, scenes of coursing and trotting: all the things that had made up a traditional Gypsy life.

But these little sketches of community life were themselves witnesses to change. They harked back to the culture of waggontime, of the days before the watershed of the 1968 Act, but they did so in a new spirit of nostalgia. In the old days, a graiengro had made a living buying and selling horses, the motive engine of the countryside: quite a different thing from a successful businessman keeping a few cobs in the field behind his bungalow. The old waggons had been trundled over heath and common until they fell apart; now the surviving vehicles, or their lovingly crafted replicas, were painted carefully for display at fairs and special occasions. Gypsies had successfully adapted to modernity, but there was something a little self-conscious about traditional identity in a modern world.

Besides, there had been another change which left people reaching for cultural definition: the arrival of other groups which resembled Gypsies, and yet weren't. After the Second World War, nomadic families began to come over from the Republic of Ireland, where they had formed a distinct ethnic group for centuries.[41] To authority, they were Irish Travellers; among themselves, they were Pavees; for English Romanichals, they were simply the Irish. The British economy was flourishing in those years, that of the Republic was not, and hearing there was work over here in construction and road building, along with door-to-door jobs such as roofing and laying patios, many more families came to try their fortune. Like any incoming group, they were tempted to undercut prices and offer cheaper equivalents. They began as long travellers – in town today, gone

Floral tributes at Epsom, 2014.

tomorrow – and moved in larger convoys than English Gypsies, because they were in a strange land and there was safety in numbers. Initially they had no country in the travelling sense, no long-standing relationships with local customers or decent-minded gavvers, which meant that there was no risk in being as confrontational as possible when someone came to move them on.

Anxiety and dismay was the commonest response to these strangers, like the group that pulled onto the Leatherhead site in the 1970s. 'They were Irish people: travellers of the roughest kind. Their trailers were old wrecks, dented, many with smashed-out windows and doors hanging loosely from their hinges.' The crowding, the mess, the uncontrolled dogs and children: it was too much. 'All around us pandaemonium reigned, for they were noisy people, and all seemed to prefer short, shouted conversations in peculiarly aggressive tones.'[42] These Irish looked to the Gypsies like an incursion of sheer anarchy, just as Gypsies had appeared to gorjers.

The irony of these comparisons was not lost on the early Gypsy Council, which at its fourth meeting decided to include the Irish in campaigns. The decision was not popular, and it took all Grattan Puxon's charisma and tact to make it work at all.[43] In following decades political organizations came and went, splitting, rebranding and re-emerging from the grassroots, but the ethnic division remained much the same. The only lasting change was semantic. Whereas up to the 1960s the Romany had preferred to be known to the gorjer world as Travellers rather than Gypsies, now the arrival of another ethnic group who were unquestionably of the road meant that the word Traveller shifted its sense and became an umbrella term: Romanichals, Irish, Showfolk, hippies ('New Age Travellers' to the bureaucrats), they were Travellers all.

When it came to real life, these classifications tended to blur as people met and shared interests and married: the same forces which had turned Irish Mahoneys into Romany Marneys at the beginning of the twentieth century were still at work. The real distinction, not so widely acknowledged, was between the rough and combative ways of the poor and the polite confidence of flash travellers, and that was a matter of money, not breed. In most other respects the Irish were like Gypsies, trading, gambling, racing and fighting at the same fairs. Though they spoke their own language – once called Shelta, now Gammon – its words were dropped into English just like the vocabulary of Romanes. Though they were Catholic not Pentecostal, the same lavish floral tributes and gleaming monuments appeared in shared cemeteries.

In this they were quite different from those other new arrivals, the Roma. For much of the twentieth century, Roma people remained in southeast Europe, trapped by a communist ideology which also guaranteed them some rights as citizens. After 1989, the restrictions on travel were lifted, but so were the restraints on gorjer aggression, and many took the chance to escape to countries such as England which, if not exactly welcoming, did at least discourage murder by vigilante mobs. These newly arrived Roma were the ancestors made flesh – they were dark, they spoke the old language, they were strict in their avoidance of anything mogadi. But they were not Travellers; they had been settled in their home villages for centuries before the great disruption, and that meant they had little in common culturally with Romanichal Gypsies.

The real impact of the newcomers was not personal, but imaginative. They bore witness to an international Romani nation of which English Gypsies were just part, a nation with its own flag, language and anthem and, most important, with a previously unimagined history of persecution. People had already known, in a general way, that the Nazis had rounded up and killed Roma; indeed, Fred Wood had told how his paratroop unit had advanced through Germany in April 1945, and participated in the liberation of Belsen, where

We faced something terrible. Heaps of unburied bodies and unbearable stench. When I saw the surviving Romanies, with small children amongst them, I was shaken. Then I went over to the ovens and found on one of the steel stretchers the half-charred body of a girl and I understood in one awful minute what had been going on there.[44]

But Fred Wood was a storyteller, and not everyone took notice of his testimony. Not until Ian Hancock started stirring things up in the 1980s was it common knowledge that the Holocaust had targeted Roma for extinction along with Jews.[45] After that, English Gypsies began to think of themselves as one blood with the victims of the Porraimos.[46] When the documentary *A People Uncounted* was shown on Holocaust Memorial Day at Leatherhead, everyone wanted to talk afterwards and there were bitter complaints about the harassments of daily life; someone walked out dramatically shouting 'for us, it's still 1945!'; but nobody placed any distance between themselves and the people in the film. Everyone was Romany, everyone was a potential victim of racism.[47]

That kind of Gypsy identity drew on more than family skills and tales around the yog; it implied access to a wider world, it needed education. At Ash Manor School the annual trip abroad was modified so that the Gypsy pupils could go to see Auschwitz and learn at first hand about the tragedy: but then Ash Manor was special in many ways. Between 7 and 10 per cent of its intake came from the community, it had policies which paid more than lip service to integration, and above all it had Billie-Jo Sines. Without her skills as an intermediary, it would have been impossible to persuade families to let their children go to Germany, leaving the security of the only world they'd ever known, but they knew Billie was going to be on the plane so that made it alright.

With her help, and some smart thinking from the head Jo Luhmann, Ash Manor became a model of how to bring secondary education to the community. It hadn't always been that kind of school; it used to be a place where Gypsy girls would make it to year eleven and boys only as far as year nine before they were pulled out, their parents saying that they were wanted at home. It used to be a school from which boys were kept away because they were going to be self-employed and needed to learn the family business. In those days it was as if sending your children to secondary school was a disloyalty to the community. At one site there were three chavvies who wouldn't put on their uniform to go to school, not even dare to walk through the site in it; they'd walk out in their ordinary clothes and then get changed outside, because they wanted to go that badly. This was at a time when fathers would burn the uniforms, but the kids would turn up all the same, uniforms or not, because their mothers would make sure they were delivered to the front door. And that was the spirit which changed Ash Manor.[48]

Not every school was like this. As soon as people began to think that education might be an asset rather than a nuisance, they asked whether it was being withheld from the Romany – deliberately or by bungled institutional malpractice. This was one of the results of settling down; as Harry Lee said at Woking, 'We want to get our kids into school and to have a good education because most of the older ones never had much of an education, because they don't seem to have settled.'[49] Before then, few had made their compulsory appearance, and most of those who did weren't learning much, not even reading and writing; at the showing of *A People Uncounted*, interpreters were needed to read out the subtitles. Meanwhile, the wider culture was finding technologies that could bring you knowledge without literacy. Television brought a glimpse of the world outside, even if early channel-hopping was confined to anything with horses in it.[50] When mobile phones came out in 1984, Tony Marshall made a killing buying them wholesale and selling them on to people he knew; they were God's gift to Gypsies: 'within hours of reaching home we had a hundred orders.'[51]

But what did an education mean, beyond the ability to key in someone's phone number? Many people stopped at the basics, letting their kids learn enough to get by but pulling them out before the gorjer world could corrupt or assimilate them. In the 1990s, about 80 per cent of children were attending primary school but only 20 per cent went on to secondary.[52] And just as parents were reluctant to hand their children over, so schools could be unwilling to take them. Education was being used as a weapon in the battle between migrant and settled. In 1988 Croydon Local Education Authority turned some children out of school: because they were stopping at an unauthorized encampment, even acknowledging the existence of the children might have legitimized the presence of their families. As time wore on, and the 1994 Criminal Justice Act undid the slender gains of the 1968 Caravan Act, problems increased for anyone who kept up the travelling life.

But even for family who lived on sites or had gone into brick, school was not easy: often children would give it a go and then come back to their parents disillusioned. The main problem was bullying, and not just from other pupils. 'Recently my daughter was being called "pikey" at school,' Rosie Smith remembered. 'She told a teacher and the teacher simply said well you are one. My daughter answered no, I'm not a "pikey" or Gypo, I am a Romany Gypsy traveller.'[53] It took pride and self-confidence, more than many children possess at a vulnerable age, to stand up to this emotional and psychological bullying, especially in schools where there were no other Gypsies in the playground to offer support.

But for those who found a good school, or who had the stamina to survive a bad one, education opened new pathways for self-assertion. The first secretary to the Gypsy Council was an unexpected graduate, Elizabeth Easton. She came from Redskin Village in Mitcham and had passed the eleven-plus, which meant that she could stay in school, though it involved putting up with the discrimination. That lasted until the day that she went out for a drink with her cousins and found herself next morning called to the headmaster's office. We know about you, girl, they said; we know about your family background, and let me tell you, if you carry on like this, you'll be on the streets by the time you're sixteen. I won't be talked to like that, she said, and left, and got a job as a secretary. Her employer was very attentive and offered her a training course – not to worry about the expense, he said, because she could always pay it off in kind. Go siv your dai, you bald-headed bastard, said Elizabeth, and left, qualifying for the training course anyway. It was a revelation: the first time she'd met people who were educated but treated her decently. She liked it so much that she went on to attend LSE, where she got a 2:1 in French and Law.[54]

Apart from its secretary, the Gypsy Council was a mush's world: 26 men to four women at that first meeting in the Bull. But the generations which followed were not so happy to leave things in the hands of the menfolk. Modernization had changed the position of women, reducing the size of families and increasing the allocation of money-making work to men. Where once both sexes would have gone calling and selling, now he was out roofing or tarmacing or gardening or whatever offered itself, while she stayed behind in a gleaming trailer. As Billie-Jo said before she took up the transformation of Ash Manor, you can get tired of cooking and cleaning after a while. So there was a great deal of unused female talent in the community, and inevitably some of it would find its way into politics.

It began in 1996, when Ann Wilson teamed up with Hilda Brazil. They were related – Hilda's grandmother Celia was the sister-in-law of Ann's great-aunt Mary – but more importantly they had grown up

Ann Wilson
receiving her MBE,
2014.

together in Effingham. The village, where Hilda was later parish coun-
cillor, had a reputation for involving Gypsies in public business, and it
was to her friends at Effingham that Linda Goodman came when she
needed help. She was a gorjer teacher who had met with a couple that had
a disabled child, and couldn't get her any education, simply because she
was a Gypsy. Clearly something needed to be done. So the three women
set up a group, the Surrey Gypsy Traveller Communities Forum, which
would get the best deal possible for the community. It was less pugna-
cious than the Gypsy Council, more concerned to coordinate health and
benefits and education and law, all the services offered by a dwindling
public sector which needed to learn about the special requirements of
the community. The group took off, holding public meetings, organizing
training sessions, holding cultural events and even sponsoring a historian.
Recognition for the forum, and for its most tireless worker, came in 2014
when Ann was presented with an MBE for services to her people. The
ceremony itself, held at Windsor Castle, was intimidating to begin with:

> We were lined up, it was all very formal, and of course I was
> frightened of tripping on the brocade or something. There was
> a guardsman organizing the queue, and he said: They'll announce

you as Ann, Mrs Wilson – and on the W you step forward – and if you don't I'll punch you in the back. Well, thank you, I thought, but it all went alright. The Queen said, 'Is this the award for Gypsies and Travellers?' and I said 'Yes, ma'm'; and she said 'How are things for your people?' and I said 'Better in some ways, but worse in others'; and she said 'How are the children?' and I said 'They're staying longer in school, ma'm, which is better'; and then I went down, being careful to walk backwards, because that's what you have to do. Everyone was asking 'What did she say to you? – she was smiling!'[55]

Ann talked about her day in Windsor at the forum that November. The medal was passed round, shiny and new, and we all admired it; Ann was almost apologetic for having received an honour, wanting everyone to know how supportive Michael and the girls had been. How bright the future seemed, how full of hope.

GLOSSARY

This is not a comprehensive vocabulary, but simply a list of many of the Romanes words which appear in this book, with some notes on their background. A reasonably confident speaker would have a core vocabulary five times as large as this.

Anglo-Romani is an oral language, and even when it has been written down, this was done by people already familiar with English, so it follows the rules of written English rather than those found in other Romani dialects, where one letter always represents one sound. I've harmonized it to the extent of always using the same letters for the same sound in the same situation, following practices which come naturally to an English speaker, such as silent letters. So in *gavver*, for instance, the double *v* and final *r* don't indicate additional sounds, but vowel quantity.

The vowel sounds should be unambiguous to a southern English speaker, except that *u* is invariably the sound in *put* not *putt*. The diphthong in *dai* rhymes with English *die*; the diphthong in *kaulo* with English *call*. A final *-o* has come to be pronounced as a schwa or weak vowel: thus *baulo* is homophonous with English *bawler*.

I have benefitted from James Hayward's *Gypsy Jib* and from the generosity of the late Jim Penfold, who entrusted me with his as yet unpublished dictionary of Romanes. I have also learnt a great deal from the comprehensive online dictionary by Yaron Matras at http://romani.humanities.manchester.ac.uk.

adoi	'there', from Old Romani *odoi*. Often pronounced with two syllables, *ado-i*
adrey	'in, into', from Old Romani *andre*. Following the loss of a word for 'to' (*kate* in the old language), *adrey* is extending its sense to this, and to 'among'. Often found in the clipped form *'drey*
akai	'here', from Old Romani *akai*
aley	'down', from Old Romani *tale*. Apparently phrases like *besh tele* were rationalized as *besh te aley* (with the emphatic enclitic *te* which follows imperative verbs) to create a new form resembling *adoi*, *akai* and so on
ambrol	'pear', as in Old Romani
atch	'to stay, to stop', from Old Romani *ač-*, used in the standard phrase *atchin tan*, 'stopping place', which appears with a south-of-England

prosthetic *h* in the Hatchingtan, a site at Woking. *Atch*, like its English counterpart, has a second sense of 'desist' (already present in Old Romani) and a children's campaign was called *Atch Poggering Mande* (Stop Bullying Me)

av   'to come', as in Old Romani. Uniquely this exists in parallel with another form, *vel*, 'to come', from the inflected form *avela*, 'he comes'

bango   'crooked' and 'left', as in Old Romani, though the form *bongo* also appears in Romanes. 'Crooked' appears to be the older sense; several languages and dialects have used similar imagery for left-handedness

bar   'pound', as in Old Romani where it means 'rock, stone'. First the sense was transferred from stone weights to the unit they represented, and then to the pound as currency

baulo   'pig', from Old Romani *balo*. *Ballovas*, 'bacon', is a compound from *baulo mas*, 'pig meat'

Beng   'Devil', as in Old Romani. An origin in *bango*, 'crooked', would make semantic if not phonological sense, but John Sampson thinks it derives from a word for 'toad', implying some confusion between devils, dragons and toads when the Roma first encountered Christianity. *Bengtail*, one of the euphemisms for 'rat', may allude to the Devil's tail, though the more literal English compounds 'longtail' and 'ringtail' are also found

besh   'to sit, to lie down', from Old Romani *beš*

bikkin   'to sell', from Old Romani *bikin-*

bitcher   'to send', from Old Romani *bičav-*. The past participle *bitchado*, 'sent', was retained in the special sense 'transported'

bitti   'little', either from French *petit* or the same word transmitted through English Cant

bok   'luck', from Old Romani *baxt*, probably ultimately from Iranian. The *t* survives in the adjective *boktalo*, 'lucky', where it is needed to distinguish the word from *bokalo*. *Kushti bok*, 'good luck', is a standard farewell

bokalo   'hungry', from Old Romani *bokhalo*, the adjectival form of *bokh*

boro   'great, big', from Old Romani *bauro*. The feminine form *bori* was retained in the special sense 'great with child, pregnant'. Some years ago a concert was announced as the *Bori Rat*, a translation presumably meant as 'big night' rather than 'pregnant blood'

bosh   'fiddle, violin'. You would have thought that the word *boshamengro*, 'fiddle-player' ('fiddler' is not idiomatic Gypsy English), came from *bosh* but in fact it's the other way round. *Boshamengro* was originally 'musician', from Old Romani *bašav-*, 'to play an instrument'; later it was confined to the fiddle-player, the king of musicians; and then it was treated as if derived from the word *bosh*, 'him of the fiddle'

boshto   'saddle', a noun formation from Old Romani *beš*, 'to sit'

budika   'shop', a loanword from French *boutique*

charro   'plate', from Old Romani *čauro*

chavvi   'child', from Old Romani *čavo/čavi*, 'boy/girl'. The feminine form became the standard one, and the word is now gender neutral

chin   'to cut', from Old Romani *čin*; also 'to write', I suppose by analogy with cutting signs with a knife on tree bark. So a *chinamengro* is not, as you might have thought, a sculptor, but a postman, 'him of the writings'

chiriklo   'bird', from Old Romani *čeriklo*

chitti   'tripod', specifically the three iron bars from which pots are hung over a fire. I may be making a fool of myself listing it here (like the lexicographers who solemnly reported *kazi* and *trolli* as Romanes for 'loo' and 'cart') but there is a *chitti* meaning 'chain' in Bath Smart and Henry Thomas Crofton, *The Dialect of the English Gypsies* (London, 1875), which may be related

chokka   'shoe', from Old Romani *čiox*, ultimately from Greek (see *chuffa* below)

chop   to exchange goods with some money thrown in the deal

chor   'to steal', from Old Romani *čor-*, also used as a noun, 'thief'. This is now homophonous with *chor*, 'grass', *čaur* in Old Romani; the collapse of the old sound system has created an ambiguity which wasn't there before

chuffa   'coat', from Old Romani *čoxa*, ultimately from Greek. The voiced velar fricative *x* in Old Romani yields *f*, *g* or *k* in Romanes; *čiox*, 'shoe', has become *chokka*, so the reflexes of *čoxa* tend to have *f* rather than *k*, to avoid confusion

chukni   'whip', from Old Romani *čupni*, perhaps ultimately from Iranian

dadus   'father', as in English Cant. On the other hand, Old Romani marks loanwords with an *-os* ending, so **dados* could be a Romani formation from English *dad* that was borrowed by Cant

dai   'mother', from Old Romani *dai*. The vocative *daia* is still sometimes used

del   'to give', from the Old Romani stem *da-* in the inflected form *dela*, 'he gives'. Generations of weary mothers shouting 'I'll del you one' have given it a second sense of 'hit'

didikai   'Gypsy' or 'Traveller', usually of lower status than the speaker. Of unknown origin, this word appears so often as an English dialect term for Gypsies that its origin must be in that language, not in Romanes

dik   'see, look', from Old Romani *dikh-*. This has a second sense of 'appear', modelled on the other sense of English 'look': a *kushti-dikking rakli* is a good-looking girl, not one with excellent eyesight

diklo   'scarf', specifically the bright silk scarf worn round the neck by men. In Old Romani it meant both 'neckerchief' and 'shawl'

dinilo   'fool, idiot', as in Old Romani; often contracted to *dinlo*. The other word for 'fool', *div* – a substantive form from *divvi*, Old Romani *divio*, 'wild' – is not quite a synonym. You could say of yourself 'I am a div, I left the skid on the wheel,' but *dinilo* is more contemptuous and mostly reserved for gorjers

divvus   'day', from Old Romani *dives*. *Kushti divvus*, 'good day', is a standard greeting

dordi   'Well!', an expression of surprise, of unknown origin. Once universal, it is now regarded as very old-fashioned by some families but in others is used routinely, even by the children

drab   'medicine, poison', as in Old Romani. Perhaps there was some semantic influence from Greek *pharmakon*, which has the same double sense, or perhaps it's an independent development of ideas

drom	'road', as in Old Romani, ultimately from Greek; also 'way, manner', either modelled on the other sense of English 'way' or an independent development. *Latcho drom*, 'good road', is a standard farewell, one of the few phrases in Romanes which has no English equivalent, though it resembles French *bon voyage*
dukker	'to tell fortunes', from Old Romani *durker*. The derived noun *dukkcripen* is found metathesized as *durrekipen* and this has given a back-formed verb *durrek*
Duvvel	'God', from Old Romani *devel*. Presumably the first vowel was changed to avoid gorjers confusing the word with English *devil*. Also found in the pious form *miDuvvel*, 'my God'
foki	'people', from English *folk*. This had become a dialect rather than a standard word and must have seemed obscure enough not to be understood by gorjers
gad	'shirt', as in Old Romani
gatter	'beer', from English Cant
gaujo	'non-Gypsy', from Old Romani *gaudžo*, *gadžo* in the Continental forms. This word is spelt differently by different authors: *gorgio* by literary types, following Borrow; *gadje* by anthropologists, loftily ignoring the difference between Continental and Anglo-Romani; *gaujo* by Gypsies who are used to writing the language, *gorja* or *gorgia* by those who aren't; *gorjer* by genealogists. The last spelling seemed the one least likely to be mispronounced, so I've used it throughout this book
gav	'town, village', as in Old Romani. London is the *Boro Gav*, 'big city'
gavver	'policeman'. Matras thinks this is a substantive use of *garav-*, 'to hide', but policemen are not known for their inconspicuousness. I suspect that *gav-mush* was originally 'man of the town', 'parish constable', later extended to the regular police force. It is a southern English term; in the north and in Wales people say *muskro*
gil	'sing', from the inflected form of Old Romani *giav-*. *Gilli* is 'song', but also 'newspaper', which may go back to the days when a horrible murder or the latest battle would be versified in a broadside
gorjer	an English-style spelling of *gaujo* (above)
grai	'horse', as in Old Romani, ultimately from Armenian. *Graiengro* is a horse-dealer. *Saster grai*, 'iron horse', is a train
granza	'barn, stable', from French *grange*
gruvni	'cow', from Old Romani *guruv* with the female suffix *-ni*. 'Bull' is *gruvno*, an attempted masculine from *gruvni* after the true one was forgotten
gudli	'noise, racket', from Old Romani *godli*. This is now homophonous with *gudli*, 'sugar, sweets', *gudlo* in Old Romani
gui	'pudding', the sort that you boil in a bag, from Old Romani *goi*, 'sausage'
haw	'to eat', from Old Romani *xa-*; sometimes *hol*, from the inflected form *xala*, 'he eats'. The derived noun is *hawben* or more commonly *hobben*, 'food'
hokker	'to lie', from Old Romani *xoxav-*. The derived noun is *hokkiben*, 'lie'
holova	'stocking', from Old Romani *xolov*, ultimately from Slavic. In Continental Romani this is now the word for 'trousers', which didn't

exist at the time of the Arrival; 'trousers' in Romanes is *rokkunyas*,
from Old Romani *raxuni*, 'coat'

horro   'shilling', from German *Heller*, 'penny'. This change in meaning may
reflect the shortage of silver pennies in the sixteenth century

hotchi   'hedgehog', more common in the pet-form *hotchiwitchi*. There is also
a verb form, 'to burn' (Old Romani *xačer-*), and the noun seems to be
a play on words between this and the English *urchin*, 'hedgehog'

jank   'shit', apparently English Cant or slang, but influenced by *hin* from
Old Romani *xin-*, 'to shit'

jell   'to go', from the Old Romani stem *dža-* in the inflected form *džala*,
'he goes'. In the Midlands and north people still say *jall*, but in the
south it has become *jell*, perhaps by analogy with *vell*

jib   'tongue', from Old Romani *čib*, but more often in a second sense
'language'. Although this matches the semantics of English 'tongue',
the double sense was already present in Old Romani

jiv   'to live', from Old Romani *dživ-*. The derived noun is *jivaben*, 'life',
also 'lifestyle' in phrases such as *Romani jivaben*

jota   'call', from Old Romani *dyuta*; specifically, a two-note whistle which
lets it be known that a Gypsy wants others to come over without
attracting the interest of gorjers

jub   'louse', from old Romani *džuv*

jukkel   'dog', from Old Romani *džukel*; more common now in the
abbreviation *jukk*. A fox is a *veshni-jukkel*

juvvel   'woman', from Old Romani *džuvli*; usually a young woman. If Louie's
eldest daughter is also called Louie, she will be known as Louie Juvvel
to distinguish her from her mother

kair   'house', from Old Romani *kher*. The pronunciation is now *ker*,
a homophone for *ker*, 'do', but I've kept the variant spelling as a
distinction. *Kairengro* is 'house dweller'

kam   'sun', from Old Romani *kham*. *Kam-divvus* is 'Sunday' in some
families; among others it is *Mas-divvus*, literally 'day of meat', a
tribute to the Sunday roast

kan   'ear', from Old Romani *kand*. A hare is *kanengro*, 'him of the ears',
to distinguish him from a *shushi*, 'rabbit'

kanni   'chicken', from Old Romani *kani*. A pheasant is a *veshni-kanni*

kas   'cheese', from Dutch. This loanword may have been adopted when Old
Romani *kiral*, 'cheese', and *khil*, 'butter', had fallen together to produce
Romanes *kil*, which was ambiguous, but is now usually 'butter'

kaulo   'black', as in Old Romani. By extension this meant 'Gypsy'; *kaulo
rat*, or 'black blood', is a sign of good family. The arrival of African
Caribbeans, who really are Black, has made this usage archaic

kek   'not', as in Old Romani, where it is the adjective 'none'. In Romanes
it is increasingly used for all kinds of negation. *Kek-ker*, 'Don't!',
abbreviated to *kekka*, is so common it sometimes replaces *kek*

ken   'house', from English Cant. The derived noun, also adopted from
Cant, is *kennick*, 'house dweller'

ker   'to do', as in Old Romani. A hard-working verb which can mean
'make' (as in the old language) but also 'reach', 'put', 'finish' and
other senses

kil   'butter', from Old Romani *khil* (see *kas* above)

kipsi   'basket', apparently from English dialect *skep*; the form *skipsi* is sometimes used. A *kipsiengro* is a basket maker. Claims that English *skip* (for building waste) is a loanword from Romanes have got things the wrong way round

kissi   'purse', from Old Romani *kisi*, ultimately from Arabic via Persian

kokkero   'alone', from Old Romani *kokoro*, but more common in the sense *mi kokkero, tu kokkero* – 'myself', 'yourself' – often with the pronoun omitted

kolla   'shilling', of uncertain origin, perhaps from English *dollar*

kolliko   'nearest day', from Old Romani *kaliko*. One of the few Romanes words without an English synonym, this refers to the day next to today, which could be either 'tomorrow' or 'yesterday'. Under the influence of English, 'yesterday' is predominating

kor   'to fight', from Old Romani *kur-*, 'to beat'. *Koromengro* is either 'soldier' or 'bare-knuckle fighter', the words having evidently been coined separately

kosh   'wood', from Old Romani *kašt*. Some families distinguish *kosh*, 'wood' in a collective sense (*yog-kosh* is 'firewood'), from *koshti*, 'stick'

krallis   'king', from Old Romani *kralis*, ultimately from Slavic. A much-travelled word, in its earliest Germanic sense 'freeman' and used as the name Karl. Among the Anglo-Saxons, the *ceorl* sank to be a peasant, just above a slave; among the Slavs, the name of Charlemagne their Frankish enemy became the archetype for 'king'; and so, a thousand years later, the cognates *krallis* and *churl* met again on English soil with diametrically opposite meanings

kushti   'fine', from Old Romani *kuško*, a word found only in Britain; it may be a metathesis of Continental Romani *šukar*, 'good'. Since the word entered London street slang as *cushty* from Romanes, some families have taken to saying *kushki*, not wanting to be mistaken for Del Boy

latch   'to catch', from Old Romani *lhat-*

latcho   'good', from Old Romani *lačo*. Interchangeable with *kushti* in some phrases such as *latcho/kushti divvus*, 'good day'; it has a second sense, 'cheap', which suggests the Tudor English phrase *good cheap*

lell   'to take', from the Old Romani stem *la-* in the inflected form *lala*, 'he takes'

leste   'he/him, she/her, it', used for all cases, though in Old Romani *leste* is the instrumental case which (as with *mande* and *tutte*) forms the standard in Romanes. *Len* is 'they, them'; in Old Romani *len* is the root of the plural

levvina   'beer', from Old Romani *lovina*, ultimately from Slavic. *Levvinengroes* are hops; the code-name for Kent is *Levvinengresko Tem*, 'Hop County'

lur   'to steal', as in Old Romani. To *chor* is to pilfer or pick pockets; to *lur* is to rob with violence. The derived noun *luripen* has been coined twice separately, once meaning 'theft' and once meaning 'booty'

mande   'I, me', used for all cases, although in Old Romani it was the prepositional form of *me*. The inflection is still correct in phrases like *Del mande pansh bar*, 'give me five quid', and usage was probably

	extended from this because *mande* was less intelligible to gorjers. Now, even as a nominative, it always takes English 'is' rather than 'am': *Mande's bokalo*, 'I'm hungry', not **Mande am bokalo*
marro	'bread', from old Romani *mauro*
mas	'meat', as in Old Romani. A *kekmasengro* is a vegetarian
matcho	'fish', from Old Romani *mačo*. An oyster is a *bar-matcho*, 'stone fish'
mer	'to die', as in Old Romani, which has the separate word *mar-*, 'to kill'; this has now fallen together with *mer* though the second sense can also be expressed by *muller*, a substantive use of *mullo*, 'to make dead'. The derived noun *meriben* has, I think, the sense 'a death', rather than 'death' in the abstract. But it also means 'a life', because the whole of your existence can be summed up by its end; another case where Romanes differs in its idiom from English
meski	'tea', a contraction of *pimeskri*, 'him of the drink'. Also known as *muttermengri*, 'him of the piss', which at first sight looks like a pun on English *pee*, but the English word is not recorded until long after the Romani one. It is more likely a reference to the green colour of China tea. Curiously, some families use the word *chai* from Continental Romani *čajo*, cognate with *tea* itself. Since the Arrival took place long before tea-drinking, this word must be a later import
miro	'my', as in Old Romani, although this has mostly given way to a contracted *mi*, which sounds like the short form of English 'my'. *Mande's* is also used
mishto	'well', from Old Romani *mišto*. *Mishto, parrak' tutte*, 'fine, thank you', will answer *Sar shan?*, 'How are you?' On its own, the word can function as 'Well done!' or 'Bravo!'
mogadi	'foul', in the specific sense of being indecently unclean, from Old Romani *maxado*. Further north, this is always *mokkadi*. It is contrasted with *chiklo*, meaning 'dirty' but in the ordinary way of work, as with field dirt or engine grease
mol	'wine', as in Old Romani, ultimately from the Indic word for 'mead'. Christmas was formerly known as *Mol-divvus*, 'day of wine', possibly because it was one of the rare occasions when Georgian and Regency churches celebrated communion – though this suggests a religious participation not always found among Gypsies
mong	'to beg', in a specifically Gypsy way, with charm and confidence, from Old Romani *mang-*. So spelt traditionally, but now pronounced to rhyme with sung not song
mort	'woman', from English Cant. Perhaps because of its origin, this can refer to either a Gypsy or a gorjer woman, whereas *juvvel* and *rakli* are used only for Gypsies
motto	'drunk', from Old Romani *mato*. *Motto jukkel*, 'drunken dog', has been a boozy term of endearment ever since the Arrival
mui	'mouth', as in Old Romani, and also 'face', a second sense already present in Old Romani. *Ma-mui*, literally 'not-facing', has been coined for 'opposite'
mullo	'dead person', from Old Romani *mulo*. Used both for the corpse that is buried and for the idea of the dead person that might return; it is a much more physical concept than English 'ghost'. The adjective

mullerdi is, according to context, 'funereal', 'spooky' or 'tainted by death'. The *Mullo-mush* is Death personified

mush   'man', from Old Romani *murš*. It is used, as in English, as the head in compounds: *yogger-mush*, literally 'gun-man', is 'gamekeeper'. If John's eldest son is also called John, he will be known as Mushy John to distinguish him from his father

muskro   'policeman', found in the Winchester Confessions and therefore likely to be the earliest term. Nationally, there are about ten synonyms for 'police', a necessary precaution as even the slowest-witted constable would notice if the same word was used in Romanes every time he turned up

needie   'Gypsy', from Shelta but used as a self-designation by Romanies

nevi   'new', from Old Romani *nevo*. *Nevi Vesh* (or *Wesh*) is the New Forest, not the most logical of translations as the forest was centuries old at the time of the Arrival

oprey   'on, above', from Old Romani *apre*. In the slogan *Oprey Roma* it functions as an adverb: 'Upwards, the Romany!'

pal   'brother', from Old Romani *phral*. The vocative *prala* (retaining an *r*) was used until recently

palai   'behind', from Old Romani *palal*. Like many words placing something in physical space, it has developed a temporal sense of 'after'

pani   'water', as in Old Romani. The cognate word in Gujarati is pronounced the same, and it used to be a regular stunt in Indian restaurants to order a glass of water in the native language

parrako   'thanks', from *pariker-*, 'to thank'. Normally used as an indeclinable element in the courtesy phrase *parrak' tute*, 'thank you'

patrin   'leaf', as in Old Romani, specifically the broken leaves or tufts of grass left as an unobtrusive marker of the route that other Gypsies have taken. In the form *patteran* this has become the primary sense

paudel   'across', from Old Romani *pardal*

pauni   'white', from Old Romani *paurno*. Also used as a substantive for 'flour', by extension from *pauno marro*, 'white bread'

pen   'sister', from Old Romani *phen*

pi   'to drink', as in Old Romani. A parallel form *peev* has developed from the inflected *pjava*, 'I drink'

pirri   'boiler', the large flat-bottomed cast-iron pot in which stews are cooked, from Old Romani *piri*

plashta   'cloak', from Old Romani *plašta*, ultimately from Slavic

pogger   'to break', from Old Romani *phager-*. Also 'to hit', with the secondary sense 'bully'. The participle is *poggadi*, 'broken': Anglo-Romani is *poggadi jib*, 'broken language'

poov   'field', from Old Romani *phuv*. A farmer is *poovengro*, 'him of the field'. It is used as a verb in *poov the grai*, 'put the horse in the field', specifically to do so overnight so that he gets some grazing without being seen

posh   'half', from Old Romani *paš*, ultimately from the Indic word for 'side'. The children of a marriage between Gypsy and gorjer are referred to as *posh-rats*, 'half-bloods' – though not in their hearing. *Posh-divvi* (see *dinilo* entry) is a nickname: Poshy Frank was a debt

collector, something for which a reputation of being 'half-crazed' had
its advantages

puro   'old', from Old Romani *phuro*. The female inflection survives in *puri jib*, 'old language', meaning Old Romani

purrum   'onion', from Old Romani *purum*, ultimately from Latin via Slavic; also 'leek', 'wild garlic' and so on

putsi   'pocket', from old Romani *potsi*. There were no pockets at the time of the Arrival; like its English equivalent, *putsi* developed a new sense from the old one of 'pouch'

rai   'gentleman', as in Old Romani. Any gorjer who looked well-dressed or official, or both, was a *rai*; *Romano rai*, 'gentleman who knows the ways of Gypsies', was a self-ascription for early scholars of the culture

rakli   'girl', as in Old Romani; much more common than *raklo*, 'boy', as Romanes tends to avoid relying on gendered inflections to distinguish meaning. In the old language it meant specifically 'gorjer girl/boy' but now it has swung to the opposite, presumably from the feeling that Gypsy words must imply Gypsy people

rashai   'clergyman', from Old Romani *rašai*, and also acceptable as 'pastor', although groups like the Life and Light Church have reservations about the idea of clergy

rat   'blood', as in Old Romani, and also 'race, breed'. *Ratvalo*, the swearword 'bloody', was a calque on English and has become as old-fashioned as its equivalent

rati   'night', as in Old Romani. *Rati* always has a long vowel, *rat* a short one, although confusingly forms like *ratti* for 'blood' are not uncommon

rauni   'lady', from Old Romani *rauni*, which is *rai* with a feminine suffix. Like English 'lady', it is being extended to women more generally

rig   'to carry', 'to keep', from Old Romani *riger-*

rinkeni   'beautiful', from Old Romani *rangkano*, apparently originally *ranikano*, 'ladylike'. It applies to people, not things, which are *kushti*

rokker   'to talk', from Old Romani *raker-*. Normally understood as 'to speak Romanes'; the antonym *gaujikanes*, 'English', would be useful but is obsolete. A phone is *rokkermengro*, 'him of the talk'

rom   'husband', from the ethnonym *Rom*, plural *Roma*. In early times every man was a husband, and Gypsies were the only true men. *Mush* has now taken the semantic space of 'man', while 'Gypsy man' is expressed by *Romanichal*, 'boy of the Roma'; the female version is *Romanichai*. *Romni*, with the feminine suffix, is 'wife'

Romanes   'in the Romani way', specifically 'in the Romani language'. A rare survival of an adverbial form, it is often treated as a noun, 'the Romani language'

saster   'iron', from Old Romani *saster*, ultimately from Greek, like most words to do with metalworking; it was in the Byzantine lands that the Romany first learned to work as smiths

scran   'food', from English Cant

shav   'to leave', apparently from English Cant; the original sense of 'run away, escape' has been extended

sherro   'head', from Old Romani *šero*. *Sherengro* – or *sherro rom*, which looks like a modern loanword from Continental Romani – is a leader, specifically someone who has earned enough respect in the community to be able to command

shoon 'to hear', from Old Romani *šun-*; also 'to listen'

shushi 'rabbit', from Old Romani *šošoi*, 'hare'. At the time of the Arrival, rabbits had not naturalized themselves as a wild species and one word covered both 'rabbit' and 'hare'. Later 'hare' was distinguished by *kanengro*

si standard form for 'is, are', used singular and plural, except for *shom*, which is known but not always used for 'I am', and *shan*, 'you are', which has survived thanks to the phrase *sar shan?*, literally 'how are you?' but implying 'so you're a Gypsy, too'. *Sas* is used for all past forms

smentini 'cream', from Old Romani *smentana*, ultimately from Slavic

stadi 'hat', as in Old Romani, ultimately from Greek. Two separate forms from the same etymon, *kadi* and *stadi*, have been used for 'man's hat' and 'woman's hat', but this is not common

starripen 'prison', from old Romani *stariben*, the derived noun from *star*, 'catch'. The metathesized form *stirrapen* has given rise to the abbreviation *stir*

suv 'to sleep', from Old Romani *sov-*. *Suv te mishto*, an imperative with enclitic *te*, is the equivalent of 'rest in peace'. But by analogy with English 'sleep with', *suv* has acquired the sense 'screw'; I have a notion that the near-homophone *siv*, 'sew', can be used in this case; more often, embarrassment is avoided by using the adjective *sutti*, 'sleepy', as both verb and noun

swegla 'pipe', from German

tan 'place', from Old Romani *than*. Romanes words are usually understood in terms of Gypsy life, so *tan* becomes 'place to stop', and then 'tent', influenced by the English word

tatcho 'true', from Old Romani *tačo*. It has an extended sense 'right, proper of its kind': a *tatcho grai* is everything you would expect a horse to be. As in English, it also has the sense 'righthand'. In conversation, an occasional *tatcho* implies agreement – 'right, OK'

tem 'country', from Old Romani *them*. There is a set of code-names in *-tem* for countries and counties. Heaven is *Oprey-tem*, 'the land above'

tikni 'baby', from Old Romani *tikno*, 'child'. In Continental Romani the word means 'little', but this sense was now supplied in Britain by the loanword *bitti*

tober 'road', from Shelta. A synonym for *drom* in its literal sense, but without the same range of associations. Among Showfolk, the *tober* is not the road but the fairground

tov 'to wash', from Old Romani *thov-*. Like *mong*, this has changed its vowel sound, which is now that of *tut* not *tot*

tulo 'fat', from Old Romani *thulo*. The original sense seems to have been 'plump', but this is now expressed by *boro* while *tulo* is specifically the fat on meat. The derived noun *tulipen* is used for 'grease'

tutte 'you', used for all cases (singular and plural) although in old Romani it was the prepositional form of the singular *tu*. An adjective *tiro*, 'your', was formerly used but seems now to have been ousted by *tutte's vardo* — 'waggon', specifically a Gypsy living-waggon, from Old Romani *verdo*, ultimately from Iranian. In early days the word meant 'cart'; the living-waggon was at first *kair-vardo*, 'house-cart', and was later abbreviated. Unlike most words ending in *-o*, it is often given a long end vowel, rhyming with *Fado* rather than *harder*. This is probably a spelling pronunciation

vast — 'hand', as in Old Romani. *Vastimengros*, 'them of the hands', are handcuffs

vesh — 'wood', from Old Romani *veš*, ultimately from Iranian. Also found as *wesh*: initial *v-* and *w-* commonly alternate, probably reflecting the London dialect of Dickens's time rather than anything older. *Veshengro*, 'him of the woods', is a gamekeeper

veshni — adjectival form of *vesh*

vonga — 'coal', from Old Romani *vangar*, but commonly 'money'. The semantic shift is a calque on eighteenth-century English slang, possibly reflecting folklore in which fairy money turns into coal. The variant *wonga* is now frowned on after it was adopted by an unloved gorjer loan firm

wafodi — 'bad', from German *böse*. Forms range from *basavo* through *vasavo* and *vaffado* but it is still curious why this word should show so much phonetic variation

wavver — 'other', from Old Romani *vaver*; unlike other *w-* words, this is never found with an initial *v-* in Romanes. *Wavvertemeskros* are foreigners, 'them of the other lands'

welgorus — 'fair, festival', perhaps ultimately from Greek. Welsh Romani has *valgora* but English seems to have kept the *-us* ending used in the old language for loanwords

yek — 'one', from Old Romani *yekh*. The numerals continue through *dui*, *trin*, *star* and *pansh*

yog — 'fire', from old Romani *yag*. Also used as a verb, 'to burn', or under the influence of the English word, 'to fire'. The agentive *yogger*, 'that which fires', is a gun; a *yogger mush* is a gamekeeper

yorro — 'egg', from Old Romani *yauro*. *Ballovas and yorros*, 'bacon and eggs', is for some reason a song refrain

zi — 'heart', a clipped form of Old Romani *ozi*. The sense is extended very widely, to 'mind', understanding', 'mood', 'memory'; to *rig in zi* is to remember

REFERENCES

Abbreviations

CR   'Convicts Transported to Australia between 1787 and 1867', database at https://convictrecords.com.au

CWG   The Commonwealth War Graves Commission, www.cwgc.org

EEH   Epsom and Ewell Local and Family History Society, https://eehe.org.uk

GLS   'The Historical Archive and Library Collections of the Gypsy Lore Society' at the University of Liverpool, https://libguides.liverpool.ac.uk/library/sca/gypsyloresociety

GPT   *Gypsies Passing Through*, a database of parish register data collected by Jackie Blackman. The original site has closed but the data can be accessed at http://gypsyjib.com/page/Gypsies+Passing+Through+Web-Site (membership site)

OB   'The Proceedings of the Old Bailey, 1674–1913', searchable text at www.oldbaileyonline.org

QS   Surrey Quarter Sessions. These survive from 1659: Order Books and Sessions Rolls down to 1668 were published in a series of four books by Surrey Record Society and Surrey County Council (1934–51) while transcripts of Order Books to 1672 and Sessions Rolls to Michaelmas 1691 are available at Surrey History Centre (shelved as 347.2). Process books and gaol calendars 1780–1820 have been published by the Centre as a CD

QVJ   'The Complete On-line Collection of Queen Victoria's Journals from the Royal Archives', www.queenvictoriasjournals.org

SHC   Surrey History Centre, catalogue at www.surreyarchives.org.uk

WWI   'British Army WWI service records 1914–20 (Soldiers)', www.greatwar.co.uk/research/military-records/british-soldiers-wwi-service-records.htm

Introduction: Meetings on Epsom Downs

1 The Gypsy presence at the Derby was a popular subject for travel writers, photographers and artists between the wars as well as for the national newspapers. Good journalistic accounts can be found in the *Birmingham Dispatch*, 31 May 1921; *Daily Sketch*, 23 May 1933; and *Daily Mail*, 1 June 1934.

2 *Daily Herald*, 19 May 1939.
3 *News Chronicle*, 30 May 1938.
4 *Daily Express*, 30 May 1938.
5 *Daily Mail*, 22 May 1939.
6 *Daily Express*, 30 May 1935.
7 *Daily Mail*, 6 June 1929.

1 Entertaining Strangers: Tudor England

1 John Coulter, *Norwood Pubs* (Stroud, 2006), pp. 45–8. In business from the 1840s, this was a different pub from the Old Gipsy House on Hall Green.
2 Percy Lane Oliver, 'Surrey Gypsies', *Surrey Magazine*, 1 (1899/1900), pp. 15–18, at p. 17. Cf. the summer entertainments provided for visitors to Oxshott Common in 1900, which included chaise rides: Alan Wright, *Their Day Has Passed: Gypsies in Victorian and Edwardian Surrey* (Tolworth, 2017), pp. 90–91.
3 Richard Bright, *Travels from Vienna through Lower Hungary* (Edinburgh, 1818), pp. 529–30.
4 Ibid., p. 531.
5 Ibid., appendix, pp. lxxviii–ix; discussed in Alexander Russell, 'Bright's Anglo-Romani Vocabulary', *Journal of the Gypsy Lore Society*, 2nd series, IX (1915–16), pp. 165–85. I've standardized the language in line with the later, better records of English Romani.
6 I have used 'Old Romani' to describe the language which Gypsies know as the *puri jib* and linguists call British Romani, and which gave rise to the two successor dialects – again, using the linguists' terms – of English and Welsh Romani. So my term isn't the standard one, but I hope it will be less confusing for the ordinary reader, who otherwise has to remember that British (English) Romani and Anglo-Romani are in effect different languages.
7 Anthony Sampson, *The Scholar Gypsy: The Quest for a Family Secret* (London, 1997), pp. 53–4.
8 Eldra Jarman and A.O.H. Jarman, *The Welsh Gypsies: Children of Abram Wood* (Cardiff, 1991), pp. 46–56.
9 With *av, jell* and so on I've used the contemporary forms of these words in southeastern Anglo-Romani, not the Old Romani words.
10 The grammar of Old British Romani has been summarized by Ian Hancock, 'Romani and Angloromani', in *Language in the British Isles*, ed. Peter Trudgill (Cambridge, 1984), pp. 366–83, and the international variations of the language are set out by Yaron Matras, *Romani: A Linguistic Introduction* (Cambridge, 2004).
11 See the table of derivations in John Sampson, *The Dialect of the Gypsies of Wales: Being the Older Form of British Romani Preserved in the Speech of the Clan of Abram Wood* (Oxford, 1926), pp. 411–19. The English word *ambrol* is closer to its Indo-Aryan origins than Welsh Gypsy *brol* – one of the few words (along with *surralo* and *Anglaterra*) which are preserved better in Anglo-Romani than in the pure language of the Woods.
12 Sampson, *Dialect of the Gypsies*, p. 344.

13 Eric Otto Winstedt, 'Anglo-Romani Gleanings from the Northern Counties', *Journal of the Gypsy Lore Society*, 3rd series, XXVII (1948), pp. 83–110, at p. 105.

14 Henry Thomas Crofton, 'Borde's Egipt Speche', *Journal of the Gypsy Lore Society*, 2nd series, I (1907–8), pp. 157–68. The original text (it is only a single page) is reproduced in Angus Fraser, *The Gypsies* (Oxford, 1992), pl. 2.

15 The tapestry is in the Castle Museum, Gaasbeck: Guy Delmarcel, *Flemish Tapestry*, trans. Alastair Weir (London, 1999), p. 166. It is discussed in A. E. Hamill, 'A Fifteenth-Century Tapestry', *Journal of the Gypsy Lore Society*, 3rd series, XXVIII (1949), pp. 41–2.

16 This was the second inquiry into the death of Richard Hunne, held not in 1514 as usually stated, but March or April 1515, after the original inquest in December 1514 and before Thomas More left England in May of the next year: see Arthur Ogle, *The Tragedy of the Lollards' Tower* (Oxford, 1949), p. 94.

17 Thomas More, *The Complete Works of St Thomas More*, vol. VI: *A Dialogue concerning Heresies*, ed. Thomas M. C. Lawler, Germain Marc'hadour and Richard C. Marius (New Haven, CT, 1981), vol. I, p. 321.

18 *Patent Rolls: Philip and Mary* (Richmond, 1936–9), vol. III, p. 67.

19 The Lowestoft party is in *Patent Rolls: Philip and Mary*, vol. III, p. 112; Chilton, in *Patent Rolls: Elizabeth* (Richmond, 1939–86), vol. III, p. 134. Philippe Lazar is in *Acts of the Privy Council of England* (Richmond, 1890–1907), 2nd series, vol. I, p. 320. There are some useful maps in Richard Edmunds, *Gypsies in Tudor England, 1485–1603* (privately printed, 2018), pp. 57–60.

20 Fraser, *Gypsies*, pp. 114–15.

21 Edward Hall, *Hall's Chronicle*, ed. Henry Ellis (London, 1809), p. 514. This was the lady Mary, sister of Henry VIII.

22 Folger Shakespeare Library L.b. 319; published in *The Loseley Manuscripts*, ed. Alfred John Kempe (London, 1835), p. 77.

23 John Skelton, *The Complete English Poems*, ed. John Scattergood (New Haven, CT, 1983), p. 216.

24 Fraser, *Gypsies*, p. 114.

25 *Acts of the Privy Council of England*, 2nd series, vol. II, p. 452.

26 Romney Marsh in *Letters and Papers of Henry VIII* (Richmond, 1862–1932), vol. XIV, part II, p. 21; Dover in *Acts of the Privy Council of England*, 2nd series, vol. I, p. 358.

27 *Letters and Papers of Henry VIII*, vol. XVIII, part I, p. 106, *Acts of the Privy Council of England*, 2nd series, vol. I, p. 88; the letters were sent to George Paullet and John Norton.

28 Alan McGowan, *On the Gypsy Trail: Sources for the Family History of Gypsies* (Swindon, 1998), p. 4.

29 *State Papers Domestic: Edward VI to James I* (Richmond, 1856–72), vol. I, pp. 137, 139.

30 *7th Report of the Royal Commission on Historical MSS* (Richmond, 1879), p. 620 (the letters were sent to Thomas Browne, John Stidolfe, John Agmondesham and William Moore) and SHC 6729/11/52.

31 St George Kieran Hyland, *A Century of Persecution under Tudor and Stuart Sovereigns from Contemporary Records* (London, 1920), pp. 346–7 (the MS

is Folger Shakespeare library L.b.210); reading 'begge' for the original 'besse' and 'thing' for 'thiting' – odd spellings, as if an original draft had been copied by someone who had no English.

32 SHC LM/COR/3/561.

33 *Acts of the Privy Council of England*, 2nd series, vol. XXVI, p. 325.

34 I find no sentences under the Egyptians Act in *Calendar of Assize Records: Surrey Indictments, Elizabeth I*, ed. J. S. Cockburn (Richmond, 1980), and although 171 people were presented as vagrants between 1562 and 1603, none of them are recognizable as Romany. David Cressy puts the deaths nationally under the Act at 'several dozen': *Gypsies: An English History* (Oxford, 2018), pp. 95, 100. There were four people killed in Middlesex by this law: *Middlesex County Records I, 1550–1603*, ed. John Cordy Jeaffreson (London, 1886), pp. 221, 253, 267. Two more got away, two were released, and one pleaded her belly. Four judicial murders in forty years is four too many, but it is not genocide.

35 *Christ's Hospital Admissions*, ed. George T. Allan (London, 1937), vol. I, p. 64.

36 But, as David Cressy has pointed out (*Gypsies*, pp. 75–6), 'counterfeit' in Tudor English meant that they were making a living through deception; it doesn't imply that they were natives pretending to be Gypsies.

37 A. L. Beier, *Masterless Men: The Vagrancy Problem in England, 1560–1640* (London, 1985), pp. 16–28, discusses pauperization.

38 See ibid., p. 74, for following fairs and markets; p. 88, harvest work; p. 97, musicians; p. 101, healers; p. 103, fortune tellers. In this period it is the native transients who exhibit what one had thought were typically Gypsy traits. They winter in London, p. 76; are divided between long and short travellers, p. 71; beg aggressively and curse those who fail to give, pp. 120–21, 142; are accused of child theft, p. 67; and even practise co-marriage, p. 65.

39 Thomas Dekker, 'Lanthorne and Candle-Light' (1609), in *The Non-Dramatic Works of Thomas Dekker*, ed. Alexander B. Grosart (privately printed, 1884–6), vol. III, pp. 252–62.

40 *The Winchester Confessions, 1615–1616: Depositions of Travellers, Gypsies, Fraudsters and Makers of Counterfeit Documents, including a Vocabulary of the Romany Language*, ed. Alan McGowan (Swindon, 1996), with Romani standardized to modern forms. Peter Bakker, 'An Early Vocabulary of British Romani (1616): A Linguistic Analysis', *Romani Studies*, 12 (2002), pp. 75–97 ends his careful study of the text (p. 86) with 'we can easily conclude . . . that the Winchester Confessions represent a form of Romani like Angloromani and not like Welsh Romani.'

41 Dekker, 'Lanthorne and Candle-Light', p. 264.

42 Cressy, *Gypsies*, pp. 107–8.

43 Dekker, 'Lanthorne and Candle-Light', p. 262.

44 Humphrey Crouch, 'The Welch Traveller' (1671), in *Remaines of the Early Popular Poetry of England*, ed. W. Carew Hazlitt (London, 1866), vol. IV, pp. 344–7.

45 Daniel Lysons, *The Environs of London* (London, 1792–6), vol. I, pp. 489–90. It was Dr Johnson who found him shrewd.

46 Abiezer Coppe, *A Fiery Flying Roll* (London, 1649), part II, pp. 8–9.

47 *Report of the Historical MSS Commission on Manuscripts in Various Collections* (Richmond, 1901–13), vol. I, p. 136, from the Wiltshire Quarter Sessions.

48 QS Order Book 1659, p. 28, published in *Surrey Quarter Sessions: The Order Book for 1659–1661*, ed. Dorothy Powell and Hilary Jenkinson (London, 1934), pp. 12–13, and discussed by Eric Otto Winstedt, 'The Squires Family', *Journal of the Gypsy Lore Society*, 3rd series, XVI (1937), pp. 146–8. In the end, for whatever reason, no case was brought against them at Sessions. To give an idea of the cost of prosecution, I calculated a day's pay at 1s 6d and multiplied it by the closest estimate of the village population, the 54 people in the 1662 Hearth Tax return.

49 QS Michaelmas 1677 and Michaelmas 1689.

50 Beier, *Masterless Men*, pp. 172–5.

2 Long Travellers: Georgian Britain

1 The contemporary literature on Canning and Squires is intimidating, as can be seen from the bibliography by Lillian Bueno McCue, 'Elizabeth Canning in Print', *University of Colorado Studies*, B2 (1945), pp. 223–32, but most of it is just polemics. John Treherne, *The Canning Enigma* (London, 1989), is a clear account based on the key sources, with a bibliography but no references. Judith Moore, *The Appearance of Truth: The Story of Elizabeth Canning and Eighteenth-Century Narrative* (Newark, DE, 1994), presents the case as it developed, while all other accounts construct (differing) sequences of the real-life events. The latest summary is in David Cressy, *Gypsies: An English History* (Oxford, 2018), pp. 126–39.

2 Eric Otto Winstedt, 'Review: *The Canning Wonder* by Arthur Machen', *Journal of the Gypsy Lore Society*, 3rd series, VI (1927), pp. 35–45.

3 The itinerary that follows is based on Treherne, *Canning Enigma*, pp. 54–64, 87–94, and Moore, *Appearance of Truth*, pp. 87–96, 94–5, 138–44.

4 George Squires's failure to identify most of his route is in marked contrast to his exact recollection of the Dorset episodes. If I could add another conjecture to this already conjectural case, it would be that until South Perrott the Squires were not travelling alone, but with other Gypsies who needed to get from London to the far west in a hurry, and it was understood that one Gypsy would not report the movements of another – certainly not in court.

5 *London Evening News*, 20–23 February 1762. Winstedt, 'Review', mistaking the date, identified Mary Squires with the Jane Fielder who appears in Farnham burial register, 26 February 1762. She was in fact buried as 'Mary Moore, stranger' on 26 January: Cressy, *Gypsies*, p. 139.

6 Some of the pamphlet literature draws on prejudice against Gypsies – for example, Treherne, *Canning Enigma*, p. 48; Moore, *Appearance of Truth*, p. 123; Cressy, *Gypsies*, p. 138 – but anyone familiar with today's online hate speech will be surprised at the comparative decency of the Georgians.

7 John Aubrey, *The Natural History and Antiquities of the County of Surrey*, ed. Richard Rawlinson (London, 1718–19), vol. V, p. 136. Powell's burial is recorded in the Newington burial register, from which it appears that the epitaph has the incorrect date 1704, Eric Otto Winstedt, 'The Norwood Gypsies and Their Vocabulary', *Journal of the Gypsy Lore Society*, 2nd series, IX (1915–16), pp. 129–65, at p. 130, n. 5. They spelled 'Desember' wrong too; maybe it was a cheap job.

8 Richard Edmunds, *The Early Romany Boswells: A Family History, 1650–1810* (Swindon, 2017–18), vol. I, p. 28.

9 *Report of the Historical MSS Commission on Manuscripts in Various Collections* (Richmond, 1901–13), vol. I, p. 136, from the Wiltshire Quarter Sessions.

10 There was a travelling woman called Finch who stopped in 1667 at Cranford, where she had three short-lived triplets, Winstedt, 'Norwood Gypsies', p. 133; this might be Margaret's mother.

11 Letterpress for 1742 engraving of Margaret Finch in Winstedt, 'Norwood Gypsies', pp. 132–3. Surrey is *tem wesh* in Juliette De Baïracli Levy, *As Gypsies Wander* (London, 1953), p. 101.

12 James Caulfield, *Portraits, Memoirs and Characters of Remarkable Persons* (London, 1820), vol. III, p. 249.

13 *London Chronicle*, 4–6 August 1768; Daniel Lysons, *The Environs of London* (London, 1792–6), vol. I, p. 107.

14 Lysons, *Environs of London*, vol. IV, p. 302, though he does not name Margaret's granddaughter. She is called Elizabeth by Winstedt, 'Norwood Gypsies', p. 135, but Margaret by Alan Warwick, *The Phoenix Suburb: A South London Social History* (Richmond, 1972), p. 29. An incident reported in the *English Chronicle*, 4 August 1789, suggests that Elizabeth is the right name.

15 Robert Borrowman, *Beckenham Past and Present* (privately printed, 1910), pp. 31–2.

16 *Annual Register*, 16 (1773), pp. 142–3; *Jackson's Oxford Journal*, 30 October 1773.

17 *London Chronicle*, 20–22 August 1771; and Winstedt, 'Norwood Gypsies', p. 136.

18 *Mist's Weekly Journal*, 12 March 1726. This gang may have been connected with the Mary Poole who in 1699 talked a gentleman of Lincoln's Inn Fields into entrusting her with £10, which was not seen again until she appeared at the Old Bailey: Cressy, *Gypsies*, p. 115.

19 Lysons, *Environs of London*, vol. IV, p. 302.

20 *Annual Register*, 13 (1770), p. 102; *London Chronicle*, 4–6 August 1768.

21 *Jackson's Oxford Journal*, 3 June 1769.

22 *London Chronicle*, 29 August 1769.

23 This famous print (there is a copy in the British Museum, 1851,0308.274) has often been reproduced, sometimes in reverse. The artist's name is given implausibly as 'Jno. Sraeho'. Perhaps the engraver misread 'Starke'.

24 *Annual Register*, 54 (1812), *Chronicle*, p. 45; however, it appears from QS Michaelmas 1797 that Thomas's father, Adam Lee, was married to an Eleanor, so the family details may have been confused.

25 Borrowman, *Beckenham*, pp. 31–2.

26 'A Southern Faunist', 'On the Origin and Present State of the Gipsies', *Gentleman's Magazine*, 72 (1802), pp. 407–9, at p. 408.

27 Lysons, *Environs of London*, vol. IV, p. 302.

28 The 1803 'View of the Gipsy-House, in Norwood, Surrey' published in John Coulter, *Norwood Past* (London, 1996), fig. 4, seems more reliable than the print of *c.* 1800 'The Gipsey House at Norwood – during the time a Lady was hearing her Fortune from a Gipsey', Coulter's fig. 5. The first

shows the frontage onto the road (such as it was) and the second seems to be a rear view from the pleasure gardens.

29 Coulter, *Norwood Past*, pp. 39, 73, and *Norwood Pubs* (Stroud, 2006), pp. 68–9; Jacob Larwood and John Camden Hotten, *The History of Signboards* (London, 1867), p. 508.

30 Gillian Rickard, *Vagrants, Gypsies and 'Travellers' in Kent, 1572–1948* (privately printed, 1995), p. 41. For the family background, see Eric Trudgill, 'William Cooper's Children', *Romany Routes*, 10 (2010–12), pp. 21–4.

31 *Jackson's Oxford Journal*, 3 June 1769; this refers twice to 'Kent-street, Seven Dials', but Kent Street was nowhere near Seven Dials; apparently the journalist confused these two different areas of cheap, dense housing.

32 Una Broadbent and Ronald Latham, *Coulsdon: Downland Village* (London, 1976), p. 33; she died a fortnight later.

33 This can be pieced together from *Courier*, 13 October 1795; *London Chronicle*, 13–15 October 1795; *The Oracle*, 16 October 1795; *Jackson's Oxford Journal*, 17 October 1795; and *The Sun*, 20 January 1796.

34 The best numbers from the pantomime were published by James Messinck, *Airs, Duets &c. in the New Pantomime, Called the Norwood Gypsies, Performing at the Theatre-Royal in Covent-Garden* (London, 1777). The critics were unimpressed (*Public Advertiser*, 26 November 1777). Oh no they weren't! (*London Chronicle*, 25 November 1777). Oh yes they were! (*Morning Chronicle*, 26 November 1777).

35 George Bubb Doddington, *The Diary of the Late George Bubb Doddington*, ed. Henry Penruddocke Wyndham (London, 1828), p. 47.

36 *The Life of Miss Anne Catley* (London, 1888), p. 23.

37 Maureen O'Sullivan, 'Settlement Examination Dated 26 July 1740', *East Surrey Family History Journal*, XXVIII/3 (2005), p. xiv, citing Quarter Sessions at Cheshire RO QJF 168/3/123–4.

38 The original painting by Francis Hayman is lost but survives as a print (for example, British Museum 1862, 1011.613, 1877,0210.404, and Cc,3.169); it is reproduced in David Coke and Alan Bord, *Vauxhall Gardens: A History* (New Haven, CT, 2011), pp. 385–6.

39 Frances Burney, *The Early Diary of Frances Burney, 1768–1778, with a Selection from Her Correspondence, and from the Journals of Her Sisters Susan and Charlotte Burney*, ed. Annie Raine Ellis (London, 1889), vol. II, pp. 264–6.

40 Stephen Doe, 'From Viking Longboat to Gypsy Caravan: I', *Romany Routes*, 8 (2006–8), pp. 319–21, at p. 319.

41 QS Epiphany 1794.

42 Rickard, *Vagrants, Gypsies and 'Travellers'*, p. 40.

43 Winstedt, 'Norwood Gypsies', pp. 137–8, reconciles accounts of the Norwood family in *Jackson's Oxford Journal*, 17 October 1795, and Thomas Frost, *Reminiscences of a Country Journalist* (London, 1886), pp. 7–16. I'm assuming that these were the same Lees that were travelling in Kent.

44 Rickard, *Vagrants, Gypsies and 'Travellers'*, p. 46.

45 'A Gentleman of the Inner-Temple', *De Toryismo Liber; or, A Treatise on Toryism* (London, 1748), pp. 11–13; this is a skit, not a serious treatise (he makes the Gypsies come over from Grand Cairo with William the Conqueror), but even a parody will refer to reality.

46 John Barrell, *The Dark Side of the Landscape: The Rural Poor in English Painting, 1730–1840* (Cambridge, 1980), p. 95.

47 Pierce Egan, *Boxiana; or, Sketches of Ancient and Modern Pugilism from the Days of the Renowned Broughton and Slack, to the Championship of Cribb* (London, 1812–29), 2nd series, vol. I, p. 136.

48 *London Chronicle*, 22–4 January 1761.

49 F. C. Wellstood, 'Foreign Gypsies in England, 1761', *Journal of the Gypsy Lore Society*, 2nd series, IV (1901–11), p. 307.

50 Although Christopher Griffin, *Nomads under the Westway: Irish Travellers, Gypsies and Other Traders in West London* (Hatfield, 2008), pp. 138ff., suggests that the surname is a development of an earlier Brazier, citing Mortlake marriage register 1657. However, the Thomas Brazier and Mary Smeth of this parish who married then cannot have been travellers of any kind, since they went on to have six children all christened at the same church. See *Mortlake Parish Register (1599–1678)*, ed. Maurice S. Cockin and David Gould (London, 1958).

51 Rickard, *Vagrants, Gypsies and 'Travellers'*, pp. 43–4.

52 Eric Otto Winstedt, 'The Valentines', *Journal of the Gypsy Lore Society*, 2nd series, IX (1915–16), pp. 222–4; Cressy, *Gypsies*, pp. 78, 80, 89, 95.

53 *Patent Rolls: Elizabeth* (Richmond, 1939–86), vol. VIII, p. 134; QS Michaelmas 1791. In the later source Bastin isn't identified as a Gypsy, but an itinerant razor grinder found near the Old Wells at two in the afternoon could hardly be anything else.

54 Baptismal registers of Guildford St Nicholas, 19 February 1670, and Godalming, 23 September 1683, and burial register of Woking, 3 November 1688, for which I am grateful to Hazel Ballan; Hale baptismal register, 12 September 1858, noted in GPT.

55 Thomas William Thompson, 'Gleanings from Constables' Accounts and Other Sources', *Journal of the Gypsy Lore Society*, 3rd series, VII (1928), pp. 30–47.

56 Dorking burial register, 6 December 1649, noted in GPT.

57 Janet Keet-Black, 'A Keet Family Tree', *Romany Routes*, 3 (1996–8), pp. 20–21. The forms without a prosthetic *s* are probably older.

58 C. H. Fielding, *Memories of Malling and Its Valley* (West Malling, 1893), p. 166; their daughter was 'Cliff', or at least that's what it says in the West Malling baptismal register – surely an error for some Gypsy name.

59 Compton burial register, 30 April 1754; Great Bookham burial register, 29 January 1755; both noted in GPT.

60 Charles Godfrey Leland, *The Gypsies* (London, 1882), pp. 305–6, notes the use of *purrum* as a code-name for Lee.

61 Eric Trudgill, *The Family Trees of Damon and Thomas Lee from about 1750 to about 1900, Mainly the English Southern Counties* (Swindon, 2007), pp. 1–2, 4. 'Child' might also have included miscarriages.

62 Eric Otto Winstedt, 'Gypsies as Highwaymen and Footpads', *Journal of the Gypsy Lore Society*, 3rd series, VI (1927), pp. 68–88, at pp. 74–6.

63 Eric Otto Winstedt, 'Gypsies in Political Disturbances', *Journal of the Gypsy Lore Society*, 3rd series, IX (1930), pp. 47–8.

64 John Cobley, *The Crimes of the First Fleet Convicts* (Sydney, 1970), p. 259; James Hugh Donohoe, *The Forgotten Australians: The Non Anglo or Celtic*

Convicts and Exiles (privately printed, 1991), pp. 63–5; Ruth MacDonald, 'Romanichal Gypsies Bitchedi Pawdel to Australia', *Romany Routes*, 5 (2000–2002), pp. 295–300.

65 Rickard, *Vagrants, Gypsies and 'Travellers'*, pp. 39–41.

66 Alan McGowan, *On the Gypsy Trail: Sources for the Family History of Gypsies* (Swindon, 1998), pp. 11, 29; Jeremy Harte, 'Just Enough: Petty Crime at Quarter Sessions in Three Surrey Parishes, 1780–1820', *Surrey History*, 13 (2014), pp. 1–15, at pp. 11–12. The name is not military in origin, however; it is a Yorkshire form of Mauger.

67 'Britannicus', in *St James's Chronicle*, 19 March 1795.

68 QS Michaelmas 1764, noted in Janet Keet-Black, 'Miscellany', *Romany Routes*, 5 (2000–2002), p. 329.

69 William Bartlett, *The History and Antiquities of Wimbledon* (London, 1865), pp. 139–40.

70 Kenneth Ross, *A History of Malden* (New Malden, 1947), p. 107; this was evidently a different James Squire/Squires from the Australian, who was alive and well in 1790, and whose first wife was Martha.

71 Bartlett, *History and Antiquities of Wimbledon*, p. 114, discussed in Eric Otto Winstedt, 'A Gypsy Christening', *Journal of the Gypsy Lore Society*, 2nd series, VI (1912–13), p. 65. The godfather (?) is named as 'Dr. Eliz. Pitchford'.

72 *Annual Register*, 12 (1769), p. 126; *London Chronicle*, 29 August 1769; Alan Crosby, *A History of Woking* (Chichester, 2003), p. 48. Bagshot Park was the seat of George Keppel, Third Earl of Albemarle.

73 *European Magazine*, 8 (1785), p. 398, referring to 'very near thirty years ago'. I haven't checked the Assize records, but I'm doubtful. It sounds too much like the story of Damon Lee and his brothers.

3 Lucky for Some: Regency Days

1 QVJ, 3 December 1836–8 January 1837. This represents vols XII, pp. 292–340, and XIII, pp. 1–26, of the original journal for 1836; 1837 survives only in Lord Esher's transcript, where the entries are III, pp. 11–41. Extracts were published in *The Girlhood of Queen Victoria: A Selection from Her Majesty's Diaries between the Years 1832 and 1840*, ed. Brett Reginald, Viscount Esher (London, 1912), vol. I, pp. 180–84, and the episode is discussed by F. G. Ackerley, 'Queen Victoria and the Gypsies', *Journal of the Gypsy Lore Society*, 2nd series, VII (1913–14), pp. 149–50, and Janet Keet-Black, 'Princess Victoria's Gypsies', *Romany Routes*, 7 (2004–6), pp. 254–5. I have followed the standardized spelling and punctuation used by Lord Esher. Diana, Job and Nelson were the children of Leonard and Phyllis; Britannia, of Nelson and Bella. Emmeline and Helen (?) have not been identified.

2 Not unreasonably, given that Matty had been involved in the theft of two horses from the stables at Claremont not long before; the story is given anonymously in George Hall, *The Gypsy's Parson: His Experiences and Adventures* (London, 1915), pp. 248–9, and names are named in Eric Otto Winstedt, Thomas William Thompson and Fred Shaw, 'Anglo-Romani Gleanings from London-Side Gypsies', *Journal of the Gypsy Lore Society*, 3rd series, III (1924), pp. 110–36, at p. 118.

3 This foreign accent was also noticed in the Lees at Kew: Richard Phillips, *A Morning's Walk from London to Kew* (London, 1817), pp. 363–76.

4 And 'so unlike the gossiping, fortune-telling race-gipsies', wrote Victoria naively (25 December). She was probably remembering her experiences at the 1831 Derby, for which see *The Spectator*, 21 May 1831.

5 On 1 January, Lehzen had said 'we could not walk by the camp now'; reading between the lines, I wonder if she felt that her princess was getting a bit too involved with the Coopers, and had them warned off.

6 Charles Godfrey Leland, Edward Henry Palmer and Janet Tuckey, *English-Gypsy Songs* (London, 1875), pp. 8–16.

7 James Crabb, *The Gipsies' Advocate* (London, 1831), pp. 67–8 (pp. 64–71 of the 1832 edn). Crabb does not provide names, but we know that the man sentenced to death at the Assizes in 1827 was Francis Proudley (sometimes Stanley). Thanks to the generous help of Anne-Marie Ford, I found that Francis (born 1802) was the son of Edward Stanley and Sara Saunders, who also had a daughter Sarah (1799) and son Edward (1801), and that he married Patience, the daughter (1805) of Reuben Stanley, who had married Lydia; the children of Francis and Patience were Francis (1823–6), Elizabeth (1825–8) and Vandaloe (1826–9).

8 The two Farnhams are occasionally confused, for example, in Thomas Acton, *Gypsy Politics and Social Change* (London, 1974), p. 104.

9 Crabb, *Gypsies' Advocate*, pp. 125–9 (pp. 159–63 of 1832 edn).

10 Ibid., pp. 118–22 (pp. 151–6 of 1832 edn).

11 James Caulfield, *Portraits, Memoirs and Characters of Remarkable Persons* (London, 1820), vol. III, p. 248.

12 'Norwood', in Samuel Howell, *The Wandering Minstrel: A Collection of Original Poems* (London, 1827), pp. 118–19.

13 Edward Thurlow was not a popular man in the neighbourhood – see *The World*, 26 June and 11 August 1787 – though this may reflect the newspaper's animus towards him rather than the facts.

14 John Coulter, *Norwood Past* (London, 1996), p. 13; W. E. Tate, 'Enclosure Acts and Awards Relating to Lands in the County of Surrey', *Surrey Archaeological Collections*, 48 (1943), pp. 118–49, at pp. 142–5.

15 The story is in Alan Warwick, *The Phoenix Suburb: A South London Social History* (Richmond, 1972), pp. 30–31; this cannot, as he claims, have been the raid of 1797, but the events might have happened in 1795, when the Lees were first taken, since the *London Chronicle*, 13–15 October 1795, says that 'they were apprehended on a Sunday evening by . . . a party of the patrole'.

16 *The Times*, 22 August 1797; names are listed in QS Michaelmas 1797. According to QS the raid was made by Thomas Cave (presumably the parish constable) on 14 August.

17 *London Chronicle*, 13–15 October 1803; QS Michaelmas 1803; the charge also included Harriett Lee and John Lovell, who were charged only with vagrancy, but may have arranged the set-up for the others.

18 John Hoyland, *A Historical Survey of the Customs, Habits and Present State of the Gypsies* (York, 1816), p. 180, and *The Traveller*, 24 July 1815. The charges, brought by John May on Monday, 17 July, appear in QS Michaelmas 1815. This queen cannot be the granddaughter of Margaret Finch, who must therefore have been dead by 1815. Remembering that

Coopers were later assigned this status, it might be Tryphena, who was certainly based at Norwood and had sons Jack and Thomas.

19 'Union Hall police court', noted in Eric Otto Winstedt, 'The Norwood Gypsies and Their Vocabulary', *Journal of the Gypsy Lore Society*, 2nd series, IX (1915–16), p. 146. This must be a newspaper report from the court, but I didn't find it in *The Times*.

20 J.P.P.C., 'The Norwood Gypsies', *Literary Lounger*, 2 (1826), pp. 88–96, at p. 92.

21 Hoyland, *Historical Survey*, p. 180. His local informant was Edward Morris, who had run the Old Gipsy House until 1808 but still featured as 'the landlord at the Gypsey house', presumably a new establishment with the old name.

22 *London Chronicle*, 19–21 and 21–3 January 1796, noted by Winstedt, 'Norwood Gypsies', p. 138.

23 *The Times*, 12 October 1821. This was before horsedrawn transport, so presumably they needed it for bedding.

24 Dora Yates, 'T. L. Busby's "Jemmy Lovel" (1819)', *Journal of the Gypsy Lore Society*, 3rd series, XXXV (1956), p. 97.

25 J. Horsfall Turner, 'The Gypsies', *Notes and Queries*, 6th series, I (1880), p. 258.

26 Hoyland, *Historical Survey*, pp. 182–5, with further details of individuals from Winstedt, 'Norwood', pp. 138–9, 145–6.

27 Hoyland, *Historical Survey*, p. 187.

28 *Gentleman's Magazine*, LXXIII/1 (1803), p. 86.

29 The Turnpike Roads Act of 1822 had set the precedent, but only for roads maintained by a turnpike trust. The effect of the 1835 Highways Act was to make Gypsy life illegal in any area where access to land was denied by farmers, and where there were no commons.

30 *The Times*, 1 August 1823.

31 *The Times*, 11 August 1823, 16 October 1832.

32 David Cox, *Gipsies on Dulwich Common*, c. 1808, in Birmingham Museum & Art Gallery. This is the only one of the many Gypsy paintings by Cox in an identified setting. They are discussed by S. Wilcox, *Sun, Wind and Rain: The Art of David Cox* (New Haven, CT, 2008); see also M. Neale Solly, *Memoir of the Life of David Cox* (London, 1873), p. 21.

33 J.P.P.C., 'Norwood Gypsies', p. 90; 'A Gipsy Ballad' first published by Wolcot (1793), afterwards in Walter Scott, ed., *English Minstrelsy* (Edinburgh, 1810), vol. II, pp. 156–7.

34 William Cobbett, 'To a Correspondent in America', *Cobbett's Political Register*, 26 (1814), col. 641–60, at col. 658; one would like to know exactly which North American savages he'd seen.

35 *The Times*, 14 August 1811; these stage Gypsies may nevertheless have been real local members of the community, as this would have been cheaper than dressing up actors. Other early donkeys appear in Phillips, *A Morning's Walk*, p. 375, and Richard Bright, *Travels from Vienna through Lower Hungary* (Edinburgh, 1818), p. 530.

36 East Hoathly baptismal register, 7 May 1815, noted in Kevin Doyle, 'From Sussex Parish Registers', *Romany Routes*, I (1994–5), p. 12, where 'Hawkern Common, Dorking' appears to be Hawkhurst; Etchingham baptismal

register, 22 July 1821, noted in Doyle, 'Sussex Parish Registers'; Long Ditton baptismal register, 29 June 1828, noted in GPT, where the father, 'Righteous Jones', was surely a Lee using a cover name; and Eversley baptismal register, 25 March 1832, 22 November 1835 and 19 February 1837, noted in Carol Murphey, 'From Parish Registers', *Romany Routes*, 7 (2004–6), p. 162.

37 Eric Trudgill, *The Family Trees of Damon and Thomas Lee from about 1750 to about 1900, Mainly the English Southern Counties* (Swindon, 2007), p. 7; Trudgill, 'William Cooper's Children', *Romany Routes*, 10 (2010–12), p. 21.

38 William Howitt, *The Rural Life of England* (London, 1840), p. 184; he lived near the Bookhams.

39 Their examinations are in QS Michaelmas 1815. Susan Deacons appears in the indictment as Sarah.

40 All these locations are given in QS – assuming that the 'Upman' of the depositions is Up Marden and 'Hadleigh' is Hadlow – except for Burstow, where Edmund's baptism can be found in the baptismal register, 17 October 1813.

41 The Nichols were first identified by Eric Otto Winstedt, 'Notes on English Gypsy Christian Names: 1', *Journal of the Gypsy Lore Society*, 3rd series, 1 (1921), pp. 64–90, at p. 84. Janet Keet-Black has made a study of them, begun in 'So You've Found Great Granny's Baptism?', *Romany Routes*, 2 (1995–6), pp. 108–11, and 'Nichols by Any Other Name?', *Romany Routes*, 2 (1995–6), pp. 172–3, and summed up in 'The Continuing Saga of the Nichols', *Romany Routes*, 14 (2018–20), pp. 150–54, which quotes a description of Elizabeth in action at Tavistock in 1838. They were discovered independently by H. V. Carter, 'Multiple Baptisms by a Traveller', *Genealogists' Magazine*, 28 (2005), pp. 197–200.

42 *The Times*, 24 November 1834.

43 *Boro hokkiben* is an Anglo-Romanization of the phrase *hokkano baro* used by Borrow; this is in fact Caló, and misunderstood at that, *hokkano* being 'liar' not 'lie': Ian Hancock, *Danger! Educated Gypsy: Selected Essays*, ed. Dileep Karanth (Hatfield, 2010), p. 170.

44 OB 6 December 1797. This is Plunkett's account, which is contradicted by the prosecution witnesses; however, as the witnesses also contradicted each other, he was acquitted.

45 Contemporary reports from *Jackson's Oxford Journal*, 4 January 1834, and *The Observer*, 6 January 1834, and tradition from Charles Rose's 'Recollections', in *Memorials of Old Dorking*, ed. Margaret Kohler (Dorking, 1977), p. 107. It was argued in court that the youngsters took horses for joyriding, not for deliberate theft. In the absence of any record of execution, I assume they were transported.

46 Cobbett, 'To a Correspondent, col. 658.

47 Much depended on local circumstances. In Epsom only 10 per cent of committals were made on charges of vagrancy and poverty, while for Sir George Glyn, the sole magistrate in neighbouring Ewell, these constituted 56 per cent of his work: Jeremy Harte, 'Just Enough: Petty Crime at Quarter Sessions in Three Surrey Parishes, 1780–1820', *Surrey History*, 13 (2014), p. 7.

48 *Gentleman's Magazine*, LXXIII/1 (1803), pp. 84–6, 280; *The Times*, 10 August 1818; *The Times*, 21 October 1826.

49 Charles Robert Leslie (as 'A Resident in England'), 'The Gipsies: A Slight Sketch', pp. 145–51 of Eliza Leslie, *The Gift: A Christmas and New Year's Present for 1837* (Philadelphia, PA, 1836), p. 146. Leslie wrote anonymously as 'a resident in England' but is identified in George Fraser Black, *A Gypsy Bibliography* (Edinburgh, 1909), entry 3333. Though it was published in 1836, it is clear from the chronology of his life of Charlotte Lee, afterwards Cooper, that he wrote the piece ten years earlier.

50 Bright, *Travels*, pp. 528, 530, 543.

51 Furzebind was tormentil (*Potentilla erecta*); waspweed was water figwort (*Scrophularia auriculata*); burvine came in two sorts, yellow and purple, which sounds as if it might be toadflax (*Linaria* spp.).

52 John Clare, *The Prose of John Clare*, ed. John W. and Anne Tibble (London, 1951), pp. 35–8, with spelling standardized and some punctuation added; discussed by Angus Fraser, 'John Clare's Gypsies', *Journal of the Gypsy Lore Society*, 3rd series, L (1971), pp. 85–100.

53 Systematic discussion begins with Eric Otto Winstedt, 'Notes on English Gypsy Christian Names: I', pp. 64–90, and 'Notes on English Gypsy Christian Names: II', *Journal of the Gypsy Lore Society*, 3rd series, II (1922), pp. 16–39. Baptismal registers suggest that the fashion for distinctive names had its first beginnings *c.* 1700. The names of parents, which would have been given some twenty or thirty years previously, include Dedimiaj Dannils (the Spanish Dedamaia) at Fetcham, 11 June 1726, Jasper Wood at Chaldon, 5 July 1747, and Mashach Gardener at Capel, 21 April 1751; all noted in GPT. Among the names of children are Onslow Eyres at Wilmington in Kent, 1713, noted in Alan McGowan, *On the Gypsy Trail: Sources for the Family History of Gypsies* (Swindon, 1998), p. 9, and Hercules Stone at Bisley, 28 March 1741, noted in GPT.

54 Trudgill, *The Family Trees of Damon and Thomas Lee*, pp. 4–12.

55 Turner, 'Gypsies'. This is the only woman's name to hint at Eastern romance; there are no Gypsy Cleopatras or Zenobias, which suggests that the community did not think of themselves as 'Oriental'.

56 QS Midsummer 1782. The name, already current among gorjers in the seventeenth century, may have been adopted by Gypsies as a pun on Stanley, since the Stanleys were earls of Derby. It cannot refer to the race as that was established in 1780.

57 '"Sampson, sit down to hear the gentleman"; "Onslow, come here"; "Solomon, there's a good boy"': Crabb, *Gipsies' Advocate* (1832 edn), p. 140 (not in 1831 edn).

58 There was a Perram Brickwell, recorded as the victim of a theft at Southwark in QS Michaelmas 1799, but nothing apart from his first name identifies him as a Gypsy. The name is also found with a Romani ending as Perramos, sometimes written Pyramus under the influence of its Latin lookalike.

59 The Cinderella story is traditional, but the name itself first appeared in print, as an English translation of the French Cendrillon, in 1729. Cinderella Wood, the wife of Shadrach Boswell, was born in about 1751 – Richard Edmunds, 'The Life of Shadrach Boswell: II', *Romany Routes*, II (2012–14), pp. 209–302 – so it took only twenty years for the name to be adopted.

60 In Spain *La vida de Lazarillo de Tormes* was published in 1554.

61 In 1772 a Kentish Gypsy claimed to speak Romani but not English, a claim which may have had something to do with his summons to court: *Parliamentary History of England* (T. C. Hansard, London, 1776–1833), vol. XVII, coll. 449–50.

62 Hancock, *Educated Gypsy*, pp. 47–53, discusses the first recognition of Romani as an Indic language. The year is traditionally put down as 1763 but I suspect that it was a repeated discovery.

63 Joseph Farington, *The Diary of Joseph Farington*, ed. Kenneth Garlick, Angus Macintyre and Kathryn Cave (London, 1978–98), vol. III, p. 1051, discussed by Henry Thomas Crofton, 'Thomas Daniell and Romani', *Journal of the Gypsy Lore Society*, 3rd series, VII (1928), p. 48.

64 Crabb, *Gypsies' Advocate*, p. 17 (p. 18 of 1832 edn). This was Lord Teignmouth, assistant to the board of revenue in West Bengal; more on his Romani researches can be found in Charles John Shore, *Memoir of the Life and Correspondence of John Lord Teignmouth* (London, 1843), vol. II, pp. 373–6.

65 Phillips, *A Morning's Walk*, pp. 363–76. Winstedt, 'Norwood Gypsies', pp. 145–6, thought that this group included the Diana, Mansfield and Zachariah Lee known to Hoyland, *Historical Survey*, p. 185. The location is discussed in Charles Hailstone, *Alleyways of Mortlake and East Sheen* (London, 1983), pp. 31–3.

66 Percy Lane Oliver, 'Surrey Gypsies', *Surrey Magazine*, 1 (1899–1900), pp. 15–18. We know that 'Mrs. Cooper' was taken in by a Sam Cooper, married his youngest son and stayed mostly at Norwood, from which I assume that her adopter was Norwood Sam.

67 *Morning Post*, 7, 8 and 11 June 1802, and *Jackson's Oxford Journal*, 19 June 1802.

68 *Morning Post*, 19 September 1835.

69 Leslie, 'The Gipsies', p. 146. Like Crabb, *Gypsies' Advocate*, pp. 51–2 (pp. 55–6 of 1832 edn), he was convinced that accusations of the theft of babies were simply a rumour legend. David Cressy, *Gypsies: An English History* (Oxford, 2018), pp. 255–64, deals at length with this, and agrees.

70 St Luke's Norwood marriage register, 27 August 1827; *The Times*, 1 September 1827.

71 H. G. Ward, 'A German Professor on the Norwood Gypsies', *Journal of the Gypsy Lore Society*, 3rd series, XV (1936), pp. 94–6.

72 Thomas William '"My Friend's Gypsy Journal"', *Journal of the Gypsy Lore Society*, 3rd series, XIV (1935), pp. 108–11, at p. 109.

73 Frances Brown, *Fairfield Folk: A History of the British Fairground and Its People* (Upton upon Severn, 1988), p. 10, with dialect spelling standardized. The story, though treasured for many generations, is not true – Lydia was not a parson's daughter, and her surname was not Gowan. Her parents were Charles Reynolds and Mary Brewer: Robert Dane Matthews, 'My Matthews Family: II', *Romany Routes* 15 (2020–22), pp. 261–3.

74 'A Clown', 'The Poor Man's friend', *Christian Guardian*, 4 (1812), p. 99.

75 Hoyland, *Historical Survey*, pp. 173–4. I've taken a liberty in presenting the metaphor of the bird as Trinity's own, though Hoyland attributes it to her teacher. It is a traditional Romany expression, found, for example, in Augustus John, *Finishing Touches* (London, 1964), p. 68.

4 Test Your Strength: Early Victorian Times

1 OB 2 March 1840. I am fairly sure that this is indeed the transportation of Fighting Jack Cooper (though his age is given as 35, when in fact it was 40), but there is no mention of his ethnicity at the trial, neither does it seem to have attracted any media attention, perhaps because by 1840 Jack was yesterday's news.

2 CR John Cooper, 8 July 1840; Mary Ann Hart, 28 March 1840.

3 Eric Trudgill, 'William Cooper's Children', *Romany Routes*, 10 (2010–12); they were both baptized at Old Windsor.

4 Thus on William Kemp's plan of 1823, in Patricia Connor, *Derby Day 200* (London, 1979), p. 40.

5 Pierce Egan, *Boxiana; or, Sketches of Ancient and Modern Pugilism from the Days of the Renowned Broughton and Slack, to the Championship of Cribb* (London, 1812–29), 1st series, vol. III, p. 418.

6 Egan refers simply to 'the Gypsy's sister' but this must have been Trinity as she was the only girl in the family.

7 Egan, *Boxiana*, 2nd series, vol. I, pp. 194–202.

8 Ibid., p. 597.

9 Ibid., pp. 600–603; *Sporting Magazine*, 69 (1827), pp. 400–401.

10 *The Times*, 24 June 1825 (where 'Mr Fitzclarence' is one of the sons of Dorothy Jordan and the future William IV).

11 *Morning Post*, 4 September 1833; *The Times*, 5 December 1833; *Essex Standard*, 25 January 1834. The *Essex Standard* gives Tom Cooper's age as 31, which seems to be a year or two out.

12 George Hall, *The Gypsy's Parson: His Experiences and Adventures* (London, 1915), p. 250.

13 Terence Lee, *The Lee Family Tree* (privately printed, 1992), vol. I, p. 13, vol. II, p. 24. Jim Beaney, 'Aspects of Jack Cooper', *Romany Routes*, 5 (2000–2002), pp. 360–68, is wrong in identifying her as the daughter of Righteous Lee and Penny Cooper.

14 Charles Godfrey Leland, 'A Gypsy Beauty', *The Century*, 32 (1886), pp. 539–42.

15 Charles Robert Leslie (as 'A Resident in England'), 'The Gipsies: A Slight Sketch', pp. 145–51 of Eliza Leslie, *The Gift: A Christmas and New Year's Present for 1837* (Philadelphia, PA, 1836), p. 148. This description matches his portrait of Charlotte, now lost, but preserved through the engraving in Leland.

16 George Borrow, *Romano Lavo-Lil* (London, 1874), p. 210 – though she may have shrunk a bit over the years.

17 Egham St John baptismal register, 6 February 1820.

18 Not everybody felt this way; Enoch Lee spoke scornfully of Jack for selling out to the gorjers, *Sunday Times*, 6 May 1838.

19 Charles Godfrey Leland, 'Visiting the Gypsies', *The Century*, 25 (1883), pp. 905–12, at pp. 908–9, with Romani standardized.

20 Thomas Frost, *Reminiscences of a Country Journalist* (London, 1886), p. 4; *The Sun*, 20 January 1796.

21 George Sanger, *Seventy Years a Showman* (London, 1908), p. 47.

22 QVJ 5 January 1837.

23 *The Times*, 22 September 1829.

24 Costume is often described in QVJ – Sarah on 15 December 1836 and 1 January 1837, Bella on 18 December; the descriptions are accompanied by watercolours.

25 William Howitt, *The Rural Life of England* (London, 1840), p. 195; this passage was written while he was living at Stoke d'Abernon (p. 192).

26 Charles Dickens, 'Epsom', *Household Words*, 3 (1851), pp. 241–6, at p. 245.

27 Evelyn Richards, 'Old Folk's Memories of Wimbledon', *Wimbledon and Merton Annual*, 4 (1910), pp. 91–101, at p. 96.

28 Howitt, *Rural Life*, p. 195.

29 This is commented on by Edward Bradley, as 'Cuthbert Bede', 'In Gipsy Tents', *Notes and Queries*, 6th series, 2 (1880), pp. 362–4, at p. 363.

30 Eric Trudgill, *The Family Tree of Benjamin and Thomas Hearn from about 1740 to about 1900, Mainly Counties to the North, West and South of London* (Swindon, 2009), pp. 3–4.

31 'Beautiful oriental china' was on show, along with solid silver plate, at a wedding of 1822 in Buckinghamshire: *Jackson's Oxford Journal*, 31 August 1822.

32 *The Observer*, 25 March 1832.

33 *Croydon Chronicle*, 22 March 1856.

34 *The Times*, 10 August 1818.

35 *Morning Chronicle*, 1 October 1825; *The Times*, 11 July 1833; Sanger, *Seventy Years*, p. 125.

36 *The Observer*, 21 March 1831, evidently the vehicle 'formerly an advertising van for Astley's theatre' and appearing (slightly worse for wear) in Mary Bayly, 'The Gipsy Family', *The British Workman*, 9 (1863), p. 418; *The Era*, 2 June 1850.

37 *Illustrated London News*, 22 May 1858. Except that the stovepipe is shown on the wrong side (probably an engraver's error), the waggon is of the standard kite/Reading design.

38 Borrow, *Romano Lavo-Lil*, pp. 218–19.

39 'The Missionary to the Gypsies', 'Annual Reports, 1858 and 1859', *London City Mission Magazine*, 25 (1860), pp. 1–36, at p. 18.

40 Alan Wright, *Their Day Has Passed: Gypsies in Victorian and Edwardian Surrey* (Tolworth, 2017), p. 68. Until 1861 census enumerators were told not to record travellers by name, so this is a rare exception.

41 He had moved into 22 Hereford Square in 1860: David Williams, *A World of His Own: The Double Life of George Borrow* (Oxford, 1982), p. 166.

42 Not called this at the time: 'bender' is a regional term, first recorded quite late, in *The Times*, 10 June 1934. Peter Ingram, *Wagtail Tale: Gypsy Life of Bygone Days* (privately printed, 2014), p. 310, speaks of 'rod and blanket tents, commonly referred to in the south of England as "Benders"'.

43 The description in Borrow, *Romano Lavo-Lil*, pp. 217–18 can be compared with more jaundiced but otherwise confirmatory accounts by 'The Missionary', 'Annual Reports', pp. 17, 30, and *Surrey Mirror*, 24 December 1881.

44 A correspondent of George Smith, *Gipsy Life: Being an Account of Our Gipsies and Their Children* (London, 1880), p. 51, estimated five children to a tent.

45 OB 6 May 1850; the transcriber writes 'libbet' for what is later called a livett.

46 *The Times*, 25 August 1864.

47 Benjamin Ward Richardson, *Vita Medica: Chapters of Medical Life and Work* (London, 1897), p. 145.

48 A common service, delicately expressed in *New Monthly Magazine*, 35 (1832), p. 376: 'Gipsies are subject to but few diseases: they seldom ask the doctor's assistance but for one friendly office, and that serves a man his lifetime.'

49 *Parliamentary Debates*, 4th series, 187 (1908), col. 453.

50 Jenny Hamilton-Sneath, *A Glimpse of Old England: Surrey by the Tillingbourne* (London, 1997), pp. 74–5.

51 *Surrey Advertiser*, 10 February 1883, from a correspondence discussed in Stanley Alder, *Work among the Gypsies* (Chobham, 1893), p. 8.

52 Christine Nunweek, 'The Christmas Holly Wreath', *Romany Routes*, 9 (2008–10), pp. 11–12; this was in 1903, later than the other examples, but the spirit is the same.

53 Epsom burial register, 28 May 1853, noted in GPT. He might have been a son or grandson of James Methuselah Lee, who lived to a more creditable eighty: Lee, *Lee Family*, p. 25, and Sandra Smith, 'My Gypsy Family', *Romany Routes*, 8 (2006–8), pp. 326–30, at p. 327.

54 James Crabb, *The Gipsies' Advocate* (London, 1831), p. 34 (p. 36 of 1832 edn): 'melancholy instances of children being burnt and scalded to death are not unfrequent.'

55 Charles Godfrey Leland, *The Gypsies* (London, 1882), p. 100.

56 'The Orchard and the Hearth', in George Meredith, *Poems and Lyrics of the Joys of Earth* (London, 1883), first published in *Macmillan's Magazine*, 17 (1867–8), pp. 362–6. Meredith had recently moved to Box Hill.

57 Based on a sample of 47 people with recorded dates of birth/baptism and death/burial from the genealogies of three families travelling in the southeast: Eric Trudgill, *The Family Trees of Damon and Thomas Lee from about 1750 to about 1900, Mainly the English Southern Counties* (Swindon, 2007), Trudgill, *The Family Tree of Benjamin and Thomas Hearn*, and Roger Baker, *The Family Tree of Samson and Celia Scamp* (Swindon, 2007). The sample was confined to those who died aged 20 and upwards in the nineteenth century, and the average age at death was found to be 59.8 years.

58 Benjamin Ward Richardson, *The Asclepiad* (London, 1884–95), vol. II, pp. 211–15. Doctors in 1909 reported on the rarity of infectious disease among Gypsies: Wright, *Their Day Has Passed*, pp. 138–40.

59 Sarah Lamb's daughter was another survivor, 'pitted with the small pox', *The Times*, 16 October 1832.

60 *The Standard*, 28 July 1827; this appears to be the case mentioned by Crabb, *Gypsies' Advocate*, p. 53 (p. 57 of 1832 edn).

61 Charles Godfrey Leland, *The English Gypsies and Their Language* (London, 1873), p. 51 (I have not found a record of Job's death; he is last recorded in the 1861 census, at Clewer); Wisley burial register, 28 July 1845.

62 *Open Spaces (Metropolis) Select Committee: First Report* (Richmond, 1865), vol. I, p. 82.

63 *Penny Illustrated Paper*, 24 November 1866.

64 Kerry Hawkins, 'My Ancestors at Hampton Wick in the 1861 and 1871 Census Returns: 1', *Romany Routes*, 4 (1998–2000), pp. 298–300.

65 Frances Brown, *Fairfield Folk: A History of the British Fairground and Its People* (Upton upon Severn, 1988), pp. 22–3.

66 Ibid., p. 86, refers to the death from scarlet fever of Carrie, daughter of Charles/Chorley Matthews, at Horsham Fair in about 1874.

67 Ibid., p. 19.

68 Frost, *Reminiscences*, p. 4.

69 Crabb, *Gypsies' Advocate* (1832), pp. 37–8 (not in 1831 edn).

70 'The Missionary', 'Annual Reports', p. 31.

71 Frost, *Reminiscences*, p. 15.

72 One version in Frost, *Reminiscences*, and the other in the contemporary newspapers cited by Keith Chandler, 'Trinity Cooper: From Attentive Scholar to Battered Wife', *Romany Routes*, 10 (2010–12), pp. 213–19; combine them how you will!

73 The *Essex Standard*, 22 September 1832, says it was a quarrel, while tradition remembered him as being 'too fond' of her: Thomas William Thompson, 'Borrow's Gypsies', *Journal of the Gypsy Lore Society*, 2nd series, III (1909–10), pp. 162–72, at p. 165.

74 *The Times*, 21 May 1836, *The Standard*, 21 May 1836, noted with other sources in Eric Otto Winstedt, 'Gypsies as Highwaymen and Footpads', *Journal of the Gypsy Lore Society*, 3rd series, VI (1927), pp. 68–88, at p. 80. The arrested man 'is said to be the brother of a pugilist who is now transported for felony' (Tom Cooper), but his name is given as James Cooper. Since there is no other evidence that Elisha had a son James, this may be Jack.

75 *The Observer*, 3 June 1844.

76 *The Times*, 28 August 1846, noted in Chandler, 'Trinity Cooper', pp. 215–17.

77 *The Times*, 10 July 1856. John and Thomas Stevens both kept booths at different fairs: OB 18 September 1837.

78 Rowland Baker and Gwendoline Baker, *Thameside Molesey: A Towpath Ramble from Hampton Court to Hampton Reach* (Buckingham, 1989), pp. 117–19.

79 *London City Mission Magazine*, 46 (1881), p. 233.

80 *The Observer*, 1 June 1823.

81 Michael Wynn Jones, *The Derby* (London, 1979), p. 96.

82 *Illustrated London News*, 22 May 1858, pp. 511–14.

83 'The Missionary', 'Annual Reports', p. 23. There were limits to people's toleration, even of gentlemen, and two missionaries were attacked on Epsom Downs in the 1850s: Wright, *Their Day Has Passed*, p. 108.

84 Samuel Roberts, *The Gypsies: Their Origin, Continuance and Destination* (London, 1836), pp. 64–8, and Borrow, *Romano Lavo-Lil*, pp. 241–2. Roberts says she was with him for eight days; Borrow, six weeks; I have taken an average.

85 Borrow, *Romano Lavo-Lil*, pp. 242–3. The first husband was Cornelius Smith, who parted with Clara at some time after 1855, while the daughters would have been Phoebe, born in 1841, and Patience, in 1848: Anne-Marie Ford, 'Tinker of Hargrave', *Romany Routes*, 12 (2014–16), pp. 253–5.

86 I've divided the 1,000 to 1,500 people estimated to be present on the night before the Derby in the *Illustrated London News*, 22 May 1858, p. 513, by the 70 to 80 Gypsy tents enumerated in 'The Missionary', 'Annual Reports', p. 23, assuming an average of two adults per tent.

87 Brown, *Fairfield Folk*, p. 25; Elizabeth Robins Pennell, *Charles Godfrey Leland* (London, 1906), vol. II, pp. 155–6.

88 From a newspaper interview quoted in Brown, *Fairfield Folk*, p. 25. The date appears to have been 25 September 1922 but the paper was not, as cited on pp. 32, 54–6, the *Aldershot Gazette and Military News*.

89 Brown, *Fairfield Folk*, p. 33.

90 Note, however, that Brown treats her family – all the way back – not as Romany but as a dynasty of showfolk initially misidentified as Gypsies. Other descendents of Chewbacca and Liddy, such as Robert Dane Matthews, think otherwise, and I have followed their lead.

91 Sanger, *Seventy Years*, p. 46.

92 Plato is the father in Christ Church Battersea baptismal register, 31 December 1911, Concelleta the mother in 12 August 1902 and 14 March 1910; noted in Jenifer Edmonds, *Gypsies, Tramps and . . . Strangers* (privately printed, 2004–5), vol. V, pp. 31, 28.

93 *Daily News*, 27 May 1875.

94 Coconuts appear in a print of 'Epsom Downs on a Derby Morning' in the *Illustrated London News*, 23 May 1863. Alan Wright has found what must be their first appearance, at Battersea in 1860: *Their Day Has Passed*, p. 93.

95 *The Times*, 17 June 1843.

96 Until the end of the prize-fighting era Gypsies didn't supply more fighters than any other sector of the working class. After this come the references to prize-fighting in a specifically Gypsy milieu, such as a fight at Sydenham in 1881 'surrounded by a gang of about 400 navvies and gipsies': *The Times*, 28 September 1881.

97 *The Standard*, 23 June 1845; *The Times*, 23 June 1845.

98 Sanger, *Seventy Years*, p. 49. *The Standard*, 23 June 1845, talks of seven policemen facing 'a mob of between 300 and 400 persons, consisting of gipsies and other desperadoes' , numbers which are so disproportionate that you wonder how there could have been any kind of fight at all.

99 *Morning Post*, 1 July 1845, and *Lloyd's Weekly Newspaper*, 6 July 1845, name the men who were arrested (there was also a seventh, James Porter). The sudden flight appears only in Sanger; the newspapers do not mention it.

100 Remembered in the *Pall Mall Gazette*, 25 May 1871; 1844 is an approximate date.

101 J. G. Taylor, *Our Lady of Batersey* (London, 1925), p. 290; *The Survey of London 49–50: Battersea* (English Heritage, 2013), vol. I, p. 260.

102 This figure appears in *The Times*, 5 September 1848, as part of the prosecution of Thomas and Silvester Lee, who had lured a young donkey rider behind a hedge and relieved him of his silver watch.

103 *Daily News*, 3 April 1858.

104 Crabb, *Gipsies' Advocate* (1832 edn), p. 137 (not in 1831 edn). Cf. a reference of 1825 to 'the numerous tribe of Gypsies' on the common: *Morning Chronicle*, 18 June 1825.

105 *The Observer*, 21 March and 3 April 1831.

106 Edward Page Gaston, 'Gypsy Associations of Wimbledon Common', *Wimbledon and Merton Annual*, 3 (1905), pp. 67–76, at p. 69; Guy Boas, *Wimbledon – Has It a History?* (London, 1947), p. 15.

107 *The Times*, 20 July 1841. It was common for gorjers to rent stopping places to Gypsies: Wright, *Their Day Has Passed*, pp. 76–7.

108 Richard Milward, *Historic Wimbledon: Caesar's Camp to Centre Court* (London, 1989), pp. 132–7; Dorian Gerhold, ed., *Putney and Roehampton Past* (London, 1999), pp. 89–91.

109 *First Report of the Open Spaces Committee*, vol. I, pp. 28, 37. These figures should be taken with some caution since they are estimates by householders with an axe to grind. James Britten said that he had never seen more than three families of the 'persecuted tribe' together (*The Standard*, 16 January 1865).

110 John Pateman, *Hoo, Hops and Hods: The Life and Times of Robert Pateman* (privately printed, 2007), pp. 73, 78. Pateman argues that the brothers (born in 1821) were sons of a gorjer agricultural labourer, another John, who lived at Hoo, 1772–1849. This seems unlikely, and it is possible that they came instead from a Chiltern Gypsy family of Patemans.

111 As he wrote in a letter of 1861: Thomas Acton, *Gypsy Politics and Social Change* (London, 1974), pp. 105–6, David Mayall, *Gypsy-Travellers in Nineteenth-Century Society* (Cambridge, 1988), p. 158. In *First Report of the Open Spaces Committee*, vol. I, p. 18, he refers to complaints 'within the last six or seven years'.

112 *First Report of the Open Spaces Committee*, vol. I, p. 55.

113 Ibid., pp. 50, 55; Blanchard Jerrold, *The Life and Remains of Douglas Jerrold* (London, 1859), p. 258.

114 James Douglas, *Theodore Watts-Dunton: Poet, Novelist, Critic* (London, 1904), p. 100.

115 *First Report of the Open Spaces Committee*, vol. I, p. 43; Richards, 'Old Folk's Memories', p. 96.

116 *The Graphic*, 18 June 1870. In 1914 George Chapman was running classes at Godalming, teaching the gorjers how to make baskets: Wright, *Their Day Has Passed*, p. 82.

117 Hedge stakes and straying horses in *First Report of the Open Spaces Committee*, vol. I, pp. 27, 82, and *Lloyd's Weekly Newspaper*, 17 January 1858; children in *First Report of the Open Spaces Committee*, vol. I, pp. 49, 55, 82.

118 Jacqueline Loose, *Roehampton: The Last Village in London* (London, 1979), p. 61.

119 *First Report of the Open Spaces Committee*, vol. II, p. 144; this was Wandsworth, not Wimbledon, although the parishes had contiguous common ground.

120 Thus his letter of 1861: Acton, *Gypsy Politics*, pp. 105–6, Mayall, *Gypsy-Travellers*, p. 158.

5 Waggons Roll: The Victorian Age

1 Charles Godfrey Leland, *The English Gypsies and Their Language* (London, 1873), pp. 112–15, says this was 'an old acquaintance, named Brown', who is also 'White George', while his wife knew 'the Cooper clan, to which she was allied'. I believe that Brown is a cover name, and the couple were in fact George White, born *c.* 1823 at Upton Grey, and Mary, born *c.* 1828 at Fordingbridge, who appear together in the censuses of 1851 (Binfield) and 1861 (Isleworth).

2 Ibid., pp. 112–17. From his accompanying sketch it is clear that the chairs were loose, not ledge seats; the same is implied by *Open Spaces (Metropolis) Select Committee: First Report* (Richmond, 1865), vol. 1, p. 44, and can be seen in the sketch made inside a van at Latimer Road, *Illustrated London News*, 13 December 1879.

3 John Thomson and Adolphe Smith, *Street Life in London* (London, 1876–7), photo accompanying vol. 1, pp. 1–3, supplemented by the dimensions given by 'Router', 'How to Make a Showman's Caravan', *Work: The Illustrated Weekly Journal for Mechanics*, 12 (1896/7), pp. 409–11 – despite the title, this is a straightforward kite waggon.

4 The early history of showman's waggons is discussed by Paul Braithwaite, *A Palace on Wheels* (White Waltham, 1999), pp. 22–31. Vehicles of some sort appear to have been in use from the 1810s at least, with the conventional Burton form emerging by mid-century.

5 Cyril Ward-Jackson and Denis Harvey, *The English Gypsy Caravan: Its Origins, Builders, Technology and Conservation* (Newton Abbot, 1972), p. 136, note the fact about door styles; the explanatory story is in Denis Harvey, *The Gypsies: Waggon-Time and After* (London, 1979), p. 97.

6 Tom Francis, *Old Mitcham*, ed. Eric Montague (Chichester, 1993), figs 143, 147; the ledge waggon, dated *c.* 1910, is in Eric Montague, *Mitcham: A Pictorial History* (Chichester, 1991), fig. 74.

7 Ward-Jackson and Harvey, *English Gypsy Caravan*, pp. 101–2, 146; John Barker and Peter Ingram, *Romany Relics: The Wagon Album* (privately printed, 2010), pp. 277–9.

8 J.W.B., in *May's Aldershot Advertiser*, 13 September 1879, refers to '£100 for a new travelling van'; the original newspaper is now apparently lost, but survives excerpted in George Smith, *Gipsy Life: Being an Account of Our Gipsies and Their Children* (London, 1880), pp. 87–90.

9 E. Brewer, 'Gipsy Encampments in the Heart of London', *The Sunday at Home*, 1896, pp. 113–14.

10 I owe this detail to Kerry Hawkins.

11 The protection of wheels appears in a postcard, '"The Gipsies" in the Pines, Woking' (SHC PX/160/30), reproduced in Ian Wakeford, *Woking as It Was* (Chichester, 1985), fig. 88. A good example of a striped awning was photographed at the 1936 Derby: Robert Dawson, *Times Gone: Gypsies and Travellers* (privately printed, 2007), p. 42.

12 James Greenwood, *Low-Life Deeps: An Account of the Strange Fish to Be Found There* (London, 1876), p. 215.

13 D. L. Woolmer, 'Gipsies in Their Winter Quarters', *The Quiver*, 1903, pp. 530–35, at p. 530; Cloudesley Willis, *A Brief History of Ewell and Nonsuch* (Epsom, 1931), p. 90.

14 As in the 1896 oil painting by Charles Collins, *Gypsies with Cattle and Horses*, Collection of the Field House Nursing Home, Shepton Mallet. Collins painted in the Dorking area.

15 *Sunday Times*, 17 May 1863; Bisley baptismal and burial registers noted in Lesley Doe, 'From Parish Registers', *Romany Routes*, 6 (2002–4), p. 341, to which add burials of 21 May 1867, 8 March 1882 and 3 December 1883.

16 John Pateman, *Hoo, Hops and Hods: The Life and Times of Robert Pateman* (privately printed, 2007), p. 175.

17 Woolmer, 'Winter Quarters', p. 533.

18 T. W. Wilkinson, 'Van Dwelling London', in *Living London*, ed. George R. Sims (London, 1904–6), vol. III, pp. 319–23, at p. 321.

19 Dorian Gerhold, ed., *Putney and Roehampton Past* (London, 1999), p. 116.

20 *Parliamentary Debates (Fifth Series: House of Lords)*, 7 (1911), col. 109; *Surrey Mirror*, 15 May 1908.

21 SHC CC28/101, noted in David Mayall, *Gypsy-Travellers in Nineteenth-Century Society* (Cambridge, 1988), p. 201.

22 Trevor White and Jeremy Harte, *Epsom: A Pictorial History* (Chichester, 1992), pl. 190; Willis, *History of Ewell*, p. 1.

23 Charles Godfrey Leland, 'The Derby Race of 1885', *Outing*, 8 (1885), pp. 337–42, at p. 338.

24 'The Missionary to the Gypsies', 'Annual Reports, 1858 and 1859', *London City Mission Magazine*, 25 (1860), p. 30.

25 Sung by Jasper Smith on *The Travelling Songster*, TOPIC 12TS304, and quoted in Tim Coughlan, *Now Shoon the Romano Gillie: Traditional Verse in the High and Low Speech of the Gypsies of Britain* (Cardiff, 2001), p. 389. This is Jasper's variation on a gorjer folksong, 'The Irish Familie': Peter Kennedy, *Folksongs of Britain and Ireland* (London, 1975), no. 275 on pp. 607–8, and notes p. 626.

26 'The Missionary', 'Annual Reports', p. 25.

27 Leland, 'Derby Race of 1885', p. 342.

28 Stove types are discussed by Ward-Jackson and Harvey, *English Gypsy Caravan*, pp. 162–4, and Braithwaite, *Palace on Wheels*, pp. 64–8.

29 Harvey, *Waggon-Time*, p. 48.

30 Walter Johnson and William Wright, *Neolithic Man in North-East Surrey* (London, 1903), p. 177.

31 Charles Godfrey Leland, Edward Henry Palmer and Janet Tuckey, *English-Gypsy Songs* (London, 1875), pp. 97–100, and Elizabeth Robins Pennell, *Charles Godfrey Leland* (London, 1906), vol. II, p. 137. The Bokelo Gilli, as placed on record by Leland, begins '*Mándy's chávvis shan bokelo – ókelo – kokelo*' and continues with nonsense rhymes at each line. But the text seems to have had some editorial improvement, since it uses inflections (*púderla*, 'it blows', and *shúnova*, 'I hear') which never appear in the direct transcripts of Matty's Romani.

32 Charles Godfrey Leland, *The Gypsies* (London, 1882), p. 193 – evidently the same meal (beefsteak for Leland, pork for Matty) as described in Pennell.

33 Gentilla was born in 1819 – Eric Trudgill, 'William Cooper's Children', *Romany Routes*, 10 (2010–12), p. 23 – and was therefore younger than Leonard, Nelson, Matty and Sarah; she does not seem to have been travelling with them at Esher in 1836.

34 Leland, *The Gypsies*, p. 297.

35 Leland, Palmer and Tuckey, *English-Gypsy Songs*, p. 87.

36 The fable of the hedgehogs is in Leland, *English Gypsies*, pp. 203–4.

37 Woolmer, 'Winter Quarters', p. 534.

38 This method certainly existed, since it is described by a man who travelled with Gypsies at Knutsford. 'If we got a hen or goose . . . we used to roll it up in clay, with the feathers on, and put it down at a fire, letting it roast itself with its own fat; when the clay was baked hard feathers and clay

would come off together; and on cutting it open the entrails would come out in a lump': *The Times*, 14 December 1839.

39 Pennell, *Charles Godfrey Leland*, vol. II, p. 383; presumably the same dog as in Leland, *English Gipsies*, p. 163.

40 *Moveable Dwellings Bill Select Committee of the House of Lords: Report* (Richmond, 1909), p. 41; Silvester Gordon Boswell records the same, *The Book of Boswell: Autobiography of a Gypsy*, ed. John Seymour (London, 1970), p. 47.

41 Leland, *English Gipsies*, p. 164.

42 Dorothy Una Ratcliffe, 'A Gypsy Belief', *Journal of the Gypsy Lore Society*, 3rd series, XVI (1937), p. 93, and 'My Gypsy Acquaintances', *Journal of the Gypsy Lore Society*, 3rd series, XLIII (1964), pp. 131–8, at p. 133. Similar boundary hopping is recorded from Walton on Thames and West Molesey, and from Mitcham and Croydon: Alan Wright, *Their Day Has Passed: Gypsies in Victorian and Edwardian Surrey* (Tolworth, 2017), pp. xvii, 165.

43 Amabel Strachey, 'The Gipsy Scandal and the Danger to the Commons', *National Review*, 59 (1912), pp. 459–72, at p. 461.

44 The first picture of a kettle iron that I have seen is in *The Queen*, 16 November 1861; George Borrow mentions them in *Romano Lavo-Lil* (London, 1874), p. 218.

45 Chittis were first observed in the early twentieth century: Frank Cuttriss, *Romany Life: Experienced and Observed during Many Years of Friendly Intercourse with the Gypsies* (London, 1915), pp. 32, 35. I'm told that they were rare until people began to stop on places with hard standing, where you couldn't drive in a kettle iron.

46 Cf. the 'caravan with a big family boiler slung at the axle-tree' arriving at Epsom: *Daily News*, 28 May 1888.

47 Raphael Samuel, 'Comers and Goers', in *The Victorian City: Images and Realities*, ed. H. J. Dyers and Michael Wolff (London, 1973), pp. 123–60; pp. 131ff. is the best account of the collective annual migration out of London, which involved many other groups as well as Gypsies.

48 Grant Allen, 'Eclogues of Arcady XII', *Illustrated London News*, 23 March 1895.

49 Not all horses were reduced to furze; on the day after the Derby, 22 horses and a donkey mysteriously appeared in a clover field at Croydon, *Reynold's Newspaper*, 5 August 1883.

50 Harvey, *Waggon-Time*, p. 32: a waggon travels at 4 miles per hour, or brisk walking speed. He estimates 10 miles a day as an average speed, 15 to 18 miles as exceptional.

51 *Parliamentary Debates (Fifth Series): House of Lords*, 7 (1911), col. 109.

52 Six months is the figure recorded by Wilkinson, 'Van Dwelling London', p. 323. Compare the very local travelling circuits found by David Cressy in his analysis of the people stopping at Epsom in 1891: *Gypsies: An English History* (Oxford, 2018), p. 202.

53 Jenifer Edmonds, *Gypsies, Tramps and . . . Strangers* (privately printed, 2004–5), vol. IV, pp. 16–22. Two-thirds of these pupils are girls, an indication that education was still regarded as women's business.

54 Stanley Alder, *Work among the Gypsies* (Chobham, 1893), p. 26. He does not name the family, but says they were married at Chobham, 1 October

1887. Eric Hall, 'Work among the Gypsies', *Root and Branch*, 19 (1992), p. 120, made the identification.

55 Mary Ann Bennett, *Life and Work on Surrey Heath* (Chichester, 2007), pp. 31–3. I am assuming that the James and Mary Ann Lamb of the 1881 census returns are James Lamb and Ann Lynch. In this and the following examples, the circuit in which people travelled has been deduced from the birthplaces of their children.

56 Dennis Coombe, 'Help Sought', *Romany Routes*, 6 (2002–4), pp. 178–9; see also Alan Banks, 'How Dobbin the Gypsy Horse Was Saved from an Untimely End', *Newdigate Society Magazine*, 22 (1991), pp. 13–15. Henry makes brief appearances in Wright, *Their Day Has Passed*, pp. 83, 149.

57 'The Moon Shines Bright' was also sung by Wharton children in Herefordshire in the 1880s: Ella Leather, 'Collecting Folk-Melodies from Gypsies in Herefordshire', *Journal of the Gypsy Lore Society*, 3rd series, IV (1925), pp. 59–72, at p. 64.

58 Kate Lee, 'Some Experiences of a Folk-Song Collector', *Journal of the Folk-Song Society*, 1 (1899–1904), pp. 1–3 (referring only to 'a very extraordinary gipsy', but surely to one of the Gobeys); Lucy Broadwood, 'Songs', *Journal of the Folk-Song Society*, 1 (1899–1904), pp. 139–225, at pp. 176–7, 183–4.

59 Terry Doe, 'Albert Doe, 1869–1964', *Romany Routes*, 6 (2002–4), pp. 105–7.

60 J.W.B., in *May's Aldershot Advertiser*, 13 September 1879; the original newspaper is now apparently lost, but survives excerpted in Smith, *Gipsy Life*, pp. 87–90. Other locations for agricultural work are given in Wright, *Their Day Has Passed*, pp. 98–9.

61 Alder, *Work among the Gypsies*, pp. 2, 12, 25. He would give up preaching in May, as his congregation dwindled. The Gypsies that Alder had persuaded to move into cottages continued paying rent during the months they were away, as you do on a site nowadays.

62 *The Times*, 22 September 1874.

63 Sue Bellord, 'Picking "Hurts" on Hurtwood Common', *Romany Routes*, 9 (2008–10), pp. 159–60.

64 Or 'harts': *Moveable Dwellings Bill Select Committee of the House of Lords: Report* (Richmond, 1909), p. 57. The dictionary form is whortleberry, or more frequently bilberry.

65 Muriel Gibson, ed., *Surrey within Living Memory* (Newbury, 1992), p. 54; Jenny Overton, ed., *Peaslake: Story of a Surrey Village* (privately printed, 2003), pp. 26, 93.

66 Campbell Smith, 'Memories of a Lower Kingswood Resident', *Lower Kingswood Village News*, Summer 2014, pp. 15–16. For more of these woodland crafts, see Wright, *Their Day Has Passed*, pp. 78–82.

67 *Croydon Chronicle*, 22 November 1879.

68 Edgar Wakeman in *Leeds Mercury*, 21 November 1896. Wakeman was an idealist; he opens by telling us that 'An ugly word is never heard in a gipsy camp or band. A selfish act is never seen.' On the subject of crafts, however, he appears to be accurate.

69 Robert Smith, *A History of Sutton, AD 675–1960* (privately printed, 1960), p. 85.

70 *Surrey Mirror*, 24 December 1881, with dialect spelling standardized. Job Lee, towards the end of a long and eventful life which included

seeing seventy Derbys, remembered making 1,000 skewers a day, him and his father; I make that to be 1 skewer every 18 seconds incessantly for 5 hours. He and his family could also turn out four hundred pegs in a day. The weekly take for these efforts was only 12s, about the same rate as on Holmwood Common: *Evening News*, 28 August 1908.

71 Leland, *English Gypsies*, pp. 167–8; the Old Henry of this episode must be the Henry James mentioned by Leland, *The Gypsies*, p. 45.

72 Brewer, 'Gipsy Encampments', p. 113.

73 Letter from Bramley, written in 1949 but describing things as they were *c.* 1900, noted in Osbert Sitwell, 'Guildford Gypsies', *Journal of the Gypsy Lore Society*, 3rd series, XXIX (1950), pp. 150–52. A family at Caterham in 1881 specialized in 'fancy baskets of oak apples strung on wires': Wright, *Their Day Has Passed*, p. 80.

74 Alder, *Work among the Gypsies*, pp. 5–6, 7–8, 10–11, 22; Bennett, *Surrey Heath*, p. 33; thanks also to the historians of St Saviours church, Valley End.

75 Kevin Pearce, 'Sampson and Amelia Tarrant', *Romany Routes*, 8 (2006–8), pp. 414–15. Another repair craft was umbrella-mending: it was Ernest Nunn's main occupation at Worplesdon in 1911, and saplings were cut for umbrella handles as well as for walking sticks: Wright, *Their Day Has Passed*, pp. 83, 87.

76 Andrew McFarlane, 'Matty Cooper and the Windsor Rats', *Journal of the Gypsy Lore Society*, 3rd series, XX (1941), pp. 41–2.

77 Juliette de Baïracli Levy, *Wanderers in the New Forest* (London, 1958), p. 89.

78 *Westminster Gazette*, 2 June 1908; McFarlane, 'Matty Cooper'.

79 Pateman, *Hoo, Hops and Hods*, p. 174. Of the 106 adults identified by a trade, 68 were hawkers, pedlars or general dealers; 2 labourers and 4 miscellaneous; and the 32 trades as given. Hawkers were issued with licences, but as these were handed out to gorjer traders as well, it is difficult to use them as evidence for the Gypsy economy: Wright, *Their Day Has Passed*, pp. 84–6.

80 *Lloyd's Weekly Newspaper*, 19 July 1857. Caroline's surname is given as Penfred, but this is surely a copyist's error.

81 Thomson and Smith, *Street Life*, p. 3.

82 Although people in the Londonside settlements could keep goods there: Wilkinson, 'Van Dwelling London', p. 321, mentions huts storing stock for firewood dealers.

83 Angus McMillan, *Gipsy Hawkins* (London, 1946), pp. 9–18.

84 See, for instance, the 1861 census returns for Palmers Field in Wandsworth, noted in Jacqui Gomm, 'From the Census', *Romany Routes*, 5 (2000–2002), pp. 380–81, where out of eight families, five had a husband with a trade and a wife who sold the goods.

85 Mary Attwell, *Childhood Memories of Barnes Village*, ed. Nicholas Dakin (London, 1996), pp. 40–41. The cabins were in what was to become Railway Side. Mignonette was, I suppose, the 'M. L.' of Barnes who left her husband when she got religion, because they had not had a church wedding – one of the less appealing fruits of grace: *London City Mission Magazine*, 46 (1881), p. 235.

86 Francis, *Old Mitcham*, fig. 46; Montague, *Mitcham*, fig. 74.

87 Kennedy, *Folksongs*, no. 356 on pp. 786–7, and notes pp. 801–2.
88 William Stewart, *Characters of Bygone London* (London, 1960), pp. 49–50.
89 Charles Payne, 'Bikk'ning Raklies', *Journal of the Gypsy Lore Society*, 3rd series, xxx (1951), pp. 151–3, at p. 151, with Romani standardized. Payne was a queer fish, one of those overly romantic types who flourished in the post-war Gypsy Lore Society. His everyday observations, which seem quite reliable, are coupled with marvellous fabricated accounts of superstition and ritual.
90 Thomson and Smith, *Street Life*, p. 3.
91 Leland, *English Gipsies*, p. 179. On the other hand, Frank Vinson was Grand Master of the Stepney Temperance Society: Wright, *Their Day Has Passed*, p. 110.
92 The average daily takings for dukkering were 5s or 6s, but at the races it went up to £2 2s: *London City Mission Magazine*, 34 (1869), p. 141.
93 Payne, 'Bikk'ning Raklies', p. 151; Henry Thomas Crofton, 'Affairs of Egypt, 1907', *Journal of the Gypsy Lore Society*, 2nd series, II (1908–9), pp. 121–41, at p. 129.
94 Brewer, 'Gipsy Encampments', p. 113, says '28s a week'; I'm assuming a six-day week.
95 Charles Godfrey Leland, 'Three Gipsy Songs', *Hood's Comic Annual*, 19 (1887), pp. 65–7, with Romani standardized. The original is in any case full of transcription errors – *kusliti* for *kushti* and so on.
96 Gibson, *Surrey*, p. 54; she says 1s a pint but I think this is an error for 1s a quart, as recorded elsewhere, for example, Bellord, 'Hurtwood Common'.
97 *The Times*, 22 September 1874; *The Standard*, 6 September 1893.
98 J.W.B., in *May's Aldershot Advertiser*, 13 September 1879; the original newspaper is now apparently lost, but survives excerpted in Smith, *Gipsy Life*, pp. 87–90.
99 Leland, *Gypsies*, p. 117.
100 *The Times*, 26 November 1872. Drusilla, who also appeared as Mrs Smith, may be the Drucella Smith of Barnes Common who assaulted Cinderella Beldam ten years earlier in a fight over a straying husband: *Sunday Times*, 6 April 1862.
101 Londonside Gypsies would sell the horse in winter and buy a new one in spring, for about £15 each: Henry Thomas Crofton, 'Affairs of Egypt, 1907', *Journal of the Gypsy Lore Society*, 2nd series, II (1908–9), p. 129.
102 F. Anstey, 'A Gypsy Fair in Surrey', *Harper's Monthly Magazine*, 76 (1888), pp. 625–33, at p. 625; George Sturt, *A Small Boy in the Sixties* (Cambridge, 1927), pp. 104, 107.
103 *Morning Post*, 3 May 1881.
104 Leland, *Gypsies*, pp. 126–8, 136–8; Pennell, *Charles Godfrey Leland*, vol. II, p. 155. Cobham Fair was held on 11 December, old St Andrew's Day.
105 Importing horses: Sturt, *A Small Boy in the Sixties*, p. 107, Woolmer, 'Winter Quarters', p. 532. Horse-doctoring: Juliette de Baïracli Levy, *As Gypsies Wander* (London, 1953), pp. 88, 125; Edwin Smith (as 'Lavengro'), *The Gypsy: Poems and Ballads* (Tunbridge Wells, 1973), p. 40.
106 Edward Page Gaston, 'Gypsy Associations of Wimbledon Common', *Wimbledon and Merton Annual*, 3 (1905), p. 75.
107 This is one of Matty Cooper's stories: Leland, *English Gipsies*, pp. 224–5.

108 I am leaving out a few extremely wealthy individuals, such as old Mo in Battersea whose waggon was robbed of bags of money amounting to a reputed £1,400: Thomson and Smith, *Street Life*, p. 3.

109 *Evening News*, 1 May 1919. The family row over who should have the money was long and bitter, which shows why there were usually community strictures against inherited wealth.

110 *Motherwell Times*, 16 September 1921, noted in Stephen Doe, 'Newspaper Finds', *Romany Routes*, 12 (2014–16), p. 68. For people who had invested their money in housing, the returns were higher. Rebecca Gess of Wardley Street left £1,300 of landed property in her will: Wright, *Their Day Has Passed*, p. 84.

111 *West Surrey Times*, 18 October 1884.

112 *The Times*, 27 March 1878; Thomas William Thompson, 'Affairs of Egypt, 1909', *Journal of the Gypsy Lore Society*, 2nd series, v (1911–12), pp. 113–35, at p. 121.

113 Taken from the list in David Mayall, *English Gypsies and State Policies* (Hatfield, 1995), pp. 56–7. Alan Wright has analysed Gypsy crime in Surrey newspapers from 1880 to 1914, and finds 421 regulatory offences, 23 cases of violent resistance to police, 81 minor crimes (if we include horse theft in this category), 26 fights, and 10 crimes of serious violence: *Their Day Has Passed*, pp. 130–31.

114 Hubert Rendell records moving Gypsies twice in his 22 months at Ockham and twice in 18 months at Ripley: Les Bowerman, 'Hubert H. Rendell, Ripley Police Sergeant 1922/3', *Journal of the Send and Ripley History Society*, 5 (2000), pp. 14–19.

115 The figure of 227 prosecutions in *Moveable Dwellings Bill: Report*, p. 88, can be matched with the 1907 county census of nomads which recorded 294 men above the age of 21: Wright, *Their Day Has Passed*, p. 82. Both figures refer to administrative Surrey, excluding the areas in the London County Council, and while the census no doubt excludes a large number of ethnic Gypsies not travelling, the people that it did count were those most likely to have been stopped by the police for offences.

116 PRO HO45/10995/158231/9, noted by Mayall, *Gypsy-Travellers*, p. 161.

117 PRO ED 18/225, noted by Paul Bowen, 'The Schooling of Gypsy Children in Surrey 1906–1933', *Journal of Educational Administration and History*, 36 (2004), pp. 57–67, at p. 60.

118 Gertrude Jekyll, *Old West Surrey* (London, 1904), pp. 313–14.

119 Overton, *Peaslake*, p. 125.

120 *London City Mission Magazine*, 34 (1869), pp. 138, 148.

121 Epsom Christ Church baptismal register, 3 July 1881, 20 August 1882.

122 Ted Dowman, et al., eds, *Epsom Common* (Epsom Common Association, 1981), pp. i, 39–40. Oakshott died in 1935: *Evening News*, 9 April 1935.

123 Memories in the Cranleigh Women's Institute scrapbook (SHC: 1605/1, p. 26).

124 'Until recently [it] was not a favourite place for gipsies: they cannot make any use of the Scotch fir trees': *Moveable Dwellings Bill: Report*, p. 56.

125 *The Spectator*, 79 (1897), p. 895.

126 Elizabeth Cotton, *Our Coffee Room* (London, 1876), pp. 33–4.

127 Alder, *Work among the Gypsies*, p. 48. He attributes the problems to the arrival of some fourteen strangers who pulled on one hard winter and went wooding in the hedges nearby, and regrets that his 'old families' should have got caught up in the general attack; but it is doubtful whether the villagers made any such distinction. There was a vigilante attack at Effingham in 1909 and another on twelve waggons at Holmwood in 1912 when, in the reporters' understated phrase, 'some blows were struck': Wright, *Their Day Has Passed*, pp. 157, 164, 166.

128 *Surrey Mirror*, 15 June 1889.

129 This is a brief summary of events dealt with in much more detail by Mayall, *Gypsy-Travellers*; Mayall, *English Gypsies and State Policies*, pp. 69–74, Becky Taylor, *A Minority and the State: Travellers in Britain in the Twentieth Century* (Manchester, 2008), pp. 55–63, and Wright in *Their Day Has Passed*, pp. 142–63, and his introduction to *Surrey Census of Nomads, 1913* (London, 2020). The principal Surrey actors were Thomas Cecil Farrer, 2nd Baron Farrer, of Abinger Hall; Dr Henry Morris Chester of Pyle Park in Seale; Reginald Bray of the Manor House, Shere; and Mowbray Lees Sant, Chief Constable.

130 Not all landowners were prepared to do this. C. S. Loch, giving evidence to a Parliamentary Committee, was bitter about an (unidentified) common in Surrey where Gypsies were tolerated – 'they use the commons as a sort of neutral territory . . . All Surrey is an attraction from this point of view; there is so much space': *Vagrancy Departmental Committee: Report* (Richmond, 1906), vol. I, p. 290.

6 Between Two Fires: The Early Twentieth Century

1 Barbara Walsh in Janet Keet-Black, *Gypsies of Britain* (Oxford, 2013), p. 43; cf. Barbara Walsh, 'The Ripleys', *Romany Routes*, 5 (2000–2002), p. 263, and 'Around the Fire', *Romany Routes*, 13 (2016–18), p. 378.

2 CWG service nos G/40970 and 51313. Both men are commemorated on the war memorial at Hailsham in Sussex.

3 EEH War Memorials, Parker.

4 J. A. Brown, 'Romany Girl', *Romany Routes*, 10 (2010–12), pp. 166–7.

5 From research undertaken on Surrey's Gypsy war dead by Alan Wright, featured on www.surreyinthegreatwar.org.uk.

6 Alan McGowan, 'Henry Ayres: Killed in Action in WWI', *Romany Routes*, 12 (2014–16), pp. 161–2.

7 CWG service number 47235.

8 Alan Wright, *Their Day Has Passed: Gypsies in Victorian and Edwardian Surrey* (Tolworth, 2017), pp. 199, 203–5; Debbie Ayres, 'Lance Corporal Sidney Harris: "A Gypsy Warrior"', *Romany Routes*, 14 (2018–20), p. 26. George's Sidney had a second cousin of the same name, son of Eli Harris and Emily Gregory, who served in the war – also born in Surrey, also dying on 25 March 1918: Paula Wrigley, 'They Say "Truth Is Stranger Than Fiction": The Case of Two Soldiers Called Sidney Harris', *Romany Routes*, 14 (2018–20), pp. 58–9.

9 Stuart Petre Brodie Mais, *It Isn't Far from London* (London, 1930), pp. 312, 314.

10 Mary Jo Nye, *Blackett: Physics, War, and Politics in the Twentieth Century* (Cambridge, MA, 2004), p. 16. Certainly some soldiers were literate – Lance Corporal Sidney Harris, for instance, filled in the Short Form of Will in his paybook.

11 Information courtesy of Janet Keet-Black, whose work on Gypsies in the WWI set me on the right path for much of this section. Another nagsman, Matthew Brazil of the Quadrant, served for two years in the Royal Army Service Corps assessing horses for the front; he features in the Great War section of Wright, *Their Day Has Passed*, pp. 207–8.

12 Terry Doe, 'Walter Doe: Royal Navy Boy Signaller of World War 1', *Romany Routes*, 12 (2014–16), pp. 114–15.

13 WWI regimental number 28394. In the 1901 and 1911 censuses he appears as 'hawker' in Walford Road, a popular Gypsy area of Croydon.

14 Rosie Smith and Lindsey Marsh, *Old Ways, New Days: A Family History of Gypsy Life in South London and Kent* (London, 2009), p. 64.

15 Manfri Frederick Wood, *In the Life of a Romany Gypsy* (London, 1973), p. 86. But everything Fred Wood says should be taken with a pinch of salt.

16 Jimmy Stockin, with Martin King and Martin Knight, *On the Cobbles: The Life of a Bare-Knuckle Gypsy Warrior* (Edinburgh, 2000), p. 14. Three years after the war he was an army pensioner, though evidently an able-bodied one as he was arrested after a fracas at the White Post in East Coker: *Western Chronicle*, 29 April 1921.

17 Headley marriage register, 19 May 1919. My thanks to Janet Keet-Black for this reference.

18 Sylvia Smith, pers. comm.

19 Hilda Brazil, pers. comm.

20 Walsh, 'The Ripleys'.

21 *South Wales Echo*, 26 August 1916; *West Surrey Gazette*, 31 August 1916.

22 Rachel Clay, 'Gypsies of the Surrey Hills', *Countryman*, 45 (1952), pp. 293–7, at p. 296. Other reluctant recruits can be found in Wright, *Their Day Has Passed*, pp. 208–9.

23 Is it possible to quantify Gypsy involvement in the war? Given that in 1911 the community numbered about 1,000 in administrative Surrey, and given that villages with a similar population have an average of ten men each on their war memorials, you would expect similar numbers of Surrey Gypsies. A total of nine are identified above, several of them found largely by happenstance. Systematic work on war memorials would certainly increase that number.

24 This was told to me at the 2012 Derby. Aaron is presumably the 'Hiram Hoadley', who, according to Eleanor Smith, was recognized as head man during the 1933 Derby, and kept order in the encampment (*Daily Mirror*, 30 May 1933); he was born at Mitcham in 1884 (Wright, *Their Day Has Passed*, p. 55).

25 I am grateful to Alan Wright for his studies of the 1911 census, which were exhibited at the 2012 Romany Day. A Gypsy, in his analysis, is anyone who appears in the record with two out of a potential five distinguishing features – characteristic first name, characteristic surname, typical occupation, reported itinerancy and a history of having been in many places. He discusses population with more detail in *Their Day Has Passed*, pp. 12–24.

26 In 1901, when 'barns and sheds' and 'tents, caravans, and open air' were
added up separately, the latter formed 80 per cent of the total of itinerants.
I have therefore divided the 1911 cumulative total of 1,518 by this proportion.
Earlier, in the 1891 census, tents and caravans had been 70 per cent. The
figures from the 1911 census are those gathered by David Mayall, *Gypsy-
Travellers in Nineteenth-Century Society* (Cambridge, 1988), p. 159, with
the error of '1,918' corrected to 1,518.

27 Statistics were given in the *Moveable Dwellings Bill Select Committee
of the House of Lords: Report* (Richmond, 1909), p. 71. The second
census has been published in full as *Surrey Census of Nomads, 1913*
(London, 2020).

28 SHC 85/29/21 and *Surrey Times*, 8 June 1907, noted in Mayall, *Gypsy-
Travellers*, pp. 160, 163. Sant gives the 1907 figures in *Moveable Dwellings
Bill: Report*, p. 71. The Surrey police district was not co-extensive with the
administrative county of Surrey; some parishes, such as Epsom, belonged
to Surrey County Council but the Metropolitan Police. The date for the
first census was fixed for May, while the second was to be made twice,
in June and August (*Surrey Census of Nomads*, pp. 20, 39). However,
Hubert Rendell has the entry under 1907 '9 March. V wet ride to Wisley
Common etc. to carry out a census of gipsies' (Les Bowerman, 'Hubert
H. Rendell, Ripley Police Sergeant 1922/3', *Journal of the Send and Ripley
History Society*, 5 (2000)) and in 1913 he went to Wood Street on 19 May and
Stringers Common on 20 May, evidently for the count (SHC 6815/1/11).
Other officers may have anticipated the date in the same way.

29 They began by quoting 10,000: *The Spectator*, 1897, p. 894.

30 *Moveable Dwellings Bill: Report*, p. 65. The previous year there had been fifty.

31 PRO HO45/10995/158231/15, noted by Mayall, *Gypsy-Travellers*, p. 162.

32 I am grateful to Alan Wright for sharing his statistical breakdown of the
1911 census: 9.4 per cent at Croydon, 7.9 per cent at Ash, 6.9 per cent at
Chobham, 6.4 per cent at Shere, 6.3 per cent at West Horsley, 6.3 per cent at
Woking, 5.2 per cent at Farnham. He discusses distribution with more detail
in *Their Day Has Passed*, pp. 25–43. It is surprising that few people (only
eighteen) are recorded as stopping at Epsom: a considerable falling-off from
the numbers in the 1891 census.

33 George Sturt (as 'George Bourne'), *The Bettesworth Book: Talks with a
Surrey Peasant* (London, 1901), p. 164. 'Frederick Bettesworth' is Frederick
Grover: Chapters 17 and 29 record his discussions of Gypsies. The original
record of the conversation is in E. D. Mackerness, ed., *The Journals of George
Sturt, 1890–1927* (Cambridge, 1967), vol. I, p. 239.

34 Marjorie Mack, *Hannaboys Farm* (London, 1942), pp. 20, 51. Juliette
De Baïracli Levy, *As Gypsies Wander* (London, 1953), p. 93, knew many
instances of children being burnt.

35 Rupert Croft-Cooke, *The Moon in My Pocket: Life with the Romanies*
(London, 1948), p. 165.

36 The three girls appear in Laura Knight's *The Gyppos*, Ferens Art Gallery,
Hull. Kathleen afterwards married a man called Towle and moved to Hull:
Patricia Connor, *Derby Day 200* (London, 1979), p. 117. She and Melanie
appear with their grandmother in a 1931 photo by Fred Shaw, GLS Shaw
p. 248; another photo of the girls with their father, taken at the same time,

has not survived in Shaw's archive but appears in Denis Harvey, *The Gypsies: Waggon-Time and After* (London, 1979), p. 30.

37 Christopher Griffin, *Nomads under the Westway: Irish Travellers, Gypsies and Other Traders in West London* (Hatfield, 2008), pp. 142–9.

38 Geoff Boyce, 'Joe Who?', *Romany Routes*, 5 (2000–2002), pp. 77–81, and *The Boyce and Beckett Trail* (Swindon, 2016), pp. 4ff.

39 Mack, *Hannaboys Farm*, p. 45, says simply that *didikai* 'is the Surrey word for Gypsies', but ten years later Lawrence Boswell was using the term in a much less complimentary fashion: 'The Blackpool Gypsies', *Journal of the Gypsy Lore Society*, 3rd series, XXXIV (1955), pp. 42–5, at p. 44.

40 Robert Phillimore, 'Songs of Luriben and Curiben', *Journal of the Gypsy Lore Society*, 2nd series, VI (1912–13), pp. 67–8.

41 Tim Coughlan, *Now Shoon the Romano Gillie: Traditional Verse in the High and Low Speech of the Gypsies of Britain* (Cardiff, 2001), p. 226.

42 From the vocabulary in Smith and Marsh, *Old Ways, New Days*, pp. 8–10. Smith also includes among her Romani rokker a number of dialect English words – *clammed*, *ding*, *whittle* and the mysterious *ark*, 'listen', which turns out to be *hark*.

43 Frederick Cowles, *Gypsy Caravan* (London, 1948), pp. 139–47. 'Patrick Stanley' is a pseudonym.

44 Ted Dowman et al., eds, *Epsom Common* (Epsom Common Association, 1981), pp. i, 39; *Lincoln Echo*, 5 June 1920.

45 Mack, *Hannaboys Farm*, pp. 54–5. Earlier, there were Irish 'Gypsies' at the Derby (*The Standard*, 17 May 1866; 23 May 1867), although they may have been slum girls made up for the occasion rather than Travellers.

46 George Hall, *The Gypsy's Parson: His Experiences and Adventures* (London, 1915), pp. 201–2.

47 Croft-Cooke, *Moon in My Pocket*, p. 78.

48 Elizabeth Robins Pennell, *Charles Godfrey Leland* (London, 1906), vol. II, p. 178.

49 For Redskin Village, see Wood, *Romany Gypsy*, p. 86, and Wright, *Their Day Has Passed*, p. 56; for Indians Wood, Jenny Overton, ed., *Peaslake: Story of a Surrey Village* (privately printed, 2003), p. 93.

50 *Daily News*, 3 May 1919 ('a touch of Fenimore Cooper on the Downs'); *Leeds Mercury*, 9 June 1920 and 5 May 1921.

51 Henry Thomas Crofton, 'Affairs of Egypt, 1907', *Journal of the Gypsy Lore Society*, 2nd series, II (1908–9), pp. 132–3; Colin Holmes, 'The German Gypsy Question in Britain, 1904–06', *Journal of the Gypsy Lore Society*, 4th series, I (1974), pp. 248–67, at pp. 262–3; David Cressy, *Gypsies: An English History* (Oxford, 2018), p. 210.

52 Eric Otto Winstedt, 'The Gypsy Coppersmiths' Invasion of 1911–13', *Journal of the Gypsy Lore Society*, 2nd series, VI (1912–13), pp. 244–303, is the principal, and extremely thorough, source; Michael O'hAodha, 'Romany Aristocrats Invade London Suburbs', *Romany Routes*, 2 (1995–6), pp. 158–62, summarizes newspaper cuttings kept by the GLS, although the press occasionally got details wrong; Tom Francis, *Old Mitcham*, ed. Eric Montague (Chichester, 1993), figs 47, 159, has some local photos.

53 The Tšórons professed to be Catholics, while carrying out a number of Orthodox rituals, which is what you would expect in people coming from Galicia and Ruthenia: Winstedt, 'Gypsy Coppersmiths', p. 293.

54 Augustus John, *Finishing Touches* (London, 1964), pp. 52–3. This took
   place, he says, in the days of gold sovereigns: these were withdrawn from
   circulation in 1914.

55 Dora Yates, 'The "Greek" Nomad Gypsies in Britain, 1929–40: 1', *Journal
   of the Gypsy Lore Society*, 3rd series, XXI (1942), pp. 87–110, pp. 107–8; for her
   later retrospect on the family, see *My Gypsy Days: Recollections of a Romani
   Rawnie* (London, 1953), pp. 131ff. Bibi Dora was no fool, and once she found
   their con tricks were as competent as their Romani, she kept her distance.

56 Eric Otto Winstedt, 'The Funeral of Mārya Yevanovič', *Journal of the
   Gypsy Lore Society*, 3rd series, XXII (1943), p. 59.

57 Andrew McFarlane, 'Rudari and "Greek" Gypsy Death Customs', *Journal
   of the Gypsy Lore Society*, 3rd series, XXII (1943), p. 60.

58 Crofton, 'Affairs of Egypt, 1907'; Ted Rudge, *Brumroamin: Birmingham
   and Midland Romany Gypsy and Traveller Culture* (Birmingham, 1988),
   pp. 38–9.

59 Jim Moody, 'Help Sought', *Romany Routes*, 4 (1998–2000), pp. 232–3, and
   'Collecting Gypsy Postcards', *Romany Routes*, 11 (2012–14), pp. 310–14. She
   was Urania Buckland in her younger days and Selina Smith later.

60 Laura Knight, *The Magic of a Line* (London, 1965), p. 253. For the
   identification of Lilo Smith, see Ferdinand Gerard Huth, 'Dame Laura
   Knight's "Gypsy Family"', *Journal of the Gypsy Lore Society*, 2nd series, XXII
   (1943), p. 61.

61 Muriel Gibson, ed., *Surrey within Living Memory* (Newbury, 1992), p. 54.
   'Morella' is either a variant or a misremembering of Mirelli; she had a son
   called Mark, but no other details are given.

62 Robert Bunyan, *A Lad in the Village of Ash* (Ash, Surrey, 2003), p. 19.
   I assume this is the same funeral as reported (from Farnham) in Chris
   Shepheard, *The Lost Countryside: Images of Rural Life* (Derby, 2001), p. 163.

63 *The Times*, 20 January 1955.

64 Angela Clifford and Hazel Walker, eds, *Langley Vale: Memories of a Surrey
   Village* (privately printed, 2001), p. 46.

65 *Mokadi* or *moxadi* is the dictionary form, but *mogadi* is the usual Surrey
   pronunciation.

66 Linda Webb, 'Memories of My Grandmother, Alice Emma Matthews
   (Totty)', *Romany Routes*, 10 (2010–12), pp. 203–4.

67 W. W. Gill, 'Told in a Vardo', *Journal of the Gypsy Lore Society*, 3rd series,
   XIX (1940), pp. 60–62.

68 Sarah Ann Eastwood, from Garratt Lane in Wandsworth, said her sister-
   in-law Lydia Dixey was a witch and threatened to beat her up: *Lloyd's
   Weekly Newspaper*, 12 January 1879.

69 Mack, *Hannaboys Farm*, p. 58.

70 Knight, *Magic of a Line*, p. 252.

71 Sturt, *Bettesworth Book*, p.164; Poll is identified in the *Journals of George Sturt*.

72 We catch a glimpse of this arrangement when Mrs Dixey, to amuse a little
   girl, 'lifted up her apron and underneath was a small sack full of trinkets
   and jewellery': Webb, 'Memories of My Grandmother', p. 203.

73 *Surrey Advertiser*, 10 October 1917.

74 Knight, *Magic of a Line*, pp. 251, 255. Mary Ann Smith was the wife of
   Christopher (Willy) Smith and mother of young Gilderoy, travelling with

Lilo Smith and family; Mary and Gilderoy appear in Knight's *The Little Beggar*. I'm grateful to Rosie Broadley of the National Portrait Gallery, who forwarded this family information from John Haggar.

75 Epsom version from Phillimore, 'Luriben and Curiben', p. 67, collated with others sung by Jasper Smith and Mary Ann Haynes: Michael Yates, 'English Gypsy Songs', *Folk Music Journal*, 3 (1975–9), pp. 63–80, at p. 71.

76 Surrey data taken from Janet Keet-Black, *Some Travellers in the 1891 Census* (Swindon, 2000–2002), vol. II, pp. 16–28. Since there is no way of telling when a couple began living together, I took the 38 families where the mother was under 35, and therefore would still have had all her children around her, and calculated her age at the birth of the first child, which would most likely be a year after the marriage; the median age was 20, the extremes being 16 and 30.

77 De Baïracli Levy, *As Gypsies Wander*, pp. 131–2, with Romani standardized, and what seems to be an omitted 'he' added after 'Ain't'.

78 Phoebe Barney, *Memories* (privately printed, n.d. (*c.* 1995)).

79 E. Brewer, 'Gipsy Encampments in the Heart of London', *The Sunday at Home*, 1896, p. 114.

80 Kerry Hawkins, 'My Ancestors at Hampton Wick in the 1861 and 1871 Census Returns: II', *Romany Routes*, 5 (2000–2002), pp. 13–17.

81 Eric Parker, *Highways and Byways in Surrey* (London, 1908), p. 279; he does not give a date, but it must have been the snows of April 1908, recorded in Mark Davison and Ian Currie, *The Surrey Weather Book: A Century of Storms, Floods and Freezes* (Coulsdon, 1993), p. 15.

82 De Baïracli Levy, *As Gypsies Wander*, p. 78.

83 Mack, *Hannaboys Farm*, pp. 48–50.

84 Paul Bowen, 'The Schooling of Gypsy Children in Surrey, 1906–1933', *Journal of Educational Administration and History*, 36 (2004), pp. 59–60.

85 *The Schoolmaster*, 77 (1910), p. 398; *School Government Chronicle*, 84 (1910–11), p. 346. *Surrey Advertiser*, 7 May 1910, has reports from Stoke D'Abernon, New Malden, Esher and elsewhere. Some schools knew their local chavvies and had no problems with them; others were prejudiced. Their choice language is quoted in Wright, *Their Day Has Passed*, pp. 174–8.

86 SHC CEM/186/1, 12 October 1909, noted in Bowen, 'Schooling of Gypsy Children', p. 59.

87 Logbook of Ewell Girls School (SHC CES/15/1–2), 12 October 1910; 15 May 1911.

88 *School Government Chronicle*, 84 (1910–11), p. 346; *Surrey Advertiser*, 22 October 1910; Sheila Brown and David Porter, *Two Surrey Village Schools: The Story of Send and Ripley Village Schools* (Ripley, 2002), p. 84; Wright, *Their Day Has Passed*, p. 179.

89 Cranleigh Women's Institute Scrapbook, 1949 (SHC 1605/1); Clay, 'Gypsies of the Surrey Hills'.

90 *West Sussex Gazette*, 31 August 1921.

91 Cranleigh Women's Institute Scrapbook, 1949 (SHC 1605/1); Overton, *Peaslake*, p. 67.

92 Hurtwood School is discussed by Bowen, 'Schooling of Gypsy Children', and Becky Taylor, *A Minority and the State: Travellers in Britain in the Twentieth Century* (Manchester, 2008), pp. 89–91, with local memories in

Clay, 'Gypsies of the Surrey Hills'. Details can be found in Circular E495 of Surrey Education Committee (SHC 6246/4/1); Report to Elementary Education Committee, minutes of 7 July 1926, appendix E1 (SHC CC767/40/1/9); *The Times*, 12 January 1926.

93 Census for 1911. She married Harold Fagence in October 1928, Guildford registration district.

94 *Surrey Weekly Press*, 11 January 1926; *Surrey Advertiser*, 16 January 1926. The first day of Hurtwood School was also recorded in film by Pathé News.

95 *Daily Express*, 21 May 1926; A. J. Lynch, 'A Gipsy School', *The Schoolmaster and Woman Teacher's Chronicle*, 113 (1928), p. 335.

96 GLS 5/4/5, p. 82, an unprovenanced newspaper cutting.

97 George Salt, 'England's School for Gipsy Children', *Millgate Monthly*, 30 (1934–5), pp. 387–8.

98 *Surrey Times*, 8 December 1933.

99 *Times Educational Supplement*, 13 January 1934; *Surrey Advertiser*, 13 January 1934; *Surrey Herald*, 26 January 1934. The burning of the tents was filmed by Pathé, and the fact that they were there on time, despite assurances by landowners that no such event was going to take place, suggests that it was orchestrated by the Gypsies.

100 *Yorkshire Herald*, 30 May 1921.

101 Harvey, *The Gypsies*, p. 57.

102 Lisa Hutchins, *Esher and Claygate Past* (London, 2001), fig. 68; Mais, *It Isn't Far from London*, p. 310.

103 *News Chronicle*, 25 May 1936.

104 Worcester County Museum at Hartlebury has a square bow, apparently the only one to survive in a museum, although others have been seen at auction.

105 Joe Mitchell, pers. comm.

106 Postcards of the Derby issued between 1900 and 1914 – for example, 'Derby Day, Epsom', Valentine no. 39510 – show occasional waggons with mollicrofts as the new fashion became available.

107 Paul Braithwaite, *A Palace on Wheels* (White Waltham, 1999), pp. 61–3. If the word mollicroft was, as he suggests, originally Malakoff, then the design must date from the Crimean War.

108 Cyril Ward-Jackson and Denis Harvey, *The English Gypsy Caravan: Its Origins, Builders, Technology and Conservation* (Newton Abbot, 1972), pp. 133–4, 173–5, describing waggons by Duntons of Reading; but the same is true, with modifications, of the other types.

109 Edward Harvey, 'English Gypsy Caravan Decoration', *Journal of the Gypsy Lore Society*, 3rd series, XVII/part 3 (v) (1938), pp. 38–46, at p. 44. My thanks to Lindsey Marsh, who identified the other two women as her great-great-aunts; they appear in other photos of the period, together with Emily, their sister Eliza's daughter by Derby Smith.

110 The military authorities moved Gypsies off the Downs in 1915: SHC CC98/14/7.

111 Alfred Munnings, *The Second Burst* (London, 1951), pp. 80–81, 278–82, supplemented by his recollections in *Morning Post*, 30 May 1922. According to Reginald Pound, *The Englishman: A Biography of Sir Alfred Munnings* (London, 1962), p. 75, he paid 2s 6d a session. Family details have been supplied from the memories of Ken Boyd on datchethistory.org.uk. It turns

out that Munnings is not a very reliable guide to the names of his 'select family' (p. 80); he remembered Loveridge as Loveday (p. 282), Moocher Wingfield, the brother-in-law of Alfred Gregory, as a Gregory (p. 80), and Comfort Gregory, the wife of Thomas Stevens, as 'Mark Stevens's wife' (p. 282). To be fair, he was writing from memory, 25 years after their last contact; and some of these people may have been using more than one name.

112 The white mare may be the same one painted in 1925, almost at the tea table, in Munnings's *Gypsies on Epsom Downs, Derby Week*.

113 Lionel Lindsay, *A. J. Munnings, R. A.: Pictures of Horses and English Life* (London, 1939), visited the Gypsies with Munnings and thought 'they have a high regard' for him (p. 19); this comes out in the letters he received (as 'Mr. Money'), noted by Jean Goodman, *What a Go! The Life of Alfred Munnings* (London, 1988), pp. 115–16. A. Egerton Cooper, who also accompanied Munnings to the Downs, said he was concerned that 'his real name should not be known to the gipsies' (Pound, *Englishman*, p. 75), but this is contradicted by Munnings's own recollections and is incompatible with the fact that people identified his pictures in shops and wrote letters to him.

114 Moocher has been identified as the man standing by the horse in Munnings's *Epsom Downs, City and Suburban Day* and leading in his *Arrival at Epsom Downs for Derby Week*; he is presumably among the male figures in Munnings's *Gypsies on the Downs* (a Binsted picture) and *Gypsy Life*.

115 Lindsay, *Munnings*, p. 20.

116 Comfort Gregory, or Stevens, appears in *Epsom Downs, City and Suburban Day*, in *Gypsies on the Downs*, in *Gypsy Life* (a preliminary sketch, of 'Mrs. Mark Stevens', is in the Munnings Museum at Dedham), in *Arrival at Epsom Downs for Derby Week* (where she is driving the trolley), and in the pair of pictures *Before the Races, Derby Day* and *Gypsies on Epsom Downs, Derby Week*. These last two were evidently contemporary, since people are wearing the same clothes in both; *Gypsies on Epsom Downs, Derby Week* was exhibited at the Royal Academy in 1926 and would therefore have been begun at the previous year's Derby. Ocean is with her sister in *Epsom Downs, City and Suburban Day*, in *Before the Races, Derby Day* and in *Gypsies on Epsom Downs, Derby Week*.

117 Goodman, *What a Go!*, p. 116. Note how Nell, even though she is writing in English, automatically signs off with a translation of *kushti bok*.

7 The End of the Road: Post-War Britain

1 I'm identifying the traditional Bluenose with the historical Charles Mayes whose diaries are at SHC 8537/1/1/9 to 11, which I summarized in 'Gypsies at Salfords, Surrey: Captured by a PC's Diary', *Romany Routes*, 13 (2016–18), pp. 166–70.

2 Rosie Smith and Lindsey Marsh, *Old Ways, New Days: A Family History of Gypsy Life in South London and Kent* (London, 2009), p. 75.

3 Juliette De Baïracli Levy, *As Gypsies Wander* (London, 1953), p. 135.

4 Marjorie Mack, *Hannaboys Farm* (London, 1942), pp. 52–3; *Daily Express*, 20 November 1939; *News Chronicle*, 22 November 1939. A note in a cuttings book at Liverpool (5/3/17, p. 134) says: 'This George Devall is said to be

really John White', but the name Devall is an old one, found in the 1891 census.

5 *Journal of the Commons, Open Spaces and Footpaths Preservation Society*, 2 (1931–2), pp. 2–3. This report covers all transients and their equipment, including three ice-cream barrows and a steam engine, but it is clear from the order and wording of the list that the vans and benders belonged to Gypsies.

6 Good relations are a recurrent motif in Gill Willis, ed., *I Remember Chobham* (privately printed, 1999), pp. 19, 20, 28.

7 *Surrey Herald*, 1 February 1935; *Evening Standard*, 29 March 1935; *Daily Express*, 30 March 1935.

8 Minutes of the Chobham Commons Preservation Committee, 1936–57, courtesy of the committee.

9 *The Times*, 16 April 1932; for further newspaper sources, see David Cressy, *Gypsies: An English History* (Oxford, 2018), p. 216.

10 *Daily Herald*, 24 and 26 April 1929; Stuart Petre Brodie Mais, *It Isn't Far from London* (London, 1930), p. 311.

11 *West Sussex Gazette*, 4 February 1937, *West Sussex Gazette*, 11 March 1937.

12 *Daily Sketch*, 13 April 1937; *News Chronicle*, 14 April 1937; *Morning Post*, 22 April 1937.

13 *The Times*, 27 May 1937. There is an overview of the 1937 incident in Becky Taylor, *A Minority and the State: Travellers in Britain in the Twentieth Century* (Manchester, 2008), pp. 67–9.

14 *New Chronicle*, 28 May 1937.

15 *West Sussex Gazette*, 10 June 1937; Eric Otto Winstedt, 'Gypsies on Epsom Downs', *Journal of the Gypsy Lore Society*, 3rd series, XVI (1937), pp. 204–5; Trevor White and Jeremy Harte, *Epsom: A Pictorial History* (Chichester, 1992), pl. 162.

16 *The Times*, 19 May 1938; the name Harber has been mistranscribed as 'Harker'.

17 *News Chronicle*, 1 June 1938.

18 De Baïracli Levy, *As Gypsies Wander*, pp. 77–8, with dialect spelling standardized.

19 J. E. Daniels, *Heathcote Memorial School, Ash, 1860–1950* (privately printed, n.d. (*c.* 1976)), p. 117.

20 *Daily Express*, 20 November 1939.

21 Terry Doe, 'Walter Doe: Royal Navy Boy Signaller of World War I', *Romany Routes*, 12 (2014–16), pp. 114–15.

22 Mack, *Hannaboys Farm*, p. 49. In the first photo that he sent home, rimmed with flags and crowns, Jasper still looks vulnerably young: Smith and Marsh, *Old Ways, New Days*, p. 80.

23 Ronald Searle and Kaye Webb, *Looking at London and People Worth Meeting* (London, 1953), p. 11.

24 *Daily Telegraph*, 6 March 1944.

25 Vivien Cooper, 'Tales My Family Told Me: Barriers to Understanding', *Romany Routes*, 12 (2014–16), pp. 75–6.

26 *Picture Post*, 25 May 1939.

27 Ross Gordon, 'It's the Gypsy in Them', *Photo World: Picturing Today*, VI/5 (1946), pp. 31–5, at pp. 34–5.

28 *Slough, Eton and Windsor Observer*, 22 October 1943.

29 Jane Bartlett, ed., *Ripley and Send Looking Back: Surrey Village Life and Its People, 1890s–1940s* (Ripley, 1987), pp. 30–31.

30 Smith and Marsh, *Old Ways, New Days*, p. 80. Emily was born in 1927 and was sent away to live with her aunts on the Cooper side when her mother died (p. 59), which is why she did not appear with the other children at Gincox Farm.

31 Frederick Cowles, *Gypsy Caravan* (London, 1948), p. 14.

32 Smith and Marsh, *Old Ways, New Days*, p. 81.

33 P. J. Teesdale, 'Move On!', *Journal of the Gypsy Lore Society*, 3rd series, XXVII (1948), pp. 158–9. In those days Jasper travelled as a Cooper, under his mother's name.

34 Brian Vesey-FitzGerald, 'Houses Not Meant for Tent-Dwellers', *Journal of the Gypsy Lore Society*, 3rd series, XXIX (1950), pp. 70–72; Angus Fraser, 'The Gypsy Problem: A Survey of Post-War Developments', *Journal of the Gypsy Lore Society*, 3rd series, XXXII (1953), pp. 82–100, at pp. 86–7; Thomas Acton, *Gypsy Politics and Social Change* (London, 1974), pp. 140–41. Eventually the Does were rehoused, but in a bungalow and not a site.

35 I am grateful to Terry Masterson for this passage from his song.

36 De Baïracli Levy, *As Gypsies Wander*, p. 142, with other details from pp. 124, 135.

37 Even Jim Penfold, who was a master waggon builder when he had the time and materials, spoke of using these tea chests: Jeremy Sandford, *Gypsies* (London, 1973), p. 79.

38 This was evidently recorded at the time of the accident in 1962, perhaps by John Brune, who was at Stone near Dartford and spent time with the Smiths: Peter Kennedy, *Folksongs of Britain and Ireland* (London, 1975), p. 748. It was published in Denise Stanley and Rosy Burke, *The Romano Drom Song Book* (Brentwood, 1986); an earlier copy seems to have been sent to Henry Sherriff as it appears in his collection of Gypsy songs, *Henry Dry-Bread: The Richard Wade Papers*, ed. Robert Dawson (privately printed, 1988), pp. 90–91.

39 Tony Marshall, *The Prince of Gypsies* (London, 2014), p. 35.

40 *Illustrated London News*, 4 June 1927.

41 *North Eastern Daily Gazette*, 22 April 1935; previous Derbies from *Everybody's Weekly*, 10 June 1933; *Daily Mail*, 1 June 1934.

42 Judy Cannon, 'Gentleman Gypsy', *Guildford Today*, II/10 (1963), pp. 22–3; they married in October 1953, Ashford registration district.

43 P. Saunders et al., eds, *Gypsies and Travellers in Their Own Words: Words and Pictures of Travelling Life* (Leeds, 2000), p. 139.

44 Bridget Plowden et al., *Children and Their Primary Schools: A Report of the Central Advisory Council for Education (England)* (Richmond, 1967), p. 596; Ian Hancock, 'Romanes Numerals and Innovations', *Journal of the Gypsy Lore Society*, 3rd series, XLVIII (1969), pp. 19–29, at p. 19.

45 Lawrence Boswell, 'The Blackpool Gypsies', *Journal of the Gypsy Lore Society*, 3rd series, XXXIV (1955), p. 44, and see also Brian Heppell, 'Daisy Boswell: The Generous Fortune-Teller on the Tober at Newcastle', *Romany Routes*, 13 (2016–18), pp. 58–9.

46 Kerry Hawkins, pers. comm.

47 Sandford, *Gypsies*, p. 85.

48 Dominic Reeve, *Beneath the Blue Sky: Four Decades of a Travelling Life in Britain* (Nottingham, 2007), p. 4.

49 Brian Raywid, 'Notes on Life on the Road', *Journal of the Gypsy Lore Society*, 3rd series, LI (1972), pp. 102–15, at p. 112.

50 Dominic Reeve, *Green Lanes and Kettle Cranes* (Marshwood, 2010), pp. 147–54. Reeve's friend is simply 'Wisdom': I'm guessing he was a Penfold, since they and the Smiths are the only families I know where the name Wisdom is common. Reeve's 'little black town' must be Woking, and presumably the 'not too distant Scrap Metals Merchant', run by a Gypsy woman, was Matthews of Guildford, for which see *Surrey Advertiser*, 24 October 2003, reproduced and discussed in David Rose, 'Plenty of Scrap Metal and Friendly Chat Too', *Romany Routes*, 6 (2002–4), pp. 244–7.

51 Michael Johnson, *A History of Outwood* (Outwood, 1997), p. 47.

52 *Gypsies and Other Travellers: A Report of a Study Carried out in 1965 and 1966 by a Sociological Research Section of the Ministry of Housing and Local Government* (Richmond, 1967), p. 83. There were similar arrangements at Well Lane, outside Woking, where each plot was held in the name of a different Gypsy, not necessarily the one who lived there. Such a complex arrangement sounds intended to make things difficult for the local authority, and probably was: SHC 6198/3/191.

53 Eric Montague, *Mitcham Histories 8: Phipps Bridge* (London, 2006), p. 119.

54 Alan Banks, 'How Dobbin the Gypsy Horse Was Saved from an Untimely End', *Newdigate Society Magazine*, 22 (1991).

55 Pauline Guildford, 'Letters', *Romany Routes*, 5 (2000–2002), pp. 3–4.

56 Denis Harvey, 'Hook-Up at Clandon', *Journal of the Gypsy Lore Society*, 3rd series, XXXI (1952), pp. 81–3. Harvey's 'Dūi' is I think Job, in which case he thought that Jasper was Ceni's brother rather than her cousin.

57 De Baïracli Levy, *As Gypsies Wander*, p. 133, adapted slightly from my own knowledge of how it's done, though unusually Bill Smith used a potato peeler rather than a knife.

58 Jenny Overton, ed., *Peaslake: Story of a Surrey Village* (privately printed, 2003), p. 93; Tony Boxall, *Gypsy Camera* (Croydon, 1992), p. 30.

59 Vivien Cooper, 'Tales My Family Told Me: Porridge for Christmas', *Romany Routes*, 12 (2014–16), p. 215.

60 De Baïracli Levy, *As Gypsies Wander*, pp. 101–3, 113.

61 Saunders et al., *Gypsies and Travellers in Their Own Words*, p. 140.

62 Hilda Brazil, pers. comm.

63 De Baïracli Levy, *As Gypsies Wander*, pp. 89, 101; the encounter took place in the year before she left for Mexico, which seems to have been 1948.

64 Keziah Cooper, *Favourite Romany Recipes* (Sevenoaks, 2004), p. 29.

65 Searle and Webb, *Looking at London*, p. 12.

66 De Baïracli Levy, *As Gypsies Wander*, p. 129.

67 Cooper, *Romany Recipes*, pp. 4, 32.

68 Brian Raywid's introduction to Boxall, *Gypsy Camera*, pp. 32–3; see De Baïracli Levy, *As Gypsies Wander*, p. 110, for sawing the legs off chairs.

69 Jimmy Stockin, with Martin King and Martin Knight, *On the Cobbles: The Life of a Bare-Knuckle Gypsy Warrior* (Edinburgh, 2000), p. 49.

70 Sandford, *Gypsies*, pp. 80–81, with Romani standardized.

71 De Baïracli Levy, *As Gypsies Wander*, p. 93.

72 I don't know why it's called Joe Gray, and haven't come across any early references: the name first appears (as 'jogray') in Sandford, *Gypsies*, p. 80.

73 Smith and Marsh, *Old Ways, New Days*, pp. 54–5; cf. a similar story about Jasper Smith coming to the rescue with a couple of rabbits, p. 81.

74 Manfri Frederick Wood, *In the Life of a Romany Gypsy* (London, 1973), p. 59.

75 Stanley and Burke, *Romano Drom*, p. 10, with Romani standardized. In the *Song Book* both metre and language seem to have been revised once already, at least compared to other versions in which Jasper uses the cant word *morg* rather than *kanengro*: Tim Coughlan, *Now Shoon the Romano Gillie: Traditional Verse in the High and Low Speech of the Gypsies of Britain* (Cardiff, 2001), pp. 442–6.

76 Boxall, *Gypsy Camera*, pp. 71, 116; Sandford, *Gypsies*, p. 84.

77 Vivien Cooper, 'Tales My Family Told Me: Waxie, a Faithful Friend', *Romany Routes*, 12 (2014–16), p. 269.

78 De Baïracli Levy, *As Gypsies Wander*, pp. 80, 90, 123.

79 Brian Raywid's introduction to Boxall, *Gypsy Camera*, p. 36.

80 Jasper Smith, pers. comm.

81 Vivien Cooper, 'Tales My Family Told Me: The Roar of the Lion', *Romany Routes*, 10 (2010–12), pp. 333–4.

82 Smith and Marsh, *Old Ways, New Days*, pp. 53, 66.

83 De Baïracli Levy, *As Gypsies Wander*, pp. 126, 129.

84 Ibid., pp. 140–46.

85 Christine Aziz, 'Romany Women: Forced to Move with the Times', *Marie Claire* (February 1995), pp. 42–8. There is a general analysis of health in the 1980s and '90s in Colin Clark and Margaret Greenfields, *Here to Stay: The Gypsies and Travellers of Britain* (Hatfield, 2006), pp. 182–212, but I have not been able to find earlier figures or anything specific to Surrey.

86 Peter Cox, *Set into Song: Ewan MacColl, Charles Parker, Peggy Seeger and the Radio Ballads* (Cambridge, 2008), p. 157. This was the story behind Ewan MacColl's 'Moving On Song', written in 1960 for the *Travelling People* episode of the 'Radio Ballads'.

87 Shirley Lee, Kingston, 1950s, in Saunders, *Gypsies and Travellers in Their Own Words*, p. 140.

88 Sandford, *Gypsies*, p. 78.

89 Augustus John, *Finishing Touches* (London, 1964), p. 68, with spelling standardized.

90 Boxall, *Gypsy Camera*, pp. 12–19.

91 De Baïracli Levy, *As Gypsies Wander*, pp. 115, 139.

92 Boxall, *Gypsy Camera*, pp. 25–6.

93 Stockin, *On the Cobbles*, p. 77.

94 Reeve, *Beneath the Blue Sky*, p. 21; Beshlie, *Romany Road: Life on Wheels* (Marshwood, 2011), pp. 119–20.

95 Stockin, *On the Cobbles*, pp. 96–101; also briefly mentioned by Joe Smith, *Gypsy Joe: Bare-Knuckle Fighter, Professional Golfer* (London, 2009), p. 32.

8 New Ways: The Modern World

1 Thomas Acton, *Gypsy Politics and Social Change* (London, 1974), pp. 162–3, 280–81.

2 Norman Dodds, *Gypsies, Didikois and Other Travellers* (London, 1966), pp. 140–63.

3 Donald Kenrick and Colin Clark, *Moving On: The Gypsies and Travellers of Britain* (Hatfield, 2000), p. 176.

4 Sven Berlin, *Dromengro: Man of the Road* (London, 1971), pp. 181–2. He says he was moved on by police, but I think they were uniformed security guards.

5 Acton, *Gypsy Politics*, p. 170. Legal business was handled by the solicitor Peter Kingshill.

6 David Hunn, *Epsom Racecourse: Its Story and Its People* (London, 1973), pp. 15, 167–8, 176.

7 *Epsom and Walton Downs: A Report on Their Regulation* (Epsom, 1980), pp. 21–2.

8 Brian Vesey-Fitzgerald, *Gypsies of Britain* (Newton Abbot, 1973), p. 250; Kenrick and Clark, *Moving On*, p. 91. The legal loophole by which district councils could block county council sites by refusing to license them was closed shortly afterwards.

9 Christine Aziz, 'Romany Women: Forced to Move with the Times', *Marie Claire* (February 1995).

10 SHC 6128/3/80.

11 John E. Salmon, *The Surrey Countryside: The Interplay of Land and People* (Guildford, 1975), p. 204.

12 Thomas Acton, *Scholarship and the Gypsy Struggle: Commitment in Romani Studies* (Hatfield, 2000), p. 109; *The Times*, 15 April, 21 April and 1 September 1971.

13 Kenrick and Clark, *Moving On*, pp. 137–8; enforcement notice now in the archives of Mole Valley District Council, 1970/002/ENF.

14 Denis Harvey, *The Gypsies: Waggon-Time and After* (London, 1979), p. 138; Beshlie, *Romany Road: Life on Wheels* (Marshwood, 2011), p. 104.

15 Albert Jack, *That's Bollocks! Urban Legends, Conspiracy Theories and Old Wives' Tales* (London, 2006), pp. 10–12.

16 Martin Francis, 'The Villager and the Gypsy', *Surrey Villager*, 6 (1980), pp. 3–5.

17 Kenrick and Clark, *Moving On*, p. 138; Rosie Smith and Lindsey Marsh, *Old Ways, New Days: A Family History of Gypsy Life in South London and Kent* (London, 2009), pp. 69–70; SHC 6288/2/1.

18 Denis Harvey, 'A Wafodi English Grai', *Journal of the Gypsy Lore Society*, 3rd series, LI (1972), pp. 58–9, and 'Little Egypt and the Stillborn Child', *Countryman*, XCV/3 (1990), pp. 98–101.

19 Ann Wilson, pers. comm.

20 Dominic Reeve, *Beneath the Blue Sky: Four Decades of a Travelling Life in Britain* (Nottingham, 2007), pp. 86–97; Beshlie, *Romany Road*, pp. 110–11.

21 Sue Locke, *Travelling Light: The Remarkable Story of Gypsy Revival* (London, 1997), p. 102.

22 Ibid., pp. 97–107; cf. Tom Wilson, *The Secret Revival* (privately printed, 1998). For a different view of Tommy and his mission, see Reeve, *Beneath the Blue Sky*, p. 88.

23 *Gypsies and Other Travellers: A Report of a Study Carried Out in 1965 and 1966 by a Sociological Research Section of the Ministry of Housing and Local Government* (Richmond, 1967), pp. 30, 48, 51, 83. The Caravan Sites Act of 1960 (confusingly named the same as its successor of 1968) controlled low-level development; it was not targeted at Gypsies as such.

24 *House of Commons Debates*, 19 July 1988, vol. CXXXVII, CC1074–80; Kenrick and Clark, *Moving On*, p. 160. The officer in charge of the raid later wrote it up in detail: Nick Brent, 'Operation Checkmate', *Surrey Constabulary History Journal*, 12 (2015), pp. 5–13.

25 Joe Smith, *Gypsy Joe: Bare-Knuckle Fighter, Professional Golfer* (London, 2009), pp. 38–61.

26 Ibid., pp. 81–2.

27 Jimmy Stockin, with Martin King and Martin Knight, *On the Cobbles: The Life of a Bare-Knuckle Gypsy Warrior* (Edinburgh, 2000), pp. 106–7.

28 Coursing was finally made illegal under the Hunting Act 2004.

29 Bluey Bagley, pers. comm.

30 Ambrose Cooper, pers. comm.

31 *Dorking Advertiser*, 7 May 1965, noted in Alan Banks, 'How Dobbin the Gypsy Horse Was Saved from an Untimely End', *Newdigate Society Magazine*, 22 (1991).

32 Stockin, *On the Cobbles*, p. 81.

33 Roger Crowhurst, 'The Gypsy King', *London Police Pensioner*, 114 (2004), pp. 38–9; Jasper is thinly disguised as 'Rueben Smiff'. Aaron is not named, but an Aaron Smith dealing with motors appears in Brent, 'Operation Checkmate'.

34 Chris Shepheard, *The Lost Countryside: Images of Rural Life* (Derby, 2001), p. 163.

35 Smith and Marsh, *Old Ways, New Days*, pp. 20–21; Smith, *On the Cobbles*, pp. 105–6.

36 Reeve, *Beneath the Blue Sky*, p. 210; the race was 'near Staines'.

37 Harvey, *Waggon-Time*, p. 125.

38 *Epsom and Ewell Herald*, 5, 12 April 2000.

39 *Epsom Post*, 7 May 2003, and personal recollection.

40 From the graves of Jasper Edward Smith, died 1996, at Epsom; Albert Chapman, died 2014, at Lingfield; Tommy Boswell, died 1988, at Epsom.

41 David Cressy, *Gypsies: An English History* (Oxford, 2018), pp. 224–5.

42 Reeve, *Beneath the Blue Sky*, pp. 88–90.

43 Acton, *Gypsy Politics*, pp. 166–8.

44 Donald Kenrick and Grattan Puxon, *The Destiny of Europe's Gypsies* (Brighton, 1972), pp. 187–8.

45 Ian Hancock, *Danger! Educated Gypsy: Selected Essays*, ed. Dileep Karanth (Hatfield, 2010), pp. 226–63.

46 Porrajmos in Continental Romani; I have spelt it in an English way, as usual in Anglo-Romani.

47 *A People Uncounted* was made in 2011; I was at the 2016 showing.

48 Noted at the meeting of the Surrey Gypsy Forum at Ash Manor, 26 February 2018.

49 Rib Davis, ed., *Woking: Living Words* (Woking, 2007), p. 14; 'don't seem to settle' in the original but I've changed it to make the meaning clearer.

50 Stockin, *On the Cobbles*, p. 50.

51 Tony Marshall, *The Prince of Gypsies* (London, 2014), pp. 110–12.

52 Mary Waterson, '"I Want More than Green Leaves for My Children": Some Developments in Gypsy/Traveller Education, 1970–96', in *Romani Culture and Gypsy Identity*, ed. Thomas Acton and Gary Mundy (Hatfield, 1997), pp. 127–49, at p. 139.

53 Smith and Marsh, *Old Ways, New Days*, p. 75.

54 Thomas Acton, pers. comm.; matched by the slightly less colourful account in Andrew Ryder, Sarah Cemlyn and Thomas Acton, eds, *Hearing the Voices of Gypsy, Roma and Traveller Communities* (Bristol, 2014), pp. 35–6.

55 Ann Wilson, pers. comm.

BIBLIOGRAPHY

'A Clown', 'The Poor Man's Friend', *Christian Guardian*, 4 (1812), pp. 98–101

'A Gentleman of the Inner-Temple', *De Toryismo Liber; or, A Treatise on Toryism* (London, 1748)

'A Southern Faunist', 'On the Origin and Present State of the Gipsies', *Gentleman's Magazine*, 72 (1802), pp. 407–9

Ackerley, F. G., 'Queen Victoria and the Gypsies', *Journal of the Gypsy Lore Society*, 2nd series, VII (1913–14), pp. 149–50

Acton, Thomas, *Gypsy Politics and Social Change* (London, 1974)

—, *Scholarship and the Gypsy Struggle: Commitment in Romani Studies* (Hatfield, 2000)

Alder, Stanley, *Work among the Gypsies* (Chobham, 1893)

Allen, Thomas, *The History and Antiquities of the Parish of Lambeth* (London, 1826)

Anstey, F., 'A Gypsy Fair in Surrey', *Harper's Monthly Magazine*, 76 (1888), pp. 625–33

Attwell, Mary, *Childhood Memories of Barnes Village*, ed. Nicholas Dakin (London, 1996)

Aubrey, John, *The Natural History and Antiquities of the County of Surrey*, ed. Richard Rawlinson (London, 1718–19)

Ayres, Debbie, 'Lance Corporal Sidney Harris: "A Gypsy Warrior"', *Romany Routes*, 14 (2018–20), p. 26

Aziz, Christine, 'Romany Women: Forced to Move with the Times', *Marie Claire* (February 1995), pp. 42–8

Baker, Roger, *The Family Tree of Samson and Celia Scamp* (Swindon, 2007)

Baker, Rowland, and Gwendoline Baker, *Thameside Molesey: A Towpath Ramble from Hampton Court to Hampton Reach* (Buckingham, 1989)

Bakker, Peter, 'An Early Vocabulary of British Romani (1616): A Linguistic Analysis', *Romani Studies*, 12 (2002), pp. 75–97

Banks, Alan, 'How Dobbin the Gypsy Horse Was Saved from an Untimely End', *Newdigate Society Magazine*, 22 (1991), pp. 13–15

Barker, John, and Peter Ingram, *Romany Relics: The Wagon Album* (privately printed, 2010)

Barney, Phoebe, *Memories* (privately printed, n.d. (*c.* 1995))

Barrell, John, *The Dark Side of the Landscape: The Rural Poor in English Painting, 1730–1840* (Cambridge, 1980)

Bartlett, Jane, ed., *Ripley and Send Looking Back: Surrey Village Life and Its People, 1890s–1940s* (Ripley, 1987)

Bartlett, William, *The History and Antiquities of Wimbledon* (London, 1865)

Bayly, Mary, 'The Gipsy Family', *The British Workman*, 9 (1863), p. 418

Beaney, Jim, 'Aspects of Jack Cooper', *Romany Routes*, 5 (2000–2002), pp. 360–68

Beier, A. L., *Masterless Men: The Vagrancy Problem in England, 1560–1640* (London, 1985)

Bellord, Sue, 'Picking "Hurts" on Hurtwood Common', *Romany Routes*, 9 (2008–10), pp. 159–60

Bennett, Alfred Rosling, *London and Londoners in the Eighteen-Fifties and Sixties* (London, 1924)

Bennett, Mary Ann, *Life and Work on Surrey Heath* (Chichester, 2007)

Berlin, Sven, *Dromengro: Man of the Road* (London, 1971)

Beshlie, *Romany Road: Life on Wheels* (Marshwood, 2011)

Black, George Fraser, *A Gypsy Bibliography* (Edinburgh, 1909)

Boas, Guy, *Wimbledon – Has It a History?* (London, 1947)

Borrow, George, *Romano Lavo-Lil* (London, 1874)

Borrowman, Robert, *Beckenham Past and Present* (privately printed, 1910)

Boswell, Lawrence, 'The Blackpool Gypsies', *Journal of the Gypsy Lore Society*, 3rd series, XXXIV (1955), pp. 42–5

Boswell, Silvester Gordon, *The Book of Boswell: Autobiography of a Gypsy*, ed. John Seymour (London, 1970)

Bowen, Paul, 'The Schooling of Gypsy Children in Surrey, 1906–1933', *Journal of Educational Administration and History*, 36 (2004), pp. 57–67

Bowerman, Les, 'Hubert H. Rendell, Ripley Police Sergeant 1922/3', *Journal of the Send and Ripley History Society*, 5 (2000), pp. 14–19

Boxall, Tony, *Gypsy Camera* (Croydon, 1992)

Boyce, Geoff, 'Joe Who?', *Romany Routes*, 5 (2000–2002), pp. 77–81

—, *The Boyce and Beckett Trail* (Swindon, 2016)

Bradley, Edward, as 'Cuthbert Bede', 'In Gipsy Tents', *Notes and Queries*, 6th series, 2 (1880), pp. 362–4

Braithwaite, Paul, *A Palace on Wheels* (White Waltham, 1999)

Brent, Nick, 'Operation Checkmate', *Surrey Constabulary History Journal*, 12 (2015), pp. 5–13

Brewer, E., 'Gipsy Encampments in the Heart of London', *The Sunday at Home* (1896), pp. 113–14

Bright, Richard, *Travels from Vienna through Lower Hungary* (Edinburgh, 1818)

Broadbent, Una, and Ronald Latham, *Coulsdon: Downland Village* (Surrey, 1976)

Broadwood, Lucy, 'Songs', *Journal of the Folk-Song Society*, 1 (1899–1904), pp. 139–225

Brown, Frances, *Fairfield Folk: A History of the British Fairground and Its People* (Upton upon Severn, 1988)

Brown, J. A., 'Romany Girl', *Romany Routes*, 10 (2010–12), pp. 166–7

Brown, Sheila, and David Porter, *Two Surrey Village Schools: The Story of Send and Ripley Village Schools* (Ripley, 2002)

Bunyan, Robert, *A Lad in the Village of Ash* (Ash, Surrey, 2003)

Burney, Frances, *The Early Diary of Frances Burney, 1768–1778, with a Selection from Her Correspondence, and from the Journals of Her Sisters Susan and Charlotte Burney*, ed. Annie Raine Ellis (London, 1889)

Cannon, Judy, 'Gentleman Gypsy', *Guildford Today*, 11/10 (1963), pp. 22–3

Carter, H. V., 'Multiple Baptisms by a Traveller', *Genealogists' Magazine*, 28 (2005), pp. 197–200

Caulfield, James, *Portraits, Memoirs and Characters of Remarkable Persons* (London, 1820)

Chandler, Keith, 'Trinity Cooper: From Attentive Scholar to Battered Wife', *Romany Routes*, 10 (2010–12), pp. 213–19

Clare, John, *The Prose of John Clare*, ed. John W. and Anne Tibble (London, 1951)

Clark, Colin, and Margaret Greenfields, *Here to Stay: The Gypsies and Travellers of Britain* (Hatfield, 2006)

Clay, Rachel, 'Gypsies of the Surrey Hills', *Countryman*, 45 (1952), pp. 293–7

Clifford, Angela, and Hazel Walker, eds, *Langley Vale: Memories of a Surrey Village* (privately printed, 2001)

Cobbett, William, 'To a Correspondent in America', *Cobbett's Political Register*, 26 (1814), col. 641–60

Cobley, John, *The Crimes of the First Fleet Convicts* (Sydney, 1970)

Coke, David, and Alan Bord, *Vauxhall Gardens: A History* (New Haven, CT, 2011)

Connor, Patricia, *Derby Day 200* (London, 1979)

Coombe, Dennis, 'Help Sought', *Romany Routes*, 6 (2002–4), pp. 178–9

Cooper, Keziah, *Favourite Romany Recipes* (Sevenoaks, 2004)

Cooper, Vivien, 'Tales My Family Told Me: The Roar of the Lion', *Romany Routes*, 10 (2010–12), pp. 333–4

—, 'Tales My Family Told Me: Barriers to Understanding', *Romany Routes*, 12 (2014–16), pp. 75–6

—, 'Tales My Family Told Me: Porridge for Christmas', *Romany Routes*, 12 (2014–16), p. 215

—, 'Tales My Family Told Me: Waxie, a Faithful Friend', *Romany Routes*, 12 (2014–16), p. 269

Coppe, Abiezer, *A Fiery Flying Roll* (London, 1649)

Cotton, Elizabeth, *Our Coffee Room* (London, 1876)

Coughlan, Tim, *Now Shoon the Romano Gillie: Traditional Verse in the High and Low Speech of the Gypsies of Britain* (Cardiff, 2001)

Coulter, John, *Norwood Past* (London, 1996)

—, *Norwood Pubs* (Stroud, 2006)

Cowles, Frederick, *Gypsy Caravan* (London, 1948)

Cox, Peter, *Set into Song: Ewan MacColl, Charles Parker, Peggy Seeger and the Radio Ballads* (Cambridge, 2008)

Crabb, James, *The Gipsies' Advocate*, 1st edn (London, 1831)

—, *The Gipsies' Advocate*, 2nd edn (London, 1832)

Cressy, David, *Gypsies: An English History* (Oxford, 2018)

Croft-Cooke, Rupert, *The Moon in My Pocket: Life with the Romanies* (London, 1948)

Crofton, Henry Thomas, 'Borde's Egipt Speche', *Journal of the Gypsy Lore Society*, 2nd series, 1 (1907–8), pp. 157–68

——, 'Affairs of Egypt, 1907', *Journal of the Gypsy Lore Society*, 2nd series,
  II (1908–9), pp. 121–41

——, 'Thomas Daniell and Romani', *Journal of the Gypsy Lore Society*, 3rd series,
  VII (1928), p. 48

Crosby, Alan, *A History of Woking* (Chichester, 2003)

Crowhurst, Roger, 'The Gypsy King', *London Police Pensioner*, 114 (2004),
  pp. 38–9

Cuttriss, Frank, *Romany Life: Experienced and Observed during Many Years
  of Friendly Intercourse with the Gypsies* (London, 1915)

Daniels, J. E., *Heathcote Memorial School, Ash, 1860–1950* (privately printed, n.d.
  (*c.* 1976))

Davis, Rib, ed., *Woking: Living Words* (Woking, 2007)

Davison, Mark, and Ian Currie, *The Surrey Weather Book: A Century of Storms,
  Floods and Freezes* (Coulsdon, 1993)

Dawson, Robert, *Times Gone: Gypsies and Travellers* (privately printed, 2007)

De Baïracli Levy, Juliette, *As Gypsies Wander* (London, 1953)

——, *Wanderers in the New Forest* (London, 1958)

Dekker, Thomas, *The Non-Dramatic Works of Thomas Dekker*, ed. Alexander
  B. Grosart (privately printed, 1884–6)

Delmarcel, Guy, *Flemish Tapestry*, trans. Alastair Weir (London, 1999)

Dickens, Charles, 'Epsom', *Household Words*, 3 (1851), pp. 241–6

Doddington, George Bubb, *The Diary of the Late George Bubb Doddington*,
  ed. Henry Penruddocke Wyndham (London, 1828)

Dodds, Norman, *Gypsies, Didikois and Other Travellers* (London, 1966)

Doe, Lesley, 'From Parish Registers', *Romany Routes*, 6 (2002–4), p. 341

Doe, Stephen, 'From Viking Longboat to Gypsy Caravan: I', *Romany Routes*,
  8 (2006–8), pp. 319–21

——, 'Newspaper Finds', *Romany Routes*, 12 (2014–16), p. 68

Doe, Terry, 'Albert Doe, 1869–1964', *Romany Routes*, 6 (2002–4), pp. 105–7

——, 'Walter Doe: Royal Navy Boy Signaller of World War I', *Romany Routes*,
  12 (2014–16), pp. 114–15

Donohoe, James Hugh, *The Forgotten Australians: The Non Anglo or Celtic
  Convicts and Exiles* (privately printed, 1991)

Douglas, James, *Theodore Watts-Dunton: Poet, Novelist, Critic* (London, 1904)

Dowman, Ted, et al., eds, *Epsom Common* (Epsom, 1981)

Doyle, Kevin, 'From Sussex Parish Registers', *Romany Routes*, 1 (1994–5), p. 12

Edmonds, Jenifer, *Gypsies, Tramps and . . . Strangers* (privately printed, 2004–5)

Edmunds, Richard, 'The Life of Shadrach Boswell: II', *Romany Routes*, 11
  (2012–14), pp. 209–302

——, *The Early Romany Boswells: A Family History, 1650–1810* (Swindon, 2017–18)

——, *Gypsies in Tudor England, 1485–1603* (privately printed, 2018)

Egan, Pierce, *Boxiana; or, Sketches of Ancient and Modern Pugilism from the
  Days of the Renowned Broughton and Slack, to the Championship of Cribb*
  (London, 1812–29)

Farington, Joseph, *The Diary of Joseph Farington*, ed. Kenneth Garlick, Angus
  Macintyre and Kathryn Cave (London, 1978–98)

Fielding, C. H., *Memories of Malling and Its Valley* (West Malling, 1893)

Ford, Anne-Marie, 'Tinker of Hargrave', *Romany Routes*, 12 (2014–16),
  pp. 253–5

Francis, Martin, 'The Villager and the Gypsy', *Surrey Villager*, 6 (1980), pp. 3–5

Francis, Tom, *Old Mitcham*, ed. Eric Montague (Chichester, 1993)

Fraser, Angus, 'The Gypsy Problem: A Survey of Post-War Developments', *Journal of the Gypsy Lore Society*, 3rd series, XXXII (1953), pp. 82–100

—, 'John Clare's Gypsies', *Journal of the Gypsy Lore Society*, 3rd series, L (1971), pp. 85–100

—, *The Gypsies* (Oxford, 1992)

Frost, Thomas, *Reminiscences of a Country Journalist* (London, 1886)

Gaston, Edward Page, 'Gypsy Associations of Wimbledon Common', *Wimbledon and Merton Annual*, 3 (1905), pp. 67–76

Gerhold, Dorian, ed., *Putney and Roehampton Past* (London, 1999)

Gibson, Muriel, ed., *Surrey within Living Memory* (Newbury, 1992)

Gill, W. W., 'Told in a Vardo', *Journal of the Gypsy Lore Society*, 3rd series, XIX (1940), pp. 60–62

Gomm, Jacqui, 'From the Census', *Romany Routes*, 5 (2000–2002), pp. 380–81

Goodman, Jean, *What a Go! The Life of Alfred Munnings* (London, 1988)

Gordon, Ross, 'It's the Gypsy in Them', *Photo World: Picturing Today*, VI/5 (1946), pp. 31–5

Greenwood, James, *Low-Life Deeps: An Account of the Strange Fish to Be Found There* (London, 1876)

Griffin, Christopher, *Nomads under the Westway: Irish Travellers, Gypsies and Other Traders in West London* (Hatfield, 2008)

Guildford, Pauline, 'Letters', *Romany Routes*, 5 (2000–2002), pp. 3–4

Hailstone, Charles, *Alleyways of Mortlake and East Sheen* (London, 1983)

Hall, Edward, *Hall's Chronicle*, ed. Henry Ellis (London, 1809)

Hall, Eric, 'Work among the Gypsies', *Root and Branch*, 19 (1992), p. 120

Hall, George, *The Gypsy's Parson: His Experiences and Adventures* (London, 1915)

Hamill, A. E., 'A Fifteenth-Century Tapestry', *Journal of the Gypsy Lore Society*, 3rd series, XXVIII (1949), pp. 41–2

Hamilton-Sneath, Jenny, *A Glimpse of Old England: Surrey by the Tillingbourne* (London, 1997)

Hancock, Ian, 'Romanes Numerals and Innovations', *Journal of the Gypsy Lore Society*, 3rd series, XLVIII (1969), pp. 19–29

—, 'Romani and Angloromani', pp. 366–83 of Peter Trudgill, ed., *Language in the British Isles* (Cambridge, 1984)

—, *Danger! Educated Gypsy: Selected Essays*, ed. Dileep Karanth (Hatfield, 2010)

Harte, Jeremy, 'Just Enough: Petty Crime at Quarter Sessions in Three Surrey Parishes, 1780–1820', *Surrey History*, 13 (2014), pp. 1–15

—, 'Gypsies at Salfords, Surrey: Captured by a PC's Diary', *Romany Routes*, 13 (2016–18), pp. 166–70

Harvey, Denis, 'Hook-Up at Clandon', *Journal of the Gypsy Lore Society*, 3rd series, XXXI (1952), pp. 81–3

—, 'A Wafodi English Grai', *Journal of the Gypsy Lore Society*, 3rd series, LI (1972), pp. 55–9

—, *The Gypsies: Waggon-Time and After* (London, 1979)

—, 'Little Egypt and the Stillborn Child', *Countryman*, XCIII/3 (1990), pp. 98–101

Harvey, Edward, 'English Gypsy Caravan Decoration', *Journal of the Gypsy Lore Society*, 3rd series, XVII/part 3 (v) (1938), pp. 38–46

Hawkins, Kerry, 'My Ancestors at Hampton Wick in the 1861 and 1871 Census Returns: I', *Romany Routes*, 4 (1998–2000), pp. 298–300

—, 'My Ancestors at Hampton Wick in the 1861 and 1871 Census Returns: II', *Romany Routes*, 5 (2000–2002), pp. 13–17

Hayward, James, *Gypsy Jib: A Romany Dictionary* (Wenhaston, 2003)

Hazlitt, W. Carew, ed., *Remaines of the Early Popular Poetry of England* (London, 1866)

Heppell, Brian, 'Daisy Boswell: The Generous Fortune-Teller on the Tober at Newcastle', *Romany Routes*, 13 (2016–18), pp. 58–9

Holmes, Colin, 'The German Gypsy Question in Britain, 1904–6', *Journal of the Gypsy Lore Society*, 4th series, I (1974), pp. 248–67

Howell, Samuel, *The Wandering Minstrel: A Collection of Original Poems* (London, 1827)

Howitt, William, *The Rural Life of England* (London, 1840)

Hoyland, John, *A Historical Survey of the Customs, Habits and Present State of the Gypsies* (York, 1816)

Hunn, David, *Epsom Racecourse: Its Story and Its People* (London, 1973)

Hutchins, Lisa, *Esher and Claygate Past* (London, 2001)

Huth, Ferdinand Gerard, 'Dame Laura Knight's "Gypsy Family"', *Journal of the Gypsy Lore Society*, 2nd series, XXII (1943), p. 61

Hyland, St George Kieran, *A Century of Persecution under Tudor and Stuart Sovereigns from Contemporary Records* (London, 1920)

Ingram, Peter, *Wagtail Tale: Gypsy Life of Bygone Days* (privately printed, 2014)

J.P.P.C., 'The Norwood Gypsies', *Literary Lounger*, 2 (1826), pp. 88–96

Jack, Albert, *That's Bollocks! Urban Legends, Conspiracy Theories and Old Wives' Tales* (London, 2006)

Jarman, Eldra, and A.O.H. Jarman, *The Welsh Gypsies: Children of Abram Wood* (Cardiff, 1991)

Jekyll, Gertrude, *Old West Surrey* (London, 1904)

Jerrold, Blanchard, *The Life and Remains of Douglas Jerrold* (London, 1859)

John, Augustus, *Finishing Touches* (London, 1964)

Johnson, Michael, *A History of Outwood* (Outwood, 1997)

Johnson, Walter, and William Wright, *Neolithic Man in North-East Surrey* (London, 1903)

Keet-Black, Janet, 'So You've Found Great Granny's Baptism?', *Romany Routes*, 2 (1995–6), pp. 108–11

—, 'Nichols by Any Other Name?', *Romany Routes*, 2 (1995–6), pp. 172–3

—, 'A Keet Family Tree', *Romany Routes*, 3 (1996–8), pp. 20–21

—, 'Miscellany', *Romany Routes*, 5 (2000–2002), p. 329

—, *Some Travellers in the 1891 Census* (Swindon, 2000–2002)

—, 'Princess Victoria's Gypsies', *Romany Routes*, 7 (2004–6), pp. 254–5

—, *Gypsies of Britain* (Oxford, 2013)

—, 'The Continuing Saga of the Nichols', *Romany Routes*, 14 (2018–20), pp. 150–54

Kennedy, Peter, *Folksongs of Britain and Ireland* (London, 1975)

Kenrick, Donald, and Colin Clark, *Moving On: The Gypsies and Travellers of Britain* (Hatfield, 2000)

Kenrick, Donald, and Grattan Puxon, *The Destiny of Europe's Gypsies* (Brighton, 1972)

Knight, Laura, *The Magic of a Line* (London, 1965)

Kohler, Margaret, ed., *Memorials of Old Dorking* (Dorking, 1977)

Larwood, Jacob, and John Camden Hotten, *The History of Signboards* (London, 1867)

Leather, Ella, 'Collecting Folk-Melodies from Gypsies in Herefordshire', *Journal of the Gypsy Lore Society*, 3rd series, IV (1925), pp. 59–72

Lee, Kate, 'Some Experiences of a Folk-Song Collector', *Journal of the Folk-Song Society*, 1 (1899–1904), pp. 1–3

Lee, Terence, *The Lee Family Tree* (privately printed, 1992)

Leland, Charles Godfrey, *The English Gypsies and Their Language* (London, 1873)

—, *The Gypsies* (London, 1882)

—, 'Visiting the Gypsies', *The Century*, 25 (1883), pp. 905–12

—, 'The Derby Race of 1885', *Outing*, 8 (1885), pp. 337–42

—, 'A Gypsy Beauty', *The Century*, 32 (1886), pp. 539–42

—, 'Three Gipsy Songs', *Hood's Comic Annual*, 19 (1887), pp. 65–7

Leland, Charles Godfrey, Edward Henry Palmer and Janet Tuckey, *English-Gypsy Songs* (London, 1875)

Leslie, Charles Robert (as 'A Resident in England'), 'The Gipsies: A Slight Sketch', in Eliza Leslie, *The Gift: A Christmas and New Year's Present for 1837* (Philadelphia, PA, 1836), pp. 145–51

Lindsay, Lionel, *A. J. Munnings, R. A.: Pictures of Horses and English Life* (London, 1939)

Locke, Sue, *Travelling Light: The Remarkable Story of Gypsy Revival* (London, 1997)

Loose, Jacqueline, *Roehampton: The Last Village in London* (London, 1979)

The Loseley Manuscripts, ed. Alfred John Kempe (London, 1835)

Lynch, A. J., 'A Gipsy School', *The Schoolmaster and Woman Teacher's Chronicle*, 113 (1928), p. 335

Lysons, Daniel, *The Environs of London* (London, 1792–6)

McCue, Lillian Bueno, 'Elizabeth Canning in Print', *University of Colorado Studies*, B2 (1945), pp. 223–32

MacDonald, Ruth, 'Romanichal Gypsies Bitchedi Pawdel to Australia', *Romany Routes*, 5 (2000–2002), pp. 295–300

McFarlane, Andrew, 'Matty Cooper and the Windsor Rats', *Journal of the Gypsy Lore Society*, 3rd series, XX (1941), pp. 41–2

—, 'Rudari and "Greek" Gypsy Death Customs', *Journal of the Gypsy Lore Society*, 3rd series, XXII (1943), p. 60

McGowan, Alan, *On the Gypsy Trail: Sources for the Family History of Gypsies* (Swindon, 1998)

—, 'Henry Ayres: Killed in Action in WW1', *Romany Routes*, 12 (2014–16), pp. 161–2

McGowan, Alan, ed., *The Winchester Confessions, 1615–1616: Depositions of Travellers, Gypsies, Fraudsters and Makers of Counterfeit Documents, including a Vocabulary of the Romany Language* (Swindon, 1996)

Mack, Marjorie, *Hannaboys Farm* (London, 1942)

McMillan, Angus, *Gipsy Hawkins* (London, 1946)

Mais, Stuart Petre Brodie, *It Isn't Far from London* (London, 1930)

Marshall, Tony, *The Prince of Gypsies* (London, 2014)

Matras, Yaron, *Romani: A Linguistic Introduction* (Cambridge, 2004)

Matthews, Robert Dane, 'My Matthews Family: 11', *Romany Routes*, 15 (2020–22), pp. 261–3

Mayall, David, *Gypsy-Travellers in Nineteenth-Century Society* (Cambridge, 1988)

—, *English Gypsies and State Policies* (Hatfield, 1995)

Meredith, George, *Poems and Lyrics of the Joys of Earth* (London, 1883)

Messinck, James, *Airs, Duets &c. in the New Pantomime, Called the Norwood Gypsies, Performing at the Theatre-Royal in Covent-Garden* (London, 1777)

Milward, Richard, *Historic Wimbledon: Caesar's Camp to Centre Court* (Wimbledon, 1989)

'The Missionary to the Gypsies', 'Annual Reports, 1858 and 1859', *London City Mission Magazine*, 25 (1860), pp. 1–36

Montague, Eric, *Mitcham: A Pictorial History* (Chichester, 1991)

—, *Mitcham Histories 8: Phipps Bridge* (London, 2006)

Moody, Jim, 'Help Sought', *Romany Routes*, 4 (1998–2000), pp. 232–3

—, 'Collecting Gypsy Postcards', *Romany Routes*, 11 (2012–14), pp. 310–14

Moore, Judith, *The Appearance of Truth: The Story of Elizabeth Canning and Eighteenth-Century Narrative* (Newark, DE, 1994)

More, Thomas, *The Complete Works of St Thomas More*, vol. VI: *A Dialogue concerning Heresies*, ed. Thomas M. C. Lawler, Germain Marc'hadour and Richard C. Marius (New Haven, CT, 1981)

Munnings, Alfred, *The Second Burst* (London, 1951)

Murphey, Carol, 'From Parish Registers', *Romany Routes*, 7 (2004–6), p. 162

Nunweek, Christine, 'The Christmas Holly Wreath', *Romany Routes*, 9 (2008–10), pp. 11–12

Nye, Mary Jo, *Blackett: Physics, War, and Politics in the Twentieth Century* (Cambridge, MA, 2004)

Ogle, Arthur, *The Tragedy of the Lollards' Tower* (Oxford, 1949)

O'hAodha, Michael, 'Romany Aristocrats Invade London Suburbs', *Romany Routes*, 2 (1995–6), pp. 158–62

Oliver, Percy Lane, 'Surrey Gypsies', *Surrey Magazine*, 1 (1899/1900), pp. 15–18

O'Sullivan, Maureen, 'Settlement Examination Dated 26 July 1740', *East Surrey Family History Journal*, XXVIII/3 (2005), p. xiv

Overton, Jenny, ed., *Peaslake: Story of a Surrey Village* (privately printed, 2003)

Parker, Eric, *Highways and Byways in Surrey* (London, 1908)

Pateman, John, *Hoo, Hops and Hods: The Life and Times of Robert Pateman* (privately printed, 2007)

Payne, Charles, 'Bikk'ning Raklies', *Journal of the Gypsy Lore Society*, 3rd series, XXX (1951), pp. 151–3

Pearce, Kevin, 'Sampson and Amelia Tarrant', *Romany Routes*, 8 (2006–8), pp. 414–15

Pennell, Elizabeth Robins, *Charles Godfrey Leland* (London, 1906)

Phillimore, Robert, 'Songs of Luriben and Curiben', *Journal of the Gypsy Lore Society*, 2nd series, 6 (1912–13), pp. 67–8

Phillips, Richard, *A Morning's Walk from London to Kew* (London, 1817)

Plowden, Bridget, et al., *Children and Their Primary Schools: A Report of the Central Advisory Council for Education (England)* (Richmond, 1967)

Pound, Reginald, *The Englishman: A Biography of Sir Alfred Munnings* (London, 1962)

Ratcliffe, Dorothy Una, 'A Gypsy Belief', *Journal of the Gypsy Lore Society*, 3rd series, XVI (1937), p. 93

—, 'My Gypsy Acquaintances', *Journal of the Gypsy Lore Society*, 3rd series, XLIII (1964), pp. 131–8

Raywid, Brian, 'Notes on Life on the Road', *Journal of the Gypsy Lore Society*, 3rd series, LI (1972), pp. 102–15

Reeve, Dominic, *Beneath the Blue Sky: Four Decades of a Travelling Life in Britain* (Nottingham, 2007)

—, *Green Lanes and Kettle Cranes* (Marshwood, 2010)

Reginald, Brett, Viscount Esher, ed., *The Girlhood of Queen Victoria: A Selection from Her Majesty's Diaries between the Years 1832 and 1840* (London, 1912)

Richards, Evelyn, 'Old Folk's Memories of Wimbledon', *Wimbledon and Merton Annual*, 4 (1910), pp. 91–101

Richardson, Benjamin Ward, *The Asclepiad* (London, 1884–95)

—, *Vita Medica: Chapters of Medical Life and Work* (London, 1897)

Rickard, Gillian, *Vagrants, Gypsies and 'Travellers' in Kent, 1572–1948* (privately printed, 1995)

Roberts, Samuel, *The Gypsies: Their Origin, Continuance and Destination* (London, 1836)

Rose, David, 'Plenty of Scrap Metal and Friendly Chat Too', *Romany Routes*, 6 (2002–4), pp. 244–7

Ross, Kenneth, *A History of Malden* (New Malden, 1947)

'Router', 'How to Make a Showman's Caravan', *Work: The Illustrated Weekly Journal for Mechanics*, 12 (1896/7), pp. 409–11

Rudge, Ted, *Brumroamin: Birmingham and Midland Romany Gypsy and Traveller Culture* (Birmingham, 1988)

Russell, Alexander, 'Bright's Anglo-Romani Vocabulary', *Journal of the Gypsy Lore Society*, 2nd series, IX (1915–16), pp. 165–85

Ryder, Andrew, Sarah Cemlyn and Thomas Acton, eds, *Hearing the Voices of Gypsy, Roma and Traveller Communities* (Bristol, 2014)

Salmon, John E., *The Surrey Countryside: The Interplay of Land and People* (Guildford, 1975)

Salt, George, 'England's School for Gipsy Children', *Millgate Monthly*, 30 (1934–5), pp. 387–8

Sampson, Anthony, *The Scholar Gypsy: The Quest for a Family Secret* (London, 1997)

Sampson, John, *The Dialect of the Gypsies of Wales: Being the Older Form of British Romani Preserved in the Speech of the Clan of Abram Wood* (Oxford, 1926)

Samuel, Raphael, 'Comers and Goers', in *The Victorian City: Images and Realities*, ed. H. J. Dyers and Michael Wolff (London, 1973), pp. 123–60

Sandford, Jeremy, *Gypsies* (London, 1973)

Sanger, George, *Seventy Years a Showman* (London, 1908)

Saunders, P., et al., eds, *Gypsies and Travellers in Their Own Words: Words and Pictures of Travelling Life* (Leeds, 2000)

Scott, Walter, ed., *English Minstrelsy* (Edinburgh, 1810)

Searle, Ronald, and Kaye Webb, *Looking at London and People Worth Meeting* (London, 1953)

Shepheard, Chris, *The Lost Countryside: Images of Rural Life* (Derby, 2001)

Sherriff, Henry, *Henry Dry-Bread: The Richard Wade Papers*, ed. Robert Dawson (privately printed, 1988)

Shore, Charles John, *Memoir of the Life and Correspondence of John Lord Teignmouth* (London, 1843)

Sitwell, Osbert, 'Guildford Gypsies', *Journal of the Gypsy Lore Society*, 3rd series, XXIX (1950), pp. 150–52

Skelton, John, *The Complete English Poems*, ed. John Scattergood (New Haven, CT, 1983)

Smart, Bath, and Henry Thomas Crofton, *The Dialect of the English Gypsies* (London, 1875)

Smith, Campbell, 'Memories of a Lower Kingswood Resident', *Lower Kingswood Village News* (Summer 2014), pp. 15–16

Smith, Edwin (as 'Lavengro'), *The Gypsy: Poems and Ballads* (Tunbridge Wells, 1973)

Smith, George, *Gipsy Life: Being an Account of Our Gipsies and Their Children* (London, 1880)

Smith, Joe, *Gypsy Joe: Bare-Knuckle Fighter, Professional Golfer* (London, 2009)

Smith, Robert, *A History of Sutton, AD 675–1960* (privately printed, 1960)

Smith, Rosie, and Lindsey Marsh, *Old Ways, New Days: A Family History of Gypsy Life in South London and Kent* (London, 2009)

Smith, Sandra, 'My Gypsy Family', *Romany Routes*, 8 (2006–8), pp. 326–30

Solly, M. Neale, *Memoir of the Life of David Cox* (London, 1873)

Stanley, Denise, and Rosy Burke, *The Romano Drom Song Book* (Brentwood, 1986)

Stewart, William, *Characters of Bygone London* (London, 1960)

Stockin, Jimmy, with Martin King and Martin Knight, *On the Cobbles: The Life of a Bare-Knuckle Gypsy Warrior* (Edinburgh, 2000)

Strachey, Amabel, 'The Gipsy Scandal and the Danger to the Commons', *National Review*, 59 (1912), pp. 459–72

Sturt, George (as 'George Bourne'), *The Bettesworth Book: Talks with a Surrey Peasant* (London, 1901)

—, *A Small Boy in the Sixties* (Cambridge, 1927)

—, *The Journals of George Sturt, 1890–1927*, ed. E. D. Mackerness (Cambridge, 1967)

The Survey of London 49–50: Battersea (Swindon, 2013)

Tate, W. E., 'Enclosure Acts and Awards Relating to Lands in the County of Surrey', *Surrey Archaeological Collections*, 48 (1943), pp. 118–49

Taylor, Becky, *A Minority and the State: Travellers in Britain in the Twentieth Century* (Manchester, 2008)

Taylor, J. G., *Our Lady of Batersey* (London, 1925)

Teesdale, P. J., 'Move On!', *Journal of the Gypsy Lore Society*, 3rd series, XXVII (1948), pp. 158–9

Thompson, Thomas William, 'Borrow's Gypsies', *Journal of the Gypsy Lore Society*, 2nd series, III (1909–10), pp. 162–72

——, 'Affairs of Egypt, 1909', *Journal of the Gypsy Lore Society*, 2nd series,
   V (1911–12), pp. 113–35
——, 'Gleanings from Constables' Accounts and Other Sources', *Journal of the
   Gypsy Lore Society*, 3rd series, VII (1928), pp. 30–47
——, '"My Friend's Gypsy Journal"', *Journal of the Gypsy Lore Society*, 3rd series,
   XIV (1935), pp. 108–11
Thomson, John, and Adolphe Smith, *Street Life in London* (London, 1876–7)
Treherne, John, *The Canning Enigma* (London, 1989)
Trudgill, Eric, *The Family Trees of Damon and Thomas Lee from about 1750
   to about 1900, Mainly the English Southern Counties* (Swindon, 2007)
——, *The Family Tree of Benjamin and Thomas Hearn from about 1740 to about
   1900, Mainly Counties to the North, West and South of London* (Swindon,
   2009)
——, 'William Cooper's Children', *Romany Routes*, 10 (2010–12), pp. 21–4
Turner, J. Horsfall, 'The Gypsies', *Notes and Queries*, 6th series, 1 (1880), p. 258
Vesey-FitzGerald, Brian, 'Houses Not Meant for Tent-Dwellers', *Journal of the
   Gypsy Lore Society*, 3rd series, XXIX (1950), pp. 70–72
——, *Gypsies of Britain* (Newton Abbot, 1973)
Wakeford, Ian, *Woking as It Was* (Chichester, 1985)
Walsh, Barbara, 'The Ripleys', *Romany Routes*, 5 (2000–2002), p. 263
——, 'Around the Fire', *Romany Routes*, 13 (2016–18), p. 378
Ward, H. G., 'A German Professor on the Norwood Gypsies', *Journal of the
   Gypsy Lore Society*, 3rd series, XV (1936), pp. 94–6
Ward-Jackson, Cyril, and Denis Harvey, *The English Gypsy Caravan: Its
   Origins, Builders, Technology and Conservation* (Newton Abbot, 1972)
Warwick, Alan, *The Phoenix Suburb: A South London Social History*
   (Richmond, 1972)
Waterson, Mary, '"I Want More than Green Leaves for My Children": Some
   Developments in Gypsy/Traveller Education, 1970–96', in *Romani
   Culture and Gypsy Identity*, ed. Thomas Acton and Gary Mundy (Hatfield,
   1997), pp. 127–49
Webb, Linda, 'Memories of My Grandmother, Alice Emma Matthews (Totty)',
   Romany Routes, 10 (2010–12), pp. 203–4
Wellstood, F. C., 'Foreign Gypsies in England, 1761', *Journal of the Gypsy Lore
   Society*, 2nd series, IV (1901–11), p. 307
White, Trevor, and Jeremy Harte, *Epsom: A Pictorial History* (Chichester, 1992)
Wilcox, S., ed., *Sun, Wind and Rain: The Art of David Cox* (New Haven, CT,
   2008)
Wilkinson, T. W., 'Van Dwelling London', in *Living London*, ed. George R.
   Sims (London, 1904–6), vol. III, pp. 319–23
Williams, David, *A World of His Own: The Double Life of George Borrow*
   (Oxford, 1982)
Willis, Cloudesley, *A Brief History of Ewell and Nonsuch* (Epsom, 1931)
Willis, Gill, ed., *I Remember Chobham* (privately printed, 1999)
Wilson, Tom, *The Secret Revival* (privately printed, 1998)
Winstedt, Eric Otto, 'A Gypsy Christening', *Journal of the Gypsy Lore Society*,
   2nd series, VI (1912–13), p. 65
——, 'The Gypsy Coppersmiths' Invasion of 1911–13', *Journal of the Gypsy Lore
   Society*, 2nd series, VI (1912–13), pp. 244–303

——, 'The Norwood Gypsies and Their Vocabulary', *Journal of the Gypsy Lore Society*, 2nd series, IX (1915–16), pp. 129–65

——, 'The Valentines', *Journal of the Gypsy Lore Society*, 2nd series, IX (1915–16), pp. 222–4

——, 'Notes on English Gypsy Christian Names: I', *Journal of the Gypsy Lore Society*, 3rd series, I (1921), pp. 64–90

——, 'Notes on English Gypsy Christian Names: II', *Journal of the Gypsy Lore Society*, 3rd series, II (1922), pp. 16–39

——, 'Review: *The Canning Wonder* by Arthur Machen', *Journal of the Gypsy Lore Society*, 3rd series, VI (1927), pp. 35–45

——, 'Gypsies as Highwaymen and Footpads', *Journal of the Gypsy Lore Society*, 3rd series, VI (1927), pp. 68–88

——, 'Gypsies in Political Disturbances', *Journal of the Gypsy Lore Society*, 3rd series, IX (1930), pp. 47–8

——, 'The Squires Family', *Journal of the Gypsy Lore Society*, 3rd series, XVI (1937), pp. 146–8

——, 'Gypsies on Epsom Downs', *Journal of the Gypsy Lore Society*, 3rd series, XVI (1937), pp. 204–5

——, 'The Funeral of Mārya Yevanovič', *Journal of the Gypsy Lore Society*, 3rd series, XXII (1943), p. 59

——, 'Anglo-Romani Gleanings from the Northern Counties', *Journal of the Gypsy Lore Society*, 3rd series, XXVII (1948), pp. 83–110

——, Thomas William Thompson and Fred Shaw, 'Anglo-Romani Gleanings from London-Side Gypsies', *Journal of the Gypsy Lore Society*, 3rd series, III (1924), pp. 110–36

Wolcot, John, as 'Peter Pindar', 'A Gipsy Ballad', *Kentish Register and Monthly Miscellany*, I (1793), p. 194

Wood, Manfri Frederick, *In the Life of a Romany Gypsy* (London, 1973)

Woolmer, D. L., 'Gipsies in Their Winter Quarters', *The Quiver* (1903), pp. 530–35

Wright, Alan, *Their Day Has Passed: Gypsies in Victorian and Edwardian Surrey* (Tolworth, 2017)

Wrigley, Paula, 'They Say "Truth Is Stranger Than Fiction": The Case of Two Soldiers Called Sidney Harris', *Romany Routes* 14 (2018–20), pp. 58–9

Wynn Jones, Michael, *The Derby* (London, 1979)

Yates, Dora, 'The "Greek" Nomad Gypsies in Britain, 1929–40: II', *Journal of the Gypsy Lore Society*, 3rd series, XXI (1942), pp. 87–110

——, *My Gypsy Days: Recollections of a Romani Rawnie* (London, 1953)

——, 'T. L. Busby's "Jemmy Lovel" (1819)', *Journal of the Gypsy Lore Society*, 3rd series, XXXV (1956), p. 97

Yates, Michael, 'English Gypsy Songs', *Folk Music Journal*, 3 (1975–9), pp. 63–80

Further Sources

A comprehensive listing of further sources can be found in Jeremy Harte, *A Surrey Gypsy Bibliography* (Swindon, 2019).

LIST OF ILLUSTRATIONS

p. 92: Percy Roberts, after a drawing by Read, *Jack Cooper (the Gypsey)*, 1824, engraving. Museum of London z6752 © Museum of London.

p. 97: Andrew Duncan, after Charles Robert Leslie, *The Gypsy Belle*, 1830, etching *c.* 1826. © The Trustees of the British Museum.

p. 109: 'The morning of the Derby – the Gipsy quarter', engraving in *Illustrated London News*, 22 May 1858.

p. 111: 'Sketches of Gipsy life: inside a tent on Mitcham-Common', engraving in *Illustrated London News*, 6 December 1879.

p. 116: 'Epsom Downs on a Derby morning', engraving in *Illustrated London News*, 23 May 1863.

p. 122: 'William Hampton's waggon at Battersea', photograph in John Thomson and Adolphe Smith, *Street Life in London* (1876–7).

p. 127: J. Barnard Davis, 'Donovan's Yard at Battersea', drawing in *The Quiver* (1903).

p. 136: 'Getting supper at the Derby', photograph in *Illustrated Sporting and Dramatic News*, 31 May 1913.

p. 141: W. H. Humphris, 'Listening to the teacher', drawing in *The Graphic*, 4 June 1910.

p. 149: C. H. Taffs, 'Faced with the Surrey Anti-Vagrants Association', drawing in *The Graphic*, 24 April 1909.

p. 157: 'Ted Baker in wartime', *c.* 1914, photograph. Family photo. Bourne Hall Museum OP 9812, kindly provided by Genty Lee.

p. 159: 'Aaron Hoadley in peacetime', 1920, photograph. Bourne Hall Museum OP 9791.

p. 163: 'Darkus Price with her grandchildren on Epsom Downs', 1931, photograph. Photo by Fred Shaw, 1931. University of Liverpool SMGC Shaw P248, kindly provided by University of Liverpool Special Collections and Archives.

p. 176: *School for Gypsy Children* (1926). Hurtwood Gypsy School. Film 446.05, footage supplied by British Pathé.

p. 180: 'Families on Arbrook Common', *c.* 1910, photograph. Kingston History Centre K2-0700, by permission of Kingston Heritage Service.

p. 189: 'Threatened off Epsom Downs', 1929, photograph. Photo by Ross Gordon, in *Photo World* 6v (1946).

p. 191: 'Gathering in Lady Sybil's field', 1937, photograph. Bourne Hall Museum OP 4986.

p. 195: 'Ernest Williams spreading the message', 1944, photograph. Photo in *Today* (May 1944).

p. 210: 'White Will Smith and family at Banstead', 1952, photograph. Photo by Juliette de Baïracli Levy, 1952. University of Liverpool SMGC 1/2 PX Baïracli Levy, kindly provided by University of Liverpool Special Collections and Archives.

p. 213: 'Overtaken by the modern world', 1940s, photograph. Glass slide. Bourne Hall Museum 2014.042-001.

p. 221: 'Jasper Smith', 1999, photograph. Photo by Jo McGuire, 1999. Bourne Hall Museum GP 3753.

p. 222: 'Jimmy and Mary Wilson at Little Egypt', 1976, photograph. Photo by Kenneth Gill, 1976, kindly provided by gillfoto.

p. 231: 'Dave Stacey's funeral', 2000, photograph. Bourne Hall Museum FM 0785.21.

p. 235: 'Floral tributes at Epsom', 2014, photograph. Bourne Hall Museum DP 1407.19.

p. 240: 'Ann Wilson receiving the MBE', 2014, photograph. Family photo, 2014, kindly provided by Jean Howey.

INDEX

Page numbers in *italics* indicate illustrations

Buckland family 168, 198
Buckley family 107
burglary 56, 72
Burstow 77
Bushnell family 108
Byfleet 144, 193

Camberwell 43, 69
Canning, Elizabeth 39–40
Cant language 164
Capel 134, 202, 228–9
carts 99, 200, 212
Caterham 217, 220
chair-mending 106, 119, 138, 139, 140, 164
Chapman family 185, 201, 218
Charlwood 76, 134, 212
Chelsham 152
Cherry family 105
Chertsey 83, 124–5, 155, 172
Chessington 50, 231–2
Chilcott family 50, 88
childbirth 102–3, 169, 211
children 32, 103–4, 120, 137, 139, 141–2, 143, 172–8, 192, 203, 209, 210
chimney-sweeping 51, 139
china-mending 42, 119
Chipstead 49
Chislehurst 54
Chobham 103, 133, 135, 139, 151–2, 161, 169, 188, 201
Christmas trade 103, 134, 136, 138, 203
churches
    Anglican 61, 120
    Nonconformist 175
    Pentecostal 223
    Wesleyan 66
circuses 166–7, 176, 201
Clandon 51
Clare, John 81–2
Claygate 83, 132
cleanliness 10, 34, 64, 126–8, 209
    ritual 15, 103, 205, 208–9, 228
Clifford family 32
Cobham 83, 98, 166, 112, 146
cock-fighting 227
cock-shies 113, 117, 147, 150
coconut-shies 114
Cole family 72

Collins family 57, 158
common land 68–9, 109, 117
Compton 55
confidence tricks 78, 145
continental Gypsies 21, 26, 53, 162, 166–8, 193, 215, 219, 236
conversion of Gypsies 66–7, 79, 111–12, 139, 150, 175, 222–3
cookery 34, 58, 81–2, 104, 131–2, 135, 136, 204–7
Cooper family 18, 48, 53, 61, 63–4, 65, 71, 72, 75, 83, 84, 86, 87, 88, 90–96, 92, 98, 99, 101, 105, 107–8, 109, 115, 121–2, 129–31, 139–40, 144, 150, 156, 165, 174, 182, 190, 193, 203, 204–5, 206, 208, 228
Costa family 203
costume 11, 27, 32, 34, 64, 95, 96–8, 134, 183–4
Crabb, James 65–6
Cranford 226
Cranleigh 76
Crondall 28
Croydon 69, 76, 103, 156, 161, 162, 186–7, 193, 230, 238
Curder family 105
curses 219–20

dancing 87, 106–7, 174, 178, 210
Davis family 147
de Baïracli Levy, Juliette 204
Deacons family 76
death
    burning clothes after 46
    burning waggons after 168–9
    Devil comes at 169
decoration
    of lorries 200–201
    of waggons 181–2
Denewe family 25
The Derby 9–16, 11, 15, 98, 99–100, 103, 105, 107, 109–12, 109, 113–14, 116, 116, 126, 127–8, 129, 136, 140, 159, 167, 168, 170, 179, 189–91, 191, 199, 200, 216–17, 229–30
deserters from army 158
Devall family 186–7, 192
disease 73, 95, 104–5, 211